HISTORY

OF

SOUTHERN FICTION

EDITOR:

EDWIN MIMS, M. A., Ph. D.,

*Professor of English, University of
North Carolina.*

THE SOUTH *in the* Building *of the* Nation

HISTORY OF THE SOUTHERN STATES DESIGNED *to* RECORD *the* SOUTH'S PART *in the* MAKING *of the* AMERICAN NATION; *to* PORTRAY *the* CHARACTER *and* GENIUS, *to* CHRONICLE *the* ACHIEVEMENTS *and* PROGRESS *and to* ILLUSTRATE *the* LIFE *and* TRADITIONS *of the* SOUTHERN PEOPLE

VOLUME VIII

COMPLETE IN TWELVE VOLUMES

PELICAN PUBLISHING COMPANY
Gretna 2002

Manufactured in the United States of America
Published by Pelican Publishing Company, Inc.
1000 Burmaster Street, Gretna, Louisiana 70053

CONTENTS OF VOLUME VIII.

CONTENTS.

PREFACE.

THE selections from the writings of Southern novelists and story-writers found in this volume have an absolute value from the standpoint of pure fiction. In some cases short stories have been given in full, while the selections from novels have an inherent interest independent of the complete stories. They serve also as an interpretation of various phases of Southern life; for this reason, longer selections have been made from Kennedy's *Swallow Barn* and Baldwin's *Flush Times in Alabama and Mississippi* than would otherwise have been given. Furthermore, a certain unity may be seen in the volume in that it suggests the main tendencies of Southern fiction and the characteristics of some distinct groups of writers.

If there should seem to be an undue proportion of ante-bellum fiction, it must be borne in mind that the earlier writings are inaccessible to the general reader, either because they are now out of print or are found only in expensive editions. A sufficient reason for the absence of some recent writings is that the publishers have in some cases refused the right to use selections, and in other cases have limited the publishers of this volume to very fragmentary selections. It is particularly to be regretted that for this reason selections could not be given from Richard Malcolm Johnston and Mr. James Lane Allen, though there is some compensation in the case of the latter in the admirable study by the late Professor John Bell Henneman. Some of the most popular of the contemporary writers have had to be omitted for lack of space. Adequate selections from a few representative writers have been made rather than short selections from a greater number.

The Introduction attempts to give some idea of the main tendencies of Southern fiction—tendencies that are found to be those of American fiction as well. Part One treats of Southern fiction before the War of Secession, and Part Two of Southern fiction after the war. While the lives of the writers have not been given in full, the principal events in the life of each writer have been suggested as essential to the proper understanding of his works. The Introduction is also an interpretation of the selections. Frequently the full story of a novel is suggested in order that the context of the selection may be seen. The reader should therefore refer constantly to the Introduction before reading the different selections. Notes have been sparingly used because this volume is intended, not for school-children nor specialists, but for the general reader.

The editor has profited by all the books referred to in the bibliographical note at the end of the Introduction, but he is under special obligations to Professor Trent's *William Gilmore Simms* and *Southern Writers,* Henry Watterson's *Oddities of Southern Life and Character,* Link's *Pioneers of Southern Literature,* and Baskervill's *Southern Writers.* To the following publishers he would express his keen appreciation of their kindness in permitting him to use selections from copyright material: Houghton, Mifflin Company, Charles Scribner's Sons, D. Appleton and Company, The Century Company, G. P. Putnam's Sons, and Doubleday, Page and Company.

E. M.

INTRODUCTION.

I.—SOUTHERN FICTION PRIOR TO THE WAR OF SECESSION.

NOTHING was more striking about the recent centenary celebrations in memory of Edgar Allan Poe than the effort to relate him to international, national, and even Southern tendencies of his time. It was for a long time popular to consider him as "a world artist, unrelated to his local origin, unindebted to it, and existing in a cosmopolitan limbo, denationalized, almost dehumanized." In contradistinction to this prevailing opinion, different writers, from widely different standpoints, have insisted upon the influence of his Southern environment.

Though born in Boston, he spent his youthful days in Richmond, as an adopted son in a family that was in close touch with the best elements of Southern life. At a Richmond classical school he received that classical training which was particularly characteristic of the ante-bellum South. He resided for a few months at the newly established University of Virginia, where his training in classical, as well as in modern literature, was noteworthy. President Alderman in an address at the Poe celebration held at the University of Virginia felicitously suggested the probable influence of the University on its most renowned alumnus. There is perhaps a conceit in his words, but one that may be accepted as a half truth:

"It is probably true that 'Annabel Lee' and the 'Ode to Helen' would have sung themselves out of Poe's heart and throat if he had never seen the University of Virginia; but surely there was genuine inspiration in the place in that time of its dim beginning. There were noble books here, few in number and great in quality. Coleridge, Byron, Shelley, Keats, and the great Greeks were all here; sincere scholars from the old world and the new had set up their homes here. Here were unbeaten youths with young hearts and passions; here hopes gleamed and ambitions burned. And then, as now, beauty dwelt upon the venerable hills encircling the horizon, and the university itself lay new and chaste in its simple lines upon the young lawn. I venture to think sometimes that when our poet wrote those stateliest lines of his—

> To the glory that was Greece,
> And the grandeur that was Rome—

perhaps there flashed into his mind's eye the vision of the Rotunda upon some such night as this, with its soaring columns whitened by the starlight and vying with the beauty and witchery of the white winter about us."

It is certain that in Baltimore Poe received his first recognition, when the committee, of which John P. Kennedy was a member, discovered his genius as a poet and as a writer of short stories.

In Richmond, after years of wandering, Poe became editor of the most distinctively Southern magazine, the *Southern Literary Messenger*. In this he published his earliest poems and prose tales, and here also he published the criticism of contemporary writings which made him famous. Poe's critical writings indicate, perhaps better than any of his other writings, his Southern bent of mind; for here he manifested a characteristic prejudice against New England writers and a corresponding sympathy with Southern writers. In a criticism of Lowell he wrote a striking defense of slavery. In such sentences as the following, written in 1848, he seemed to align himself definitely with Southern men of letters: "Pinckney was born too far South"; "Had the 'George Balcombe' of Beverley Tucker been the work of any one born north of Mason's and Dixon's line, it would have been long ago recognized as one of the very noblest pictures ever written by an

American"; "It is high time that the literary South took its own interest into its own charge."

Other writers have not hesitated to go even farther than Poe's education and early environment and criticism to find the influence of the South on him. Prof. G. E. Woodberry in his *America in Literature* contends that Poe was as much a product of the South as Whittier was of New England:

"His breeding and education were Southern; his manners, habits of thought and moods of feeling were Southern; his sentimentalism, his conception of womanhood and its qualities, of manhood and its behavior, his weaknesses of character, have the stamp of his origin; his temperament, even his sensibilities, his gloom and dream, his response in color and music, were of his race and place. When he came to the North, where he spent his mature life, he brought his Southern endowment with him. * * * No stranger meeting him could have failed to recognize him as a Southerner. * * * He always lived in the North as an alien, somewhat on his guard, somewhat contemptuous of his surroundings, always homesick for the place that he well knew would know him no more though he were to return to it. In his letters, in his conversation, in all reminiscences of him, this mark of the South on him is as plain as in his color, features and personal bearing. * * * Are not all his women elaborations of suggestions from Southern types? Is not the 'House of Usher' a Southern tale at the core?"

From a very different standpoint Prof. C. Alphonso Smith suggests that the intellectual qualities of Poe are Southern, commenting especially on his critical views and on his power of artistic construction as manifest in his clear-cut, logical tales. He says:

"Poe's formative years, therefore, were spent in a society rarely trained in subtle analysis, in logical acumen, and in keen philosophic interpretation. Though Poe does not belong to politics or to statesmanship, there was much in common between his mind and that of John C. Calhoun, widely separated as were their characters and the arenas on which they played their part. Both were keenly alive to the implication of a phrase. Both reasoned with an intensity born not of impulsiveness but of sheer delight in making delicate distinctions. Both showed in their choice of words an element of the pure classicism that lingered longer in the South than in New England or Old England; and both illustrated an individual independence more characteristic of the South then than would be possible amid the levelling influences of to-day."*

In all of these suggestions there is perhaps a note of special pleading, a stretching of the facts in the case, but the statements may well serve to indicate the particular Southern quality of Poe's work, at least in its intellectual aspects. Certainly no apology is needed for including in a volume of Southern fiction two of the typical stories of Poe. When he is compared with other writers of America, there is enough of the Southern environment and character in even his most romantic tales to suggest his Southern breeding and training.

When, however, Prof. Woodberry goes so far as to say that the South is manifest "in the temper of Poe's imagination, characterization, incident, atmosphere and landscape," one may well dissent. For, after all, Poe's imagination was of neither time nor place. One of the striking things about his stories is that they suggest in no way any distinctively Southern landscape. The first part of his *Tale of the Ragged Mountains* is laid in the country around Charlottesville, Virginia, where the local color would seem to be especially fine; and yet Poe has scarcely begun to tell the story before a suggestion of certain weird aspects of the scenery leads him to place the main body of the story in far-away India:

"I found myself at the foot of a high mountain, looking down into a vast plain, through which wound a majestic river. On the margin of this river stood an eastern-looking city such as we read of in the 'Arabian Tales,' but of character even more singular than any there described. * * * The houses were wildly picturesque. On every hand was a wilderness of balconies, of verandas, of minarets, of shrines, and fantastically carved oriels. Besides these things were seen, on all sides, banners and palanquins, litters with stately dames closely veiled, elephants gorgeously caparisoned, idols grotesquely hewn. * * * Beyond the limits of the city arose, in frequent majestic groups, the palm and cocoa, with other gigantic

*Address at the Poe Centenary Celebration, University of Virginia, 1909.

and weird trees of vast age; and here and there might be seen a field of rice, the thatched hut of a peasant, a tank, a stray temple, a gypsy camp, or a solitary graceful maiden taking her way, with a pitcher upon her head, to the banks of the magnificent river."

The scene of *The Gold Bug* is Sullivan's Island near Charleston, and yet there is only a slight suggestion of one of the most picturesque backgrounds that might be imagined. Poe's interest in the story is in the mathematical puzzle with which Legrand's mind is entirely infatuated. Baudelaire once said that America was only a vast prison which Poe traversed with the feverish agitations of a being made to breathe in a rare world; his inner life was a ceaseless effort to escape the influence of this antipathetic atmosphere. All American writers with romantic tendency have felt the need of an antique background for their stories. Some of them have found it in the vanished life of the colonial era and in certain legends and traditions found in out-of-the-way places. But Poe could find backgrounds for his strange and weird tales only in far-off lands, sometimes even in the middle ages, or yet again in the fantastic creations of his own mind as it went voyaging through strange seas of imagination alone. "He haunted a borderland between the visible and the invisible, a land of waste places, ruined battlements and shadowy forms, wrapped in a melancholy twilight."

Sometimes, as in *The Fall of the House of Usher*, the story has no definite location on the map. One of the strong points of this story is the wonderful picture, in the first two paragraphs and in the concluding, of the strange house and its enveloping landscape. Every detail of the background contributes to the climax of the story. The singularly dreary tract of country, the black and lurid tarn, the vacant eye-like windows, the few rank sedges,

the white trunks of decayed trees, the gothic archway of the hall, the sombre tapestries of the walls,
the ebon blackness of the floors, the phantasmagoric
armorial trophies, the encrimsoned light and
trellissed panes of the windows—all these serve to
render the total effect of the story startlingly impressive.

Noteworthy also are the backgrounds of the
stories which are laid in different European countries, which Poe had never seen. *The Mask of
the Red Death* is a story of northern Italy, *The
Assignation* of Venice, *The Cask of Amontillado* of
the Roman catacombs, *Metzengerstein* of Hungary,
The Pit and the Pendulum of the Spanish Inquisition, and *Hop Frog* of France. Of these *The Assignation* may best serve to illustrate Poe's exquisite
handling of foreign background:

(How different is Poe's Venice from that of
Bryan or Ruskin!)

"It was at Venice, beneath the covered archway there called the
Ponte di Sospiri, that I met for the third or fourth time the person
of whom I speak. It is with a confused recollection that I bring to
mind the circumstances of that meeting. Yet I remember—ah! how
should I forget?—the deep midnight, the Bridge of Sighs, the
beauty of woman, and the Genius of Romance that stalked up and
down the narrow canal.

"It was a night of unusual gloom. The great clock of the Piazza
had sounded the fifth hour of the Italian evening. The square of
the Campanile lay silent and deserted, and the lights in the old
Ducal Palace were dying fast away. I was returning home from
the Piazzetta, by way of the Grand Canal. But as my gondola
arrived opposite the mouth of the canal San Marco, a female voice
from its recesses broke suddenly upon the night, in one wild,
hysterical and long-continued shriek. Startled at the sound, I
sprang upon my feet, while the gondolier, letting slip his single oar,
lost it in the pitchy darkness beyond a chance of recovery, and we
were consequently left to the guidance of the current which here
sets from the greater into the smaller channel. Like some huge and
sable-feathered condor, we were slowly drifting down towards the
Bridge of Sighs, when a thousand flambeaus flashing from the
windows, and down the staircases of the Ducal Palace, turned all
at once that deep gloom into a livid and preternatural day."

As his backgrounds are in no sense American or Southern, so his characters are even more delocalized. The use of the negro character in *The Gold Bug* clearly suggests Poe's inability to individualize flesh and blood characters. His various women characters—the Eleanoras, Ligeias and Morellas—are mere tapestry figures and his men are "the Alastors of a doleful land where gloomed his own valley of the shadow." "His favorite hero is the descendant of a race of visionaries, brooding over occult books, in a vaulted, tapestried chamber of his hereditary halls, in some 'dim, decaying city by the Rhine.'" Of his women and men characters Usher and his sister may be taken as types which are repeated with varying effect in all his other stories. The type of woman is most concisely and imaginatively presented in *Ligeia:*

"There is one dear topic, however, on which my memory fails me not. It is the *person* of Ligeia. In stature she was tall, somewhat slender, and, in her latter days, even emaciated. I would in vain attempt to portray the majesty, the quiet ease, of her demeanor, or the incomprehensible lightness and elasticity of her footfall. She came and departed as a shadow. I was never made aware of her entrance into my closed study, save by the dear music of her low sweet voice, as she placed her marble hand upon my shoulder. In beauty of face no maiden ever equalled her. It was the radiance of an opium-dream—an airy and spirit-lifting vision more wildly divine than the fantasies which hovered about the slumbering souls of the daughters of Delos. Yet her features were not of that regular mould which we have been falsely taught to worship in the classical labors of the heathen. 'There is no exquisite beauty,' says Bacon, Lord Verulam, speaking truly of all the forms and genera of beauty, 'without some *strangeness* in the proportion.' Yet, although I saw that the features of Ligeia were not of a classic regularity—although I perceived that her loveliness was indeed 'exquisite,' and felt that there was much of 'strangeness' pervading it, yet I have tried in vain to detect the irregularity and to trace home my own perception of 'the strange.' I examined the contour of the lofty and pale forehead: it was faultless—how cold indeed that word when applied to a majesty so divine!—the skin rivalling the purest ivory, the commanding extent and repose, the gentle prominence of the regions above the temples; and then the raven-black, the glossy, the luxuriant and naturally-curling tresses, setting forth the full

force of the Homeric epithet, 'hyacinthine!' I looked at the delicate outlines of the nose—and nowhere but in the graceful medal-
lions of the Hebrews had I beheld a similar perfection. There were
the same luxurious smoothness of surface, the same scarcely perceptible tendency to the aquiline, the same harmoniously curved
nostrils speaking the free spirit. I regarded the sweet mouth. Here
was indeed the triumph of all things heavenly—the magnificent turn
of the short upper lip—the soft, voluptuous slumber of the under—
the dimples which sported, and the color which spoke—the teeth
glancing back, with a brilliancy almost startling, every ray of the
holy light which fell upon them in her serene and placid, yet most
exultingly radiant of all smiles. I scrutinized the formation of the
chin: and here, too, I found the gentleness of breadth, the softness
and the majesty, the fulness and the spirituality, of the Greek—
the contour which the god Apollo revealed but in a dream to Cleo-
menes, the son of the Athenian. And then I peered into the large
eyes of Ligeia.

"For eyes we have no models in the remotely antique. It might
have been, too, that in these eyes of my beloved lay the secret to
which Lord Verulam alludes. They were, I must believe, far larger
than the ordinary eyes of our own race. They were even fuller than
the fullest of the gazelle eyes of the tribe of the valley of Nourja-
had. Yet it was only at intervals—in moments of intense excitement—that this peculiarity became more than slightly noticeable
in Ligeia. And at such moments was her beauty—in my heated
fancy thus it appeared perhaps—the beauty of beings either above
or apart from the earth, the beauty of the fabulous Houri of the
Turk. The hue of the orbs was the most brilliant of black, and, far
over them, hung jetty lashes of great length. The brows, slightly
irregular in outline, had the same tint. The 'strangeness,' however, which I found in the eyes, was of a nature distinct from the
formation, or the color, or the brilliancy of the features, and must,
after all, be referred to the *expression*. Ah, word of no meaning!
behind whose vast latitude of mere sound we intrench our ignorance
of so much of the spiritual. The expression of the eyes of Ligeia!
How for long hours have I pondered upon it! How have I, through
the whole of a midsummer night, struggled to fathom it! What was
it—that something more profound than the well of Democritus—
which lay far within the pupils of my beloved? What *was* it? I
was possessed with a passion to discover. Those eyes! those large,
those shining, those divine orbs! they became to me twin stars of
Leda, and I to them devoutest of astrologers."

Perhaps his own Virginia Clemm was the model
of his fragile and hauntingly beautiful women.
Certainly there is a suggestion in all of Poe's tales
of his own weird and strongly-marked personality.
If one should make a composite picture of William

Wilson, William Legrand and Usher, he would have
an adequate picture of Poe—the morbid conscience,
the acute intellect, the romantic imagination. After
all, the suggestion of one's own personality is one
of the greatest effects in literature. In his characters, as in his style, Poe makes one aware of his own
individuality. One would have no difficulty in
detecting some hitherto undiscovered story or poem
of his. In this respect, as in so many others, Poe
is closely identified with the romantic movement of
his century, for, as a brilliant critic has said, "the
very essence of romanticism lies in the passionate
assertion of literary or artistic individuality."

No better characterization of Poe has been written
than his own words in the story, *Berenice:*

"My baptismal name is Egæus; that of my family I will not mention. Yet there are no towers in the land more time-honored than
my gloomy, gray, hereditary halls. Our line has been called a race
of visionaries; and in many striking particulars—in the character
of the family mansion, in the frescoes of the chief saloon, in the
tapestry of the dormitories, in the chiselling of some buttresses in
the armory, but more especially in the gallery of antique paintings,
in the fashion of the library chamber, and, lastly, in the very peculiar
nature of the library contents—there is more than sufficient evidence
to warrant the belief.

"The recollections of my earliest years are connected with that
chamber, and with its volumes. * * * There is a remembrance of
aerial forms, of spiritual and meaning eyes, of sounds musical yet
sad; a remembrance which will not be excluded; a memory like a
shadow—vague, variable, indefinite, unsteady. * * * The realities
of the world affected me as visions, and as visions only, while the
wild ideas of the land of dreams became, in turn, not the material
of my every-day existence, but in very deed that existence utterly
and solely itself.

"To muse for long, unwearied hours with my attention riveted
to some frivolous device on the margin or in the typography of a
book; to become absorbed, for the better part of a summer's day, in
a quaint shadow falling aslant upon the tapestry or upon the floor;
to lose myself for an entire night in watching the steady flame of a
lamp or the embers of a fire; to dream away whole days over the
perfume of a flower * * * —such were a few of the most common and least pernicious vagaries induced by a condition of the
mental faculties, not, indeed, altogether unparalleled, but certainly
bidding defiance to anything like analysis or explanation."

Aside from all questions of background or characterization, Poe's stories make yet another appeal
to the reader and the critic. His great contribution
to American literature, and indeed to world literature, aside from his poetry, was his preëminent success as a writer of short stories. Both by theory and
by practice, he served to fix forever what was practically a new form of literature—a form that has
come to occupy a commanding place in the contemporary literature of all nations. Fortunately
he has left to us a complete statement of his ideal
of this form of fiction—a statement that is similar
to his plea for the short poem in his "Philosophy of
Composition." In a review of Hawthorne's *Twice
Told Tales in* 1842, he says:

"The ordinary story is objectionable from its length, for reasons
already stated in substance. As it cannot be read at one sitting, it
deprives itself, of course, of the immense force derivable from
totality. Worldly interests intervening during the pauses of perusal
modify, annul, or contract, in a greater or less degree, the impressions of the book. But simply cessation in reading would, of itself,
be sufficient to destroy the true unity. In the brief tale, however,
the author is enabled to carry out the fulness of his intention, be
it what it may. During the hour of perusal the soul of the reader
is at the writer's control. There are no external or extrinsic influences—resulting from weariness or interruption.

"A skillful literary artist has constructed a tale. If wise, he has
not fashioned his thoughts to accommodate his incidents; but having
conceived, with deliberate care, a certain unique or single *effect* to
be wrought out, he then invents such incidents—then combines such
events as may best aid him in establishing this preconceived effect.
If his very initial sentence tend not to the outbringing of this effect,
then he has failed in his first step. In the whole composition there
should be no word written of which the tendency, direct or indirect,
is not to the one preëstablished design. As by such means, with
such care and skill, a picture is at length painted which leaves in
the mind of him who contemplates it with a kindred art a sense
of the fullest satisfaction. The idea of the tale has been presented
unblemished, because undisturbed; and this is an end unattainable
by the novel. Undue brevity is just as exceptionable here as in the
poem; but undue length is yet more to be avoided."

This "totality of effect" which Poe insisted upon
in both his stories and poems is produced in the

most impressive way in all his best stories and in none more so than in the two which are herewith published. It is not necessary here to analyze the technical aspects of short story writing. Perhaps it is well to call attention to the various kinds of short stories which Poe wrote. There is no better classification than that used in the Stedman-Woodberry edition of his complete works. We have first the Romances of Death, such as *The Fall of the House of Usher, Berenice, Ligeia* and *Eleanora,* all of which present that most characteristic note in all Poe's work—the passing away of a beautiful and fragile woman. Interesting, too, are those dialogues, the most notable of which is the *Colloquy of Mona and Una,* which suggests the point of view of spirits who have just arrived in the other world. There was a strange fascination for Poe in the thought of death and immortality—not the healthy and even spiritual aspects of either, but the somewhat morbid and abnormal view of the borderland between the visible and the invisible. Of the Old World Romances mention has already been made. It is only necessary to add here that each of them is marked by singularly fine reproductions of certain antique backgrounds. Of the Tales of Conscience the most notable are *William Wilson, The Black Cat* and *The Imp of the Perverse.* In these stories comparison with Hawthorne is most obvious. Both romancers wrote with singular power—and yet in what different ways!—of the haunting effect of sin on the human soul. The stories by which Poe has most directly affected contemporary writers in England and France are those Tales of Ratiocination, as Poe called them, or detective stories, as they are more commonly called, such as *The Gold Bug, Murder in Rue Morgue* and *The Purloined Letter.* Far less successful but typical of certain intellectual characteristics of Poe are the Tales of Pseudo-science, in which he exercised his strange power of scientific analysis. Poe undoubtedly affected scholarship, and nowhere so much as in these efforts to bring current scientific discoveries into the domain of fiction, and nowhere did he exercise his ingenuity with better effect. Of these stories *The MS. Found in a Bottle* is perhaps the best. The least successful of all his efforts are those characterized by his editors as Tales of Extravaganza and Caprice, such as *A Tale of Jerusalem, The Angel of the Odd* and *Lionizing.* Poe had no sense of humor, and wherever he attempted it, whether as caricature or satire, he failed. Equally unsuccessful is his long story of Adventure and Exploration, *Arthur Gordon Pym.*

In all except these last stories Poe was nearly always master of a style marked by distinction and beauty. If in his poetry he suggests comparison oftenest with Coleridge, in his prose one inevitably thinks of De Quincey, especially in the tendency towards apostrophes and ejaculations. Poe can be at times as clear-cut in his style as the most extreme realist, but at other times there is all the charm of melody and color. The pursuit of perfection in phrase and form was one of his most characteristic passions. After all, this is his great bequest to American literature, and especially to Southern. Nowhere else in this Introduction will there be such an opportunity to comment on felicity and finality of style and perfection of literary form. In no other Southern stories is there such haunting beauty of style or such steadfast adherence to the demands of art for art's sake.

. If it was Poe's part to introduce Southern fiction by his own faultless stories, it was also his duty as editor of the *Southern Literary Messenger* to write the first noteworthy reviews of the books of South-

ern writers who were to play an important part in
the furtherance of creative writing in the South.
In May, 1835, he wrote an enthusiastic review of
Kennedy's *Horse-Shoe Robinson,* in January, 1836,
a very critical notice of Simms's *The Partisan,* and
in March, 1836, a highly laudatory review of Longstreet's *Georgia Scenes*—the first two books destined
to open up the field of historical romance, and the
last to inaugurate a series of sketches of contemporary life in the southwest. These books, along
with Poe's own stories, some of which appeared the
same year (1835), may well serve to define the three
kinds of fiction written in the ante-bellum South—
the purely romantic short story, the historical romance, and the humorous portrayal of contemporary
life in pioneer sections.

Of *Horse-Shoe Robinson,* to the author of which he
was under special obligation, Poe says:

"If ever volumes were entitled to be called original—these are so
entitled. We have read from beginning to end with the greatest
attention, and feel very little afraid of hazarding our critical
reputation, when we assert that they will place Mr. Kennedy at once
in the very first ranks of American novelists. * * * The novelist
has been peculiarly fortunate in the choice of an epoch, a scene and
a subject. We sincerely think that he has done them all the fullest
justice, and has worked out, with these and with other materials,
a book of no ordinary character. * * * We have called the style
of Mr. K. a style simple and forcible, and we have no hesitation in
calling it, at the same time, richly figurative and poetical."

Poe afterwards wrote more favorable criticisms
of Simms, but in his review of *The Partisan* he was
extremely severe, criticising its ungrammatical
language, the great majority of the characters, the
confused and ill-arranged story, and the general
failure of the author to produce the effects of a
genuine historical romance. "Instances of bad
taste—villainously bad taste—occur frequently in
the book." He closes, however, by saying, "In spite,

however, of its manifest and manifold blunders and
impertinences, *The Partisan* is no ordinary work.
Its historical details are replete with interest. The
concluding scenes are well drawn. Some passages
descriptive of swamp scenery are exquisite.''

Never was a writer more different from Poe than
Longstreet, and never was there a better illustration of catholicity in criticism than Poe's criticism
of the *Georgia Scenes,* nor a better evidence of Poe's
ability to apply right standards to a contemporary
book. He says:

"The author is a clever fellow, imbued with a spirit of the truest
humor, and endowed, moreover, with an exquisitely discriminative
and penetrating understanding of character in general, and of
southern character in particular. * * * If this book were printed
in England it would make the fortune of its author. * * * Seldom
—perhaps never in our lives—have we laughed as immoderately
over any book as over the one now before us. If these scenes have
produced such effect upon our cachinnatory nerves—upon us who are
not 'of the merry mood,' and, moreover, have not been used to the
perusal of somewhat similar things—we are at no loss to imagine
what a hubbub they would occasion in the unitiated region of
Cockaigne. * * * The whole anecdote is told with a raciness and
vigor which would do honor to the pages of Blackwood. * * * Altogether this very humorous, and very clever, book forms an era in
our reading. It has reached us per mail, and without a cover.
We will have it bound forthwith, and give it a niche in our library
as a sure omen of better days for the literature of the South."

Thus did Poe welcome into the realm of letters
three men who were destined to play important rôles
in Southern literary history. Let us now consider
them more in detail.

William Gilmore Simms was in striking contrast
with Poe in many respects. Every thing that Poe
wrote has the touch of finality upon it—it is characterized by discipline and restraint. Simms left
behind a great mass of material—essays, poems, bi-
ographies, short stories and novels—but scarcely
any one of his writings gives evidence of either discipline or restraint. Poe cultivated a scanty plot of

ground, but the harvest was full and bountiful. Simms cultivated an immense estate, but the returns were meagre. The permanent result was out of all proportion to the quantity of labor bestowed upon it. Poe made little conscious effort in behalf of Southern literature; Simms, during his long and eventful life, did everything in his power to make use of the material that was at hand in the South and to encourage younger Southern writers to develop their talents.

There will always attach to Simms, therefore, the interest of being a pioneer in the promotion of the literature of the South. If he had serious limitations as a creative artist, he must yet be considered the most representative man of letters of the antebellum period. The historical value of much of what seems now ephemeral writing is, therefore, very great. As a contemporary influence, as editor and essayist, he deserves the careful consideration of all students of Southern history and literature. In another volume of this publication his work as an editor of various magazines has been treated in full. What concerns us here is his work as a novelist. And, after all, it is as the author of *The Yemassee* and *The Partisan* that he will be remembered.

Simms was prepared by inheritance and by early environment for the rôle of a romancer. His grandmother, who, after the death of his mother, reared him, told him many stories of the Revolutionary War, and especially many of the incidents of the British capture of Charleston.* She was also fond of telling him weird tales of ghosts and witches, some of which had been told her by her father. Simms's own father came to this country from Ireland, and, after living for awhile in Charleston, moved out to the border region, finally settling on

*Simms was born in Charleston April 17, 1806, and died there June 11, 1870.

a plantation in Mississippi. On a visit to Charleston he told his son many stories of the southwest. He had been in the battle of New Orleans and was a close friend of Andrew Jackson. "The man who had killed his own horse for food, and lived on it for seven days, was no ordinary hero in the eyes of his son." In 1824, and later in 1830, Simms visited his father in Mississippi, going partly by boat and partly on horseback. His father had just returned from a trip of 300 miles into the heart of the Indian country. The son rode with his father to visit the Creek and Cherokee Indians, and one night slept on a grave which he always believed was that of one of De Soto's followers. One may easily see the effect of this first-hand observation of pioneer and Indian life on his later romances. Some of the characters he met with in his travels are thus suggested by his biographer, Prof. W. P. Trent:

"The broken-down aristocrat from the older state, planting his first crop of cotton with the aid of lazy slaves and still lazier Indians; the hardy North Carolina mountaineer, building a cabin similar to the one left behind, and still supporting himself and family on what his rifle could bring down; the half-breed, as slimy as the swamp in which he took up his abode; the flashy gambler compelled to fly from Mobile or New Orleans, and amusing himself while in hiding by practicing on the simple-shrewd inhabitants of a cross-roads settlement; the rascally pettifogger; the pompous and absurd justice of the peace; the Yankee peddler; the Methodist circuit rider; and, finally, the hearty sensible woodsman, now fighting like a tiger, and now as gentle as a lamb—all these he rode with, ate with, and slept with, and they live yet in his pages."*

His father strongly urged Simms to remain in the southwest, saying, that he would guarantee him a future and in ten years a seat in Congress, but the son very wisely decided to return to Charleston, which city, despite its indifference to him and his struggle to make a place for himself, had a strange fascination for him.

---

*Life of Simms in the *American Men of Letters* series.

After being an apprentice to a druggist and then studying law, he began to write poetry, publishing his first two volumes in the very same years which saw the publication of Poe's first two—1827 and 1829. In 1830, at the time of the Nullification controversy, he arrayed himself with Legaré, Petigru and others against the extreme followers of Calhoun and Hayne. This step made him unpopular. Incidentally it served to divert his attention from politics to literature, a tendency still further accentuated by a visit to the North. He was thrown in pleasant social relations with William Cullen Bryant and other literary men in New York, who encouraged him to give himself to literary work. In 1834, while on another trip to the North, he wrote *Martin Faber,* which was published by the Harpers, and in the same year *Guy Rivers,* which was published in New York and London. The latter was the first of his border romances, which later included *Richard Hurdis, Border Beagles, Beauchampe,* and others, all of which dealt with sensational incidents in the southwest. *Guy Rivers* is typical of the rest. It opens with a young aristocrat, dissipated and seemingly broken-hearted, wending his way from the East into the undiscovered forests of the West. He meets with many adventures, and himself becomes one of a band of outlaws. The public, which just at that time was tiring a bit of Cooper, turned to this sensational story with amazing gusto. Three editions were published in a year and the author received several hundred dollars. He was hailed as ''the new Southern writer.''

Returning to Charleston he worked during the winter of 1834 on *The Yemassee.* He carried the manuscript with him to New York in the spring of 1835. Drawing upon the stories and traditions which had been familiar to him from childhood and studying carefully the printed and manuscript sources of early colonial history, he was able to present as faithful a picture of Indian and colonial life as Cooper had of another section. The historical background of the romance is the period of 1715, when the Yemassee Indians, joining with the Spaniards, rose against their former allies, the English of South Carolina.

There are three Indian characters drawn with great power. Sanutee, one of the older chiefs, realizing that his own people are becoming corrupted by the English and feeling that a sort of sad fate awaits his nation, goes from the Indian capital one evening to inspect the English block-house, which is the fortress of the whites. His journey through the forest and his reflections serve as an admirable introduction to the story. His son, Occonestoga, is in thorough sympathy with the English who have taught him the use of whiskey; in his father's eye he is an illustration of what may happen to the entire nation. Matiwan, the wife of Sanutee, is one of the best Indians ever drawn in fiction. She plays a difficult rôle, drawn one way by the love of her husband and another by the love of her son. The climax of her dramatic situation is reached in the thrilling chapter which is reproduced in the selections, when she kills her son in order that he may not receive the curse of his tribe. In addition to these three characters, Simms has given vivid descriptions of the Indian council, the war dance, the wild chant of battle, and their resourcefulness in finding their way through the seemingly impenetrable forests. The conclusion of the story is an account of their attack upon the block-house and their final defeat by the English.

The white characters are not so successfully portrayed. Governor Craven, who disguises himself as an English cavalier soldier; Dr. Matthews, a serious, stern Scotch Presbyterian minister; Bess Matthews, his daughter and the beloved of the disguised Governor; and the brave woman who single-handed resists the attack of the Indians—these are some of the most significant characters.

Simms's use of dialogue is very unsatisfactory; pitiable almost is the dialect put into the mouth of the negro slave, and scarcely less so the various love scenes. But no failure of Simms to meet successfully all the demands of a novel can take away his glory as a genuine story-teller. The book is full of stirring incidents, of hairbreadth escapes. The difficulty is that there are too many such incidents— a fact that cannot destroy the effect, however, of such scenes as the escape of Harrison from the Indian guard-house, the dramatic rescue of the heroine from the rattlesnake, the final siege of the blockhouse, and, above all, the chapter which centers about the execution of the young Indian.

Scarcely less interesting and successful than *The Yemassee* is *The Partisan*, which Simms also published in 1835. By this time he had begun to see the wealth of material afforded by his state's history and traditions. In the preface he tells us how he came to write the story:

"It was while spending part of a summer with a friend in the neighborhood of the once beautiful, but now utterly decayed, town of Dorchester, that I availed myself of the opportunity to revisit the ancient ruins of the place. When a boy I had frequently rambled over the ground, and listened to its domestic chronicles, from the lips of one—now no more—who had been perfectly conversant with its local history, as with a large body of Revolutionary and traditional history besides.

"Many of its little legends were impressed upon my memory, and the fortunes of more than one of its families, of whom no record now remains, but that of the place of burial, were deeply scored upon my mind. * * * It was with the revival of old memories, and the awakening of new impulses and sentiments, that I rambled through the solemn tabernacles of decay—the dismantled church,

the steeple overgrown with ivy and tenanted by a family of owls—
the frowning fortress of the British, overgrown with vines and
shrub-trees.''

The town of Dorchester and the surrounding country had been the scene of the uprising of the partisans in 1780, at a time when the Tory ascendancy in
the state was most despotic. Simms, stirred by
every motive of patriotism and inspired by his historic imagination, entered into the telling of the
story with all his energy. The romance has not only
an historical value, but deserves to rank with the
best romances that have been written in this country. Certainly it will tend to keep alive the memory
of Marion, ''the Swamp Fox,'' and his brave followers.

One of the most attractive features of the story
is Simms's description of the cypress swamps,
whence the American soldiers would sweep out on
the unsuspecting British soldiers:

"The party followed as their guide directed, and, after some twenty
minutes' plunging, they were deep in the shadow and the shelter of
the swamp. The gloom was thicker around them, and was only
relieved by the pale and skeleton forms of the cypresses, clustering in groups along the plashy sides of the still lake. Sometimes a
phosphorescent gleam played over the stagnant pool, while on the
neighboring bank the frogs of all degrees croaked forth their in-
harmonious chant, making the scene more hideous, and certainly
adding greatly to the sense of gloom which it inspired in those who
penetrated it.''

So much for the historical background and the
scenery of the romance, both of which are still further suggested by the selections given in the text.
The incidents are not so graphic as in *The Yemassee,*
but such passages as the description of the storm
which overtakes Captain Singleton and his comrades
and the account of the rescue of Colonel Walton
from the British partisans show Simms at his best
as a romancer. An element of the weird is found

in the episode that centres about the witch and her uncanny son. The presentation of Marion and his men, though to some extent more historical than romantic, is vivid and picturesque. Perhaps the most original characters in the book is Porgy, who is a combination of Falstaff and the old-time Southern colonel. In him there is also a suggestion of Simms himself:

"Porgy was a good-looking fellow, spite of his mammoth dimensions. He had a fine, fresh, manly face, clear complexion and light blue eyes, the archness of which was greatly heightened by its comparative littleness. It was a sight to provoke a smile on the face of Mentor, to see those little blue eyes twinkling with treacherous light as he watched Dr. Oakenburg plunging from pool to pool under his false guidance, and condoling with him afterwards. * * * If Oakenburg was as lean as the Knight of La Mancha, Porgy was quite as stout as Sancho. At a glance you saw that he was a jovial philosopher—one who enjoyed his bottle with his humors, and did not suffer the one to be soured by the other. It was clear that he loved all the good things of this life, and some possibly that we may not call good with sufficient reason. His abdomen and brains seemed to work together. He thought of eating perpetually, and, while he ate, still thought. But he was not a mere eater. He rather amused himself with a hobby when he made food his topic, as Falstaff discoursed of his own cowardice without feeling it. He was a wag, and exercised his wit with whomsoever he traveled; Dr. Oakenburg, on the present occasion, offering himself as an admirable subject for victimization. To quiz the Doctor was Porgy's recipe against the tedium of a swamp progress, and the fertile humors of the wag perpetually furnished him occasions for the exercise of his faculty. He was attended by a negro body-servant—a fellow named Tom, and of humors almost as keen and lively as his own. Tom was a famous cook, after the fashion of the Southern planters, who could win his way to your affection through his soups, and needed no other argument. He was one of that class of faithful, half-spoiled negroes who will never suffer any liberties with his master except such as he takes himself."

Between 1835, which witnessed the appearance of these two striking romances, and 1842 Simms was a prolific romancer, but he never again attained the success achieved in his first ventures. He did not attempt to write further about Indians, but he wrote sequels to *The Partisan,* none of which are

successful.* His border romances, to which reference has already been made, were also unsuccessful.
The amazing thing is that Simms did not fulfill the
promise of his first two romances. He settled at
"Woodlands"—the estate of his second wife—under
conditions most favorable for his work. Here he
entertained some of the most famous writers of
his country; here he gradually gathered a large library; and here for several years he worked with
prodigious energy during the winter months. The
account of his literary habits shows that it was
his custom to write thirty pages of manuscript every
morning, whatever diversions might tempt him. His
fame was rapidly spreading throughout this country and Europe; and one might well have prophe-
sied a prosperous and constantly expanding literary
career.

Two reasons may be assigned, however, for his
failure to realize his possibilities. He was a careless writer. The story is told of him that he took
The Partisan to New York with him uncompleted.
Printers soon caught up with him. When he expressed a desire to take a holiday of a week, the
publishers told him they could not wait. "Give me
pen, ink and paper," he said, "and I will go upstairs and find a place to write." In less than half
an hour he came down again with more manuscript
than would be required during his absence. The incident is characteristic. He says in the preface to
one of his books in apologizing for its defects, "I
find it much easier to invent a new story than to repair the defects of an old one." Like Cooper and
Scott, he was unable to give the attention to the details of his work which they required; and even the
general structure of his romances suffered from his

---

*They are *Mellichampe* (1836), *Katharine Walton* (1851), *The Foragers* (1855)
and *Eutaw* (1856).

lack of discipline and restraint. Hence we have even
grammatical mistakes, to say nothing of carelessly
written dialogue and incident.

A still further reason for Simms's failure may be
seen in his gradual absorption in the great political
and social questions of his section and in the great
number of undertakings in which he was engaged.
His versatility kept him from following the true
bent of his genius. His biographer in summarizing
his activity from 1842 to 1850 says:

"The main business of his life appeared to consist in endeavoring
to put as many irons as possible into the fire. In these eight years
he edits two magazines, begins to edit a third, is his own chief con-
tributor, and favors his New York, Philadelphia and Richmond
confrères with a perennial supply of manuscript. He is equally
dexterous in dashing off satire and in delivering Fourth of July and
commencement orations. He turns biographer, and with apparently
little effort writes the lives of three American heroes, and then
adventurously tries his hand on the romantic career of Bayard. He
continues his investigations into the history of his native state,
and publishes a geography of the same. He assumes the rôle of
critic, fills his magazines with reviews long and short, and collects
the best in two volumes. He edits apocryphal plays, and serves two
years in the legislature. And in the midst of it all he finds time for
an annual visit to the North, for jauntings through the South and
Southwest, for balls and parties in Charleston, and for the duties of
a planter at Woodlands."*

The fact is that Simms saw the great possibilities
in the undeveloped resources of Southern literature,
and sought to cover the field himself, in the absence
of any who might have helped him. Furthermore,
he became more and more interested in the political
questions of his section. There is no better illustration of the fascination which public life had for
talented Southerners than the way in which Simms
dedicated his great powers in the years before the
war to the defense of Southern institutions and
political theories.

---

*W. P. Trent: *Life of Simms.*

After the war, when he might have turned again to the writing of fiction, he was a sad and broken man. He had lost his home and with it his library of ten thousand volumes. About him in his native state was the desolation of a conquered and persecuted people. He did all in his power to help the younger writers who looked to him as their leader, his reputation bolstered up for awhile many of the short-lived Southern magazines, and he even wrote two romances about pioneer life in North Carolina; but it was too late. His wand was broken, and some of the most pathetic words ever written are those which tell the story of his heroic efforts to regain the creative power of the past. He tells us that for three nights he wrote till two in the morning on his romances. He left behind an epitaph which he desired to be put upon his tomb-stone, words which suggest poignantly the pathos of his brave career: "Here lies one who, after a reasonably long life, distinguished chiefly by unceasing labors, has left all his better works undone." If beside these words we place those of Simms's friend, Paul Hamilton Hayne, we have the key to the tragedy of his life: "Simms's genius never had fair play! Circumstances hampered him! Thus, the man was greater than his works."

John P. Kennedy (1795-1870) did not take literature so seriously as did Simms. He was a man of the same type as William Wirt, whose biography he wrote (1849). He was a lawyer and public man who was interested in literature as a recreation from his severer work. And yet we should scarcely remember that he was Secretary of the Navy under Fillmore if we did not know him as the author of *Swallow Barn* and *Horse-Shoe Robinson*.

His first story, *Swallow Barn; or a Sojourn in the Old Dominion* (1832), is written in the leisurely

style of the Eighteenth century, suggesting comparison with the *Sir Roger de Coverley Papers* and Irving's *Bracebridge Hall.* His personal friendship for
Irving, to whom one of his books is dedicated, as well
as his admiration for Addison, suggested these
sketches of life in Virginia in the first part of the
Nineteenth century. The book is a series of letters
writen by Mark Littleton to a friend in New York,
giving his impressions of a Virginia home which he
is visiting. The first part is a description of the
fine old country mansion upon the James River and
a sketch of the interesting family. The story wid-
ens, however, as the author relates some of the romantic stories of the neighborhood and sketches
various characters from the surrounding estates and
villages. It is not a novel, however, but rather—to
use the words of Kennedy's preface—"a series of
detached sketches linked together by the hooks and
eyes of a traveler's notes; and although the narrative does run into some by-paths of personal adventure, it has still preserved its desultory, sketchy
character to the last. It is therefore utterly in-
artistic in plot and structure, and may be described
as variously and interchangeably partaking of the
complexion of a book of travel, a diary, a collection
of letters, a drama and a history."

The main effort of the writer is to preserve the
details of a life which even at that time seemed to
be losing its most distinctive charm in the general
uniformity of modern American life. The whole
book is written in a mood of tender reminiscence, as
of a man in the city recalling some of the charms of
country life—"the mellow, bland and sunny luxuriance of the old-time society of Virginia, its good-
fellowship, its hearty and constitutional compan-
ionableness, the thriftless gaiety of the people, a
dogged but amiable invincibility of opinion, and that

overflowing hospitality which knew no ebb.'' Rather
copious extracts are given from this book because
it gives what is perhaps the best contemporary account of the aristocratic social life of Virginia. The
reader will not fail to see in the sketches of the lord
and lady of Swallow Barn, of Prudence Meriwether
in her flower garden, of Parson Chub, a plump, rosy
old gentleman and classical pedant with his passion
for folios, and of Phillpot Wart, types that will reveal the very form and pressure of the olden time.
Certainly there is nowhere in Southern fiction such
a realistic picture of the hospitality that reigned in
the old Virginia mansions as the account of the great
dinner given by the Meriwethers to their visitors
and neighbors. Incidentally, we have interesting
side-lights on the political questions of the day, and
especially the author's pronounced national spirit
and his view of the kindlier aspects of slavery.

Very different from this leisurely book is Kennedy's stirring romance of the Revolution, *Horse-
Shoe Robinson,* which vies with Simms' *Partisan* in
being the best of the Revolutionary romances. The
two authors were interested in the same period of
history, the uprising of the partisans during the
Tory ascendency in South and North Carolina. The
novels are not duplicates, however, for the background of Simms's story is the swamps of South
Carolina, while Kennedy's story reaches its climax
in the battle of King's Mountain. Both writers give
a vivid idea of the heroism of the brave men that
followed Marion, Sumpter, Harvey, Pickens and
other partisan leaders who ''entered with the best
spirit of chivalry into the national quarrel, and
brought to it hearts as bold, minds as vigorous, and
arms as strong as ever in any clime worked out a
national redemption.'' In a nation of legendary or

poetical associates their fame "would have been re-duplicated through a thousand channels of verse."

The circumstances under which Kennedy met the principal character of the story are graphically told in his introduction to the novel. On a visit to the western section of South Carolina he spent the night at a place to which Horse-Shoe Robinson, then an old man, was summoned to give relief to a boy who had met with a serious accident.

"What a man I saw! With near seventy years upon his poll, time seemed to have broken its billows over his front only as the ocean breaks over a rock. There he stood—tall, broad, brawny and erect. The sharp light gilded his massive frame and weatherbeaten face with a pictorial effect that would have rejoiced an artist."

On that night the old gentleman told him the thrilling story of his escape from Charleston and how he took five Scotchmen prisoners—incidents that were afterwards developed in the novel. It was long after midnight before the party broke up; and when the novelist got to bed it was to dream of Horse-Shoe and his adventures. This was the beginning of what Kennedy afterwards, with the aid of historical research, elaborated in his story.

The story opens with Robinson and Captain Butler making their way from the country around Charlottesville to join the ranks of the partisans. Horse-Shoe relates to his companion the story of his perilous escape from the Tories in Charleston. The mountaineer has come to guide Butler into the mountains of western North Carolina. Soon after they reach their destination they are both captured. Horse-Shoe escapes from his captors and tries in every way to rescue his comrade. With the aid of a mountain girl and her lover he accomplishes the feat, only, however, to see him captured again. The story then centres about the numerous frays between the Tories and Whigs in the mountain sections—the hairbreadth escapes, the long midnight rides, the fierce warfare between members of the same family even. Led by Sevier, Campbell and Shelby at King's Mountain, the Whig partisans win a glorious victory.

When the original Horse-Shoe Robinson heard the story read in his old age he remarked: "It is all true and right—excepting about them women, which I disremember. That mought be true, too, but my memory is treacherous—I disremember." It was this element of a love story that served to enhance the romantic appeal of the novel. The characters of Mary Musgrove, who in her devotion to the Whig cause proves to be a heroine of great resourcefulness, and of Mildred Lindsay, who, although the daughter of a rich Tory of Pennsylvania, follows her lover, Captain Butler, to the scene of conflict, are well drawn.

There are scenes in the story that anticipate some of the stories of Charles Egbert Craddock in their suggestion of the treachery and bravery of mountaineers. The tragic death of John Ramsay is one of the episodes of the story. But, after all, the character of Horse-Shoe dominates the entire book. He is resourceful, brave, full of good humor, and has a certain elemental sympathy with right things. When at the end of the battle he comes rushing up with the rescued Butler and throws him into Mildred's arms, saying, "Take him, ma'am, I promised myself to-day that I'd give him to you. And, now you've got him," one feels that he has been in the presence of a man loyal to friendship and patriotic at a critical time in his country's history. No better conception could be given of his character than the words of Poe in the review of the book already referred to:

"Horse-Shoe Robinson is the life and soul of the drama—the bone and sinew of the book—its very breath—its everything which gives it strength, substance and vitality. Never was there a rarer fellow—a more laughable blacksmith—a more gallant Sancho. He is the very prince at an ambuscade, and a very devil at a fight. He is a better edition of Robin Hood—quite as sagacious, not half so much of a coxcomb—and infinitely more moral. In short, he is the man of all others we should like to have riding by our side in any very hazardous expedition."

Twenty years after the publication of Kennedy's novel the last of the important romances of the South before the war made its appearance—John Esten Cooke's *The Virginia Comedians, or, Old Days in the Old Dominion*. From the historical standpoint, it fills the gap between Simms's *The Yemassee* and the two Revolutionary romances of Simms and Kennedy. The historical background is that of the period just before the Revolution, when against the Established Church and the feudal system of society the new forces of freedom and democracy began to struggle. The scene of the story is laid in Williamsburg at the time when the Virginia company of comedians at the theatre near the capitol played *The Merchant of Venice*—the first dramatic representation in America. In the well-written introduction the author suggests the setting of the story:

"It was the period of the culmination of the old social régime. A splendid society had burst into flower, and was enjoying itself in the sunshine and under the blue skies of the most beautiful of lands. The chill winds of the Revolution were about to blow; life was easy and full of laughter. * * * Social intercourse was the joy of the epoch, and crowds flocked to the race course, where the good horses were running for the cup, or to the cock-fight, where the favorite spangles fought to the death. The violin seemed to be ever playing—at the Raleigh Tavern, in Williamsburg, where young Jefferson 'danced with Belinda at the Apollo' and was happy, or in the great manor-houses of the planters clustering along the lowland rivers. In town and country life was a pageant."

To this society, sketched so brilliantly by Cooke, there comes a rude shock. Beatrice Hallam, a young actress, who is a member of the troupe of Virginia

Comedians, fascinates Effingham, a descendant of one of the first families of Virginia, while John Walters, the incarnation of the new democratic tendencies in Virginia life, becomes a disturbing political factor. The struggle between the forces of conservatism and of radicalism is dramatically presented:

"A vague unrest pervaded the atmosphere and gave warning of the approaching cataclysm. Class distinctions had been immemorially looked upon as a part of the order of nature; but certain curious and restive minds began to ask if that was just, and to glance sideways at the wealthy nabob in his fine coach. * * * On all sides murmurs, mutterings as of an approaching storm! Men doubtful of the ground they walk on—new ideas dazzling them—old institutions crumbling—a hand upon the wall tracing, in fiery letters, the mysterious future."*

Meanwhile there had sprung up in the Southwest an entirely different group of writers with very different ideals of literature. It will be recalled that the year 1835 was a notable one in the history of Southern fiction. It saw the publication in the *Southern Literary Messenger* of some of Poe's short stories, of Simms's two best romances, of Kennedy's *Horse-Shoe Robinson,* and of Longstreet's *Georgia Scenes.* In this one year we have suggested all the lines along which Southern fiction was to develop. Poe, as has been seen, represents the tendency to seek in remote countries and far-away vistas for the background of his creations. Simms and Kennedy both had an eye for the picturesque traditions and romances of Southern history. Augustus Baldwin Longstreet (1790-1870) was perhaps more strikingly original than any of them when he sought to set forth the every-day life of the rural sections of Georgia—"the nether side of Southern life." In

*Cooke never again wrote so notable a romance. After the war he published a series of novels, based on his experiences during the war—*Surry of Eagle's Nest, Mohun, Hilt to Hilt,* and others. They were widely read at the time, but they were too hurriedly and carelessly written to be of permanent value. Cooke's desire to preserve the best memories of that tragic era was commendable, but the artistic interpretation of so great a struggle was not within his power—time alone could give the proper perspective.

doing so he anticipated the methods and ideals of modern realists. His book has a value out of all proportion to its absolute value. It was popular in its own day, because it was recognized at once as a faithful interpretation of the life of a primitive people. More recently it has received increasing attention because of its relation to modern tendencies in fiction.

It is surely the irony of fate that a Methodist preacher and the president of two universities (Universities of South Carolina and Mississippi) should be remembered now chiefly as the author of a series of humorous stories. As an instructor of youth, he might well feel embarrassed by the characters and language of his book; as a Methodist preacher, he might often be confronted by his realistic pictures of the dance and the horse-race. He was so ashamed of his book that his publishers could never persuade him to revise the first edition, nor did he like to have his authorship referred to. In his preface to the first edition, which was printed in Augusta, he tells of the genesis of the stories:

"The following sketches were written rather in the hope that chance would bring them to light when time would give them interest than in the belief that they would afford any interest to the readers of the present day. They consist of nothing more than fanciful combinations of real incidents and characters; and throwing into those scenes, which would be otherwise dull and insipid, some personal accident or adventure of my own. * * * Some of the scenes are as literally true as the frailties would allow them to be. I commenced the publication of them in one of the gazettes of the state, rather more than a year ago; and I was not more pleased than astonished to find that they were well received by readers generally. For the last six months I have been importuned by persons from all quarters of the state to give them to the public in the present form. * * * This volume is purely a concession to their entreaties. I have not had it in my power to superintend the publication of them, though they issue from a press in the immediate vicinity of my residence. I discovered that, if the work was delayed until I could have an opportunity of examining the proof sheets, it would linger in the press till the expenses (already large) would become intolerable.

Consequently there may be many typographical errors among them, for which I must crave the reader's indulgence.

"I cannot conclude these introductory remarks without reminding those who have taken exception to the coarse, inelegant and sometimes ungrammatical language which the writer represents himself as occasionally using, that it is *language accommodated to the capacity of the person to whom he represents himself as speaking.*"

No apology need now be made for so faithful a picture of life in Georgia. Georgia was from the first a more democratic state than Virginia or South Carolina. Its population was composed of various types of settlers, who took part in the camp-meeting, the old-field school, the county court, the races, the gander-pulling, the debating society, the militia drill and the fox hunt. All these phases of rural social life are vividly portrayed in the *Georgia Scenes.*

Longstreet had exceptional opportunities to see country life. After graduating at Yale, he settled in Georgia as a lawyer and editor, later as a preacher and educator. In wandering around the circuit of county courts and mingling with lawyers at country taverns he heard many of the stories which he later recorded in his book. The first selection given in the text will illustrate the anecdotal character of other parts of the book. Wherever two or three Georgians are gathered together even now, there is likely to be a large number of anecdotes, more or less coarse. Their public speakers have retained in these anecdotes and even in their own speeches much of the homely *patois* of the rural section. Never was there a book that grew so vitally out of the life of the people. It is clearly an anticipation of the realistic stories of Richard Malcolm Johnston and Joel Chandler Harris, and in its elemental quality suggests the humor of Mark Twain.

Among the best-known portraits of the book are those of Ned Brace and Ransy Sniffle. Of the latter the author writes, with some of Dickens's power of caricature:

"Now there happened to reside in the county just alluded to a little fellow by the name of Ransy Sniffle: a sprout of Richmond, who, in his earlier days, had fed copiously upon red clay and black-berries. This diet had given to Ransy a complexion that a corpse would have disdained to own, and an abdominal rotundity that was quite unprepossessing. His shoulders were fleshless and elevated; his head large and flat; his neck slim and translucent; and his arms, hands, fingers and feet were lengthened out of all proportion to the rest of his frame. His joints were large and his limbs small; and as for flesh he could not, with propriety, be said to have any. Those parts which nature usually supplies with the most of this article— the calves of the legs, for example—presented in him the appearance of so many well-drawn blisters. His height was just five feet nothing; and his average weight in blackberry season, ninety-five. There was nothing on this earth which delighted Ransy so much as a fight. He never seemed fairly alive except when he was witnessing, fomenting or talking about a fight. Then, indeed, his deep sunken gray eye assumed something of a living fire, and his tongue acquired a volubility that bordered upon eloquence."

Poe was prophetic in his suggestion that the *Georgia Scenes* would be the prototype of other books in Southern literature. Longstreet's friend, William Tappan Thompson (1812-1882), was joint editor with him of the Augusta *Sentinel*. He later wrote for the Madison (Ga.) *Miscellany* a series of letters entitled *Major Jones's Courtship*, which were collected in book form in 1840. In 1843 he published the *Chronicles of Pineville*, and in 1848 some humor-ous sketches of travel in the form of letters written by "Major Jones," relating his adventures in Wash-ington and Baltimore. He was editor of the Savan-nah *Morning News* (1840-1882), and as such was the first literary patron of Joel Chandler Harris.

The best book of Mr. Thompson's was his first. "In representative quality, both as to its *dramatis personæ* and its dialect, the story is genuinely racy of the soil. It is distinctively Southern and pro-vincial." Major Jones, with his innocence of heart and homely dialect, figures as the lover of a country girl, who has just returned from Wesleyan Female College, and who has much to say, to the Major's discomfort, of "Matthew Matix," "Nat. Filosofy" and "Al. Geber." After a series of humorous adventures, such as a Georgia coon hunt, he finds that his love has not been in vain. The climax of the courtship is reached in the passage which is reproduced in the selection herewith given.

Simon Suggs, the creation of Johnson Jones Hooper (1815-1862), is a much coarser character than Major Jones. "He is," as Henry Watterson says, "a gambler by nature, by habit, by preference and by occupation. Without a virtue in the world, except his good-humor and self-possession, there is something in his vices, his insolence, his swagger, his rogueries, which, in spite of the worthlessness of the man and the dishonesty of his practices, detains and amuses us." In a word, he is a sharp and vulgar, sunny and venal swash-buckler. The son of an old "hardshell" Baptist preacher, and reared according to the strictest requirements of the moral law, he reacts in the direction of extreme dissipation and coarseness. He professes conversion at a revival meeting, only to deceive the enthusiastic Christians into giving him money to establish another mission. He avoids the judgment of a court by having a fake message sent telling of the probable death of his sons, thereby winning the sympathy of the judge for the "grief-stricken old man going home to his dying children." He is in his glory while impersonating a rich Kentuckian in a venturesome raid on the "tiger"—an antiquated form of reckless gambling. He announces his philosophy of life in the following words: "Mother Wit kin beat book-larnin' at any game. * * * Human natur' and the human family is my books, and I have never seed many but what I could hold my own with. * * *

Books ain't fitten for nothin' but gist to give to children goin' to school, to keep 'em outen mischief.'' The unfailing principle on which he acts in the "flush times," of Alabama is: "It is good to be shifty in a new country.''

The author of the book, whose full title is *The History of the Life and Adventures of Captain Simon Suggs of the Tallapoosa Volunteers,* was born in North Carolina, and moved to Alabama, where he was editor of several papers, notably the Montgomery *Mail. The Adventures,* like all the other humorous books mentioned in this sketch, appeared in a Southern newspaper; it was later published in Philadelphia in 1846. Hooper was prominent in politics, being secretary to the provisional Confederate Congress. Like Longstreet, he had occasion to regret his reputation as a humorist. At an important political convention he was called upon in the capacity of "Mr. Suggs" for a speech. Link, in recording the incident, says:

"From the character which his writings inspired, he was supposed by everybody to be always ripe for a frolic and for a roar of merriment, and that he was good at telling stories as in writing his droll descriptions, and thankful for the privilege. He stirred not an inch. More than a thousand persons, in the galleries and elsewhere, were on the tiptoe of expectation at hearing "Simon Suggs" deliver his convulsive jokes. But the feast came not, when the entrance of the committee put an end to the embarrassment of Mr. Hooper. This call by Judge Jones was referred to at the hotel, in the presence of Mr. Hooper, as an evidence of the popularity of the latter, even out of his own state. He replied that a liberty had been taken with his name which was really offensive, as showing that others looked upon him as a mere story-teller, with nothing solid in his composition. He confessed and regretted that his writings had established that character in public estimation, and that he felt its depressing influence whenever he desired or aimed to soar above it to a higher rank before the public. His ambition had been to move in quite a different channel, to enjoy the respect of men, but he had unfortunately obtained a reputation which cut off all such hopes. It was an evil day to his fortunes and to his happiness when he embarked in that class of literature, or otherwise became a chronic story-teller for the diversion of his companions. He said it was probably too late to rectify the blunder, and that he must continue to suffer the consequences."*

Of distinctively better quality than any of the books by Southern humorists is *Flush Times in Alabama and Mississippi*, by Judge Joseph Glover Baldwin (1815-1864). Like all the other humorists, he had lived in other sections than that which furnished the basis of his writing, and could thereby see the pioneer life of the Southwest in a proper perspective. At the age of twenty-one he left his home at Winchester, Va., with the scant outfit of a pony and clothing sufficient to fill a pair of saddlebags, "urged by hunger and request of friends." Magnificent accounts had come to him from the Southwest—"that sunny land of most cheering and exhilarating prospects of fussing, quarrelling, murdering, violation of contracts—in fine, of a flush tide of litigation in all of its departments, civil and criminal—a legal Utopia." He settled first in Mississippi and then in Sumter, Ala., where he found a number of interesting lawyers of literary taste and culture, who often "gathered in the old Choctaw House to regale their spirits with funny anecdotes and humorous adventures, with comforting beverages and appetizing meals." His sketches, which appeared first in the *Southern Literary Messenger* (1853-54), were the natural product of "that golden era, when shinplasters were the sole currency; when bank-bills were 'as thick as autumn leaves in Vallambrosa' and credit was a franchise."

Various types figure in this well-written book— Ovid Bolus, who for a long time deceives the pioneer section with the exaggerated stories of his adventures in politics and love; the mendacious and roguish lawyer, Simon Suggs, Jr.; the young lawyer who receives a genuine hazing at the hands of a

Pioneers of Southern Literature, Vol. 2.

practiced lawyer of the old school; and, above all, the generous and hospitable and yet proud Virginian, who cannot adapt himself to an age of adventurous plunging in finance. Baldwin's style has the note of distinction—his delicate power of literary allusion and his felicitous strokes of characterization deserve far more praise than they have received.

In the course of this sketch the main reasons why Southern writers did not achieve greater success in fiction have been suggested. None of them, except Poe, and perhaps Simms, were professional men of letters; their literary work was incidental to what seemed to them more important. Most of them wrote carelessly, even slovenly. Furthermore, the absence of anything like a literary centre was a hindrance; there was little of the influence of one writer on another. Slavery, and the feudal system perpetuated thereby, militated against purely literary work. For all these reasons, and others that might be mentioned, the promise of the early thirties was not fulfilled. From 1855 to 1861 some novels, mostly sentimental or sensational, were appearing from time to time. The war itself called forth some poetry of real passion and power, but no worthy fiction.

II.—SOUTHERN FICTION AFTER THE WAR
OF SECESSION.

With the death of Simms, Kennedy, and Long-street in 1870, a distinct period of Southern fiction may be said to have closed. Of the ante-bellum writers, only John Esten Cooke and a few women novelists maintained, for a few years after the war, the ideals of romantic fiction. Cooke realized that he was fighting a losing battle against the rising tide of realism, as he and his section had fought a losing battle against the rising tide of nationalism. Richard Malcolm Johnston, who had, prior to 1860, written some sketches of social life in Georgia, published his *Dukesborough Tales* in the *Southern Magazine* of Baltimore in 1870. They made but little impression, however. Not till 1879, when he contributed to the *Century Magazine,* did he really begin to attract attention, and by that time a group of younger writers had inaugurated a new era in Southern fiction. He was thus the connecting link between Longstreet and Joel Chandler Harris, as Paul Hamilton Hayne was between Simms and Lanier.

There was in the South immediately after the war a demand, sometimes vociferously expressed, for a distinctive "Southern" literature. Magazines were started in many Southern cities, publishing houses were projected either in the South or in the North for the express purpose of promoting the sale of Southern books, and there were many men and women who wrote with the avowed aim of setting the South right before the world. Some wrote out of their extreme poverty. There was a deluge of poems, sentimental and morbid; of reminiscences carelessly put together; of histories written without

F. HOPKINSON SMITH.

reliance on documentary material; of fiction highly
romantic and sensational; and of textbooks written
because the South could "no longer trust the mental
and moral training of sons and daughters to teachers and books imported from abroad." The idea
was that patriotic men should now come forth to jus-
tify the Southern point of view.

About 1875 there began to appear in Northern
magazines short stories and poems by Southern writers which were of a distinctly different quality.
The real Southern literature—or better American
literature in the South—came almost without observation, when men began to describe in a simple
and yet artistic way the human life about them. Ir-
win Russell, listening to an old negro mammy singing a revival hymn in the back yard of his Mississippi home and fitting words to the tune, ushered
in the dialect poem and prepared the way for the
dialect story. Joel Chandler Harris began to
write for the Atlanta *Constitution* stories gathered
from the old plantation of his boyhood—and "Uncle
Remus" was soon known around the world. George
W. Cable depicted with consummate art the scenery
and romance of New Orleans. Miss Murfree, with
the background of the mountains of east Tennessee,
interpreted the life of our "contemporary ancestors." In the eighties, Thomas Nelson Page wrote
out the stories of the old times in Virginia that he
had told for a number of years in the social circles
of Richmond. Later James Lane Allen, with a finer
culture and with an added note of idealism, set forth
the remoter life of the Revolutionary days in Kentucky and the distinctive landscapes of the bluegrass
country. Still later, Miss Johnston explored the
fields of early colonial history, and Miss Ellen Glasgow represented something of the transition from
the old South to the new. Some of the most inter-

esting figures in contemporary American literature are Southerners.* It is unfortunate that there has not been a more notable fulfillment of the early promise, but this fact may be in part attributed to the general condition of American literature.

Gradually these writers, and others who might be named, portrayed practically all the picturesque phases of Southern life. The Creole, the mountaineer, the "cracker," the negro, the old Southern gentleman and his lady, the overseer, found their interpreters in a literature that was full of humor and pathos, and that was permeated with the air of kindly sympathy and freedom. Southern society that had been without expression, that had prided itself on its solidarity, suddenly revealed its secrets to men of genius. If there was a tendency to idealize the life of the past and to shut the eye to certain important phases of that life, it was but natural. The significant point is that men began to describe Southern scenery, not some fantastic world of dreamland; sentimentalism was superseded by a healthy realism touched with romance.

Some distinct causes may be assigned for the development of the new Southern fiction. First, there was abundant material calling for its interpreters. One of the writers afterwards said: "Never in the history of the country has there been a generation of writers who came into such an inheritance of material." The various picturesque characters that had been somewhat obscured by the supposed solidarity of Southern life were full of possibilities for those with seeing eyes and understanding hearts. The vanishing of the old feudal system, with its attendant spirit of caste and its sharply defined types

---

*But for lack of space and, in some cases, for failure to secure copyright privileges, it would have been a pleasure to include in this volume selections from Mr. Hopkinson Smith, Mr. John Fox, Jr., Mr. Will N. Harben, Mrs. Ruth McEnery Stuart, Mr. Harry Stillwell Edwards, Miss Sarah Barnwell Elliott, Mrs. Tiernan ("Christian Reid") and others.

of the Southern gentleman and those who lived about him; the mountaineers, living a primitive and arrested life in the most beautiful mountain section; the less picturesque but none the less interesting "crackers" of middle Georgia; the people of New Orleans, where there was the most romantic blending of French, Spanish, and Creole types; the inhabitants of the bluegrass region of Kentucky who had, amid romantic surroundings, retained so many of the characteristics of their English ancestors—all these and more lent themselves to men and women of artistic temperament.

To cope with this situation there sprang up in different parts of the South young men and women who were particularly well fitted for the art of story-writing and for the portrayal of Southern life. They began to write, not out of some desire to promote the interests of Southern literature, nor from any stress of poverty, but merely because they had the instinct of the story-teller. Born in the years from 1842 to 1850, they were old enough to have seen with the imaginative eyes of childhood the old order. They had felt the strain and stress of Reconstruction days, and had also shared the joy of a new and better day. The stories of their lives as told by the late Professor Baskervill and his pupils are the best possible introductions to their writings.*

And nothing is more interesting in their careers than the way in which they gradually drifted into literature. Long before Mr. Thomas Nelson Page

---

* *Southern Writers*, Vols. I and II. Some of the most important dates to be remembered in connection with the writers are the following: Richard Malcolm Johnston (1822–1898) published *Dukesborough Tales* (1871), *Old Mark Langston* (1884) and *Widow Guthrie* (1890); George Washington Cable (1844–), *Old Creole Days* (1879), *The Grandissimes* (1880), *Madame Delphine* (1881); Joel Chandler Harris (1848–1908), *Uncle Remus; His Songs and Sayings* (1880), *Nights with Uncle Remus* (1883), *Free Joe* (1887); Mary Noailles Murfree (1850–), *In the Tennessee Mountains* (1884), *The Prophet of the Great Smoky Mountains* (1885), *In the Clouds* (1886); Thomas Nelson Page (1853–), *In Ole Virginie* (1887), *Red Rock* (1898); James Lane Allen (1849–), *Flute and Violin* (1891), *A Kentucky Cardinal* (1895), *The Choir Invisible* (1897), *The Reign of Law* (1900); Mary Johnston (1870–), *To Have and To Hold* (1900), *Lewis Rand* (1908); Ellen Glasgow (1874–), *The Voice of the People* (1900), *The Battleground* (1902), *The Deliverance* (1904).

had become an author, his stories were the delight of the best social circles of Richmond. Says one who knew him: "In the social circles he was a great favorite and, having the ability to tell good negro stories, and his association being with that class of people whose parents had been large owners of slaves in Virginia, they kept him busy telling the humorous and pathetic side of negro life on the plantations. Every one testified to the naturalness and truthfulness of the negro character, and this led to his writing short stories from time to time."

There is no better story of the boyhood of a great writer than Joel Chandler Harris's *On the Plantation*. From runaway slaves and deserters he learned the art of story-telling and got much of the material he afterward used in his books. He wrote his first stories as space-fillers for the Atlanta *Constitution*, and also for the pure fun of it. He portrayed the life which he had seen as an imaginative boy, told simple folk stories that were found to be akin to the primitive stories of all races in their childhood. In his introduction to *Nights with Uncle Remus* he tells of the circumstances under which he secured additions to his own stock of stories. It is such a characteristic passage that I quote it at length—so full of the naturalness and simplicity of the man and such an illustration of the origin and appeal of pure art:

"One of these opportunities occurred in the summer of 1882, at Norcross, a little railroad station, twenty miles northeast of Atlanta. The writer was waiting to take the train to Atlanta, and this train, as it fortunately happened, was delayed. At the station were a number of negroes, who had been engaged in working on the railroad. It was night, and, as there was nothing better to do, they were waiting to see the train go by. Some were sitting in little groups up and down the platform of the station and some were perched upon a pile of crossties. They seemed to be in great good humor, and cracked jokes at each other's expense, in the midst of boisterous shouts of laughter. The writer sat next to one of the liveliest talkers in the party; and after listening and laughing awhile, told the *Tar Baby Story* by way of a feeler, the excuse being that someone in the crowd mentioned 'Ole Molly Har'! The story was told in a low tone as if to avoid attracting attention, but the comments of the negro, who was a little past middle age, were loud and frequent. 'Dar, now!' he would exclaim, or 'He's a honey mon!' or 'Gentermens, git out de way, an' gin 'im room!'

"These comments and the peals of unrestrained and unrestrainable laughter that accompanied them, drew the attention of the other negroes, and before the climax of the story had been reached, where Brother Rabbit is cruelly thrown into the brier-patch, they had all gathered around and made themselves comfortable. Without waiting to see what the effect of the Tar Baby legend would be, the writer told the story of *Brother Rabbit and the Mosquitoes*, and this had the effect of convulsing them. Two or three could hardly wait for the conclusion, so anxious were they to tell stories of their own. The result was that, for almost two hours, a crowd of thirty or more Negroes vied with each other to see which could tell the most and the best stories. Some told them poorly, giving only meagre outlines, while others told them passing well; but one or two, if their language and their gestures could have been taken down, would have put Uncle Remus to shame. Some of the stories had already been gathered and verified, and a few had been printed in the first volume, but the great majority were either new or had been entirely forgotten."

In such a simple way, then, were his stories collected and told. Few men have ever so transferred to words the inimitable art of story-telling. Their effect on the negroes themselves suggests the story of Cooper's reading his first sea story to an old tar whose pleasure in it was the surest evidence of the novelist's success—far more trustworthy than the judgment of a professional critic. The "Uncle Remus" stories made their appeal not only to the uncultivated negroes, but to imaginative children and childlike men and women throughout the world.

Nothing so sharply distinguishes this group of Southern writers from all their predecessors, except Poe, as their careful workmanship and the discipline of their artistic powers. Some of them have perhaps been tempted by the demands of magazines and publishers to write more than they ought to have written; but their best work is characterized by a faithful adherence to the demands of art. In their

writings we have none of the careless workmanship
of Simms or Longstreet. Even so spontaneous a
writer as Joel Chandler Harris brought to his dialect stories an almost scientific accuracy and fidelity
to fact. While the "Uncle Remus" stories were—
to use his own words—"stuff prepared during the
leisure moments of an active journalistic career and
lack of all that goes to make up a permanent literature," they have been as interesting to students of
folk-lore as to the large number of children and
childlike men and women. Mr. Page is known by
his publishers as one of the most careful revisers
of proofsheets. Mr. Cable added to his natural feeling for the romance and beauty of New Orleans a
minute study of natural history, that causes one to
wonder at his realistic pictures of swamp, bayou, and
prairie; and a study of the history, dialect, songs,
manners and customs of the Creoles, that causes
his stories and novels to assume the rôle of history
no less than of art. No detail of research or execution has escaped him. Like some of the modern
French realists, he always had with him his note-
book, so systematizing everything as to be able to
turn to it without a moment's delay. Lafcadio
Hearn, in an interesting article on the "Scenes of
Cable's Stories," has pointed out the accuracy with
which the author has reproduced all the details of
the New Orleans architecture of the older and more
romantic period.

With even greater distinction of style, if possible,
Mr. James Lane Allen has wrought out his finely
conceived stories. It is said that he wrote one of
his short stories four times, and all of his readers
have wondered at his transformation of *John Gray*
into *The Choir Invisible*. He is rightly distinguished among Southern writers, as indeed among
contemporary writers, for his mastery of pure liter-

ary English. His passages of description, as well
as of insight into the deeper interests of the spiritual life, well entitle him to the praise of the finest
literary workmanship. Such excellence of style and
such conscientious effort arise from the fact that
Mr. Allen and his co-workers have been professedly
men of letters. Literature is with them not a pastime, but a profession.

The effect produced by such writers on the Southern people was happily expressed by the Southern
scholar who took such a sympathetic interest in their
work and who wrote the best estimate of their
achievement:

"There was joy in beholding the roses of romance and poetry blossoming above the ashes of defeat and humiliation, and that too
among a people hitherto more remarkable for the masterful deeds
of warrior and statesmen than for the finer, rarer, and more artistic
creations of literary genius. To this was added the exhilaration of
fresh and novel discoveries, of making the acquaintance of new regions and new peoples. Whether the discoverers reported mere
transcriptions from contemporary life and manners or threw over
scenery, incident, situation, and character the unfading light of
idealizing and creative imagination—all were gladly welcomed."*

To the same effect wrote his colleague, now a distinguished professor in the University of Wisconsin:

"I remember very distinctly the day I was inducted into the new
cult. I was ill and confined to my room, though able to sit up.
Baskervill came to see me, and brought Cable's *Old Creole Days*.
I think I read the whole volume without rising from my chair, with
increasing appreciation and delight as I went from story to story;
and when I finished *Madame Delphine* a glow passed over me from
head to foot and back from foot to head, and I said to myself, with
profound feeling: 'It has come at last!' I meant the day of the
South's finding her expression in literature. Such a moment of
overwhelming conviction and satisfaction can come only once, I
know. I realized then that the South had the material in her old
past, and that we had the writers with the art to portray it."†

In the same spirit wrote a Northern critic, recalling the morning of youth when he read the same volume, and caught "glimpses into a new world, vistas

*Baskervill: *Southern Writers.*
†Charles Forster Smith: *Reminiscenses and Sketches*

of untravelled regions of experience and art," "en-
chanting gardens and picturesque streets." This
was but typical of the hearty response that the new
Southern literature met with in the North. Contrary to the idea which had prevailed after the war,
that Northern people would be slow to recognize
Southern genius, it must be said that Northern publishers, Northern magazines, and Northern readers
to a large degree made possible the success of Southern writers. In one number of *Scribner's Magazine*
there were no less than seven contributions by
Southerners, which led the editor to comment on
the fact of "a permanent productive force in literature in the South" and to "welcome the new writers
to the great republic of letters." The same recognition came from the *Century* and *Harper's*. An article in the *Atlantic Monthly,* which had been the
special organ of New England writers, said in 1885:

"It is not the subjects offered by Southern writers which interest
us so much as the manifestation of a spirit which seemed to be
dying out of our literature. * * * Their work is large, imaginative, and constantly responsive to the elemental movements of human
nature; and we should not be greatly surprised if the historian of
our literature, a few generations hence, should take note of an en-
largement of American letters at this time through the agency of a
New South. * * * The North refines to a keen analysis, the
South enriches through a generous imagination. * * * The
breadth which characterizes the best Southern writing, the large,
free handling, the confident imagination, are legitimate results of
the careless yet masterful and hospitable life which has pervaded
that section. We have had our laugh at the florid, coarse-flavored
literature which has not yet disappeared at the South, but we are
witnessing now the rise of a school that shows us the worth of
generous nature when it has been schooled and ordered."

It may be readily seen that the Southern writers
of fiction fell in with two marked tendencies of recent American literature—the delevopment of a new
type of magazine and of the short story, especially
the short story with local color. Soon after the War
of Secession, the illustrated magazines, as compared

with the more dignified and serious quarterlies and monthlies, made their appeal to an increasing number of readers. Along with illustrated sketches of various aspects of American life, the editors profited by the fresh emphasis put upon short stories by readers and critics. Practically all the Southern stories and novels appeared first in these magazines.

The short story has indeed become "the national mode of utterance in the things of the imagination." It may be said to be the most distinct contribution that America has made to literary forms. Bret Harte, in his stories of Western life, gave the short story, as started by Poe, a new turn. After his tremendous success of the early seventies "there came forward a host of American writers of the short story of local color, men and women, humorists and sentimentalists, fantasists and realists, Northerners and Southerners, differing in sincerity and differing in skill. For more than three score years now they have been exploring these United States; and they have been explaining the people of one state to the population of the others, increasing our acquaintance with our fellow citizens, and broadening our sympathies. In no other country has anything like this probing inquisition of contemporary humanity been attempted,—perhaps because there is no other country in which it could be as useful and as necessary."*

With their contemporaries in all sections of the country the Southern writers have wrought to this end. It may be objected that the short story is too scanty a plot of ground for the display of great artistic genius, that the use of dialect has been carried to a ridiculous excess, and that there has been far too much provincialism. But when all is said it remains true that this particular development of

---

*Brander Matthews: *The Philosophy of the Short Story.*

prose fiction has been the most marked characteristic of our contemporary literature, and that Southern writers have played a most worthy part in this
achievement.

In the matter of dialect one may admit the stric-
tures which are sometimes placed upon its excessive
use. An American critic has recently spoken of it
as "a sort of epidemic of which the most prominent
characteristics are the misspelling of words and a
plentiful scattering of apostrophes, as if the secret
of literary art lay in eccentric and intermittent or-
thography." But this criticism can scarcely be applied to the best dialect of the Southern writers,
whether we consider the life-like negro dialect of
Harris and Page, that of the mountaineers of Craddock, who has preserved so faithfully so many sur-
vivals of old English speech, or the delicately
wrought Creole dialect which Mr. Cable has used
with such consummate art. It may be that some of
these writers would have done well to reduce the
amount of dialect in their stories; but in the case of
both Harris and Page the most effective means of
interpreting the picturesque character of the old-
time negro as well as the social order which is seen
through his eyes, is the use of his distinct and original speech. Perhaps the greatest triumph in the
artistic use of dialect is seen in the novel and varied
vocal effects produced by Mr. Cable. In *The Grandissimes* he expressed the desire that a phonograph
might have reproduced the charm of his heroine's
voice and speech. Surely the author himself has
succeeded as well as man could in reproducing the
"pretty oddities,—the arch, the pathetic, the grave,
the earnest, the matter-of-fact, the ecstatic tones of
her voice,—nay the movements of her hands, the
eloquence of her eyes, or the shapings of her mouth."

When we consider the substance rather than the

form of recent Southern fiction we find that there are abundant illustrations of the three appeals, which, according to Mr. Bliss Perry, are made by short stories. In some of them the interest is almost wholly that of the character sketch—how many types there are we have yet to suggest. In some the chief attraction is that of the local setting or background; they appeal to the modern feeling for landscape, the modern curiosity as to racial conditions. "The modern reader is satisfied if the writer can discover a new corner of the world, or sketch the familiar scene to our hearts' desire." After all, however, the chief charm of the short story ought to be that of the plot or the action. It is at this point perhaps that Southern stories have been most deficient; for Poe has had no successor in his ability to tell a story which holds one without regard to background or character.

Waiving as perhaps too technical a subject for this Introduction the third of these points, let us consider briefly the various scenes and types which we find in Southern fiction. As already indicated, the Southern writers were quick to realize the wealth of natural scenery. No writer has used this with richer effect than Miss Murfree. In fact, she may be justly accused of working her moon too much and of interfering with the progress of her story by too frequent descriptions of mountain scenery. She lingers over the setting of her picture when she is getting her figures into position. The temptation was undoubtedly great, and her marked power of description is at least a partial justification for her evident delight in painting the panoramic scenes of her mountains. A series of masterly paintings might be sketched from her stories. There is this to be said with regard to her descriptive scenes: "By unity of impression nature and human nature are

constantly present to her, and even when some bold
action is in progress she can not help feeling that
the mountains, the trees, the sun, moon and stars
are not merely spectators, but participants.''

The same point may be made with regard to the
exquisite landscapes of Mr. James Lane Allen's
stories. Nature is an important character in many
of his stories—not behind the action, but involved in
it. Her influence streams through the story, sometimes serving as a background, as in his earlier
stories, but oftener as a sort of chorus to the drama
enacted. "The human figures in the *Summer in
Arcady* seem as subordinate as those which appear
in Corot's landscapes." Although Mr. Allen in later
years moved to New York he has kept in his imagination the scenery of the bluegrass region of Kentucky. It has been one of his prime beliefs that, if
a writer is ever to have that knowledge of a country
which reappears in his work as local color, he must
have gathered it in his childhood. The citations
given in Professor Henneman's study will show the
poetic glamor he has cast over those fair regions;
only the careful reading of all his stories will give
one any adequate idea of his romantic, and even
transcendental, attitude to nature.

Surely no American writer ever had a finer background for his artistic creations than George W.
Cable. Here we have the blending of scenery, architecture, and romance. Now it is the rich luxuriance
of the swamps and bayous, now the rue Royale, "a
long, narrowing perspective of arcades, lattices, balconies, dormer windows, and blue sky—of low tiled
roofs, red and wrinkled, huddled down into their
own shadows; of canvas awnings with fluttering borders, and of grimy lamp posts twenty feet in height,
each reaching out a gaunt iron arm over the narrow
street and dangling a lamp from its ends." Again

it is some large old house that survives as a re-
minder of the past:

"Among these stood the great mother mansion of the Grandissimes. Do not look for it now; it is quite gone. The round, white-
plastered brick pillars, which held the house fifteen feet up from the
leaking ground and rose on loftily to sustain the over-spreading
roof, are clustered in the cool, paved basement; the lofty halls, with
their multitudinous glitter of gilded brass and twinkle of sweet-
smelling wax candles; the immense encircling veranda where twenty
Creole girls might walk abreast; the great front stairs, descending
from the veranda to the garden, with a lofty palm on either side, on
whose broad steps forty Grandissimes could gather on a birthday
afternoon; and the belvidere, whence you could see the cathedral, the
Ursulines', the governor's mansion, and the river, far away, shinning
between the villas of Tchoupitoulas Coast—all have disappeared as
entirely as the flowers that bloomed in the garden on the day of this
fête de grandpere."

Not less artistic are the various types we find in
Mr. Cable's stories. We have the old Creole like
Jean-ah Poquelin, now pouring out his curses upon
the United States and its President, and in his old
home resisting the inevitable progress of the city;
or Agricola Fusilier, who after a life of steadfast
adherence to the old régime dies with these words
upon his lips: "The old Louisiana will rise again.
She will get back her trampled rights. Louis—
Louisan—a—for—ever!" We have the inimitable
man of the world, the pleasure-loving Jules Ange,
who is touched into a sort of finer life by the noble
old country parson, and the progressive Honoré
Grandissime who is willing to fall in with the new
order of things and has an insight into the defects of
his people. Palmyre with her barbaric and magnetic
beauty, on the defensive against what certainly was
to her an unmerciful world, is an excellent type of
the octaroon whose tragic life Cable has depicted
with dramatic art. In Bras-Coupé we have a type
of negro not found in any other Southern story, the
African prince who in his royal nature can not wear
the bonds of slavery, and who by his practice of the

art of voodooism scatters terror among whites and blacks. As if to relieve the dark intensity of these tragic characters, Cable has often drawn the Creole mother and daughter, now gay amid the scenes of the masked ball, or sad at the prospect of poverty, or radiant and charming at the final triumph of love. After all there is no finer character than that of Madame Délicieuse, who from her balcony and surrounded by a bevy of Creole beauties sees the splendid procession go by in the street below. One can not be too enthusiastic about the half gallic, half classic beauty of these radiant women. Nor can he restrain his enthusiasm in the presence of that later creation of the author, Bonaventure, the Creole schoolmaster, who, with simple heroism lifts the children of an Acadian village to a new sense of life and of power.*

A similar study of each of the Southern writers would reveal the same variety of types—as many types as there are states or even districts. From Southern stories and novels there might be gathered passages which would be a complete portrait gallery of Southern men and women. Some of them—notably the old-time negro and the Southern colonel and his charming daughter—have become somewhat conventionalized. It must be confessed that the chief writers have repeated themselves, and that the minor ones have imitated them, rather than struck out along original lines.† The promise of the years from 1875 to 1890 has not been fulfilled. The novels, with the exception of *The Grandissimes, The Prophet of the Great Smoky Mountains* and *The Choir Invisible*, are not so good as the short stories. More recently

---

*A more sympathetic portrayal of various types of New Orleans people may be found in Miss Grace King's *Balcony Stories*. It is a misfortune that the author of *Old Creole Days* and *The Grandissimes* should have in later years let his philanthropic impulse master his artistic sense.

†Exceptions may be noted in Mrs. Rice's *Mrs. Wiggs of the Cabbage Patch* and Frances Little's *Our Lady of the Decoration*.

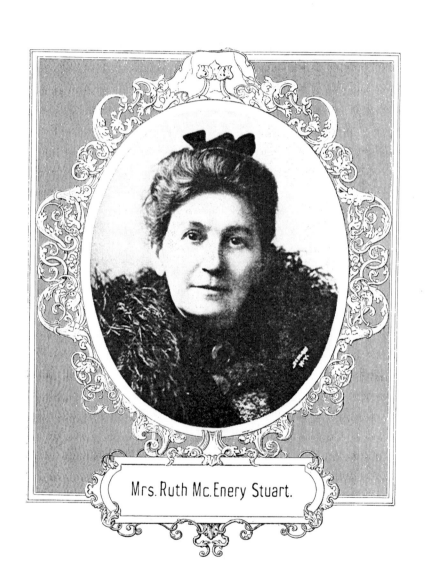

Mrs. Ruth Mc. Enery Stuart.

Miss Mary Johnston has written her stirring and at times sensational romances of colonial times, and within the past year *Lewis Rand*—a novel of real distinction and perhaps of permanent worth.

Miss Ellen Glasgow, better than any other Southern novelist has suggested the necessary transition from the old order to the new. At the end of Mr. Page's stories and novels the curtain goes down as if bringing an end to the most glorious chapter in Southern history. In Miss Glasgow's novels there is always, along with the sympathy for the old, a feeling that, despite the catastrophe of the war and reconstruction, the best is yet to be. The *Voice of the People* is a striking presentation of the rise of a new type of hero from the masses of the people, a man who brings back the better traditions of Southern statesmanship and finally gives his life as a sacrifice in his effort to prevent the lynching of a negro. In *The Deliverance* she has represented the extreme Southerner by the blind old woman who goes to her death thinking that the Southern Confederacy has been victorious. The title of the book suggests the main motive, the deliverance of the descendant of the proud family of Blakes from the spirit of caste and prejudice, while the development of the heroine, the daughter of a crude and brutal overseer, to the heights of a heroic and refined womanhood suggests in a most significant way the possibilities of the undeveloped humanity of the Southern masses. There is no better scene to illustrate the significance of the great educational development of the past few decades than the discovery by an aristocratic Southerner of the pathos of his ignorant companion learning how to read and write amid the arduous duties of camp life.

One other point may be made with regard to the general effect produced by Southern fiction since

the war. While it has been provincial, it has not
been sectional—there is in the best Southern stories
the healthy provincialism of Burns and Whittier.
But Mr. Page was right in claiming in the introduction to the Plantation Edition of his works that he
has "never wittingly written a line which he did not
hope might tend to bring about a better understanding between the North and South, and finally lead
to a more perfect Union." In his stories, when the
passion of prejudice is at its height, human nature
asserts itself. The two Little Confederates bury in
their garden the body of the Federal soldier; the
heroine of *Meh Lady,* after a long and passionate
conflict between love and patriotism, yields to the
Northern colonel; and the hero of *Red Rock*—dashing soldier and Ku Klux leader—is united with a
Northern girl.

"What does it matter," said Joel Chandler Harris, "whether I am Northerner or Southerner if I
am true to truth, and true to that larger truth, my
own true self? My idea is that truth is more important than sectionalism, and that literature that can
be labeled Northern, Southern, Western, or Eastern,
is not worth labeling at all." Again, he said, speaking of the ideal Southern writer: "He must be
Southern and yet cosmopolitan; he must be intensely
local in feeling, but utterly unprejudiced and unpar-
tisan as to opinions, tradition, and sentiment. Whenever we have a genuine Southern literature, it will
be American and cosmopolitan as well. Only let it
be the work of genius, and it will take all sections by
storm."

Such writers have been among the prime forces in
revealing the South to the nation and the nation to
the South, thus furthering one of the most important
tasks of the present generation—the promotion of
a real national spirit.

AMÉLIE RIVES CHANLER.
(Princess Troubetzkoy)

BIBLIOGRAPHICAL NOTE.—The best books for a general treatment of Southern writers are W. P. Trent's *Southern Writers* and *History of American Literature;* W. M. Baskervill's *Southern Writers;* S. A. Link's *Pioneers of Southern Literature;* Louise Manly's *Manual of Southern Literature;* Thomas Nelson Page's *Authorship in the South Before the War* (in *The Old South*); G. E. Woodberry's *America in Literature;* Barrett Wendell's *Literary History of America*.

For the study of Poe the lives by G. E. Woodberry (revised edition, 2 vols.) and J. A. Harrison (2 vols.) are essential. The best editions are the Virginia edition, edited by Harrison and Kent, and the ten-volume edition edited by E. C. Stedman and G. E. Woodberry. The Poe Centenary Book, recently published by the University of Virginia, contains some interesting addresses.

The life by W. P. Trent in the "American Men of Letters Series" is the best biography of Simms. A complete edition of his writings has recently been published by Martin and Hoyt (Atlanta). For short sketches of the lives of Kennedy, J. E. Cooke, Longstreet, Baldwin, Hooper and Thompson, Link's *Pioneers of Southern Literature* is adequate. Henry Watterson's *Oddities of Southern Humor and Character* gives full selections from the writings of the Southern humorists and story-writers, and at the same time sketches their lives and the age in which they lived.

The best account of the writers of the New South is found in Baskervill's *Southern Writers* (2 vols.). Articles on individual writers may be found by referring to Poole's *Index to Periodical Literature*. An article of special value is John B. Henneman's *The National Element in Southern Literature*, in the *Sewanee Review*, July, 1903. The editor's life of Sidney Lanier in the "American Men of Letters Series" throws sidelights on Lanier's contemporaries in poetry and fiction. References are made in the footnotes of this volume to the publishers of the best editions of the various writers.

EDWIN MIMS,

Professor of English, University of North Carolina, formerly Professor of English Literature, Trinity College.

EDGAR ALLAN POE.

THE FALL OF THE HOUSE OF USHER.

Son cœur est un luth suspendu;
Sitôt qu'on le touche il résonne.
BÉRANGER.

URING the whole of a dull, dark, and soundless day in the autumn of the year, when the clouds hung oppressively low in the heavens, I had been passing alone, on horseback, through a singularly dreary tract of country; and at length found myself, as the shades of the evening drew on, within view of the melancholy House of Usher. I know not how it was —but, with the first glimpse of the building, a sense of insufferable gloom pervaded my spirit. I say insufferable; for the feeling was unrelieved by any of that half-pleasurable, because poetic, sentiment with which the mind usually receives even the sternest natural images of the desolate or terrible. I looked upon the scene before me—upon the mere house, and the simple landscape features of the domain, upon the bleak walls, upon the vacant eye-like windows, upon a few rank sedges, and upon a few white trunks of decayed trees—with an utter depression of soul which I can compare to no earthly sensation more properly than to the after-dream of the reveller upon opium; the bitter lapse into everyday life, the hideous dropping off of the veil. There was an iciness, a sinking, a sickening of the heart,

1

an unredeemed dreariness of thought which no goad-
ing of the imagination could torture into aught of
the sublime. What was it—I paused to think—what
was it that so unnerved me in the contemplation of
the House of Usher? It was a mystery all insoluble;
nor could I grapple with the shadowy fancies that
crowded upon me as I pondered. I was forced to
fall back upon the unsatisfactory conclusion, that
while, beyond doubt, there *are* combinations of very
simple natural objects which have the power of thus
affecting us still the analysis of this power lies
among considerations beyond our depth. It was possible, I reflected, that a mere different arrangement
of the particulars of the scene, of the details of the
picture, would be sufficient to modify, or perhaps to
annihilate, its capacity for sorrowful impression;
and acting upon this idea, I reined my horse to the
precipitous brink of a black and lurid tarn that lay
in unruffled lustre by the dwelling, and gazed down
—but with a shudder even more thrilling than before
—upon the remodelled and inverted images of the
gray sedge, and the ghastly tree stems, and the
vacant and eye-like windows.

Nevertheless, in this mansion of gloom I now proposed to myself a sojourn of some weeks. Its proprietor, Roderick Usher, had been one of my boon
companions in boyhood; but many years had elapsed
since our last meeting. A letter, however, had lately
reached me in a distant part of the country—a letter from him—which in its wildly importunate nature had admitted of no other than a personal reply.
The MS. gave evidence of nervous agitation. The
writer spoke of acute bodily illness, of a mental disorder which oppressed him, and of an earnest desire
to see me, as his best and indeed his only personal
friend, with a view of attempting, by the cheerful-

ness of my society, some alleviation of his malady.
It was the manner in which all this, and much more,
was said—it was the apparent *heart* that went with
his request—which allowed me no room for hesitation; and I accordingly obeyed forthwith what I still
considered a very singular summons.

Although as boys we had been even intimate associates, yet I really knew little of my friend. His
reserve had been always excessive and habitual. I
was aware, however, that his very ancient family
had been noted, time out of mind, for a peculiar sensibility of temperament, displaying itself, through
long ages, in many works of exalted art, and manifested of late in repeated deeds of munificent yet unobtrusive charity, as well as in a passionate devotion to the intricacies, perhaps even more than to
the orthodox and easily recognizable beauties, of
musical science. I had learned, too, the very remarkable fact that the stem of the Usher race, all time-
honored as it was, had put forth at no period any
enduring branch; in other words, that the entire
family lay in the direct line of descent, and had always, with very trifling and very temporary variation, so lain. It was this deficiency, I considered,
while running over in thought the perfect keeping
of the character of the premises with the accredited
character of the people, and while speculating upon
the possible influence which the one, in the long lapse
of centuries, might have exercised upon the other—it
was this deficiency, perhaps, of collateral issue, and
the consequent undeviating transmission from sire
to son of the patrimony with the name, which had
at length, so identified the two as to merge the original title of the estate in the quaint and equivocal
appellation of the "House of Usher"—an appellation which seemed to include, in the minds of the

peasantry who used it, both the family and the family mansion.

I have said that the sole effect of my somewhat childish experiment, that of looking down within the tarn, had been to deepen the first singular impression. There can be no doubt that the consciousness of the rapid increase of my superstition—for why should I not so term it?—served mainly to accelerate the increase itself. Such, I have long known, is the paradoxical law of all sentiments having terror as a basis. And it might have been for this reason only, that, when I again uplifted my eyes to the house itself, from its image in the pool, there grew in my mind a strange fancy—a fancy so ridiculous, indeed, that I but mention it to show the vivid force of the sensations which oppressed me. I had so worked upon my imagination as really to believe that about the whole mansion and domain there hung an atmosphere peculiar to themselves and their immediate vicinity: an atmosphere which had no affinity with the air of heaven, but which had reeked up from the decayed trees, and the gray wall, and the silent tarn: a pestilent and mystic vapor, dull, sluggish, faintly discernible, and leaden-hued.

Shaking off from my spirit what *must* have been a dream, I scanned more narrowly the real aspect of the building. Its principal feature seemed to be that of an excessive antiquity. The discoloration of ages had been great. Minute fungi overspread the whole exterior, hanging in a fine tangled web-work from the eaves. Yet all this was apart from any extraordinary dilapidation. No portion of the masonry had fallen; and there appeared to be a wild inconsistency between its still perfect adaptation of parts and the crumbling condition of the individual stones. In this there was much that reminded me of the specious totality of old wood-work which has rotted for long years in some neglected vault, with no disturbance from the breath of the external air. Beyond this indication of extensive decay, however, the fabric gave little token of instability. Perhaps the eye of a scrutinizing observer might have discovered a barely perceptible fissure, which, extending from the roof of the building in front, made its way down the wall in a zig-zag direction, until it became lost in the sullen waters of the tarn.

Noticing these things, I rode over a short causeway to the house. A servant in waiting took my horse, and I entered the Gothic archway of the hall. A valet, of stealthy step, thence conducted me, in silence, through many dark and intricate passages in my progress to the studio of his master. Much that I encountered on the way contributed, I know not how, to heighten the vague sentiments of which I have already spoken. While the objects around me—while the carvings of the ceilings, the sombre tapestries of the walls, the ebon blackness of the floors, and the phantasmagoric armorial trophies which rattled as I strode, were but matters to which, or to such as which, I had been accustomed from my infancy—while I hesitated not to acknowledge how familiar was all this—I still wondered to find how unfamiliar were the fancies which ordinary images were stirring up. On one of the staircases, I met the physician of the family. His countenance, I thought, wore a mingled expression of low cunning and perplexity. He accosted me with trepidation and passed on. The valet now threw open a door and ushered me into the presence of his master.

The room in which I found myself was very large and lofty. The windows were long, narrow, and pointed, and at so vast a distance from the black oaken floor as to be altogether inaccessible from

within. Feeble gleams of encrimsoned light made
their way through the trellised panes, and served to
render sufficiently distinct the more prominent objects around; the eye, however, struggled in vain
to reach the remoter angles of the chamber, or the
recesses of the vaulted and fretted ceiling. Dark
draperies hung upon the walls. The general furniture was profuse, comfortless, antique, and tattered.
Many books and musical instruments lay scattered
about, but failed to give any vitality to the scene.
I felt that I breathed an atmosphere of sorrow. An
air of stern, deep, and irredeemable gloom hung
over and pervaded all.

Upon my entrance, Usher arose from a sofa on
which he had been lying at full length, and greeted
me with a vivacious warmth which had much in it,
I at first thought, of an overdone cordiality—of the
constrained effort of the *ennuyé* man of the world.
A glance, however, at his countenance convinced
me of his perfect sincerity. We sat down; and for
some moments, while he spoke not, I gazed upon
him with a feeling half of pity, half of awe. Surely
man had never before so terribly altered, in so brief
a period, as had Roderick Usher! It was with difficulty that I could bring myself to admit the identity
of the wan being before me with the companion of
my early boyhood. Yet the character of his face
had been at all times remarkable. A cadaverousness
of complexion; an eye large, liquid, and luminous
beyond comparison; lips somewhat thin and very
pallid, but of a surpassingly beautiful curve; a nose
of delicate Hebrew model, but with a breadth of nos-
tril unusual in similar formations; a finely moulded
chin, speaking, in its want of prominence, of a want
of moral energy; hair of a more than web-like softness and tenuity; these features, with an inordinate
expansion above the regions of the temple, made up

altogether a countenance not easily to be forgotten. And now in the mere exaggeration of the prevailing character of these features, and of the expression they were wont to convey, lay so much of change that I doubted to whom I spoke. The now ghastly pallor of the skin, and the now miraculous lustre of the eye, above all things startled and even awed me. The silken hair, too, had been suffered to grow all unheeded, and as, in its wild gossamer texture, it floated rather than fell about the face, I could not, even with effort, connect its arabesque expression with any idea of simple humanity.

In the manner of my friend I was at once struck with an incoherence, an inconsistency; and I soon found this to arise from a series of feeble and futile struggles to overcome an habitual trepidancy, an excessive nervous agitation. For something of this nature I had indeed been prepared, no less by his letter than by reminiscences of certain boyish traits, and by conclusions deduced from his peculiar physical conformation and temperament. His action was alternately vivacious and sullen. His voice varied rapidly from a tremulous indecision (when the animal spirits seemed utterly in abeyance) to that species of energetic concision—that abrupt, weighty, unhurried, and hollow-sounding enunciation—that leaden, self-balanced and perfectly modulated guttural utterance—which may be observed in the lost drunkard, or the irreclaimable eater of opium, during the periods of his most intense excitement.

It was thus that he spoke of the object of my visit, of his earnest desire to see me, and of the solace he expected me to afford him. He entered, at some length, into what he conceived to be the nature of his malady. It was, he said, a constitutional and a family evil, and one for which he despaired to find a remedy—a mere nervous affection, he immediately added, which would undoubtedly soon pass off. It displayed itself in a host of unnatural sensations. Some of these, as he detailed them, interested and bewildered me; although, perhaps, the terms and the general manner of the narration had their weight. He suffered much from a morbid acuteness of the senses; the most insipid food was alone endurable; he could wear only garments of certain texture; the odors of all floors were oppressive; his eyes were tortured by even a faint light; and there were but peculiar sounds, and these from stringed instruments, which did not inspire him with horror.

To an anomalous species of terror I found him a bounden slave. "I shall perish," said he, "I *must* perish in this deplorable folly. Thus, thus, and not otherwise, shall I be lost. I dread the events of the future, not in themselves, but in their results. I shudder at the thought of any, even the most trivial, incident, which may operate upon this intolerable agitation of soul. I have, indeed, no abhorrence of danger, except in its absolute effect—in terror. In this unnerved—in this pitiable condition, I feel that the period will sooner or later arrive when I must abandon life and reason together, in some struggle with the grim phantasm, FEAR."

I learned moreover at intervals, and through broken and equivocal hints, another singular feature of his mental condition. He was enchained by certain superstitious impressions in regard to the dwelling which he tenanted, and whence, for many years, he had never ventured forth—in regard to an influence whose supposititious force was conveyed in terms too shadowy here to be restated—an influence which some peculiarities in the mere form and substance of his family mansion, had, by dint of long sufferance, he said, obtained over his spirit—an effect which the physique of the gray walls and turrets, and of the dim tarn into which they all looked down, had, at length, brought about upon the morale of his existence.

He admitted, however, although with hesitation, that much of the peculiar gloom which thus afflicted him could be traced to a more natural and far more palpable origin—to the severe and long-continued illness, indeed to the evidently approaching dissolution, of a tenderly beloved sister—his sole companion for long years, his last and only relative on earth. "Her decease," he said, with a bitterness which I can never forget, "would leave him (him the hopeless and the frail) the last of the ancient race of the Ushers." While he spoke, the lady Madeline (for so was she called) passed slowly through a remote portion of the apartment, and, without having noticed my presence, disappeared. I regarded her with an utter astonishment not unmingled with dread, and yet I found it impossible to account for such feelings. A sensation of stupor oppressed me, as my eyes followed her retreating steps. When a door, at length, closed upon her, my glance sought instinctively and eagerly the countenance of the brother; but he had buried his face in his hands, and I could only perceive that a far more than ordinary wanness had overspread the emaciated fingers through which trickled many passionate tears.

The disease of the lady Madeline had long baffled the skill of her physicians. A settled apathy, a gradual wasting away of the person, and frequent although transient affections of a partially cataleptical character, were the unusual diagnosis. Hitherto she had steadily borne up against the pressure of her malady, and had not betaken herself finally to bed; but, on the closing in of the evening of my arrival at the house, she succumbed (as her brother told me at night with inexpressible agita-

tion) to the prostrating power of the destroyer; and
I learned that the glimpse I had obtained of her person would thus probably be the last I should obtain
—that the lady, at least while living, would be seen
by me no more.

For several days ensuing, her name was unmen-
tioned by either Usher or myself; and during this
period I was busied in earnest endeavors to allevi-
ate the melancholy of my friend. We painted and
read together; or I listened, as if in a dream, to
the wild improvisation of his speaking guitar. And
thus, as a closer and still closer intimacy admitted
me more unreservedly into the recesses of his spirit,
the more bitterly did I perceive the futility of all
attempt at cheering a mind from which darkness, as
if an inherent positive quality, poured forth upon
all objects of the moral and physical universe. in one
unceasing radiation of gloom.

I shall ever bear about me a memory of the many
solemn hours I thus spent alone with the master of
the House of Usher. Yet I should fail in any attempt to convey an idea of the exact character of
the studies, or of the occupations, in which he involved me, or led me the way. An excited and highly
distempered ideality threw a sulphurous lustre
over all. His long improvised dirges will ring forever in my ears. Among other things, I hold painfully in mind a certain singular perversion and am-
plification of the wild air of the last waltz of Von
Weber. From the paintings over which his elaborate fancy brooded, and which grew, touch by touch,
into vaguenesses at which I shuddered the more
thrillingly because I shuddered knowing not why;—
from these paintings (vivid as their images now are
before me) I would in vain endeavor to educe more
than a small portion which should lie within the compass of merely written words. By the utter simplic-

ity, by the nakedness of his designs, he arrested and overawed attention. If ever mortal painted an idea, that mortal was Roderick Usher. For me at least, in the circumstances then surrounding me, there arose, out of the pure abstractions which the hypochondriac contrived to throw upon his canvas, an intensity of intolerable awe, no shadow of which felt I ever yet in the contemplation of the certainly glowing yet too concrete reveries of Fuseli.

One of the phantasmagoric conceptions of my friend, partaking not so rigidly of the spirit of abstraction, may be shadowed forth, although feebly, in words. A small picture presented the interior of an immensely long and rectangular vault or tunnel, with low walls, smooth, white, and without interruption or device. Certain accessory points of the design served well to convey the idea that this excavation lay at an exceeding depth below the surface of the earth. No outlet was observed in any portion of its vast extent, and no torch or other artificial source of light was discernible; yet a flood of intense rays rolled throughout, and bathed the whole in a ghastly and inappropriate splendor.

I have just spoken of that morbid condition of the auditory nerve which rendered all music intolerable to the sufferer, with the exception of certain effects of stringed instruments. It was, perhaps, the narrow limits to which he thus confined himself upon the guitar, which gave birth, in great measure, to the fantastic character of his performances. But the fervid *facility* of his impromptus could not be so accounted for. They must have been, and were, in the notes, as well as in the words of his wild fantasias (for he not unfrequently accompanied himself with rhymed verbal improvisations), the result of that intense mental collectedness and concentration to which I have previously alluded as observable only

in particular moments of the highest artificial excitement. The words of one of these rhapsodies I have
easily remembered. I was, perhaps, the more forci-
bly impressed with it, as he gave it, because, in the
under or mystic current of its meaning, I fancied
that I perceived, and for the first time, a full consciousness, on the part of Usher, of the tottering of
his lofty reason upon her throne. The verses, which
were entitled "The Haunted Palace," ran very
nearly, if not accurately, thus:—

I.

"In the greenest of our valleys
    By good angels tenanted,
Once a fair and stately palace—
    Radiant palace—reared its head.
In the monarch Thought's dominion,
    It stood there;
Never seraph spread a pinion
    Over fabric half so fair.

II.

"Banners yellow, glorious, golden,
    On its roof did float and flow,
(This—all this—was in the olden
    Time long ago)
And every gentle air that dallied,
    In that sweet day,
Along the ramparts plumed and pallid,
    A wingèd odor went away.

III.

"Wanderers in that happy valley
    Through two luminous windows saw
Spirits moving musically
    To a lute's well-tunèd law,
Round about a throne where, sitting,
    Porphyrogene,
In state his glory well befitting,
    The ruler of the realm was seen.

IV.

"And all with pearl and ruby glowing
    Was the fair palace door,
Through which came flowing, flowing, flowing.
    And sparkling evermore,

A troop of Echoes whose sweet duty
  Was but to sing,
In voices of surpassing beauty,
  The wit and wisdom of their king.

V.

"But evil things, in robes of sorrow,
  Assailed the monarch's high estate;
(Ah, let us mourn, for never morrow
  Shall dawn upon him, desolate!)
And round about his home the glory
  That blushed and bloomed
Is but a dim-remembered story
  Of the old time entombed.

VI.

"And travellers now within that valley
  Through the red-litten windows see
Vast forms that move fantastically
  To a discordant melody;
While, like a ghastly rapid river,
  Through the pale door
A hideous throng rush out forever,
  And laugh—but smile no more."

I well remember that suggestions arising from this ballad led us into a train of thought, wherein there became manifest an opinion of Usher's which I mention not so much on account of its novelty, (for other men* have thought thus,) as on account of the pertinacity with which he maintained it. This opinion, in its general form, was that of the sentience of all vegetable things. But in his disordered fancy the idea had assumed a more daring character, and trespassed, under certain conditions, upon the kingdom of inorganization. I lack words to express the full extent, or the earnest *abandon* of his persuasion. The belief, however, was connected (as I have previously hinted) with the gray stones of the home of his forefathers. The conditions of the sentience had been here, he imagined, fulfilled in the method of

---

* Watson, Dr. Percival, Spallanzani, and especially the Bishop of Landaff. See "*Chemical Essays*," vol. v.

collocation of these stones—in the order of their arrangement, as well as in that of the many fungi which overspread them, and of the decayed trees which stood around—above all, in the long undisturbed endurance of this arrangement, and in its reduplication in the still waters of the tarn. Its evidence—the evidence of the sentience—was to be seen, he said (and I here started as he spoke), in the gradual yet certain condensation of an atmosphere of their own about the waters and the walls. The result was discoverable, he added, in that silent, yet importunate and terrible influence which for centuries had moulded the destinies of his family, and which made *him* what I now saw him—what he was. Such opinions need no comment, and I will make none.

Our books—the books which, for years, had formed no small portion of the mental existence of the invalid—were, as might be supposed, in strict keeping with this character of phantasm. We pored together over such works as the Ververt and Chartreuse of Gresset; the Belphegor of Machiavelli; the Heaven and Hell of Swedenborg; the Subterranean Voyage of Nicholas Klimm by Holberg; the Chiromancy of Robert Flud, of Jean D'Indaginé, and of De la Chambre; the Journey into the Blue Distance of Tieck; and the City of the Sun of Campanella. One favorite volume was a small octavo edition of the *Directorium Inquisitorum*, by the Dominican Eymeric de Gironne; and there were passages in Pomponius Mela, about the old African Satyrs and Ægipans, over which Usher would sit dreaming for hours. His chief delight, however, was found in the perusal of an exceedingly rare and curious book in quarto Gothic—the manual of a forgotten church—the *Vigiliæ Mortuorum secundum Chorum Ecclesiæ Maguntinæ.*

I could not help thinking of the wild ritual of this work, and of its probable influence upon the hypochondriac, when one evening, having informed me abruptly that the lady Madeline was no more, he stated his intention of preserving her corpse for a fortnight, (previously to its final interment,) in one of the numerous vaults within the main walls of the building. The worldly reason, however, assigned for this singular proceeding, was one which I did not feel at liberty to dispute. The brother had been led to his resolution (so he told me) by consideration of the unusual character of the malady of the deceased, of certain obtrusive and eager inquiries on the part of her medical men, and of the remote and exposed situation of the burial-ground of the family. I will not deny that when I called to mind the sinister countenance of the person whom I met upon the staircase, on the day of my arrival at the house, I had no desire to oppose what I regarded as at best but a harmless, and by no means an unnatural, precaution.

At the request of Usher, I personally aided him in the arrangements for the temporary entombment. The body having been encoffined, we two alone bore it to its rest. The vault in which we placed it (and which had been so long unopened that our torches, half smothered in its oppressive atmosphere, gave us little opportunity for investigation) was small, damp, and entirely without means of admission for light; lying, at great depth, immediately beneath that portion of the building in which was my own sleeping apartment. It had been used, apparently, in remote feudal times, for the worst purposes of a donjon-keep, and in later days as a place of deposit for powder, or some other highly combustible substance, as a portion of its floor and the whole interior of a long archway through which we reached it, were carefully sheathed with copper. The door, of massive iron, had been, also, similarly protected. Its immense weight caused an unusually sharp grating sound, as it moved upon its hinges.

Having deposited our mournful burden upon tressels within this region of horror, we partially turned aside the yet unscrewed lid of the coffin, and looked upon the face of the tenant. A striking similitude between the brother and sister now first arrested my attention; and Usher, divining, perhaps, my thoughts, murmured out some few words from which I learned that the deceased and himself had been twins, and that sympathies of a scarcely intelligible nature had always existed between them. Our glances, however, rested not long upon the dead—for we could not regard her unawed. The disease which had thus entombed the lady in the maturity of youth, had left, as usual in all maladies of a strictly cataleptical character, the mockery of a faint blush upon the bosom and the face, and that suspiciously lingering smile upon the lip which is so terrible in death. We replaced and screwed down the lid, and, having secured the door of iron, made our way, with toil, into the scarcely less gloomy apartments of the upper portion of the house.

And now, some days of bitter grief having elapsed, an observable change came over the features of the mental disorder of my friend. His ordinary manner had vanished. His ordinary occupations were neglected or forgotten. He roamed from chamber to chamber with hurried, unequal, and objectless step. The pallor of his countenance had assumed, if possible, a more ghastly hue—but the luminousness of his eye had utterly gone out. The once occasional huskiness of his tone was heard no more; and a tremulous quaver, as if of extreme terror, habitually characterized his utterance. There were times, in-

deed, when I thought his unceasingly agitated mind
was laboring with some oppressive secret, to divulge
which he struggled for the necessary courage. At
times, again, I was obliged to resolve all into the
mere inexplicable vagaries of madness, for I beheld
him gazing upon vacancy for long hours, in an attitude of the profoundest attention, as if listening to
some imaginary sound. It was no wonder that his
condition terrified—that it infected me. I felt creeping upon me, by slow yet certain degrees, the wild
influences of his own fantastic yet impressive superstitions.

It was, especially, upon retiring to bed late in the
night of the seventh or eighth day after the placing
of the lady Madeline within the donjon, that I experienced the full power of such feelings. Sleep
came not near my couch, while the hours waned and
waned away. I struggled to reason off the nervousness which had dominion over me. I endeavored to
believe that much, if not all, of what I felt was due
to the bewildering influence of the gloomy furniture
of the room—of the dark and tattered draperies
which, tortured into motion by the breath of a rising
tempest, swayed fitfully to and fro upon the walls,
and rustled uneasily about the decoration of the
bed. But my efforts were fruitless. An irrepressible tremor gradually pervaded my frame; and at
length there sat upon my very heart an incubus of
utterly causeless alarm. Shaking this off with a
gasp and a struggle, I uplifted myself upon the
pillows, and, peering earnestly within the intense
darkness of the chamber, hearkened—I know not
why, except that an instinctive spirit prompted me
—to certain low and indefinite sounds which came,
through the pauses of the storm, at long intervals,
I know not whence. Overpowered by an intense
sentiment of horror, unaccountable yet unendurable,

I threw on my clothes with haste, (for I felt that I should sleep no more during the night,) and endeavored to arouse myself from the pitiable condition into which I had fallen, by pacing rapidly to and fro through the apartment.

I had taken but few turns in this manner, when a light step on an adjoining staircase arrested my attention. I presently recognized it as that of Usher. In an instant afterward he rapped with a gentle touch at my door, and entered, bearing a lamp. His countenance was, as usual, cadaverously wan—but, moreover, there was a species of mad hilarity in his eyes—an evidently restrained hysteria in his whole demeanor. His air appalled me—but anything was preferable to the solitude which I had so long endured, and I even welcomed his presence as a relief.

"And you have not seen it?" he said abruptly, after having stared about him for some moments in silence—"you have not then seen it?—but, stay! you shall." Thus speaking, and having carefully shaded his lamp, he hurried to one of the casements, and threw it freely open to the storm.

The impetuous fury of the entering gust nearly lifted us from our feet. It was, indeed, a tempestuous yet sternly beautiful night, and one wildly singular in its terror and its beauty. A whirlwind had apparently collected its force in our vicinity; for there were frequent and violent alterations in the direction of the wind; and the exceeding density of the clouds (which hung so low as to press upon the turrets of the house) did not prevent our perceiving the lifelike velocity with which they flew careering from all points against each other, without passing away into the distance. I say that even their exceeding density did not prevent our perceiving this; yet we had no glimpse of the moon or stars, nor was there any flashing forth of the lightning. But the under surfaces of the huge masses of agitated vapor, as well as all terrestrial objects immediately around us, were glowing in the unnatural light of a faintly luminous and distinctly visible gaseous exhalation which hung about and enshrouded the mansion.

"You must not—you shall not behold this!" said I, shudderingly, to Usher, as I led him with a gentle violence from the window to a seat. "These appearances, which bewilder you, are merely electrical phenomena not uncommon—or it may be that they have their ghastly origin in the rank miasma of the tarn. Let us close this casement; the air is chilling and dangerous to your frame. Here is one of your favorite romances. I will read, and you shall listen;—and so we will pass away this terrible night together."

The antique volume which I had taken up was the "Mad Trist" of Sir Launcelot Canning; but I had called it a favorite of Usher's more in sad jest than in earnest; for, in truth, there is little in its uncouth and unimaginative prolixity which could have had interest for the lofty and spiritual ideality of my friend. It was, however, the only book immediately at hand; and I indulged a vague hope that the excitement which now agitated the hypochondriac might find relief (for the history of mental disorder is full of similar anomalies) even in the extremeness of the folly which I should read. Could I have judged, indeed, by the wild overstrained air of vivacity with which he hearkened, or apparently hearkened, to the words of the tale, I might well have congratulated myself upon the success of my design.

I had arrived at that well-known portion of the story where Ethelred, the hero of the Trist, having sought in vain for peaceable admission into the dwelling of the hermit, proceeds to make good an entrance by force. Here, it will be remembered, the words of the narrative run thus:—

"And Ethelred, who was by nature of a doughty heart, and who was now mighty withal, on account of the powerfulness of the wine which he had drunken, waited no longer to hold parley with the hermit, who, in sooth, was of an obstinate and maliceful turn, but, feeling the rain upon his shoulders, and fearing the rising of the tempest, uplifted his mace outright, and with blows made quickly room in the plankings of the door for his gauntleted hand; and now pulling therewith sturdily, he so cracked, and ripped, and tore all asunder, that the noise of the dry and hollow-sounding wood alarumed and reverberated throughout the forest."

At the termination of this sentence I started, and for a moment paused; for it appeared to me (although I at once concluded that my excited fancy had deceived me)—it appeared to me that from some very remote portion of the mansion there came, indistinctly, to my ears, what might have been, in its exact similarity of character, the echo (but a stifled and dull one certainly) of the very cracking and ripping sound which Sir Launcelot had so particularly described. It was, beyond doubt, the coincidence alone which had arrested my attention; for, amid the rattling of the sashes of the casements, and the ordinary commingled noises of the still increasing storm, the sound, in itself, had nothing, surely, which should have interested or disturbed me. I continued the story:—

"But the good champion Ethelred, now entering within the door, was sore enraged and amazed to perceive no signal of the maliceful hermit; but, in the stead thereof, a dragon of a scaly and prodigious demeanor, and of a fiery tongue, which sate in guard before a palace of gold, with a floor of silver; and upon the wall there hung a shield of shining brass with this legend enwritten—

Who entereth herein, a conqueror hath bin;
Who slayeth the dragon, the shield he shall win.

And Ethelred uplifted his mace, and struck upon the head of the dragon, which fell before him, and gave up his pesty breath, with a shriek so horrid and harsh, and withal so piercing, that Ethelred had fain to close his ears with his hands against the dreadful noise of it, the like whereof was never before heard."

Here again I paused abruptly, and now with a feeling of wild amazement; for there could be no doubt whatever that, in this instance, I did actually hear (although from what direction it proceeded I found it impossible to say) a low and apparently distant, but harsh, protracted, and most unusual screaming or grating sound—the exact counterpart of what my fancy had already conjured up for the dragon's unnatural shriek as described by the romancer.

Oppressed, as I certainly was, upon the occurrence of this second and most extraordinary coincidence, by a thousand conflicting sensations, in which wonder and extreme terror were predominant, I still retained sufficient presence of mind to avoid exciting, by any observation, the sensitive nervousness of my companion. I was by no means certain that he had noticed the sounds in question; although, assuredly, a strange alteration had during the last few minutes taken place in his demeanor. From a position fronting my own, he had gradually brought round his chair, so as to sit with his face to the door of the chamber; and thus I could but partially perceive his features, although I saw that his lips trembled as if he were murmuring inaudibly. His head had dropped upon his breast—yet I knew that he was not asleep, from the wide and rigid opening of the eye as I caught a glance of it in profile. The motion of his body, too, was at variance with this idea—for he rocked from side to side with a gentle yet constant and uniform sway. Having rapidly taken notice of all this, I resumed the narrative of Sir Launcelot, which thus proceeded:—

"And now, the champion, having escaped from the terrible fury of the dragon, bethinking himself of the brazen shield, and of the breaking up of the enchantment which was upon it, removed the carcass from out of the way before him, and approached valorously

over the silver pavement of the castle to where the shield was upon
the wall; which in sooth tarried not for his full coming, but fell
down at his feet upon the silver floor, with a mighty great and terrible ringing sound."

No sooner had these syllables passed my lips, than
—as if a shield of brass had indeed, at the moment,
fallen heavily upon a floor of silver—I became aware
of a distinct, hollow, metallic and clangorous, yet apparently muffled reverberation. Completely unnerved, I leaped to my feet; but the measured rock-
ing movement of Usher was undisturbed. I rushed
to the chair in which he sat. His eyes were bent fix-
edly before him, and throughout his whole countenance there reigned a stony rigidity. But, as I placed
my hand upon his shoulder, there came a strong shudder over his whole person; a sickly smile quivered
about his lips; and I saw that he spoke in a low hurried, and gibbering murmur, as if unconscious of
my presence. Bending closely over him, I at length
drank in the hideous import of his words.

"Not hear it?—yes, I hear it, and *have* heard it.
Long — long — long — many minutes, many hours,
many days, have I heard it—yet I dared not—oh,
pity me, miserable wretch that I am!—I dared not
—I *dared* not speak! *We have put her living in the
tomb!* Said I not that my senses were acute? I *now*
tell you that I heard her first feeble movements in
the hollow coffin. I heard them—many, many days
ago—yet I dared not—*I dared not speak!* And now
—to-night—Ethelred—ha! ha!—the breaking of the
hermit's door, and the death-cry of the dragon, and
the clangor of the shield!—say, rather, the rending
of her coffin, and the grating of the iron hinges of
her prison, and her struggles within the coppered
archway of the vault! Oh, whither shall I fly? Will
she not be here anon? Is she not hurrying to up-
braid me for my haste? Have I not heard her foot-

step on the stair? Do I not distinguish that heavy
and horrible beating of her heart? Madman!"—
here he sprang furiously to his feet, and shrieked
out his syllables, as if in the effort he were giving
up his soul—"*Madman! I tell you that she now
stands without the door!*"

As if in the superhuman energy of his utterance
there had been found the potency of a spell, the
huge antique panels to which the speaker pointed
threw slowly back, upon the instant, their ponderous
and ebony jaws. It was the work of the rushing
gust—but then without those doors there *did* stand
the lofty and enshrouded figure of the lady Madeline
of Usher. There was blood upon her white robes,
and the evidence of some bitter struggle upon every
portion of her emaciated frame. For a moment she
remained trembling and reeling to and fro upon the
threshold—then, with a low moaning cry, fell heavily
inward upon the person of her brother, and, in her
violent and now final death-agonies, bore him to the
floor a corpse, and a victim to the terrors he had
anticipated.

From that chamber, and from that mansion, I fled
aghast. The storm was still abroad in all its wrath
as I found myself crossing the old causeway. Suddenly there shot along the path a wild light, and I
turned to see whence a gleam so unusual could have
issued; for the vast house and its shadows were
alone behind me. The radiance was that of the full,
setting, and blood-red moon, which now shone vividly
through that once barely-discernible fissure, of
which I have before spoken as extending from the
roof of the building, in a zigzag direction, to the
base. While I gazed, this fissure rapidly widened—
there came a fierce breath of the whirlwind—the entire orb of the satellite burst at once upon my sight
—my brain reeled as I saw the mighty walls rush-

ing asunder—there was a long tumultuous shouting sound like the voice of a thousand waters—and the deep and dank tarn at my feet closed sullenly and silently over the fragments of the *"House of Usher."*

THE GOLD-BUG.

"What oh! what oh! this fellow is dancing mad!
He hath been bitten by the Tarantula.
All in the Wrong.

MANY years ago I contracted an intimacy with a Mr. William Legrand. He was of an ancient Huguenot family, and had once been wealthy; but a series of misfortunes had reduced him to want. To avoid the mortification consequent upon his disasters, he left New Orleans, the city of his forefathers, and took up his residence at Sullivan's Island, near Charleston, South Carolina.

This island is a very singular one. It consists of little else than the sea-sand, and is about three miles long. Its breadth at no point exceeds a quarter of a mile. It is separated from the mainland by a scarcely perceptible creek oozing its way through a wilderness of reeds and slime, a favorite resort of the marsh-hen. The vegetation, as might be supposed, is scant, or at least dwarfish. No trees of any magnitude are to be seen. Near the western extremity, where Fort Moultrie stands, and where are some miserable frame buildings, tenanted, during summer, by the fugitives from Charleston dust and fever, may be found, indeed, the bristly palmetto; but the whole island, with the exception of this western point, and a line of hard, white beach on the sea-coast, is covered with a dense undergrowth of the sweet myrtle, so much prized by the horticulturists of England. The shrub here often attains the height of fifteen or twenty feet, and forms an almost impenetrable coppice, burdening the air with its fragrance.

In the inmost recesses of this coppice, not far from the eastern or more remote end of the island, Legrand had built himself a small hut, which he occupied when I first, by mere accident, made his acquaintance. This soon ripened into friendship,— for there was much in the recluse to excite interest and esteem. I found him well educated, with unusual powers of mind, but infected with misanthropy, and subject to perverse moods of alternate enthusiasm and melancholy. He had with him many books, but rarely employed them. His chief amusements were gunning and fishing, or sauntering along the beach and through the myrtles, in quest of shells or entomological specimens;—his collection of the latter might have been envied by a Swammerdam. In these excursions he was usually accompanied by an old negro, called Jupiter, who had been manumitted before the reverses of the family, but who could be induced, neither by threats nor by promises, to abandon what he considered his right of attendance upon the footsteps of his young "Massa Will." It is not improbable that the relatives of Legrand, conceiving him to be somewhat unsettled in intellect, had contrived to instil this obstinacy into Jupiter, with a view to the supervision and guardianship of the wanderer.

The winters in the latitude of Sullivan's Island are seldom very severe, and in the fall of the year it is a rare event indeed when a fire is considered necessary. About the middle of October, 18—, there occurred, however, a day of remarkable chilliness.

Just before sunset I scrambled my way through the evergreens to the hut of my friend, whom I had not visited for several weeks,—my residence being, at that time, in Charleston, a distance of nine miles from the island, while the facilities of passage and re-passage were very far behind those of the present day. Upon reaching the hut I rapped, as was my custom, and getting no reply, sought for the key where I knew it was secreted, unlocked the door, and went in. A fine fire was blazing upon the hearth. It was a novelty, and by no means an ungrateful one. I threw off an overcoat, took an arm-chair by the crackling logs, and awaited patiently the arrival of my hosts.

Soon after dark they arrived, and gave me a most cordial welcome. Jupiter, grinning from ear to ear, bustled about to prepare some marsh-hens for supper. Legrand was in one of his fits—how else shall I term them?—of enthusiasm. He had found an unknown bivalve, forming a new genus, and, more than this, he had hunted down and secured, with Jupiter's assistance, a *scarabæus* which he believed to be totally new, but in respect to which he wished to have my opinion on the morrow.

"And why not to-night?" I asked, rubbing my hands over the blaze, and wishing the whole tribe of *scarabæi* at the devil.

"Ah, if I had only known you were here!" said Legrand, "but it's so long since I saw you; and how could I foresee that you would pay me a visit this very night of all others? As I was coming home I met Lieutenant G——, from the fort, and, very foolishly, I lent him the bug; so it will be impossible for you to see it until the morning. Stay here to-night, and I will send Jup down for it at sunrise. It is the loveliest thing in creation!"

"What?—sunrise?"

"Nonsense! no!—the bug. It is of a brilliant gold color,—about the size of a large hickory-nut,—with two jet-black spots near one extremity of the back, and another, somewhat longer, at the other. The *antennæ* are——"

"Dey ain't *no* tin in him, Massa Will, I keep a tellin' on you," here interrupted Jupiter; "de bug is a goole-bug, solid, ebery bit of him, inside and all, sep him wing,—neber feel half so hebby a bug in my life."

"Well, suppose it is, Jup," replied Legrand, somewhat more earnestly, it seemed to me, than the case demanded, "is that any reason for your letting the birds burn? The color"—here he turned to me—"is really almost enough to warrant Jupiter's idea. You never saw a more brilliant metallic lustre than the scales emit,—but of this you cannot judge till to-morrow. In the meantime I can give you some idea of the shape." Saying this, he seated himself at a small table, on which were a pen and ink, but no paper. He looked for some in a drawer, but found none.

"Never mind," said he at length, "this will answer;" and he drew from his waistcoat-pocket a scrap of what I took to be very dirty foolscap, and made upon it a rough drawing with the pen. While he did this, I retained my seat by the fire, for I was still chilly. When the design was complete, he handed it to me without rising. As I received it, a loud growl was heard, succeeded by a scratching at the door. Jupiter opened it, and a large Newfoundland, belonging to Legrand, rushed in, leaped upon my shoulders, and loaded me with caresses; for I had shown him much attention during previous visits. When his gambols were over, I looked at the paper, and, to speak the truth, found myself not a little puzzled at what my friend had depicted.

"Well!" I said, after contemplating it for some minutes, "this *is* a strange *scarabœus,* I must confess: new to me: never saw anything like it before, —unless it was a skull, or a death's-head,—which it more nearly resembles than anything else that has come under *my* observation."

"A death's-head!" echoed Legrand—"Oh—yes—well, it has something of that appearance upon paper, no doubt. The two upper black spots look like eyes, eh? and the longer one at the bottom like a mouth,—and then the shape of the whole is oval."

"Perhaps so," said I; "but, Legrand, I fear you are no artist. I must wait until I see the beetle itself, if I am to form any idea of its personal appearance."

"Well, I don't know," said he, a little nettled, "I draw tolerably,—*should* do it at least,—have had good masters, and flatter myself that I am not quite a blockhead."

"But, my dear fellow, you are joking, then," said I; "this is a very passable *skull,*—indeed, I may say that it is a very *excellent* skull, according to the vulgar notions about such specimens of physiology,—and your *scarabœus* must be the queerest *scarabœus* in the world if it resembles it. Why, we may get up a very thrilling bit of superstition upon this hunt. I presume you will call the bug *scarabœus caput hominis,* or something of that kind,—there are many similar titles in the Natural Histories. But where are the *antennœ* you spoke of?"

"The *antennœ!*" said Legrand, who seemed to be getting unaccountably warm upon the subject; "I am sure you must see the *antennœ.* I made them as distinct as they are in the original insect, and I presume that is sufficient."

"Well, well," I said, "perhaps you have,—still I

don't see them''; and I handed him the paper without additional remark, not wishing to ruffle his temper. But I was much surprised at the turn affairs
had taken; his ill-humor puzzled me; and, as for the
drawing of the beetle, there were positively *no antennæ* visible, and the whole *did* bear a very close resemblance to the ordinary cuts of a death's-head.

He received the paper very peevishly, and was
about to crumple it, apparently to throw it in the
fire, when a casual glance at the design seemed suddenly to rivet his attention. In an instant his face
grew violently red,—in another as excessively pale.
For some minutes, he continued to scrutinize the
drawing minutely where he sat. At length he arose,
took a candle from the table, and proceeded to seat
himself upon a sea-chest in the farthest corner of the
room. Here again he made an anxious examination
of the paper, turning it in all directions. He said
nothing, however, and his conduct greatly astonished me; yet I thought it prudent not to exacerbate
the growing moodiness of his temper by any comment. Presently he took from his coat-pocket a wallet, placed the paper carefully in it, and deposited
both in a writing-desk, which he locked. He now
grew more composed in his demeanor; but his original air of enthusiasm had quite disappeared. Yet
he seemed not so much sulky as abstracted. As the
evening wore away he became more and more absorbed in revery, from which no sallies of mine
could arouse him. It had been my intention to pass
the night at the hut, as I had frequently done before,
but seeing my host in this mood, I deemed it proper
to take leave. He did not press me to remain, but,
as I departed, he shook my hand with even more
than his usual cordiality.

It was about a month after this (and during the
interval I had seen nothing of Legrand) when I re-

ceived a visit, at Charleston, from his man, Jupiter.
I had never seen the good old negro look so dispir-
ited, and I feared that some serious disaster had befallen my friend.

"Well, Jup," said I, "what is the matter now?—
how is your master?"

"Why, to speak de troof, massa, him not so berry
well as mought be."

"Not well! I am truly sorry to hear it. What does
he complain of?"

"Dar! dat's it!—him neber 'plain of notin,—but
him bery sick for all dat."

"*Very* sick, Jupiter!—why didn't you say so at
once? Is he confined to bed?"

"No, dat he ain't!—he ain't 'fin'd nowhar,—dat's
just whar de shoe pinch,—my mind is got to be berry
hebby 'bout poor Massa Will."

"Jupiter, I should like to understand what it is
you are talking about. You say your master is sick.
Hasn't he told you what ails him?"

"Why, massa, 'tain't worf while for to git mad
about de matter,—Massa Will say noffin at all ain't
de matter wid him,—but den what make him go
about looking dis here way, wid he head down and he
soldiers up, and as white as a gose? And den he
keep a syphon all de time——"

"Keeps a what, Jupiter?"

"Keeps a syphon wid de figgurs on de slate,—de
queerest figgurs I ebber did see. I's gittin' to be
skeered, I tell you. Hab for to keep mighty tight
eye 'pon him 'noovers. T' odder day he gib me slip
'fore de sun up and was gone de whole ob de blessed
day. I had a big stick ready cut for to gib him
deuced good beating when he did come,—but I's
sich a fool dat I hadn't de heart arter all,—he look
so berry poorly."

"Eh?—what?—ah, yes!—upon the whole I think

you had better not be too severe with the poor fellow,—don't flog him, Jupiter,—he can't very well
stand it,—but can you form no idea of what has occasioned this illness, or rather this change of conduct? Has anything unpleasant happened since I
saw you?"

"No, massa, dey ain't bin noffin onpleasant *since*
den,—'twas *fore* den, I'm feared,—'twas de berry
day you was dare."

"How? what do you mean?"

"Why, massa, I mean de bug—dare now."

"The what?"

"De bug,—I'm berry sartain dat Massa Will bin
bit somewhere 'bout de head by dat goole-bug."

"And what cause have you, Jupiter, for such a
supposition?"

"Claws enuff, massa, and mouff too. I nebber did
see sich a deuced bug,—he kick and he bite ebery
ting what cum near him. Massa Will cotch him fuss,
but had for to let him go gin mighty quick, I tell you
—den was de time he must ha' got de bite. I didn't
like de look ob de bug mouff, myself, nohow, so I
wouldn't take hold ob him wid my finger, but I cotch
him with a piece ob paper dat I found. I rap him
up in de paper and stuff piece ob it in he mouff,—
dat was de way."

"And you think, then, that your master was really
bitten by the beetle, and that the bite made him
sick?"

"I don't tink noffin about it,—I nose it. What
make him dream 'bout de goole so much, if 'tain't
cause he bit by de goole-bug? I's heerd 'bout dem
goole-bugs 'fore dis."

"But how do you know he dreams about gold?"

"How I know? why, cause he talk about it in he
sleep,—dat's how I nose."

"Well, Jup, perhaps you are right; but to what

fortunate circumstance am I to attribute the honor
of a visit from you to-day?"

"What de matter, massa?"

"Did you bring any message from Mr. Legrand?"

"No, massa, I bring dis here pissel"; and here
Jupiter handed me a note which ran thus:

My Dear——: Why have I not seen you for so long a time? I
hope you have not been so foolish as to take offence at any little
brusquerie of mine; but no, that is improbable.

Since I saw you I have had great cause for anxiety. I have something to tell you, yet scarcely know how to tell it, or whether I
should tell it at all.

I have not been quite well for some days past, and poor old Jup
annoys me, almost beyond endurance, by his well-meant attentions.
Would you believe it?—he had prepared a huge stick, the other day,
with which to chastise me for giving him the slip, and spending the
day, *solus*, among the hills on the mainland. I verily believe that
my ill looks alone saved me a flogging.

I have made no addition to my cabinet since we met.

If you can in any way make it convenient, come over with Jupiter.
Do come. I wish to see you *to-night*, upon business of importance.
I assure you that it is of the *highest* importance. Ever yours,
                                         William Legrand.

There was something in the tone of this note
which gave me great uneasiness. Its whole style
differed materially from that of Legrand. What
could he be dreaming of? What new crotchet possessed his excitable brain? What "business of the
highest importance" could *he* possibly have to trans-
act? Jupiter's account of him boded no good. I
dreaded lest the continued pressure of misfortune
had, at length, fairly unsettled the reason of my
friend. Without a moment's hesitation, therefore, I
prepared to accompany the negro.

Upon reaching the wharf, I noticed a scythe and
three spades, all apparently new, lying in the bottom of the boat in which we were to embark.

"What is the meaning of all this Jup?" I inquired.

"Him syfe, massa, and spade."

"Very true; but what are they doing here?"

"Him de syfe and de spade wnat Massa Will sis 'pon my buying for him in de town, and de debbil's own lot of money I had to gib for 'em."

"But what, in the name of all that is mysterious, is your 'Massa Will' going to do with scythes and spades?"

"Dat's more dan I know, and debbil take me if I don't b'lieve 'tis more dan he know too. But it's all cum ob de bug."

Finding that no satisfaction was to be obtained of Jupiter, whose whole intellect seemed to be absorbed by "de bug," I now stepped into the boat and made sail. With a fair and strong breeze we soon ran into the little cove to the northward of Fort Moultrie, and a walk of some two miles brought us to the hut. It was about three in the afternoon when we arrived. Legrand had been awaiting us in eager expectation. He grasped my hand with a nervous *empressement* which alarmed me and strengthened the suspicions already entertained. His countenance was pale even to ghastliness, and his deep-set eyes glared with un-natural lustre. After some inquiries respecting his health, I asked him, not knowing what better to say, if he had yet obtained the *scarabæus* from Lieu-tenant G——.

"Oh, yes," he replied, coloring violently, "I got it from him the next morning. Nothing should tempt me to part with that *scarabæus*. Do you know that Jupiter is quite right about it?"

"In what way?" I asked, with a sad foreboding at heart.

"In supposing it to be a bug of *real gold*." He said this with an air of profound seriousness, and I felt inexpressibly shocked.

"This bug is to make my fortune," he continued, with a triumphant smile, "to reinstate me in my family possessions. Is it any wonder, then. that I

Vol. 8—3

prize it? Since Fortune has thought fit to bestow it upon me, I have only to use it properly and I shall arrive at the gold of which it is the index. Jupiter, bring me that *scarabæus!*"

"What! de bug, massa? I'd rudder not go fer trubble dat bug,—you mus' git him for your own self."

Hereupon Legrand arose, with a grave and stately air, and brought me the beetle from a glass case in which it was enclosed. It was a beautiful *scarabæus,* and, at that time, unknown to naturalists,—of course a great pride in a scientific point of view. There were two round black spots near one extremity of the back, and a long one near the other. The scales were exceedingly hard and glossy, with all the appearance of burnished gold. The weight of the insect was very remarkable, and, taking all things into consideration, I could hardly blame Jupiter for his opinion respecting it; but what to make of Legrand's concordance with that opinion I could not for the life of me tell.

"I sent for you," said he, in a grandiloquent tone, when I had completed my examination of the beetle, —"I sent for you, that I might have your counsel and assistance in furthering the views of Fate and of the bug——"

"My dear Legrand," I cried, interrupting him, "you are certainly unwell, and had better use some little precautions. You shall go to bed, and I will remain with you a few days, until you get over this. You are feverish and——"

"Feel my pulse," said he.

I felt it, and, to say the truth, found not the slightest indication of fever.

"But you may be ill and yet have no fever. Allow me this once to prescribe for you. In the first place, go to bed. In the next——"

"You are mistaken," he interposed; "I am as well as I can expect to be under the excitement which I suffer. If you really wish me well, you will relieve this excitement."

"And how is this to be done?"

"Very easily. Jupiter and myself are going upon an expedition into the hills, upon the mainland, and in this expedition we shall need the aid of some person in whom we can confide. You are the only one we can trust. Whether we succeed or fail, the excitement which you now perceive in me will be equally allayed."

"I am anxious to oblige you in any way," I replied; "but do you mean to say that this infernal beetle has any connection with your expedition into the hills?"

"It has."

"Then, Legrand, I can become a party to no such absurd proceeding."

"I am sorry—very sorry,—for we shall have to try it by ourselves."

"Try it by yourselves! The man is surely mad!—but stay!—how long do you propose to be absent?"

"Probably all night. We shall start immediately, and be back, at all events, by sunrise."

"And will you promise me, upon your honor, that when this freak of yours is over, and the bug business (good God!) settled to your satisfaction, you will then return home and follow my advice implicitly, as that of your physician?"

"Yes; I promise; and now let us be off, for we have no time to lose."

With a heavy heart I accompanied my friend. We started about four o'clock,—Legrand, Jupiter, the dog, and myself. Jupiter had with him the scythe and spades, the whole of which he insisted upon carrying,—more through fear, it seemed to me, of trusting either of the implements within reach of his master, than from any excess of industry or complaisance. His demeanor was dogged in the extreme, and "dat deuced bug" were the sole words which escaped his lips during the journey. For my own part, I had charge of a couple of dark-lanterns, while Legrand contented himself with the *scarabæus,* which he carried attached to the end of a bit of whipcord; twirling it too and fro, with the air of a conjurer, as he went. When I observed this last plain evidence of my friend's aberration of mind, I could scarcely refrain from tears. I thought it best, however, to humor his fancy; at least for the present, or until I could adopt some more energetic measures with a chance of success. In the meantime I endeavored, but all in vain, to sound him in regard to the object of the expedition. Having succeeded in inducing me to accompany him, he seemed unwilling to hold conversation upon any topic of minor importance, and to all my question vouchsafed no other reply than "We shall see!"

We crossed the creek at the head of the island by means of a skiff, and, ascending the high grounds on the shore of the mainland, proceeded in a northwesterly direction, through a tract of country excessively wild and desolate, where no trace of a human footstep was to be seen. Legrand led the way with decision, pausing only for an instant, here and there, to consult what appeared to be certain landmarks of his own contrivance upon a former occasion.

In this manner we journeyed for about two hours, and the sun was just setting when we entered a region infinitely more dreary than any yet seen. It was a species of table-land, near the summit of an almost inaccessible hill, densely wooded from base to pinnacle, and interspersed with huge crags that appeared to lie loosely upon the soil, and in many cases were prevented from precipitating themselves into the valleys below, merely by the support of the trees against which they reclined. Deep ravines, in various directions, gave an air of still sterner solemnity to the scene.

The natural platform to which we had clambered was thickly overgrown with brambles, through which we soon discovered that it would have been impossible to force our way but for the scythe: and Jupiter, by direction of his master, proceeded to clear for us a path to the foot of an enormously tall tulip-tree, which stood, with some eight or ten oaks, upon the level, and far surpassed them all, and all other trees which I had then ever seen, in the beauty of its foliage and form, in the wide spread of its branches, and in the general majesty of its appearance. When we reached this tree, Legrand turned to Jupiter, and asked him if he thought he could climb it. The old man seemed a little staggered by the question, and for some moments made no reply. At length he approached the huge trunk, walked slowly around it, and examined it with minute attention. When he had completed his scrutiny, he merely said:

"Yes, massa, Jup climb any tree he ebber see in he life."

"Then up with you as soon as possible, for it will soon be too dark to see what we are about."

"How far mus' go up, massa?" inquired Jupiter.

"Get up the main trunk first, and then I will tell you which way to go—and here—stop! take this beetle with you."

"De bug, Massa Will!—de goole-bug!" cried the negro, drawing back in dismay—"what for mus' tote de bug way up de tree—d—n if I do!"

"If you are afraid, Jup, a great big negro like

you, to take hold of a harmless little dead beetle, why you can carry it up by this string; but, if you do not take it up with you in some way, I shall be under the necessity of breaking your head with this shovel."

"What de matter now, massa?" said Jup, evidently shamed into compliance; "always want for to raise fuss wid old nigger. Was only funnin anyhow. *Me* feered de bug! what I keer for de bug?" Here he took cautiously hold of the extreme end of the string, and, maintaining the insect as far from his person as circumstances would permit, prepared to ascend the tree.

In youth, the tulip-tree, or *Liriodendron tulipiferum*, the most magnificent of American foresters, has a trunk peculiarly smooth, and often rises to a great height without lateral branches; but, in its riper age, the bark becomes gnarled and uneven, while many short limbs make their appearance on the stem. Thus the difficulty of ascension, in the present case, lay more in semblance than in reality. Embracing the huge cylinder, as closely as possible, with his arms and knees, seizing with his hands some projections, and resting his naked toes upon others, Jupiter, after one or two narrow escapes from falling, at length wriggled himself into the first great fork, and seemed to consider the whole business as virtually accomplished. The *risk* of the achievement was, in fact, now over, although the climber was some sixty or seventy feet from the ground.

"Which way mus' go now, Massa Will?" he asked.

"Keep up the largest branch,—the one on this side," said Legrand. The negro obeyed him promptly, and apparently with but little trouble; ascending higher and higher, until no glimpse of his squat figure could be obtained through the dense foliage which enveloped it. Presently his voice was heard in a sort of hallo.

"How much fudder is got for go?"

"How high up are you?" asked Legrand.

"Ebber so fur," replied the negro; "can see de sky fru de top ob de tree."

"Never mind the sky, but attend to what I say. Look down the trunk and count the limbs below you on this side. How many limbs have you passed?"

"One, two, tree, four, fibe,—I done pass fibe big limb, massa, 'pon dis side."

"Then go one limb higher."

In a few minutes the voice was heard again, announcing that the seventh limb was attained.

"Now, Jup," cried Legrand, evidently much excited, "I want you to work your way out upon that limb as far as you can. If you see anything strange, let me know."

By this time what little doubt I might have entertained of my poor friend's insanity was put finally at rest. I had no alternative but to conclude him stricken with lunacy, and I became seriously anxious about getting him home. While I was pondering upon what was best to be done, Jupiter's voice was again heard.

"'Mos' feerd for to ventur 'pon dis limb berry far,—'tis dead limb putty much all de way."

"Did you say it was a *dead* limb, Jupiter?" cried Legrand, in a quavering voice.

"Yes, massa, him dead as de door-nail—done up for sartain—done departed dis here life."

"What in the name of Heaven shall I do?" asked Legrand, seemingly in the greatest distress.

"Do!" said I, glad of an opportunity to interpose a word; "why, come home and go to bed. Come, now!—that's a fine fellow. It's getting late, and, besides, you remember your promise."

"Jupiter," cried he, without heeding me in the least, "do you hear me?"

"Yes, Massa Will, hear you ebber so plain."

"Try the wood well, then, with your knife, and see if you think it *very* rotten."

"Him rotten, massa, sure nuff," replied the negro in a few moments, "but not so berry rotten as mought be. Mought ventur out leetle way 'pon de limb by myself, dat's true."

"By yourself!—What do you mean?"

"Why I mean de bug. 'Tis *berry* hebby bug. S'pose I drop him down fuss, and den de limb won't break wid just de weight ob one nigger."

"You infernal scoundrel!" cried Legrand, apparently much relieved, "what do you mean by telling me such nonsense as that? As sure as you drop that beetle I'll break your neck. Look here, Jupiter, do you hear me?"

"Yes, massa, needn't hollo at poor nigger dat style."

"Well! now listen!—if you will venture out on the limb as far as you think safe, and not let go the beetle, I'll make you a present of a silver dollar as soon as you get down."

"I'm gwine, Massa Will,—'deed I is," replied the negro very promptly,—"mos' out to the eend now."

"*Out to the end!*" here fairly screamed Legrand; "do you say you are out to the end of that limb?"

"Soon be to de eend, massa,—o-o-o-o-oh! Lor-gol-a-marcy! what *is* dis here 'pon de tree?"

"Well!" cried Legrand, highly delighted, "what is it?"

"Why, 'tain't noffin but a skull—somebody bin lef' him head up de tree, and de crows done gobble ebery bit ob de meat off."

"A skull, you say! very well!—how is it fastened to the limb?—what holds it on?"

"Sure nuff, massa; mus' look. Why dis berry curous sarcumstance, 'pon my word,—dare's a great big nail in de skull, what fastens ob it on to de tree."

"Well, now, Jupiter, do exactly as I tell you,—do you hear?"

"Yes, massa."

"Pay attention, then!—find the left eye of the skull."

"Hum! hoo! dat's good! why, dare ain't no eye lef' at all."

"Curse your stupidity! do you know your right hand from your left?"

"Yes, I nose dat,—nose all 'bout dat,—'tis my lef' hand what I chops de wood wid."

"To be sure! you are left-handed; and your left eye is on the same side as your left hand. Now, I suppose, you can find the left eye on the skull, or the place where the left eye has been. Have you found it?"

Here was a long pause. At length the negro asked:

"Is de lef' eye of de skull 'pon de same side as de lef' hand of de skull too?—'cause de skull ain't not got a bit ob a hand at all,—nebber mind! I got de lef' eye now,—here de lef' eye! what mus' do wid it?"

"Let the beetle drop through it, as far as the string will reach,—but be careful and not let go your hold of the string."

"All dat done, Massa Will; mighty easy ting for to put de bug fru de hole,—look out for him dare below!"

During this colloquy no portion of Jupiter's person could be seen; but the beetle, which he had suffered to descend, was now visible at the end of the string, and glistened, like a globe of burnished gold, in the last rays of the setting sun, some of which still faintly illumined the eminence upon which we stood. The *scarabæus* hung quite clear of any branches, and, if allowed to fall, would have fallen at our feet. Legrand immediately took the scythe, and cleared with it a circular space, three or four yards in diameter, just beneath the insect, and having accomplished this, ordered Jupiter to let go the string and come down from the tree.

Driving a peg, with great nicety, into the ground, at the precise spot where the beetle fell, my friend now produced from his pocket a tape-measure. Fastening one end of this at that point of the trunk of the tree which was nearest the peg, he unrolled it till it reached the peg, and thence farther unrolled it, in the direction already established by the two points of the tree and the peg, for the distance of fifty feet,—Jupiter clearing away the brambles with the scythe. At the spot thus attained a second peg was driven, and about this, as a centre, a rude circle, about four feet in diameter, described. Taking now a spade himself, and giving one to Jupiter and one to me, Legrand begged us to set about digging as quickly as possible.

To speak the truth, I had no especial relish for such amusement at any time, and, at that particular moment, would most willingly have declined it; for the night was coming on, and I felt much fatigued with the exercise already taken; but I saw no mode of escape, and was fearful of disturbing my poor friend's equanimity by a refusal. Could I have depended, indeed, upon Jupiter's aid, I would have had no hesitation in attempting to get the lunatic home by force; but I was too well assured of the old negro's disposition, to hope that he would assist me, under any circumstances, in a personal contest with his master. I made no doubt that the latter had been infected with some of the innumerable Southern superstitions about money buried, and that his fantasy had received confirmation by the finding of the *scarabœus,* or, perhaps, by Jupiter's obstinacy in maintaining it to be "a bug of real gold." A mind disposed to lunacy would readily be led away by such suggestions,—especially if chiming in with favorite preconceived ideas,—and then I called to mind the poor fellow's speech about the beetle's being "the index of his fortune." Upon the whole, I was sadly vexed and puzzled, but, at length, I concluded to make a virtue of necessity,—to dig with a good will, and thus the sooner to convince the visionary, by ocular demonstration, of the fallacy of the opinions he entertained.

The lanterns having been lit, we all fell to work with a zeal worthy a more rational cause; and, as the glare fell upon our person and implements, I could not help thinking how picturesque a group we composed, and how strange and suspicious our labors must have appeared to any interloper who, by chance, might have stumbled upon our whereabouts.

We dug very steadily for two hours. Little was said; and our chief embarrassment lay in the yelpings of the dog, who took exceeding interest in our proceedings. He at length became so obstreperous that we grew fearful of his giving the alarm to some stragglers in the vicinity,—or, rather, this was the apprehension of Legrand;—for myself, I should have rejoiced at any interruption which might have enabled me to get the wanderer home. The noise was, at length, very effectually silenced by Jupiter, who, getting out of the hole with a dogged air of deliberation, tied the brute's mouth up with one of his suspenders, and then returned, with a grave chuckle, to his task.

When the time mentioned had expired, we had

reached a depth of five feet, and yet no signs of any treasure became manifest. A general pause ensued, and I began to hope that the farce was at an end. Legrand, however, although evidently much disconcerted, wiped his brow thoughtfully, and recommenced. We had excavated the entire circle of four feet diameter, and now we slightly enlarged the limit, and went to the farther depth of two feet. Still nothing appeared. The gold-seeker, whom I sincerely pitied, at length clambered from the pit, with the bitterest disappointment imprinted upon every feature, and proceeded, slowly and reluctantly, to put on his coat, which he had thrown off at the beginning of his labor. In the meantime I made no remark. Jupiter, at a signal from his master, began to gather up his tools. This done, and the dog having been unmuzzled, we turned in profound silence toward home.

We had taken, perhaps, a dozen steps in this direction, when, with loud oath, Legrand strode up to Jupiter, and seized him by the collar. The astonished negro opened his eyes and mouth to the fullest extent, let fall the spades, and fell upon his knees.

"You scoundrel," said Legrand, hissing out the syllables from between his clenched teeth,—"you infernal black villain!—speak, I tell you!—answer me this instant, without prevarication!—which—which is your left eye?"

"Oh, my golly, Massa Will! ain't dis here my lef' eye for sartain?" roared the terrified Jupiter, placing his hand upon his *right* organ of vision, and holding it there with a desperate pertinacity, as if in immediate dread of his master's attempt at a gouge.

"I thought so!—I knew it! hurrah!" vociferated Legrand, letting the negro go, and executing a series of curvets and caracoles, much to the astonishment of his valet, who, arising from his knees, looked, mutely, from his master to myself, and then from myself to his master.

"Come! we must go back," said the latter, "the game's not up yet." And he again led the way to the tulip-tree.

"Jupiter," said he, when we reached its foot, "come here! Was the skull nailed to the limb with the face outwards, or with the face to the limb?"

"De face was out, massa, so dat de crows could get at de eyes good, widout any trouble."

"Well, then, was it this eye or that through which you dropped the beetle?"—here Legrand touched each of Jupiter's eyes.

"'Twas dis eye, massa,—de lef' eye,—jis as you tell me," and here it was his right eye that the negro indicated.

"That will do,—we must try it again."

Here my friend, about whose madness I now saw, or fancied that I saw, certain indications of method, removed the peg which marked the spot where the beetle fell, to a spot about three inches to the westward of its former position. Taking, now, the tape-measure from the nearest point of the trunk to the peg, as before, and continuing the extension in a straight line to the distance of fifty feet, a spot was indicated, removed, by several yards, from the point at which we had been digging.

Around the new position a circle, somewhat larger than in the former instance, was now described, and we again set to work with the spades. I was dreadfully weary, but, scarcely understanding what had occasioned the change in my thoughts, I felt no longer any great aversion from the labor imposed. I had become most unaccountably interested,—nay, even excited. Perhaps there was something, amid all the extravagant demeanor of Legrand,—some air of forethought, or of deliberation,—which impressed me. I dug eagerly, and now and then caught myself actually looking, with something that very much resembled expectation, for the fancied treasure, the vision of which had demented my unfortunate companion. At a period when such vagaries of thought most fully possessed me, and when we had been at work perhaps an hour and a half, we were again interrupted by the violent howlings of the dog. His uneasiness, in the first instance, had been, evidently, but the result of playfulness or caprice, but he now assumed a bitter and serious tone. Upon Jupiter's again attempting to muzzle him, he made furious resistance, and, leaping into the hole, tore up the mould frantically with his claws. In a few seconds he had uncovered a mass of human bones, forming two complete skeletons, intermingled with several buttons of metal, and what appeared to be the dust of decayed woollen. One or two strokes of a spade upturned the blade of a large Spanish knife, and, as we dug farther, three or four loose pieces of gold and silver coin came to light.

At sight of these, the joy of Jupiter could scarcely be restrained, but the countenance of his master wore an air of extreme disappointment. He urged us, however, to continue our exertions, and the words were hardly uttered, when I stumbled and fell forward, having caught the toe of my boot in a large ring of iron that lay half buried in the loose earth.

We now worked in earnest, and never did I pass ten mintues of more intense excitement. During this interval we had fairly unearthed an oblong chest of wood, which, from its perfect preservation and wonderful hardness, had plainly been subjected to some mineralizing process,—perhaps that of the bichloride of mercury. This box was three feet and a half long, three feet broad, and two and a half feet deep.

It was firmly secured by bands of wrought-iron, riveted, and forming a kind of open trellis-work over the whole. On each side of the chest, near the top, were three rings of iron,—six in all,—by means of which a firm hold could be obtained by six persons. Our utmost united endeavors served only to disturb the coffer very slightly in its bed. We at once saw the impossibility of removing so great a weight. Luckily, the sole fastenings of the lid consisted of two sliding bolts. These we drew back,—trembling and panting with anxiety. In an instant, a treasure of incalculable value lay gleaming before us. As the rays of the lanterns fell within the pit, there flashed upwards a glow and a glare, from a confused heap of gold and of jewels, that absolutely dazzled our eyes.

I shall not pretend to describe the feeling with which I gazed. Amazement was, of course, predominant. Legrand appeared exhausted with excitement, and spoke very few words. Jupiter's countenance wore, for some minutes, as deadly a pallor as it is possible, in the nature of things, for any negro's visage to assume. He seemed stupefied,—thunder-stricken. Presently he fell upon his knees in the pit, and, burying his naked arms up to the elbows in gold, let them there remain, as if enjoying the luxury of a bath. At length, with a deep sigh, he exclaimed, as if in a soliloquy:

"And dis all cum ob de goole-bug! de putty goole-bug! de poor little goole-bug, what I boosed in dat sabage kind ob style! Ain't you 'shamed ob yourself, nigger?—Answer me dat!"

It became necessary, at last, that I should arouse both master and valet to the expediency of removing the treasure. It was growing late, and it behooved us to make exertion, that we might get everything housed before daylight. It was difficult to say what should be done, and much time was spent in deliberation,—so confused were the ideas of all. We finally lightened the box by removing two-thirds of its contents, when we were enabled, with some trouble, to raise it from the hole. The articles taken out were deposited among the brambles, and the dog left to guard them, with strict orders from Jupiter neither, upon any pretence, to stir from the spot, nor to open his mouth, until our return. We then hurriedly made for home with the chest; reaching the hut in safety, but after excessive toil, at one o'clock in the morning. Worn out as we were, it was not human nature to do more immediately. We rested until two, and had supper; starting for the hills immediately afterwards, armed with three stout sacks, which, by good luck, were upon the premises. A little before four we arrived at the pit, divided the remainder of the booty, as equally as might be, among us, and, leaving the holes unfilled, again set out for the hut, at which, for the second time, we deposited our golden burdens, just as the first faint streaks of the dawn gleamed from over the tree-tops in the east.

We were now thoroughly broken down; but the intense excitement of the time denied us repose. After an unquiet slumber of some three or four hours' duration, we arose, as if by preconcert, to make examination of our treasure.

The chest had been full to the brim, and we spent the whole day and the greater part of the next night in a scrutiny of its contents. There had been nothing like order or arrangement. Everything had been heaped in promiscuously. Having assorted all with care, we found ourselves possessed of even vaster wealth than we had at first supposed. In coin there was rather more than four hundred and fifty thousand dollars, — estimating the value of the

pieces, as accurately as we could, by the tables of
the period. There was not a particle of silver. All
was gold of antique date and of great variety,—
French, Spanish, and German money, with a few
English guineas, and some counters, of which we
had never seen specimens before. There were several very large and heavy coins, so worn that we
could make nothing of their inscriptions. There was
no American money. The value of the jewels we
found more difficulty in estimating. There were
diamonds,—some of them exceedingly large and
fine,—a hundred and ten in all, and not one of them
small; eighteen rubies of remarkable brilliancy;
three hundred and ten emeralds, all very beautiful;
and twenty-one sapphires, with an opal. These
stones had all been broken from their settings and
thrown loose in the chest. The settings themselves,
which we picked out from among the other gold, appeared to have been beaten up with hammers as if to
prevent identification. Besides all this, there was a
vast quantity of solid gold ornaments;—nearly two
hundred massive finger and ear rings;—rich chains,
—thirty of these, if I remember;—eighty-three very
large and heavy crucifixes;—five gold censers of
great value;—a prodigious golden punch-bowl, orna-
mented with richly chased vine-leaves and Baccha-
nalian figures; with two sword-handles exquisitely
embossed, and many other smaller articles which I
cannot recollect. The weight of these valuables ex-
ceeded three hundred and fifty pounds avoirdupois;
and in this estimate I have not included one hundred and ninety-seven superb gold watches; three of
the number being worth each five hundred dollars,
if one. Many of them were very old, and as time-
keepers valueless; the works having suffered, more
or less from corrosion; but all were richly jewelled
and in cases of great worth. We estimated the en-

tire contents of the chest, that night, at a million and a half of dollars; and, upon the subsequent disposal of the trinkets and jewels (a few being retained for our own use), it was found that we had greatly undervalued the treasure.

When, at length, we had concluded our examination, and the intense excitement of the time had in some measure subsided, Legrand, who saw that I was dying with impatience for a solution of this most extraordinary riddle, entered into a full detail of all the circumstances connected with it.

"You remember," said he, "the night when I handed you the rough sketch I had made of the *scarabœus*. You recollect, also, that I became quite vexed at you for insisting that my drawing resembled a death's-head. When you first made this assertion I thought you were jesting; but afterwards I called to mind the peculiar spots on the back of the insect, and admitted to myself that your remark had some little foundation in fact. Still, the sneer at my graphic powers irritated me,—for I am considered a good artist,—and, therefore, when you handed me the scrap of parchment, I was about to crumble it up and throw it angrily into the fire."

"The scrap of paper, you mean," said I.

"No; it had much of the appearance of paper, and at first I supposed it to be such, but when I came to draw upon it, I discovered it, at once, to be a piece of very thin parchment. It was quite dirty, you remember. Well, as I was in the very act of crumpling it up, my glance fell upon the sketch at which you had been looking, and you may imagine my astonishment when I perceived, in fact, the figure of a death's-head, just where, it seemed to me, I had made the drawing of the beetle. For a moment I was too much amazed to think with accuracy. I knew that my design was very different in detail from this,—

although there was a certain similarity in general outline. Presently I took a candle, and seating myself at the other end of the room, proceeded to scrutinize the parchment more closely. Upon turning it over, I saw my own sketch upon the reverse, just as I had made it. My first idea, now, was mere surprise at the really remarkable similarity of outline, —at the singular coincidence involved in the fact that, unknown to me, there should have been a skull upon the other side of the parchment, immediately beneath my figure of the *scarabæus,* and that this skull, not only in outline, but in size, should so closely resemble my drawing. I say the singularity of this coincidence absolutely stupefied me for a time. This is the usual effect of such coincidences. The mind struggles to establish a connection,—a sequence of cause and effect,—and, being unable to do so, suffers a species of temporary paralysis. But, when I recovered from this stupor, there dawned upon me gradually a conviction which startled me even far more than the coincidence. I began distinctly, positively, to remember that there had been *no* drawing upon the parchment when I made my sketch of the *scarabæus.* I became perfectly certain of this; for I recollected turning up first one side and then the other, in search of the cleanest spot. Had the skull been there then, of course I could not have failed to notice it. Here was indeed a mystery which I felt it impossible to explain; but, even at that early moment, there seemed to glimmer, faintly, within the most remote and secret chambers of my intellect, a glowworm-like conception of that truth which last night's adventure brought to so magnificent a demonstration. I arose at once, and putting the parchment securely away, dismissed all further reflection until I should be alone.

"When you had gone, and when Jupiter was fast

asleep, I betook myself to a more methodical investigation of the affair. In the first place I considered the manner in which the parchment had come into my possession. The spot where we discovered the *scarabæus* was on the coast of the mainland, about a mile eastward of the island, and but a short distance above high-water mark. Upon my taking hold of it, it gave me a sharp bite, which caused me to let it drop. Jupiter, with his accustomed caution, before seizing the insect, which had flown toward him, looked about him for a leaf, or something of that nature, by which to take hold of it. It was at this moment that his eyes, and mine also, fell upon the scrap of parchment, which I then supposed to be paper. It was lying half buried in the sand, a corner sticking up. Near the spot where we found it, I observed the remnants of the hull of what appeared to have been a ship's long-boat. The wreck seemed to have been there for a very great while; for the resemblance to boat timbers could scarcely be traced.

"Well, Jupiter picked up the parchment, wrapped the beetle in it, and gave it to me. Soon afterwards we turned to go home, and on the way met Lieutenant G——. I showed him the insect, and he begged me to let him take it to the fort. Upon my consenting, he thrust it forthwith into his waistcoat-pocket, without the parchment in which it had been wrapped, and which I had continued to hold in my hand during his inspection. Perhaps he dreaded my changing my mind, and thought it best to make sure of the prize at once,—you know how enthusiastic he is on all subjects connected with natural history. At the same time, without being conscious of it, I must have deposited the parchment in my own pocket.

"You remember that when I went to the table, for the purpose of making a sketch of the beetle, I found no paper where it was usually kept. I looked in the drawer, and found none there. I searched my pockets, hoping to find an old letter, when my hand fell upon the parchment. I thus detail the precise mode in which it came into my possession; for the circumstances impressed me with peculiar force.

"No doubt you will think me fanciful,—but I had already established a kind of *connection*. I had put together two links of a great chain. There was a boat lying upon a sea-coast, and not far from the boat was a parchment—*not a paper*—with a skull depicted upon it. You will, of course, ask: 'Where is the connection?' I reply that the skull, or death's-head, is the well-known emblem of the pirate. The flag of the death's-head is hoisted in all engagements.

"I have said that the scrap was parchment, and not paper. Parchment is durable,—almost imperishable. Matters of little moment are rarely consigned to parchment; since, for the mere ordinary purposes of drawing or writing, it is not nearly so well adapted as paper. This reflection suggested some meaning—some relevancy—in the death's-head. I did not fail to observe, also, the *form* of the parchment. Although one of its corners had been, by some accident, destroyed, it could be seen that the original form was oblong. It was just such a slip, indeed, as might have been chosen for a memorandum,—for a record of something to be long remembered and carefully preserved."

"But," I interposed, "you say that the skull was *not* upon the parchment when you made the drawing of the beetle. How then do you trace any connection between the boat and the skull,—since this latter, according to your own admission, must have been designed (God only knows how or by whom)

at some period subsequent to your sketching the
scarabæus?"

"Ah, hereupon turns the whole mystery; although
the secret, at this point, I had comparatively little
difficulty in solving. My steps were sure, and could
afford but a single result. I reasoned, for example,
thus: When I drew the *scarabæus,* there was no skull
apparent upon the parchment. When I had completed the drawing I gave it to you, and observed
you narrowly until you returned it. *You,* therefore,
did not design the skull, and no one else was present to do it. Then it was not done by human agency.
And nevertheless it was done.

"At this stage of my reflections I endeavored to
remember, and *did* remember, with entire distinct-
ness, every incident which occurred about the period
in question. The weather was chilly (O rare and
happy accident!), and a fire was blazing upon the
hearth. I was heated with exercise, and sat near the
table. You, however, had drawn a chair close to the
chimney. Just as I placed the parchment in your
hand, and as you were in the act of inspecting it,
Wolf, the Newfoundland, entered, and leaped upon
your shoulders. With your left hand you caressed
him and kept him off, while your right, holding the
parchment, was permitted to fall listlessly between
your knees, and in close proximity to the fire. At one
moment I thought the blaze had caught it, and was
about to caution you, but, before I could speak, you
had withdrawn it, and were engaged in its examination. When I considered all these particulars, I
doubted not for a moment *that* heat had been the
agent in bringing to light, upon the parchment, the
skull which I saw designed upon it. You are well
aware that chemical preparations exist, and have existed time out of mind, by means of which it is possible to write upon either paper or vellum, so that

the characters shall become visible only when subjected to the action of fire. Zaffre, digested in *aqua
regia*, and diluted with four times its weight of water, is sometimes employed; a green tint results.
The regulus of cobalt, dissolved in spirit of nitre,
gives a red. These colors disappear at longer or
shorter intervals after the material written upon
cools, but again become apparent upon the re-appli-
cation of heat.

"I now scrutinized the death's-head with care. Its
outer edges—the edges of the drawing nearest the
edge of the vellum—were far more *distinct* than the
others. It was clear that the action of the caloric
had been imperfect or unequal. I immediately
kindled a fire, and subjected every portion of the
parchment to a glowing heat. At first, the only effect was the strengthening of the faint lines in the
skull; but, upon persevering in the experiment, there
became visible, at the corner of the slip, diagonally
opposite to the spot in which the death's-head was
delineated, the figure of what I at first supposed to
be a goat. A closer scrutiny, however, satisfied me
that it was intended for a kid."

"Ha! ha!" said I, "to be sure I have no right to
laugh at you,—a million and a half of money is too
serious a matter for mirth,—but you are about to
establish a third link in your chain,—you will not
find especial connection between your pirates and a
goat,—pirates, you know, have nothing to do with
goats; they appertain to the farming interest."

"But I have just said that the figure was *not* that
of a goat."

"Well, a kid then,—pretty much the same thing."

"Pretty much, but not altogether," said Legrand.
"You may have heard of one *Captain* Kidd. I at
once looked upon the figure of the animal as a kind
of punning or hieroglyphical signature. I say signa-

ture, because its position upon the vellum suggested this idea. The death's-head at the corner diagonally opposite had, in the same manner, the air of a stamp, or seal. But I was sorely put out by the absence of all else—of the body to my imagined instrument—of the text for my context.''

"I presume you expected to find a letter between the stamp and the signature."

"Something of that kind. The fact is, I felt irresistibly impressed with a presentiment of some vast good fortune impending. I can scarcely say why. Perhaps, after all, it was rather a desire than an actual belief;—but do you know that Jupiter's silly words, about the bug being of solid gold, had a remarkable effect upon my fancy? And then the series of accidents and coincidences,—these were so *very* extraordinary. Do you observe how mere an accident it was that these events should have occurred upon the *sole* day of all the year in which it has been, or may be, sufficiently cool for fire, and that without the fire, or without the intervention of the dog at the precise moment in which he appeared, I should never have become aware of the death's-head, and so never the possessor of the treasure?"

"But proceed,—I am all impatience."

"Well; you have heard, of course, the many stories current—the thousand vague rumors afloat about money buried, somewhere upon the Atlantic coast, by Kidd and his associates. These rumors must have had some foundation in fact. And that the rumors have existed so long and so continuously could have resulted, it appeared to me, only from the circumstance of the buried treasure still *remaining* entombed. Had Kidd concealed his plunder for a time, and afterwards reclaimed it, the rumors would scarcely have reached us in their present unvarying form. You will observe that the stories

told are all about money-seekers, not about money-
finders. Had the pirate recovered his money, there
the affair would have dropped. It seemed to me that
some accident—say the loss of a memorandum indicating its locality—had deprived him of the means
of recovering it, and that this accident had become
known to his followers, who otherwise might never
have heard that treasure had been concealed at all,
and who, busying themselves in vain, because un-
guided, attempts to regain it, had given first birth,
and then universal currency, to the reports which
are now so common. Have you ever heard of any
important treasure being unearthed along the
coast?''

''Never.''

''But that Kidd's accumulations were immense, is
well known. I took it for granted, therefore, that
the earth still held them; and you will scarcely be
surprised when I tell you that I felt a hope, nearly
amounting to certainty, that the parchment so
strangely found involved a lost record of the place
of deposit.''

''But how did you proceed?''

''I held the vellum again to the fire, after increasing the heat; but nothing appeared. I now thought
it possible that the coating of dirt might have something to do with the failure; so I carefully rinsed the
parchment by pouring warm water over it, and, having done this, I placed it in a tin pan, with the skull
downwards, and put the pan upon a furnace of
lighted charcoal. In a few minutes, the pan having
become thoroughly heated, I removed the slip, and,
to my inexpressible joy, found it spotted, in several
places, with what appeared to be figures arranged in
lines. Again I placed it in the pan, and suffered it
to remain another minute. Upon taking it off, the
whole was just as you see it now.''

Here Legrand, having re-heated the parchment, submitted it to my inspection. The following characters were rudely traced, in a red tint, between the death's-head and the goat:

53‡‡†305))6*;4826)4‡.)4‡);806*;48†8¶60))85;1‡(;
:‡*8†83(88)5*†;46(;88*96*?;8)*‡(;485);5*†2:*‡(;49
56*2(5*—4)8¶8*;4069285);)6†8)4‡‡;1(‡9;48081;8:8
‡1;48†85;4)485†528806*81(‡9;48;8)8;4(‡?34;48)4‡;
161;:188;‡?;

"But," said I, returning him the slip, "I am as much in the dark as ever. Were all the jewels of Golconda awaiting me upon my solution of this enigma, I am quite sure that I should be unable to earn them."

"And yet," said Legrand, "the solution is by no means so difficult as you might be led to imagine from the first hasty inspection of the characters. These characters, as any one might ready guess, form a cipher—that is to say, they convey a meaning; but then, from what is known of Kidd, I could not suppose him capable of constructing any of the more abstruse cryptographs. I made up my mind, at once, that this was of a simple species—such, however, as would appear, to the crude intellect of the sailor, absolutely insoluble without the key."

"And you really solved it?"

"Readily; I have solved others of an abstruseness ten thousand times greater. Circumstances, and a certain bias of mind, have led me to take interest in such riddles, and it may well be doubted whether human ingenuity can construct an enigma of the kind which human ingenuity may not, by proper application, resolve. In fact, having once established connected and legible characters, I scarcely gave a thought to the mere difficulty of developing their import.

"In the present case,—indeed in all cases of secret writing,—the first question regards the *language* of the cipher; for the principles of solution, so far, especially, as the more simple ciphers are concerned, depend upon, and are varied by, the genius of the particular idiom. In general, there is no alternative but experiment (directed by probabilities) of every tongue known to him who attempts the solution, until the true one be attained. But, with the cipher now before us, all difficulty was removed by the signature. The pun upon the word 'Kidd' is appreciable in no other language than the English. But for this consideration I should have begun my attempts with the Spanish and French, as the tongues in which a secret of this kind would most naturally have been written by a pirate of the Spanish main. As it was, I assumed the cryptograph to be English.

"You observe there are no divisions between the words. Had there been divisions, the task would have been comparatively easy. In such case I should have commenced with a collation and analysis of the shorter words, and, had a word of a single letter occurred, as is most likely (*a* or *I*, for example), I should have considered the solution as assured. But, there being no division, my first step was to ascertain the predominant letters, as well as the least frequent. Counting all, I constructed a table, thus:

Of the character 8 there are 33.

;	"	26.
4	"	19.
‡)	"	16.
*	"	13.
5	"	12.
6	"	11.
† 1	"	8.
0	"	6.

9 2 there are 5.
: 3   "   4.
¶   "   3.
¶   "   2.
—.   "   1.

"Now, in English, the letter which most frequently occurs is *e*. Afterwards, the succession runs thus: *a o i d h n r s t u y c f g l m w b k p q x z*. *E* predominates so remarkably, that an individual sentence of any length is rarely seen in which it is not the prevailing character.

"Here, then, we have, in the very beginning, the groundwork for something more than a mere guess. The general use which may be made of the table is obvious; but, in this particular cipher, we shall only very partially require its aid. As our predominant character is 8, we will commence by assuming it as the *e* of the natural alphabet. To verify the supposition, let us observe if the 8 be seen often in couples,—for *e* is doubled with great frequency in English,—in such words, for example, as 'meet,' 'fleet,' 'speed,' 'seen,' 'been,' 'agree,' etc. In the present instance we see it doubled no less than five times, although the cryptograph is brief.

"Let us assume 8, then, as *e*. Now, of all *words* in the language, 'the' is most usual; let us see, therefore, whether there are not repetitions of any three characters, in the same order of collocation, the last of them being 8. If we discover repetitions of such letters, so arranged, they will most probably represent the word 'the.' Upon inspection, we find no less than seven such arrangements, the characters being ;48. We may, therefore, assume that ; represents *t*, 4 represents *h*, and 8 represents *e*,—the last being now well confirmed. Thus a great step has been taken.

"But, having established a single word, we are enabled to establish a vastly important point; that is to say, several commencements and terminations of other words. Let us refer, for example, to the last instance but one, in which the combination ;48 occurs,—not far from the end of the cipher. We know that the ; immediately ensuing is the commencement of a word, and, of the six characters suceeding this 'the,' we are cognizant of no less than five. Let us set these characters down, thus, by the letters we know them to represent, leaving a space for the unknown—

t eeth.

"Here we are enabled, at once, to discard the *th*, as forming no portion of the word commencing with the first *t;* since, by experiment of the entire alphabet for a letter adapted to the vacancy, we perceive that no word can be formed of which this *th* can be a part. We are thus narrowed into

t ee,

and, going through the alphabet, if necessary, as before, we arrive at the word 'tree,' as the sole possible reading. We thus gain another letter, *r,* represented by (, with the words 'the tree' in juxtaposition.

"Looking beyond these words, for a short distance, we again see the combination ;48, and employ it by way of *termination* to what immediately precedes. We have thus this arrangement:

the tree ;4(‡?34 the,

or, substituting the natural letters, where known, it reads thus:

the tree thr‡?3h the.

"Now, if, in place of the unknown characters, we leave blank spaces, or substitute dots, we read thus:

the tree thr...h the,

when the word 'through' makes itself evident at once. But this discovery gives us three new letters, *o, u,* and *g,* represented by ‡, ?, and 3.

"Looking, now, narrowly, through the cipher for combinations of known characters, we find, not very far from the beginning, this arrangement,

83(88, or egree,

which, plainly, is the conclusion of the word 'degree,' and gives us another letter *d*, represented by †.

"Four letters beyond the word 'degree,' we perceive the combination

;46(;88*.

"Translating the known characters, and representing the unknown by dots, as before, we read thus:

th.rtee.,

an arrangement immediately suggestive of the word 'thirteen,' and again furnishing us with two new characters, *i* and *n*, represented by 6 and *.

"Referring, now, to the beginning of the cryptograph, we find the combination,

53‡‡†.

"Translating, as before, we obtain

.good,

which assures us that the first letter is *A,* and that the first two words are 'A good.'

"It is now time that we arrange our key, as far as discovered, in a tabular form, to avoid confusion. It will stand thus:

5	represents	a
†	"	d
8	"	e
3	"	g
4	"	h
6	"	i
*	"	n
‡	"	o
(	"	r
;	"	t
?	"	u

"We have, therefore, no less than eleven of the most important letters represented, and it will be unnecessary to proceed with the details of the solution. I have said enough to convince you that ciphers of this nature are readily soluble, and to give you some insight into the *rationale* of their development. But be assured that the specimen before us appertains to the very simplest species of cryptograph. It now only remains to give you the full translation of the characters upon the parchment, as unriddled. Here it is:

" '*A good glass in the bishop's hostel in the devil's seat forty-one degrees and thirteen minutes northeast and by north main branch seventh limb east side shoot from the left eye of the death's-head a bee-line from the tree through the shot fifty feet out.*' "

"But," said I, "the enigma seems still in as bad a condition as ever. How is it possible to extort a meaning from all this jargon about 'devil's seat,' 'death's-heads,' and 'bishop's hotels'?"

"I confess," replied Legrand, "that the matter still wears a serious aspect, when regarded with a casual glance. My first endeavor was to divide the sentence into the natural division intended by the cryptographist."

"You mean, to punctuate it?"

"Something of that kind."

"But how was it possible to effect this?"

"I reflected that it had been a *point* with the writer to run his words together without division, so as to increase the difficulty of solution. Now, a not over-acute man, in pursuing such an object, would be nearly certain to overdo the matter. When, in the course of his composition, he arrived at a break in his subject which would naturally require a pause, or a point, he would be exceedingly apt to run his characters, at this place, more than usually close together. If you will observe the manuscript in the present instance, you will easily detect five such cases of unusual crowding. Acting upon this hint, I made the division thus:

"'*A good glass in the bishop's hostel in the devil's seat—forty-one degrees and thirteen minutes—northeast and by north—main branch seventh limb east side—shoot from the left eye of the death's-head—a bee-line from the tree through the shot fifty feet out.'*"

"Even this division," said I, "leaves me still in the dark."

"It left me also in the dark," replied Legrand, "for a few days; during which I made diligent inquiry, in the neighborhood of Sullivan's Island, for any building which went by the name of the 'Bishop's Hotel'; for, of course, I dropped the obsolete word 'hostel.' Gaining no information on the subject, I was on the point of extending my sphere of search, and proceeding in a more systematic manner, when, one morning, it entered into my head, quite suddenly, that this 'Bishop's Hostel' might have some reference to an old family, of the name of Bessop, which, time out of mind, had held possession of an ancient manor-house, about four miles to the northward of the island. I accordingly went over to the plantation, and reinstituted my inquiries among the older negroes of the place. At length one of the most aged of the women said that she had heard of such a place as *Bessop's Castle,* and thought that she could guide me to it, but that it was not a castle, nor a tavern, but a high rock.

"I offered to pay her well for her trouble, and, after some demur, she consented to accompany me to the spot. We found it without much difficulty, when, dismissing her, I proceeded to examine the place. The 'castle' consisted of an irregular assemblage of cliffs and rocks,—one of the latter being quite remarkable for its height as well as for its insulated and artificial appearance. I clambered to its apex, and then felt much at a loss as to what should be next done.

"While I was busied in reflection, my eyes fell upon a narrow ledge in the eastern face of the rock, perhaps a yard below the summit upon which I stood. This ledge projected about eighteen inches, and was not more than a foot wide, while a niche in the cliff just above it gave it a rude resemblance to one of the hollow-backed chairs used by our ancestors. I made no doubt that here was the 'devil's seat' alluded to in the manuscript, and now I seemed to grasp the whole secret.

"The 'good glass,' I knew, could have reference to nothing but a telescope; for the word 'glass' is rarely employed in any other sense by seamen. Now here, I at once saw, was a telescope to be used, and a definite point of view, *admitting no variation*, from which to use it. Nor did I hesitate to believe that the phrases. 'forty-one degrees and thirteen minutes,' and 'northeast and by north,' were intended as directions for the levelling of the glass. Greatly excited by these discoveries, I hurried home, procured a telescope, and returned to the rock.

"I let myself down to the ledge, and found that it was impossible to retain a seat upon it except in one particular position. This fact confirmed my preconceived idea. I proceeded to use the glass. Of course, the 'forty-one degrees and thirteen minutes' could allude to nothing but elevation above the visible horizon, since the horizontal direction was clearly indicated by the words, 'northeast and by north.' This latter direction I at once established by means of a pocket-compass; then, pointing the glass as

nearly at an angle of forty-one degrees of elevation
as I could do it by guess, I moved it cautiously up or
down, until my attention was arrested by a circular
rift or opening in the foliage of a large tree that
overtopped its fellows in the distance. In the centre of this rift I perceived a white spot, but could
not, at first, distinguish what it was. Adjusting the
focus of the telescope, I again looked, and now made
it out to be a human skull.

"Upon this discovery I was so sanguine as to consider the enigma solved; for the phrase, 'main
branch, seventh limb, east side,' could refer only to
the position of the skull upon the tree, while 'shoot
from the left eye of the death's-head,' admitted,
also, of but one interpretation, in regard to a search
for buried treasure. I perceived that the design was
to drop a bullet from the left eye of the skull, and
that a bee-line, or, in other words, a straight line,
drawn from the nearest point of the trunk through
'the shot' (or the spot where the bullet fell), and
thence extended to a distince of fifty feet, would indicate a definite point,—and beneath this point I
thought it at least *possible* that a deposit of value lay
concealed."

"All this," I said, "is exceedingly clear, and, although ingenious, still simple and explicit. When
you left the 'Bishop's Hotel,' what then?"

"Why, having carefully taken the bearings of the
tree, I turned homewards. The instant that I left
'the devil's seat,' however, the circular rift vanished, nor could I get a glimpse of it afterwards,
turn as I would. What seems to me the chief ingenuity in this whole business is the fact (for repeated experiment has convinced me it *is* a fact)
that the circular opening in question is visible from
no other attainable point of view than that afforded
by the narrow ledge upon the face of the rock.

"In this expedition to the 'Bishop's Hotel' I had been attended by Jupiter, who had, no doubt, observed, for some weeks past, the abstraction of my demeanor, and took especial care not to leave me alone. But, on the next day, getting up very early, I contrived to give him the slip and went into the hills in search of the tree. After much toil I found it. When I came home at night my valet proposed to give me a flogging. With the rest of the adventure I believe you are as well acquainted as myself."

"I suppose," said I, "you missed the spot, in the first attempt at digging, through Jupiter's stupidity in letting the bug fall through the right instead of through the left eye of the skull."

"Precisely. This mistake made a difference of about two inches and a half in 'the shot'—that is to say, in the position of the peg nearest the tree; and had the treasure been *beneath* 'the shot,' the error would have been of little moment; but 'the shot,' together with the nearest point of the tree, were merely two points for the establishment of a line of direction; of course the error, however trivial in the beginning, increased as we proceeded with the line, and by the time we had gone fifty feet threw us quite off the scent. But for my deep-seated impressions that treasure was here somewhere actually buried, we might have had all our labor in vain."

"I presume the fancy of the *skull*—of letting fall a bullet through the skull's eye—was suggested to Kidd by the piratical flag. No doubt he felt a kind of poetical consistency in recovering his money through this ominous insignium."

"Perhaps so; still, I cannot help thinking that common-sense had quite as much to do with the matter as poetical consistency. To be visible from the Devil's seat, it was necessary that the object, if small, should be *white;* and there is nothing like your human skull for retaining and even increasing its whiteness under exposure to all vicissitudes of weather."

"But your grandiloquence, and your conduct in swinging the beetle,—how excessively odd! I was sure you were mad. And why did you insist upon letting fall the bug, instead of a bullet, from the skull?"

"Why, to be frank, I felt somewhat annoyed by your evident suspicions touching my sanity, and so resolved to punish you quietly, in my own way, by a little bit of sober mystification. For this reason I swung the beetle, and for this reason I let it fall from the tree. An observation of yours about its great weight suggested the latter idea."

"Yes, I perceive; and now there is only one point which puzzles me. What are we to make of the skeletons found in the hole?"

"That is a question I am no more able to answer than yourself. There seems, however, only one plausible way of accounting for them,—and yet it is dreadful to believe in such atrocity as my suggestion would imply. It is clear that Kidd,—if Kidd indeed secreted this treasure, which I doubt not,—it is clear that he must have had assistance in the labor. But, this labor concluded, he may have thought it expedient to remove all participants in his secret. Perhaps a couple of blows with a mattock were sufficient, while his coadjutors were busy in the pit; perhaps it required a dozen,—who shall tell?"

his contemplated route. He lay still as the enemy approached—he heard their retreating footsteps, and again he set forward. At length, his eyes beheld the bank of the river, still ahead of his enemy; and grateful, but exhausted, he lay stretched upon the sands, and gazing upon the quiet waters before him.

He was not long suffered to remain in peace. A shot arrested his attention, and he started to his feet to behold two of his pursuers emerging at a little distance from the forest. He plunged forward into the river, and, diving down, reserved his breath until, rising, he lay in the very centre of the stream. But he arose enfeebled and overcome, and turning a look of defiance upon the two Indians who stood watching his progress from the banks which they had now gained, he raised himself breast-high from the water, and challenged their arrows to his breast, by smiting it with a fierce violence. As they saw the action, one of them lifted his bow; but the other the next instant struck it down. Half amazed, Occonestoga gave a single shout of derision, and ceased all further efforts. The brave but desponding warrior sank hopelessly, just as the little skiff of Hugh Grayson, returning from his interview with Chorley, darted over the small circle in the stream which still bubbled and broke where the young Indian had gone down. As the boat passed over the spot where the red-man had been seen to sink, the black hair suddenly grew visible again above the water, and in the next moment was clutched in the grasp of the Carolinian. With difficulty he sustained the head above the surface, still holding on by the hair. The banks were not distant, and the little paddle which he employed was susceptible of use by one hand. Though thus encumbered, he was soon enabled to get within his depth. This done, he jumped from his boat, and bore the unconscious victim to the land. The Indians on the opposite bank did not wait for the result, having disappeared in the forest just at the moment when returning consciousness, on the part of Occonestoga, had rewarded Grayson for the efforts he had made.

"Thou art safe now, Occonestoga," said the young man. "Thou wilt go with me to my cabin?"

"No! The black woods for Occonestoga. He must seek arrows and feathers for Opitchi-Manneyto."

The youth pressed him urgently, but finding him obdurate, he gave up hope of persuading him to his habitation. They separated after the delay of an hour,—Grayson in his canoe and Occonestoga plunging into the woods in the direction of the Block House.

THE DOOM OF THE YOUNG CHIEF.*

From The Yemassee (1835). Revised Edition (1853).

"The pain of death is nothing. To the chief,
The forest warrior, it is good to die—
To die as he has lived, battling and hoarse,
Shouting a song of triumph. But to live
Under such doom as this were far beyond
Even his stoic, cold philosophy."

IT was a gloomy amphitheatre in the deep forests to which the assembled multitude bore the unfortunate Occonestoga. The whole scene was unique in that solemn grandeur, that sombre hue, that deep spiritual repose, in which the human imagination delights to invest the region which has been rendered

---

* "There is a concentration of power conspicuous in this entire chapter which is hardly to be found in the pages of the two American romancers who are in most respects Simms's superiors—Cooper and Brookden Brown."—W. P. Trent in his *Life of Simms.*

remarkable for the deed of punishment or crime.
A small swamp or morass hung upon one side of the
wood, from the rank bosom of which, in numberless
millions, the flickering fire-fly perpetually darted
upwards, giving a brilliance and animation to the
spot, which, at that moment, no assemblage of life
or light could possibly enliven. The ancient oak,
a bearded Druid, was there to contribute to the due
solemnity of all occasions—the green but gloomy
cedar, the ghostly cypress, and here and there the
overgrown pine,—all rose up in their primitive
strength, and with an undergrowth around them of
shrub and flower, that scarcely, at any time, in that
sheltered and congenial habitation, had found it necessary to shrink from winter. In the centre of the
area thus invested, rose a high and venerable mound,
the tumult of many preceding ages, from the
washed sides of which might now and then be seen
protruding the bleached bones of some ancient warrior or sage. A circle of trees, at a little distance,
hedged it in,—made secure and sacred by the performance there of many of their religious rites and
offices,—themselves, as they bore the broad arrow
of the Yemassee, being free from all danger of over-
throw or desecration by Indian hands.

Amid the confused cries of the multitude, they
bore the captive to the foot of the tumulus, and
bound him backward, half-reclining, upon a tree. An
hundred warriors stood around, armed according to
the manner of the nation, each with a tomahawk and
knife, and bow. They stood up as for battle, but
spectators, simply, and took no part in a proceeding
which belonged entirely to the priesthood. In a
wider and denser circle, gathered hundreds more—
not the warriors, but the people—the old, the young,
the women, and the children, all fiercely excited and
anxious to see a ceremony, so awfully exciting to an

Indian imagination; involving, as it did, not only the
perpetual loss of human caste and national consideration, but the eternal doom, the degradation, the
denial of, and the exile from, their simple forest
heaven. Interspersed with this latter crowd, seemingly at regular intervals, and with an allotted la-
bour assigned them, came a number of old women,
not unmeet representatives, individually, for either
of the weird sisters of the Scottish Thane,

"So withered and so wild in their attire—"

and, regarding their cries and actions, of whom we
may safely affirm, that they looked like anything but
inhabitants of earth! In their hands they bore, each
of them, a flaming torch of the rich and gummy pine;
and these they waved over the heads of the multitude
in a thousand various evolutions, accompanying each
movement with a fearful cry, which, at regular periods, was chorused by the assembled mass. A bu-
gle, a native instrument of sound, five feet or more
in length, hollowed out from the commonest timber—
the cracks and breaks of which were carefully sealed
up with the resinous gum oozing from their burning
torches, and which, to this day, borrowed from the
natives, our Negroes employ on the Southern waters
with a peculiar compass and variety of note—was
carried by one of the party, and gave forth at intervals, timed with much regularity, a long, protracted,
single blast, adding greatly to the wild and picturesque character of the spectacle. At the articula-
tion of these sounds, the circle continued to contract,
though slowly; until, at length, but a brief space lay
between the armed warriors, the crowd, and the unhappy victim.

The night grew dark of a sudden, and the sky was
obscured by one of the brief tempests that usually
usher in the summer, and mark the transition, in the

South, of one season to another. A wild gust rushed
along the wood. The leaves were whirled over the
heads of the assemblage, and the trees bent downwards, until they cracked and groaned again beneath
the wind. A feeling of natural superstition crossed
the minds of the multitude, as the hurricane, though
common enough in that region, passed hurriedly
along; and a spontaneous and universal voice of
chaunted prayer rose from the multitude, in their
own wild and emphatic language, to the evil deity
whose presence they beheld in its progress:

> "Thy wing, Opitchi-Manneyto,
> It o'erthrows the tall trees—
> Thy breath, Opitchi-Manneyto,
> Makes the waters tremble—
> Thou art in the hurricane,
> When the wigwam tumbles—
> Thou art in the arrow-fire,
> When the pine is shiver'd—
> But upon the Yemassee,
> Be thy coming gentle—
> Are they not thy well-beloved?
> Bring they not a slave to thee?
> Look! the slave is bound for thee,
> 'Tis the Yemassee that brings him.
> Pass, Opitchi-Manneyto—
> Pass, black spirit, pass from us—
> Be thy passage gentle."

And, as the uncouth strain rose at the conclusion
into a diapason of unanimous and contending voices,
of old and young, male and female, the brief summer
tempest had gone by. A shout of self-gratulation,
joined with warm acknowledgments, testified the
popular sense and confidence in that especial Providence, which even the most barbarous nations claim
as forever working in their behalf.

At this moment, surrounded by the chiefs, and preceded by the great prophet or high-priest, Enoree-
Mattee, came Sanutee, the well-beloved of the Yemassee, to preside over the destinies of his son.

There was a due and becoming solemnity, but nothing of the peculiar feelings of the father visible in
his countenance. -Blocks of wood were placed around
as seats for the chiefs, but Sanutee and the prophet
threw themselves, with more imposing veneration in
the proceeding, upon the edge of the tumulus, just
where an overcharged spot, bulging out with the
crowding bones of its inmates, had formed an elevation answering the purpose of couch or seat. They
sat, directly looking upon the prisoner, who reclined,
bound securely upon his back to a decapitated tree,
at a little distance before them. A signal having
been given, the women ceased their clamours, and
approaching him, they waved their torches so closely
above his head as to make all his features distinctly
visible to the now watchful and silent multitude. He
bore the examination with stern, unmoved features,
which the sculptor in brass or marble might have
been glad to transfer to his statue in the block.
While the torches waved, one of the women now
cried aloud, in a barbarous chant, above him:

> "Is not this a Yemassee?
> Wherefore is he bound thus—
> Wherefore, with the broad arrow
> On his right arm glowing,
> Wherefore is he bound thus—
> Is not this a Yemassee?"

A second woman now approached him, waving her
torch in like manner, seeming closely to inspect his
features, and actually passing her fingers over the
emblem upon his shoulder, as if to ascertain more
certainly the truth of the image. Having done this,
she turned about to the crowd, and in the same barbarous sort of strain with the preceding, replied as
follows:—

> "It is not the Yemassee,
> But a dog that runs away.
> From his right arm take the arrow,
> He is not the Yemassee."

As these words were uttered, the crowd of women
and children around cried out for the execution of
the judgment thus given, and once again flamed the
torches wildly, and the shoutings were general
among the multitude. When they had subsided, a
huge Indian came forward, and sternly confronted
the prisoner. This man was Malatchie, the executioner; and he looked the horrid trade which he pro-
fessed. His garments were stained and smeared
with blood and covered with scalps, which, connected
together by slight strings, formed a loose robe over
his shoulders. In one hand he carried a torch, in the
other a knife. He came forward, under the instructions of Enoree-Mattee, the prophet, to claim the
slave of Opitchi-Manneyto,—that is, in our language,
the slave of hell. This he did in the following
strain:—

> " 'Tis Opitchi-Manneyto
> In Malatchie's ear that cries,
> This is not the Yemassee—
> And the woman's word is true—
> He's a dog that should be mine,
> I have hunted for him long,
> From his master he had run,
> With the stranger made his home,
> Now I have him, he is mine—
> Now I have him, he is mine—
> Hear Opitchi-Manneyto."

And, as the besmeared and malignant executioner
howled his fierce demand in the very ears of his
victim, he hurled the knife which he carried, upwards
with such dexterity into the air, that it rested, point
downward, and sticking fast on its descent into the
tree and just above the head of the doomed Occonestoga. With his hand, the next instant, he laid a
resolute grip upon the shoulder of the victim, as if
to confirm and strengthen his claim by actual possession; while, at the same time, with a sort of ma-

lignant pleasure, he thrust his besmeared and distorted visage close into the face of his prisoner. Writhing against his ligaments which bound him fast, Occonestoga strove to turn his head aside from the disgusting and obtrusive presence; and the desperation of his effort, but that he had been too carefully secured, might have resulted in the release of some of his limbs; for the breast heaved and laboured, and every muscle of his arms and legs was wrought, by his severe action, into so many ropes, hard, full, and indicative of prodigious strength.

There was one person in that crowd who sympathized with the victim. This was Hiawassee, the maiden in whose ears he had uttered a word, which, in her thoughtless scream and subsequent declaration of the event, when she had identified him, had been the occasion of his captivity. Something of self-reproach for her share in his misfortune, and an old feeling of regard for Occonestoga who had once been a favorite with the young of both sexes among his people, was at work in her bosom; and, turning to Echotee, her newly-accepted lover, as soon as the demand of Malatchie had been heard, she prayed him to resist the demand. In such cases, all that a warrior had to do was simply to join issue upon the claim, and the popular will then determines the question. Echotee could not resist an application so put to him, and by one who had just listened to a prayer of his own, so all important to his own happiness; and being himself a noble youth, one who had been a rival of the captive in his better days, a feeling of generosity combined with the request of Hiawassee, and he boldly leaped forward. Seizing the knife of Malatchie, which stuck in the tree, he drew it forth and threw it upon the ground, thus removing the sign of property which the executioner had put up in behalf of the evil deity.

"Occonestoga is the brave of the Yemassee," exclaimed the young Echotee, while the eyes of the captive looked what his lips could not have said. "Occonestoga is a brave of the Yemassee—he is no dog of Malatchie. Wherefore is the cord upon the limbs of a free warrior? Is not Occonestoga a free warrior of Yemassee? The eyes of Echotee have looked upon a warrior like Occonestoga when he took many scalps. Did not Occonestoga lead the Yemassee against the Savannahs? The eyes of Echotee saw him slay the red-eyed Suwanee, the great chief of the Savannahs. Did not Occonestoga go on the war-path with our young braves against the Edistoes, the brown foxes that came out of the swamp? The eyes of Echotee beheld him. Occonestoga is a brave, and a hunter of Yemassee—he is not the dog of Malatchie. He knows not fear. He hath an arrow with wings, and the panther he runs down in the chase. His tread is the tread of a sly serpent that comes, so that he hears him not, upon the track of the red deer fleeing down the valley. Echotee knows the warrior—Echotee knows the hunter—he knows Occonestoga, but he knows no dog of Opitchi-Manneyto."

"He hath drunk of the poison drink of the pale-faces—his feet are gone from the good path of the Yemassee—he would sell his people to the English for a painted bird. He is the slave of Opitchi-Manneyto," cried Malatchie in reply. Echotee was not satisfied to yield the point so soon, and he responded accordingly.

"It is true. The feet of the young warrior have gone away from the good paths of the Yemassee, but I see not the weakness of the chief, when my eye looks back upon the great deeds of the warrior. I see nothing but the shrinking body of Suwanee under the knee, under the knife of the Yemassee. I

hear nothing but the war-whoop of the Yemassee,
when we broke through the camp of the brown foxes,
and scalped them where they skulked in the swamp.
I see this Yemassee strike the foe and take the scalp,
and I know Occonestoga—Occonestoga, the son of
the well-beloved—the great chief of the Yemassee.''

"It is good—Occonestoga has thanks for Echotee
—Echotee is a brave warrior!'' murmured the captive to his champion, in tones of melancholy acknowledgment. The current of public feeling began to set somewhat in behalf of the victim, and an
occasional whisper to that effect might be heard here
and there among the multitude. Even Malatchie
himself looked for a moment as if he thought it not
improbable that he might be defrauded of his prey;
and, while a free shout from many attested the compliment which all were willing to pay to Echotee for
his magnanimous defense of one who had once been
a rival—and not always successful—in the general
estimation, the excutioner turned to the prophet and
to Sanutee, as if doubtful whether or not to proceed
farther in his claim. But all doubt was soon quieted,
as the stern father rose before the assembly. Every
sound was stilled in expectation of his words on this
so momentous an occasion to himself. They waited
not long. The old man had tasked all the energies
of the patriot, not less than of the stoic, and having
once determined upon the necessity of the sacrifice,
he had no hesitating fears or scruples palsying his
determination. He seemed not to regard the implor-
ing glances of his son, seen and felt by all besides in
the assembly; but, with a voice entirely unaffected
by the circumstances of his position, he spoke forth
the doom of the victim in confirmation with that
originally expressed.

"Echotee has spoken like a brave warrior with a
tongue of truth, and a soul that has birth with the

sun. But he speaks out of his own heart—and does not speak to the heart of the traitor. The Yemassee will all say for Echotee, but who can say for Occonestoga when Sanutee himself is silent? Does the Yemassee speak with a double tongue? Did not the Yemassee promise Occonestoga to Opitchi-Manneyto with the other chiefs? Where are they? They are gone into the swamp, where the sun shines not, and the eyes of Opitchi-Manneyto are upon them. He knows them for his slaves. The arrow is gone from their shoulders, and the Yemassee knows them no longer. Shall the dog escape, who led the way to the English—who brought the poison drink to the chiefs, who made them dogs to the English and slaves to Opitchi-Manneyto? Shall he escape the doom the Yemassee hath put upon them? Sanutee speaks the voice of the Manneyto. Occonestoga is a dog who would sell his father—who would make our women to carry water for the pale faces. He is not the son of Sanutee—Sanutee knows him no more. Look,—Yemassee—the well-beloved has spoken!"

He paused, and turning away, sank down silently upon the little bank on which he had before rested; while Malatchie, without further opposition—for the renunciation of his own son by one so highly esteemed as Sanutee, was conclusive against the youth —advanced to execute the terrible judgment upon his victim.

"Oh, father, chief, Sanutee, the well-beloved,"—was the cry that now, for the first time burst convulsively from the lips of the prisoner—"hear me father—Occonestoga will go on the war-path with thee, and with the Yemassee—against the Edisto, against the Spaniard—hear, Sanutee—he will go with thee against the English." But the old man bent not—yielded not, and the crowd gathered nigher in the intensity of their interest. "Wilt thou have no ear, Sanutee?—it is Occonestoga—it is the son of Matiwan that speaks to thee." Sanutee's head sank as the reference was made to Matiwan, but he showed no other sign of emotion. He moved not—he spoke not—and bitterly and hopelessly the youth exclaimed—"Oh! thou art colder than the stone house of the adder—and deafer than his ears. Father, Sanutee, wherefore wilt thou lose me, even as the tree its leaf, when the storm smites it in summer? Save me, my father." And his head sank in despair as he beheld the unchanging look of stern resolve with which the unbending sire regarded him.

For a moment he was unmanned; until a loud shout of derision from the crowd, as they beheld the show of his weakness, came to the support of his pride. The Indian shrinks from humiliation where he would not shrink from death; and, as the shout reached his ears, he shouted back his defiance, raised his head loftily in air, and with the most perfect composure, commenced singing his song of death, the song of many victories.

"Wherefore sings he his death song?" was the cry from many voices,—"he is not to die!"

"Thou art the slave of Opitchie-Manneyto," cried Malatchie to the captive—"thou shalt sing no lie of thy victories in the ear of Yemassee. The slave of Opitchi-Manneyto has no triumph"—and the words of the song were effectually drowned, if not silenced, in the tremendous clamor which they raised about him. It was then that Malatchie claimed his victim —the doom had been already given, but the ceremony of expatriation and outlawry was yet to follow, and under the direction of the prophet the various castes and classes of the nation prepared to take a final leave of one who could no longer be known among them. First of all came a band of young marriageable women, who, wheeling in a circle three times about him, sang together a wild apostrophe containing a bitter farewell, which nothing in our language could perfectly embody.

"Go,—thou hast no wife in Yemassee—thou hast given no lodge to the daughter of the Yemassee— thou hast slain no meat for thy children. Thou hast no name—the women of Yemassee know thee no more. They know thee no more."

And the final sentence was reverberated from the entire assembly—"They know thee no more—they know thee no more."

Then came a number of the ancient men—the patriarchs of the nation, who surrounded him in circular mazes three several times, singing as they did so a hymn of like import.

"Go—thou sittest not in the council of Yemassee —thou shalt not speak wisdom to the boy that comes. Thou hast no name in Yemassee—the fathers of Yemassee, they know thee no more."

And again the whole assembly cried out, as with one voice—"They know thee no more, they know thee no more."

These were followed by the young warriors, his old associates, who now, in a solemn band, approached him to go through a like performance. His eyes were shut as they came—his blood was chilled in his heart, and the articulated farewell of their wild chant failed seemingly to reach his ear. Nothing but the last sentence he heard—

> "Thou that wast a brother,
> Thou art nothing now—
> The young warriors of Yemassee,
> They know thee no more."

And the crowd cried with them—"they know thee no more."

"Is no hatchet sharp for Occonestoga?"—moaned forth the suffering savage. But his trials were only then begun. Enoree—Mattee now approached him with the words, with which, as the representative of the good Manneyto, he renounced him,—with which he denied him access to the Indian heaven, and left him a slave and an outcast, a miserable wanderer, amid the shadows and the swamps, and liable to all the dooms and terrors which come with the service of Opitchi-Manneyto.

"Thou wast the child of Manneyto"

sung the high priest in a solemn chant, and with a deep-toned voice that thrilled strangely amid the silence of the scene.

"Thou wast the child of Manneyto,
He gave thee arrows and an eye,—
Thou wast the strong son of Manneyto,
He gave thee feathers and a wing—
Thou wast a young brave of Manneyto,
He gave the scalps and a war-song—
But he knows thee no more—he knows thee no more."

And the clustering multitude again gave back the last line in wild chorus. The prophet continued his chant:

"That Opitchi-Manneyto!—
He commands thee for his slave—
And the Yemassee must hear him,
Hear, and give thee for his slave—
They will take from thee the arrow,
The broad arrow of thy people—
Thou shalt see no blessed valley,
Where the plum-groves always bloom—
Thou shalt hear no song of valour,
From the ancient Yemassee—
Father, mother, name and people,
Thou shalt lose with that broad arrow,
Thou art lost to the Manneyto—
He knows thee no more—he knows thee no more."

The despair of hell was in the face of the victim, and he howled forth, in a cry of agony, that, for a moment, silenced the wild chorus of the crowd around, the terrible consciousness in his mind of that privation which the doom entailed upon him. Every feature was convulsed with emotion; and the terrors of Opitchi-Manneyto's dominion seemed al ready in strong exercise upon the muscles of his heart, when Sanutee the father, silently approached him, and with a pause of a few moments, stood gazing upon the son from whom he was to be separated eternally—whom not even the uniting, the restoring hand of death could possibly restore to him. And he —his once noble son—the pride of his heart, the gleam of his hope, the triumphant warrior, who was even to increase his own glory, and transmit the endearing title of well-beloved, which the Yemassee had given him, to a succeeding generation,—he was to be lost forever! These promises were all blasted, and the father was now present to yield him up eternally —to deny him—to forfeit him, in fearful penalty to the nation whose genius he had wronged, and whose rights he had violated. The old man stood for a moment, rather, we may suppose for the recovery of his resolution, than with any desire for the contemplation of the pitiable form before him. The pride of the youth came back to him,—the pride of the strong mind in its desolation,—as his eye caught the inflexible gaze of his unswerving father; and he exclaimed bitterly and loud:—

"Wherefore art thou come—thou hast been my foe, not my father—away—I would not behold thee!" and he closed his eyes after the speech, as if to relieve himself from a disgusting presence.

"Thou hast said well, Occonestoga,—Sanutee is thy foe—he is not thy father. To say this in thy ears has he come. Look on him, Occonestoga,—look up and hear thy doom. The young and the old of the Yemassee—the warrior and the chief,—they have all denied thee—all given thee up to Opitchi-Manneyto! Occonestoga is no name for the Yemassee. The Yemassee gives it to his dog. The prophet of Manneyto has forgotten thee—thou art unknown to those who were thy people. And I, thy father—with this speech, I yield thee to Opitchi-Manneyto! Sanutee is no longer thy father—thy father knows thee no more"—and once more came to the ears of the victim that melancholy chorus of the multitude—"He knows thee no more—he knows thee no more." Sanutee turned quickly away as he had spoken; and, as if he had suffered more than he was willing to show, the old man rapidly hastened to the little mound where he had been previously sitting, his eyes averted from the further spectacle. Occonestoga, goaded to madness by these several incidents, shrieked forth the bitterest execrations, until Enoree-Mattee, preceding Malatchie, again approached. Having given some directions in an undertone to the latter, he retired, leaving the executioner alone with his victim. Malatchie, then, while all was silence in the crowd—a thick silence, in which even respiration seemed to be suspended,—proceeded to his duty; and, lifting the feet of Occonestoga carefully from the ground, he placed a log under them—then—addressing him, as he again bared his knife which he stuck in the tree above his head, he sung—

"I take from thee the earth of Yemassee—
I take from thee the water of Yemassee—
I take from thee the arrow of Yemassee—
Thou art no longer a Yemassee—
The Yemassee knows thee no more."

"The Yemassee knows thee no more," cried the multitude, and their universal shout was deafening upon the ear. Occonestoga said no word now—he could offer no resistance to the unnerving hands of Malatchie,—who now bared the arm more completely of its covering. But his limbs were convulsed with the spasms of that dreadful terror of the future which was racking and raging in every pulse of his heart. He had full faith in the superstitions of his people. His terrors acknowledged the full horrors of their doom. A despairing agony which no language could describe, had possession of his soul. Meanwhile, the silence of all indicated the general anxiety; and Malatchie prepared to seize the knife and perform the operation, when a confused murmur arose from the crowd around; the mass gave way and parted, and, rushing wildly into the area, came Matiwan, his mother—the long black hair streaming —the features, an astonishing likeness to his own, convulsed like his; and her action that of one reckless of all things in the way of the forward progress she was making to the person of her child. She cried aloud as she came—with a voice that rang like a sudden death-bell through the ring—

"Would you keep the mother from her boy, and he to be lost to her forever! Shall she have no parting with the young brave she bore in her bosom? Away, keep me not back—I will look upon, I will love him. He shall have the blessing of Matiwan, though the Yemassee and the Manneyto curse."

The victim heard, and a momentary renovation of mental life, perhaps a renovation of hope, spoke out in the simple exclamation which fell from his lips—

"Oh, Matiwan—oh, mother!"

She rushed towards the spot where she heard his appeal, and thrusting the executioner aside, threw her arms desperately about his neck.

"Touch him not, Matiwan," was the general cry from the crowd. "Touch him not, Matiwan—Manneyto knows him no more."

"But Matiwan knows him—the mother knows her child, though the Manneyto denies him. Oh, boy—oh, boy, boy, boy," and she sobbed like an infant on his neck.

"Thou art come, Matiwan—thou art come, but wherefore?—to curse like the father—to curse like the Manneyto?" mournfully said the captive.

"No, no, no! Not to curse—not to curse. When did mother curse the child she bore? Not to curse, but to bless thee. To bless thee and forgive."

"Tear her away," cried the prophet; "let Opitchi-Manneyto have his slave."

"Tear her away, Malatchie," cried the crowd, now impatient for the execution. Malatchie approached.

"Not yet—not yet," appealed the woman. "Shall not the mother say farewell to the child she will see no more?" and she waved Malatchie back, and in the next instant drew hastily from the drapery of her dress a small hatchet, which she had there carefully concealed.

"What wouldst thou do, Matiwan?" asked Occonestoga, as his eye caught the glare of the weapon.

"Save thee, my boy—save thee for thy mother, Occonestoga—save thee for the happy valley."

"Wouldst thou slay me, mother—wouldst strike the heart of thy son?" he asked with a something of reluctance to receive death from the hands of a parent.

"I strike thee but to save thee, my son:—since they cannot take the totem from thee after the life is gone. Turn away from me thy head—let me not look upon thine eyes as I strike, lest my hands grow weak and tremble. Turn thine eyes away—I will not lose thee."

His eyes closed, and the fatal instrument, lifted above her head, was now visible in the sight of all.

The executioner rushed forward to interpose, but he came too late. The tomahawk was driven deep into the skull, and but a single sentence from his lips preceded the final insensibility of the victim.

"It is good, Matiwan, it is good—thou hast saved me—the death is in my heart." And back he sank as he spoke, while a shriek of mingled joy and horror from the lips of the mother announced the success of her effort to defeat the doom, the most dreadful in the imagination of the Yemassee.

"He is not lost—he is not lost. They may not take the child from his mother. They may not keep him from the valley of Manneyto. He is free—he is free." And she fell back in a deep swoon in the arms of Sanutee, who by this time had approached. She had defrauded Opitchi-Manneyto of his victim, for they may not remove the badge of the nation from any but the living victim.

PARTISANS IN THE CYPRESS SWAMPS.

From The Partisan: A Tale of the Revolution.

"Do not I live for it? I have no life,
But in the hope that life may bring with it
The bitter-sweet of vengeance."

THE gloomy painter would have done much with the scene before them. The wild and mystic imagination would have made it one of supernatural terrors; and fancy, fond of the melancholy twilight, would have endowed the dim shadows, lurking like so many spectres between the bald cypresses, with a ghostly character, and a most unhallowed purpose. Though familiar with such abodes, Singleton, as he

looked upon the strange groupings thrown upon the
sombre groundwork, was impressed with a lively
sense of its imposing felicity. They stood upon an
island in the very centre of the swamp—one of those
little islands, the tribute ooze of numerous minor
watercourses, hardening into solidity at last. These,
beating their feeble tides upon a single point, in
process of time create the barrier which is to usurp
their own possessions. Here, the rank matter of
the swamp, its slime and rubbish, resolving themselves by a natural but rapid decomposition into one
mass, yield the thick luxuriance of soil from which
springs up the overgrown tree, which heaves out a
thousand branches, and seems to have existed as
many years—in whose bulk we behold an emblem of
majesty, and in whose term of life, standing in utter
defiance of the sweeping hurricane, we have an image
of strength which compels our admiration, and sometimes the more elevated acknowledgment of our awe.
Thus, gathering on this insulated bed, a hundred solemn cypresses mingled their gaunt, spectral forms
with the verdant freshness of the water-oak—the
rough simplicity and height of the pine—all inter-
twined and bound together in the common guardianship of the spot, by the bulging body of the grape-
vine, almost rivalling in thickness, and far surpassing in strength, the trees from which it depended—
these formed a natural roof to the island, circum-
scribing its limits even more effectually than did the
narrow creek by which it had been isolated and
through which the tribute waters of this wide estu-
ary found their way after a few miles of contracted
journeying, into the bed and bosom of the Ashley.
  A couple of huge fires, which they had seen in
glimpses while approaching, were in full blaze upon
the island; one, the largest, near its centre; the other
somewhat apart, upon a little isthmus which it thrust

forth into the mouth of the creek. Around the former lay a singular assemblage of persons, single, or in groups, and in every position. There were not more than twenty in all, but so disposed as to seem much more numerous to the casual spectator. Three, in the glare of the fire, sat upon a log at cards, one at either end, and the third, squat upon the ground beside it. A few slept; some were engaged in conversation, while one, more musical than his neighbors broke into a song of some length, in which the current situation of the things around him underwent improvisation. A stout negro prepared the evening meal, and passed between the card-players and the fire to their occasional inconvenience; their sharp but unheeded denunciations being freely bestowed at every repetition of the offense. The dress and accoutrements of this collection were not less novel, and certainly far more outré, than their several positions and employments. Certainly, taste had but little share in their toilet arrangements, since the hair of some of them flew dishevelled in the wind, or lay matted upon their brows, unconscious of a comb. The faces generally of the party were smeared, and some of them absolutely blackened, by the smoke of the pine-wood fires which at night were kept continually burning around them. This had most effectually begrimed their features, and their dresses had not scrupled to partake of the same coloring. These, too, were as various as the persons who wore them. The ragged coat, the round jacket, and sometimes the entire absence of both, in the case of some individual otherwise conspicuous enough, destroyed all chance of uniformity in the troop. There was but one particular in which their garb seemed generally to agree, and that was in the coonskin cap which surmounted the heads of most of them—worn jauntily upon the side of the head with slips that flapped over the ears, and the tail of the animal depending from front or rear, tassel-fashion, according to the taste of the wearer. Considering such an assemblage, so disposed, so habited, in connection with the situation and circumstances in which we find them, and we shall form no very imperfect idea of the moral effect which their appearance must have had upon the newcomers. The boisterous laugh, the angry, sharp retort, the ready song from some sturdy bacchanal, and the silent sleeper undisturbed amid all the uproar, made of themselves a picture to the mind not soon to be forgotten. Then, when we behold the flaming of the torch in the deep dark which it only for a moment dissipates, and which crowds back, as with a solid body, into the spot from which it has been temporarily driven— the light flashing along and reflected back from the sullen waters of the creek,—listening, at the same moment, to the cry of the screech-owl as the intruder scares him from his perch—the plaint of the whippoorwill, in return, as if even the clamor of the obscene bird had in it something of sympathy for the wounded spirit,—these, with the croaking of the frogs in millions, with which the swamp was a dwelling place among a thousand, were all well calculated to awaken the most indifferent regards, and to compel a sense of the solemn-picturesque even in the mind of the habitually frivolous and unthinking.

With the repeated signals which they had heard from their sentries on the appearance of the newcomers, the scattered groups had simultaneously started to their feet, and put themselves in a state of readiness. The signals were familiar, however, and spoke of friends in the approaching persons; so that, after a few moments of buzz and activity, they generally sank back sluggishly to their old occupations,—the card-players to finish their game, and the less speculative, their sleep. Their movement, however, gives us a better opportunity to survey their accoutrements. The long, cumbrous rifle seemed the favorite weapon, and in the hands of the diminutive, sallow, but black-eyed and venturous dweller in the swamps of the lowlands, across whose knee we may here and there see it resting, it may confidently be held as fatal at a hundred yards. A few of them had pistols—the common horse pistol—a weapon of little real utility under any circumstances. But a solitary musket, and that too without the bayonet, was to be seen in the whole collection; and though not one of the party present but had his horse hidden in the swamp around him, yet not one in five of the riders possessed the sabre, that only effective weapon of cavalry. These were yet to be provided, and at the expense of the enemy.

THE SWAMP FOX AND HIS FOLLOWERS.

From The Partisan: A Tale of the Revolution.

"Unfold—unfold—the day is going fast,
And I would know this old time history."

THE clouds were gathering fast—the waters were troubled—and the approaching tumult and disquiet of all things in Carolina, clearly indicated the coming of that strife, so soon to overcast the scene—so long to keep it darkened—so deeply to impurple it with blood. The continentals were approaching rapidly, and the effect was that of magic upon the long prostrated energies of the South. The people were aroused, awakened, stimulated and emboldened. They gathered in little squads throughout the coun-

try. The news was generally abroad that Gates was
to command the expected army—Gates, the conqueror at Saratoga, whose very name, at that time,
was a host. The successes of Sumpter in the up-
country, of Marion on the Peedee, of Pickens with
a troop of mounted riflemen—a new species of force
projected by himself—of Butler, of Horry, James,
and others, were generally whispered about among
the hitherto desponding whigs. These encouraging
prospects were not a little strengthened in the par-
ishes by rumors of small successes nearer at hand.
The swamps were now believed to be full of enemies
to royal power, only wanting imbodiment and arms;
and truly did Tarleton, dilating upon the condition
of things at this period in the colony, give a melancholy summary of those influences which were crowding together, as it was fondly thought by the patriots
for the overwhelming of foreign domination.

"Discontents"—according   to   his   narrative—
"were disseminated—secret   conspiracies   entered
into upon the frontier—hostilities were already begun in many places, and everything seemed to menace a revolution as rapid as that which succeeded
the surrender of Charlestown." The storm grew
more imposing in its terrors when, promising himself confidently a march of triumph through the
country, Gates, in a swelling proclamation, announced his assumption of command over the Southern army. It was a promise sadly disappointed in
the end—yet the effect was instantaneous; and with
the knowledge of his arrival the entire Black River
country was in insurrection. This was the province
of Marion, and to his active persuasion and influence
the outbreak must chiefly be ascribed. But the influence of events upon other sections was not less
immediate, though less overt and important in their
development. The fermenting excitement, which, in

men's minds, usually precedes the action of powerful, because long suppressed, elements of mischief,
had reached its highest point of forbearance. The
immediately impelling power was alone wanting,
and this is always to be found in that restless love
of change, growing with its facilities, which forms
so legitimate a portion of our original nature. There
is a wholesome stir in strife itself, which, like the
thunderstorm in the sluggish atmosphere, imparts a
renewed energy, and a better condition of health and
exercise, to the attributes and agents of the moral
man.

———

These old woods about Dorchester are famous.
There is not a wagon track—not a defile—not a
clearing—not a traverse of these plains, which has
not been consecrated by the strife for liberty; the
close strife—the desperate struggle; the contest, un-
relaxing, unyielding to the last, save only with death
or conquest. These old trees have looked down upon
blood and battles; the thick array and the solitary
combat between single foes, needing no other witnesses. What tales might they not tell us! The
sands have drunk deeply of holy and hallowed blood
—blood that gave them value and a name, and made
for them a place in all human recollection. The grass
here has been beaten down, in successive seasons, by
heavy feet—by conflicting horsemen—by driving
and recoiling artillery. Its deep green has been
dyed with a yet deeper and a darker stain—the out-
pourings of the invader's veins, mingling with the
generous streams flowing from bosoms that had but
one hope—but one purpose—the unpolluted freedom
and security of home; the purity of the threshold,
the sweet repose of the domestic hearth from the in-
trusion of hostile feet—the only objects, for which

men may brave the stormy and the brutal strife, and
still keep the "whiteness of their souls."

The Carolinian well knows the old-time places;
for every acre has its tradition in this neighborhood.
He rides beneath the thick oaks, whose branches
have covered regiments, and looks up to them with
regardful veneration. Well he remembers the old
defile at the entrance just above Dorchester village,
where a red clay hill rises abruptly, breaking pleasantly the dead level of country all around it. The
rugged limbs and trunk of a huge oak, which hung
above its brow, and has been but recently overthrown, was of itself his historian. It was notorious
in tradition as the gallows oak; its limbs being employed by both parties, as they severally obtained
the ascendency, for the purposes of summary execution. Famous, indeed, was all the partisan warfare
in this neighborhood, from the time of its commencement, with out story, in 1780, to the day, when, hopeless of their object, the troops of the invader withdrew to their crowded vessels, flying from the land
they had vainly struggled to subdue. You should
hear the old housewives dilate upon these transac-
tions. You should hear them paint the disasters, the
depression of the Carolinians; how their chief city
was besieged and taken; their little army dispersed
or cut to pieces; and how the invader marched over
the country, and called it his Anon; they would show
you the little gathering in the swamp—the small
scouting squad timidly stealing forth into the plain,
and contenting itself with cutting off a foraging
party or a baggage wagon, or rescuing a disconsolate
group of captives on their way to the city and the
prison-ships. Soon, emboldened by success, the little
squad is increased by numbers, and aims at larger
game. Under some such leader as Colonel Washington, you should see them, anon, well mounted,

streaking along the Ashley River road by the peep
of day, well skilled in the management of their
steeds, whose high necks beautifully arch under the
curb, while, in obedience to their rider's will, they
plunge fearlessly through brake and through brier,
over the fallen tree, and into the suspicious water.
Heedless of all things but the proper achievement
of their bold adventure, the warriors go onward
while the broadswords flash in the sunlight, and the
trumpet cheers them with a tone of victory. And
goodlier still is the sight, when, turning the narrow
lane, thick fringed with the scrubby oak and the
pleasant myrtle, you behold them come suddenly to
the encounter with the hostile invaders. How they
hurrah, and rush to the charge with a mad emotion
that the steed partakes—his ears erect, and his nostrils distended, while his eyeballs start forward and
grow red with the straining effort; then, how the
riders bear down all before them, and, with swords
shooting out from their cheeks, make nothing of the
upraised bayonet and pointed spear, but, striking
in, flank and front, carry confusion wherever they
go—while the hot sands drink in the life-blood of
friend and foe, streaming through a thousand
wounds. Hear them tell of these, and of the "Game
Cock," Sumpter; how, always ready for fight, with
a valour which was frequently rashness, he would
rush into the hostile ranks, and, with his powerful
frame and sweeping sabre, would single out for in-
veterate strife his own particular enemy. Then, of
the subtle "Swamp Fox," Marion, who, slender of
form, and having but little confidence in his own
physical prowess, was never seen to use his sword
in battle, gaining by stratagem and unexpected enterprise those advantages which his usual inferiority
of force would never have permitted him to gain
otherwise. They will tell you of his conduct and

his coolness; of his ability, with small means, to consummate leading objects—the best proof of military talent; and of his wonderful command of his men; how they would do his will, though it led to the most perilous adventure, with as much alacrity as if they were going to a banquet. Of the men themselves, though in rags, almost starving, and exposed to all changes of the weather, how cheerfully, in the fastnesses of the swamp, they would sing their rude song about the capacity of their leader and their devotion to his person, in some such strain as that which follows:

THE SWAMP FOX.

"We follow where the Swamp Fox guides,
    His friends and merry men are we;
And when the troop of Tarleton rides,
    We burrow in the cypress tree.
The turfy tussock is our bed,
    We burrow in the red deer's den,
Our roof, the tree-top overhead,
    For we are wild and hunted men.

"We fly by day, and shun its light;
    But, prompt to strike the sudden blow,
We mount, and start with early night,
    And through the forest track our foe.
And soon he hears our chargers leap,
    The flashing sabre blinds his eyes,
And ere he drives away his sleep,
    And rushes from his camp, he dies.

"Free bridle-bit, good gallant steed,
    That will not ask a kind caress,
To swim the Santee at our need,
    When on his heels the foemen press—
The true heart and the ready hand,
    The spirit, stubborn to be free—
The twisted bore, the smiting brand—
    And we are Marion's men, you see.

"Now light the fire, and cook the meal,
    The last, perhaps, that we shall taste;
I hear the Swamp Fox around us steal,
    And that's a sign we move in haste.

He whistles to the scouts, and hark!
  You hear his order calm and low—
Come, wave your torch across the dark,
  And let us see the boys that go.

"We may not see their forms again,
  God help 'em, should they find the strife;
For they are strong and fearless men,
  And make no coward terms for life;
They'll fight as long as Marion bids,
  And when he speaks the word to shy,
Then—not till then—they turn their steeds
  Through thickening shade and swamp to fly.

"Now stir the fire, and lie at ease,
  The scouts are gone, and on the brush
I see the colonel bend his knees,
  To take his slumbers too—but hush!
He's praying, comrades; 'tis not strange;
  The man that's fighting day by day,
May well, when night comes, take a change,
  And down upon his knees to pray.

"Break up that hoecake, boys, and hand
  The sly and silent jug that's there;
I love not it should idle stand,
  When Marion's men have need of cheer.
'Tis seldom that our luck affords
  A stuff like this we just have quaffed,
'And dry potatoes on our boards
  May always call for such a draught.

"Now pile the brush and roll the log,
  Hard pillow, but a soldier's head,
That's half the time in brake and bog,
  Must never think of softer bed.
The owl is hooting to the night,
  The cooter crawling o'er the bank,
'And in that pond the splashing light,
  Tells where the alligator sank.

"What 'tis the signal! Start so soon,
  And through the Santee swamp so deep,
Without the aid of friendly moon,
  And we, Heaven help us, half asleep!
But courage, Comrades, Marion leads,
  The Swamp Fox takes us out to-night;
So clear your swords and coax your steeds,
  There's goodly chance, I think, of fight.

"We follow where the Swamp Fox guides,
  We leave the swamp and cypress tree,
Our spurs are in our courser's sides,
  And ready for the strife are we—
The tory camp is now in sight,
  And there he cowers within his den—
He hears our shout, he dreads the fight,
  He fears, and flies from Marion's men."

And gallant men they were, taught by his precept and example, their own peculiar deeds grow famous in our story. Each forester became in time an adroit partisan; learning to practise a thousand stratagems, and most generally with a perfect success. Imbedding himself in the covering leaves and branches of the thick-limbed tree, he would lie in wait till the fall of evening; then, dropping suddenly upon the shoulders of the sentry as he paced beneath, would drive the keen knife into his heart before he could yet recover from his panic. Again, he would burrow in the hollow of the miry ditch, and crawling, Indian fashion, into the trench, wait patiently until the soldier came into the moonlight, when the silver drop at his rifle's muzzle fell with fatal accuracy upon his button, or his breastplate, and the sharp, sudden crack which followed almost invariably announced the victim's long sleep of death. And numerous besides were the practices, of which history and tradition alike agree to tell us, adopted in our war of the revolution by the Carolian partisan, to neutralize the superiority of European force and tactics. Often and again have they lain close to the gushing spring, and silent in the bush, like the tiger in his jungle, awaiting until the foragers had squatted around it for the enjoyment of their midday meal; then, rushing forth with a fierce halloo, seize upon the stacked arms, and beat down the surprised but daring soldiers who might rise up to defend them. And this sort of warfare, small though it may appear, was at last triumphant. The successes of the whigs, during the whole period of the revolutionary contest in the South, were almost entirely the result of the rapid, unexpected movement—the sudden stroke made by the little troop, familiar with its ground, knowing its object, and melting away at the approach of a superior enemy, like so many dusky shadows, secure in the thousand swamp recesses which surrounded them. Nor did they rely always upon strategem in the prosecution of their enterprises. There were gleams of chivalry thrown athwart this sombre waste of strife and bloodshed, worthy of the middle ages. Bold and graceful riders, with fine horses, ready in all cases, fierce in onset, and reckless in valour, the Southern cavalry had an early renown. The audacity with which they drove through the forest, through broad rivers, such as the Santee, by day and by night, in the face of the enemy, whether in flight or in assault the same, makes their achievements as worthy of romance as those of a Bayard or Bernado. Thousands of instances are recorded of that individual gallantry—that gallantry, stimulated by courage, warmed by enthusiasm, and refined by courtesy— which gives the only credentials of true chivalry. Such, among the many, was the rescue of the prisoners, by Jasper and Newton; the restoration of the flagstaff to Fort Moultrie, in the hottest fire, by the former; and the manner in which he got his death-wound at Savannah, in carrying off the colours which had been intrusted to him. Such were many of the rash achievements of Sumpter and Laurens, and such was the daring of the brave Conyers, who daily challenged his enemy in the face of the hostile army. These were all partisan warriors, and such were their characteristics.

JOHN PENDLETON KENNEDY.

A MARVELLOUS CAPTURE.

From Horse-Shoe Robinson: A Tale of the Tory Ascendency. Revised Edition (1852).*

DAVID RAMSAY's house was situated on a by-road, between five and six miles from Musgrove's mill, and at about the distance of one mile from the principal route of travel between Ninety-six and Blackstock's. In passing from the military post that had been established at the former place, towards the latter, Ramsay's lay off to the left, with a piece of dense wood intervening. The by-way, leading through the farm, diverged from the main road, and traversed this wood until it reached the cultivated grounds immediately around Ramsay's dwelling. In the journey from Musgrove's mill to this point of divergence, the traveller was obliged to ride some two or three miles upon the great road leading from the British Garrison, a road that, at the time of my story, was much frequented by military parties, scouts, and patroles, that were concerned in keeping up the communication between the several posts which were established by the British authorities along that frontier. Amongst the whig partisans, also, there were various occasions which brought them under the necessity of frequent passage through this same district, and which, therefore, furnished opportunities for collision and skirmish with the opposite forces.

It is a matter of historical notoriety, that immediately after the fall of Charleston, and the rapid subjugation of South Carolina that followed this

J. P. Kennedy

event, there were three bold and skilful soldiers who undertook to carry on the war of resistance to the established authorities, upon a settled and digested plan of annoyance, under the most discouraging state of destitution, as regarded all the means of offence, that, perhaps, history records. It will not detract from the fame of other patriots of similar enthusiasm and of equal bravery, to mention the names of Marion, Sumpter, and Pickens, in connection with this plan of keeping up an apparently hopeless partisan warfare, which had the promise neither of men, money, nor arms,—and yet which was so nobly sustained, amidst accumulated discomfitures, as to lead eventually to the subversion of the "Tory ascendency" and the expulsion of the British power. According to the plan of operations concerted amongst these chieftains, Marion took the lower country under his supervision; Pickens the southwestern districts, bordering upon the Savannah; and to Sumpter was allotted all that tract of country lying between the Broad and Catawba rivers, from the angle of their junction, below Camden, up to the mountain districts of North Carolina. How faithfully these men made good their promise to the country, is not only written in authentic history, but it is also told in many a legend amongst the older inhabitants of the region that was made the theatre of action. It only concerns my story to refer to the fact, that the events which have occupied my last five or six chapters, occurred in that range more peculiarly appropriated to Sumpter, and that the high road from Blackstock's towards Ninety-six was almost as necessary for communication between Sumpter and Pickens, as between the several British garrisons.

On the morning that succeeded the night in which Horse Shoe Robinson arrived at Musgrove's, the stout and honest sergeant might have been seen,

about eight o'clock, leaving the main road from Ninety-six, at the point where that leading to David Ramsay's separated from it, and cautiously urging his
way into the deep forest, by the more private path
into which he had entered. The knowledge that
Innis was encamped along the Ennoree, within a
short distance of the mill, had compelled him to make
an extensive circuit to reach Ramsay's dwelling,
whither he was now bent; and he had experienced
considerable delay in his morning journey, by finding himself frequently in the neighborhood of small
foraging parties of Tories, whose motions he was
obliged to watch for fear of an encounter. He had
once already been compelled to use his horse's heels
in what he called "fair flight"; and once to ensconce
himself, a full half hour, under cover of the thicket
afforded him by a swamp. He now, therefore, according to his own phrase, "dived into the little road
that scrambled down through the woods towards
Ramsay's, with all his eyes about him, looking out
as sharply as a fox on a foggy morning"; and with
this circumspection, he was not long in arriving
within view of Ramsay's house. Like a practised
soldier, whom frequent frays has taught wisdom, he
resolved to reconnoitre before he advanced upon a
post that might be in possession of an enemy. He
therefore dismounted, fastened his horse in a fence
corner, where a field of corn concealed him from notice, and then stealthily crept forward until he came
immediately behind one of the out-houses.

The barking of a house-dog brought out a negro
boy, to whom Robinson instantly addressed the
query—

"Is your master at home?"—

"No, sir. He's got his horse, and gone off more
than an hour ago."

"Where is your mistress?"

"Shelling beans, Sir."

"I didn't ask you," said the sergeant, "what she is doing, but where she is."

"In course, she is in the house, Sir,"—replied the negro with a grin.

"Any strangers there?"

"There was plenty on 'em a little while ago, but they've been gone a good bit."

Robinson having thus satisfied himself as to the safety of his visit, directed the boy to take his horse and lead him up to the door. He then entered the dwelling.

"Mistress Ramsay," said he, walking up to the dame, who was occupied at a table, with a large trencher before her, in which she was plying that household thrift which the negro described; "luck to you, ma'am, and all your house! I hope you haven't none of these clinking and clattering bullies about you, that are as thick over this country as the frogs in the kneading troughs, that they tell of."

"Good lack, Mr. Horse Shoe Robinson," exclaimed the matron, offering the sergeant her hand. "What has brought you here? What news? Who are with you? For patience sake, tell me!"

"I am alone," said Robinson, "and a little wettish, mistress;" he added, as he took off his hat and shook the water from it, "it has just sot up a rain, and looks as if it was going to give us enough on't. You don't mind doing a little dinner-work of a Sunday, I see—shelling of beans, I s'pose, is tantamount to dragging a sheep out of a pond, as the preachers allow on the Sabbath—ha, ha!—Where's Davy?"

"He's gone over to the meeting-house on Ennoree, hoping to hear something of the army at Camden; perhaps you can tell us the news from that quarter?"

"Faith, that's a mistake, Mistress Ramsay. Though I don't doubt that they are hard upon the

scratches, by this time. But, at this present speaking, I command the flying artillery. We have out
one man in the corps, and that's myself; and all the
guns we have got is this piece of ordnance, that
hangs in this old belt by my side (pointing to his
sword)—and that I captured from the enemy at
Blackstock's. I was hoping I mought find John Ramsay at home—I have need of him as a recruit."

"Ah, Mr. Robinson, John has a heavy life of it
over there with Sumpter. The boy is often without
his natural rest, or a meal's victuals; and the general
thinks so much of him, that he can't spare him to
come home. I hav'n't the heart to complain, as long
as John's service is of any use, but it does seem, Mr.
Robinson, like needless tempting of the mercies of
providence. We thought that he might have been
here to-day; yet I am glad he didn't come—for he
would have been certain to get into trouble. Who
should come in this morning, just after my husband
had cleverly got away on his horse, but a young
cock-a-whoop ensign, that belongs to Ninety-six, and
four great Scotchmen with him, all in red coats; they
had been out thieving, I warrant, and were now going home again. And who but they! Here they
were, swaggering all about my house—and calling
for this—and calling for that—as if they owned the
fee-simple of everything on the plantation. And it
made my blood rise, Mr. Horse Shoe, to see them
run out in the yard, and catch up my chickens and
ducks, and kill as many as they could string about
them—and I not daring to say a word: though I did
give them a piece of my mind, too."

"Who is at home with you?" inquired the sergeant eagerly.

"Nobody but my youngest boy, Andrew," answered the dame. "And then, the filthy, toping rioters—" she continued, exalting her voice.

"What arms have you in the house?" asked Robinson, without heeding the dame's rising anger.

"We have a rifle, and a horseman's pistol that belongs to John.—They must call for drink, too, and turn my house, of a Sunday morning, into a tavern."

"They took the route towards Ninety-six, you said, Mistress Ramsay?"

"'Yes,—they went straight forward upon the road. But, look you, Mr. Horse Shoe, you're not thinking of going after them?"

"Isn't there an old field, about a mile from this, on that road?" inquired the sergeant, still intent upon his own thoughts.

"There is," replied the dame; "with the old school-house upon it."

"A lop-sided, rickety log-cabin in the middle of the field. Am I right, good woman?"

"Yes."

"And nobody lives in it? It has no door to it?"

"There ha'n't been anybody in it these seven years."

"I know the place very well," said the sergeant, thoughtfully; "there is woods just on this side of it."

"That's true," replied the dame: "but what is it you are thinking about, Mr. Robinson?"

"How long before this rain began was it that they quitted this house?"

"Not above fifteen minutes.'

"Mistress Ramsay, bring me the rifle and pistol both—and the powder-horn and bullets."

"'As you say, Mr. Horse Shoe," answered the dame, as she turned round to leave the room; "but I am sure I can't suspicion what you mean to do."

In a few moments the woman returned with the weapons, and gave them to the sergeant.

"Where is Andy?" asked Horse Shoe.

The hostess went to the door and called her son, and, almost immediately afterwards, a sturdy boy of about twelve or fourteen years of age entered the apartment, his clothes dripping with rain. He modestly and shyly seated himself on a chair near the door, with his soaked hat flapping down over a face full of freckles, and not less rife with the expression of open, dauntless hardihood of character.

"How would you like a scrimmage, Andy, with them Scotchmen that stole your mother's chickens this morning?" asked Horse Shoe.

"I'm agreed," replied the boy, "if you will tell me what to do."

"You are not going to take that boy out on any of your desperate projects, Mr. Horse Shoe?" said the mother, with the tears starting instantly into her eyes. "You wouldn't take such a child as that into danger?"

"Bless your soul, Mrs. Ramsay, there ar'n't no danger about it! Don't take on so. It's a thing that is either done at a blow, or not done,—and there's an end of it. I want the lad only to bring home the prisoners for me, after I have took them."

"Ah, Mr. Robinson, I have one son already in these wars—God protect him!—and you men don't know how a mother's heart yearns for her children in these times. I cannot give another," she added, as she threw her arms over the shoulders of the youth and drew him to her bosom.

"Oh! it ain't nothing," said Andrew, in a sprightly tone. "It's only snapping a pistol, mother,—pooh! If I'm not afraid, you oughtn't to be."

"I give you my honor, Mistress Ramsay," said Robinson, "that I will bring or send your son safe back in an hour; and that he sha'n't be put in any sort of danger whatsomever: come, that's a good woman!"

"You are not deceiving me, Mr. Robinson?" asked the matron wiping away a tear. "You wouldn't mock the sufferings of a weak woman in such a thing as this?"

"On the honesty of a sodger, ma'am," replied Horse Shoe, "the lad shall be in no danger, as I said before—whatsomedever."

"Then I will say no more," answered the mother. "But Andy, my child, be sure to let Mr. Robinson keep before you."

Horse Shoe now loaded the fire-arms, and having slung the pouch across his body, he put the pistol into the hands of the boy; then shouldering his rifle, he and his young ally left the room. Even on this occasion, serious as it might be deemed, the sergeant did not depart without giving some manifestation of that light-heartedness which no difficulties ever seemed to have the power to conquer. He thrust his head back into the room, after he had crossed the threshold, and said with an encouraging laugh, "Andy and me will teach them, Mistress Ramsay, Pat's point of war—we will *surround* the ragamuffins."

"Now, Andy, my lad," said Horse Shoe, after he had mounted Captain Peter, "you must get up behind me. Turn the lock of your pistol down," he continued, as the boy sprang upon the horse's rump, "and cover it with the flap of your jacket, to keep the rain off. It won't do to hang fire at such a time as this."

The lad did as he was directed, and Horse Shoe, having secured his rifle in the same way, put his horse up to a gallop, and took the road in the direction that had been pursued by the soldiers.

As soon as our adventurers had gained a wood, at the distance of about half a mile, the sergeant re-

laxed his speed, and advanced at a pace a little above
a walk.

"Andy," he said, "we have got rather a ticklish
sort of a job before us, so I must give you your lesson, which you will understand better by knowing
something of my plan. As soon as your mother told
me that these thieving villains had left her house
about fifteen minutes before the rain came on, and
that they had gone along upon this road, I remembered the old field up here, and the little log hut in
the middle of it; and it was natural to suppose that
they had jut got about near that hut, when this rain
came up; and then, it was the most supposable case
in the world, that they would naturally go into it, as
the driest place they could find. So now, you see,
it's my calculation that the whole batch is there at
this very point of time. We will go slowly along,
until we get to the other end of this wood, in sight of
the old field, and then, if there is no one on the look-
out, we will open our first trench; you know what
that means, Andy?"

"It means, I s'pose, that we'll go right smack at
them," replied Andrew.

"Pretty exactly," said the sergeant. "But listen
to me. Just at the edge of the woods you will have
to get down, and put yourself behind a tree. I'll
ride forward, as if I had a whole troop at my heels,
and if I catch them, as I expect, they will have a
little fire kindled, and, as likely as not, they'll be
cooking some of your mother's fowls."

"Yes, I understand," said the boy eagerly—

"No, you don't," replied Horse Shoe, "but you
will when you hear what I am going to say. If I
get at them onawares, they'll be mighty apt to think
they are surrounded, and will bellow, like fine fellows, for quarter. And, thereupon, Andy, I'll cry
out, 'stand fast,' as if I was speaking to my own men,

and when you hear that, you must come up full tilt, because it will be a signal to you that the enemy has surrendered. Then it will be your business to run into the house and bring out the muskets, as quick as a rat runs through a kitchen: and when you have done that, why, all's done. But if you should hear any popping of fire-arms—that is, more than one shot, which I may chance to let off—do you take that for a bad sign, and get away as fast as you can heel it. You comprehend."

"Oh! yes," replied the lad, "and I'll do what you want, and more too, may be, Mr. Robinson."

"*Captain* Robinson,—remember, Andy, you must call me captain, in hearing of these Scotsmen."

"I'll not forget that neither," answered Andrew.

By the time that these instructions were fully impressed upon the boy, our adventurous forlorn hope, as it may fitly be called, had arrived at the place which Horse Shoe Robinson had designated for the commencement of active operations. They had a clear view of the old field, and it afforded them a strong assurance that the enemy was exactly where they wished him to be, when they discovered smoke arising from the chimney of the hovel. Andrew was soon posted behind a tree, and Robinson only tarried a moment to make the boy repeat the signals agreed on, in order to ascertain that he had them correctly in his memory. Being satisfied from this experiment that the intelligence of his young companion might be depended upon, he galloped across the intervening space, and, in a few seconds, abruptly reined up his steed, in the very doorway of the hut. The party within was gathered around a fire at the further end, and, in the corner near the door, were four muskets thrown together against the wall. To spring from his saddle and thrust himself one pace inside of the door, was a movement which the sergeant executed in an instant, shouting at the same time—

"Halt! File off right and left to both sides of the house, and wait orders. I demand the surrender of all here," he said, as he planted himself between the party and their weapons. "I will shoot down the first man who budges a foot."

"Leap to your arms," cried the young officer who commanded the little party inside of the house. "Why do you stand?"

"I don't want to do you or your men any harm, young man," said Robinson, as he brought his rifle to a level, "but, by my father's son, I will not leave one of you to be put upon a muster-roll if you raise a hand at this moment."

Both parties now stood, for a brief space, eyeing each other in a fearful suspense, during which there was an expression of doubt and irresolution visible on the countenances of the soldiers, as they surveyed the broad porportions, and met the stern glance of the sergeant, whilst the delay, also, began to raise an apprehension in the mind of Robinson that his stratagem would be discovered.

"Shall I let loose upon them, captain?" said Andrew Ramsay, now appearing, most unexpectedly to Robinson, at the door of the hut. "Come on, boys!" he shouted, as he turned his face towards the field.

"Keep them outside of the door—stand fast," cried the doughty sergeant, with admirable promptitude, in the new and sudden posture of his affairs caused by this opportune appearance of the boy. "Sir, you see that it's not worth while fighting five to one; and I should be sorry to be the death of any of your brave fellows; so, take my advice, and surrender to the Continental Congress and this scrap of its army which I command."

During this appeal the sergeant was ably seconded

by the lad outside, who was calling out first on one name, and then on another, as if in the presence of a troop. The device succeeded, and the officer, within, believing the forbearance of Robinson to be real, at length said:—

"Lower your rifle, sir. In the presence of a superior force, taken by surprise and without arms, it is my duty to save bloodshed. With the promise of fair usage, and the rights of prisoners of war, I surrender this little foraging party under my command."

"I'll make the terms agreeable," replied the sergeant. "Never doubt me, sir. Right hand file, advance, and receive the arms of the prisoners!"

"I'm here, captain," said Andrew, in a conceited tone, as if it were a mere occasion of merriment; and the lad quickly entered the house and secured the weapons, retreating with them some paces from the door.

"Now, sir," said Horse Shoe to the Ensign, "your sword, and whatever else you mought have about you of the ammunitions of war!"

The officer delivered up his sword and a pair of pocket pistols.

As Horse Shoe received these tokens of victory he asked, with a lambent smile, and what he intended to be an elegant and condescending composure, "Your name, sir, if I mought take the freedom?"

"Ensign St. Jermyn, of his Majesty's seventy-first regiment of light infantry."

"Ensign, your sarvent," added Horse Shoe, still preserving his unusual exhibition of politeness. "You have defended your post like an old sodger, although you ha'n't much beard on your chin; but, seeing you have given up, you shall be treated like a man who has done his duty. You will walk out, now, and form yourselves in line at the door. I'll engage my men shall do you no harm; they are of a marciful breed.''

When the little squad of prisoners submitted to his command, and came to the door, they were stricken with equal astonishment and mortification to find, in place of the detachment of cavalry which they expected to see, nothing but a man, a boy, and a horse. Their first emotions were expressed in curses, which were even succeeded by laughter from one or two of the number. There seemed to be a disposition on the part of some to resist the authority that now controlled them; and sundry glances were exchanged, which indicated a purpose to turn upon their captors. The sergeant no sooner perceived this, than he halted, raised his rifle to his breast, and, at the same instant, gave Andrew Ramsay an order to retire a few paces, and to fire one of the captured pieces at the first man who opened his lips.

"By my hand," he said, "if I find any trouble in taking you all five, safe away from this here house, I will thin your numbers with your own muskets! And that's as good as if I had sworn to it.''

"You have my word, sir," said the Ensign. "Lead on.''

"By your leave, my pretty gentleman, you will lead, and I'll follow," replied Horse Shoe. "It may be a new piece of drill to you; but custom is to give the prisoners the post of honor.''

"As you please, sir," answered the Ensign. "Where do you take us to?''

"You will march back by the road you came," said the sergeant.

Finding the conqueror determined to execute summary martial law upon the first who should mutiny, the prisoners submitted, and marched in double file from the hut back towards Ramsay's—Horse Shoe, with Captain Peter's bridle dangling over his arm,

and his gallant young auxiliary Andrew, laden with
double the burden of Robinson Crusoe (having all
the fire-arms packed upon his shoulders), bringing
up the rear. In this order victors and vanquished
returned to David Ramsay's.

"Well, I have brought you your ducks and chickens back, mistress," said the sergeant, as he halted
the prisoners at the door; "and, what's more, I have
brought home a young sodger that's worth his weight
in gold."

"Heaven bless my child! my brave boy!" cried the
mother, seizing the lad in her arms, and unheeding
anything else in the present perturbation of her feelings. "I feared ill would come of it; but Heaven
has preserved him. Did he behave handsomely, Mr.
Robinson? But I am sure he did."

"A little more venturesome, ma'am, than I wanted
him to be," replied Horse Shoe; "but he did excellent service. These are his prisoners, Mistress Ramsay; I should never have got them if it hadn't been
for Andy. In these drumming and fifing times the
babies suck in quarrel with their mother's milk.
Show me another boy in America that's made more
prisoners than there was men to fight them with,
that's all!"

A RETREAT AFTER THE MANNER OF XENOPHON.

*From Horse-Shoe Robinson: A Tale of the Tory Ascendency. Re-
vised Edition (1852).*

THE next morning, a little after sunrise, as Robinson was holding the watch on the outer ledge of the
rock, in a position that enabled him to survey the ap-

proaches to the spot through the valley, as well as
to keep his eye upon the ensign and Christopher
Shaw, who were both asleep under cover of the crag,
he was startled by a distant noise of something
breaking through the bushes on the margin of the
brook. At first it struck him that this was caused by
deer stalking up the stream; but he soon afterwards
descried the head and shoulders of a man, whose
motions showed him to be struggling through the
thicket towards the base of the hill. This person
at length reached a space of open ground, where he
halted and looked anxiously around him, thus revealing his figure, as he sat on horseback, to the observation of the sergeant, who, in the meantime, had
taken advantage of a low pine tree and a jutting angle of a rock to screen himself from the eager eye of
the traveller—at least until he should be satisfied as
to the other's character and purpose.

A loud and cheerful halloo, several times repeated
by the stranger, seemed to indicate his quest of a
lost companion; and this gradually drew the sergeant, with a weary motion, from his hiding-place,
until assuring himself that the comer was alone, he
stept out to the edge of the shelf of the rock, and
presenting his musket, peremptorily gave the common challenge of "Who goes there?"

"A friend to Horse Shoe Robinson," was the reply of the visitor, in whom my reader recognizes
John Ramsay.

Before further question might be asked and answered, John had dismounted from his horse and
clambered to the platform, where he greeted the sergeant and the hastily-awakened Christopher Shaw,
with a hearty shake of the hand; and then proceeded
to communicate the pressing objects of his visit, and

to relate all that he had learned of the recent events during his short stay at his father's house.

In the consultation that followed these disclosures, Ramsay earnestly urged his comrades to make instant preparation to quit their present retirement, and to attempt the enterprise of conducting the prisoner to Williams, who was supposed to be advancing into the neighborhood of a well known block-house, or frontier fortification, on the Saluda, about forty miles from their present position.

The message with which Ramsay was charged from Sumpter to Williams, made it necessary that he should endeavor to reach that officer as soon as possible; and the sergeant, rejoicing in the thought of being so near a strong body of allies who might render the most essential aid to the great object of his expedition, readily concurred in the propriety of the young trooper's proposal. This enterprise was also recommended by the necessity of taking some immediate steps to preserve the custody of the ensign, whose capture had already been so serviceable to the cause of Arthur Butler. In accordance, moreover, with John Ramsay's anxious entreaty, Christopher Shaw, it was determined, should hasten back to the mill at the earliest moment.

A speedy departure was, therefore, resolved on, and accordingly all things were made ready, in the course of an hour, to commence the march. At the appointed time the ensign was directed to descend into the valley, where he was once more bound to his horse. The conferences between the sergeant and his two comrades had been held out of the hearing of the prisoner; but it was now thought advisable to make him acquainted with the late proceedings that had transpired with regard to Butler, and especially with the respite that had been given to that officer by Innis. This communication was accompanied by an intimation that he would best consult his own comfort and safety by a patient submission to the restrictions that were put upon him, inasmuch as his captors had no disposition to vex him with any other precautions than were necessary for his safe detention during the present season of peril to Butler.

With this admonition the party began their journey. The first two or three hours were occupied in returning, by the route of the valley, to the Ennoree. When they reached the river they found themselves relieved from the toils of the narrow and rugged path by which they had threaded the wild mountain dell, and introduced into an undulating country covered with forest, and intersected by an occasional but unfrequented road leading from one settlement to another. Here Christopher Shaw was to take leave of his companions, his path lying along the bank of the Ennoree, whilst the route to be pursued by the others crossed the river and extended thence southwards to the Saluda. The young miller turned his horse's head homewards, with some reluctance at parting with his friend in a moment of such interest, and bore with him many messages of comfort and courage to those whom he was about to rejoin—and more particularly from the sergeant to Butler, in case Christopher should have the good fortune to be able to deliver them. At the same time, Horse Shoe and John Ramsay, with the prisoner, forded the Ennoree, and plunged into the deep forest that lay upon its further bank.

For several hours they travelled with the greatest circumspection, avoiding the frequented roads and the chance of meeting such wayfarers as might be abroad on their route. It was a time of great anxiety and suspense, but the habitual indifference of military life gave an air of unconcern to the conduct

of the soldiers, and scarcely affected, in any visible
degree, the cheerfulness of their demeanor.

They reached, at length, the confines of a cultivated country—a region which was known to be inhabited by several Tory families. To avoid the risk
of exposure to persons who might be unfriendly to
their purpose, they thought it prudent to delay entering upon this open district until after sunset, that
they might continue their journey through the night.
The difficulty of ascertaining their road in the dark,
and the danger of seeking information from the few
families whose habitations occurred to their view,
necessarily rendered their progress slow. The time
was, therefore, passed in weary silence and persevering labor, in the anxious contemplation of the
probability of encountering some of the enemy's
scouts.

At the break of day they stopped to refresh themselves; and the contents of Horse Shoe's wallet, un-
happily reduced to a slender supply of provisions,
were distributed amongst the party. During this
halt, John Ramsay commanded the ensign to exchange his dress with him; and our faithful ally was
converted, by this traffic, for the nonce, into a spruce,
well-looking, and gay young officer of the enemy's
line.

The most hazardous portion of their journey now
lay before them. They were within a few miles of
the Saluda, from whence at its nearest point, it was
some six or seven more down the stream to the Block-
house—the appointed rendezvous, where it was yet
a matter of uncertainty whether Williams had arrived. The space between the travellers and the
river was a fertile and comparatively thickly-peo-
pled region, of which the inhabitants were almost entirely in the Tory interest. The broad day-light having overtaken them on the confines of this tract, ex-

posed them to the greatest risk of being questioned.
They had nothing left but to make a bold effort to
attain the river by the shortest path; and thence to
pursue the bank towards the rendezvous.

"Courage, John," said Horse Shoe, smiling at the
new garb of his comrade; "you may show your pretty feathers to-day to them that are fond of looking
at them. And you, my young clodpole, ride like an
honest Whig, or I mought find occasion to do a dis-
comfortable thing, by putting a bullet through and
and through you. Excuse the liberty, sir, for these
are ticklish times; but I shall ondoubtedly be as
good as my word."

Our adventurers soon resumed their journey.
They had come within a mile of the Saluda without
interruption, and began to exchange congratulations
that the worst was passed, when they found themselves descending a sharp hill which jutted down
upon an extensive piece of pasture ground. One
boundary of this was watered by a brook, along
whose margin a fringe of willows, intermixed with
wild shrubbery of various kinds, formed a screen
some ten or fifteen feet in height. As soon as this
range of meadow was observed, our cautious soldiers
halted upon the brow of the hill to reconnoitre; and
perceiving nothing to excite their apprehension, they
ventured down upon the track of an ill-defined road,
which took a direction immediately over the broadest
portion of the field.

They had scarcely crossed the brook at the bottom
of the hill, before they heard the remote voices of
men in conversation, and the tones of a careless
laugh. On looking towards the upper section of the
stream, they were aware of a squad of loyalist cavalry, who came riding, in the shade of the willows,
directly towards the spot where the travellers had
entered upon the meadow. The party consisted of

seven or eight men, who, were, at this instant, not more than one hundred paces distant.

"They are upon us, sergeant!" exclaimed John Ramsay. "Make sure of the prisoner: retreat as rapidly as you can. Leave me to myself. Make for the Block-house—I will meet you there."

With these hasty intimations, he pricked his courser up to full speed, and shaped his flight directly across the open field, in full view of the enemy.

Horse Shoe, at the same moment, drew a pistol, cocked it, and throwing the rein of St. Jermyn's horse into the hands of the rider, he cried out:—

"Back across the branch and into the woods! Push for it, or you are a dead man! On, on!" he added, as he rode at high speed immediately beside the ensign; " a stumble, or a whisper above your breath, and you get the bullet. Fly—your life is in your horse's heels!"

The resolute tone of the sergeant had its effect upon his prisoner, who yielded a ready obedience to the pressing orders, and bounded into the thicket with as much alacrity as if flying from an enemy.

Meanwhile, the troopers, struck with the earnest haste of one whose dress bespoke a British officer, speeding across the field, did not doubt that they had afforded this timely opportunity for the escape of a prisoner from the hands of the Whigs.

"Wheel up, lads," shouted the leader of the squad, "it is the ensign! Wheel up and form a platoon to cut off the pursuit. We have him safe out of their clutches!"

Impressed with the conviction that a considerable force of Whig cavalry were at hand, the troopers directed all their efforts to cover what they believed Ensign St. Jermyn's retreat, and were now seen formed into a platoon, and moving towards the middle of the plain, in such a manner as to place themselves between the fugitive and his supposed pursuers. Here they delayed a few minutes, as if expecting an attack; until finding that the object of their solicitude had safely crossed the field and plunged into the distant woods, they rode away at a rapid pace in the same direction. When they reached the further extremity of the open ground, they halted for an instant, turned their eyes back towards the spot of their first discovery, and, finding that no attempt was made to follow, gave a hearty huzza, and rode onward in search of their prize.

The stratagem had completely succeeded: Ramsay had escaped, and Horse Shoe had withdrawn his prisoner into the neighboring wood upon the hill, where he was able to observe the whole scene. After a brief interval, the sergeant resumed his journey, and, with all necessary circumspection, bent his steps towards the river, where he arrived without molestation, and thence he continued his march in the direction of the rendezvous.

John Ramsay did not stop until he had crossed the Saluda and advanced a considerable distance on the opposite bank, where, to his great joy, he was encountered by a look-out party of Williams's regiment. Our fugitive had some difficulty in making himself known to his friends, and escaping the salutation which an enemy was likely to obtain at their hands; but when he surrendered to them, and made them acquainted with the cause of his disguise, the party instantly turned about with him, and proceeded in quest of the sergeant and his prisoner.

It was not long before they fell in with the small detachment of Connelly's troopers,—as the late masters of the meadow turned out to be—who were leisurely returning from their recent exploit. These, finding themselves in the presence of superior numbers, turned to flight. Not far behind them Ramsay and his new companions encountered Horse Shoe; and the whole party proceeded without delay to Williams's camp.

Colonel Williams had reached the Block-house on the preceding evening with a force of two hundred cavalry. Clarke and Shelby happened, at this juncture, to be with him; and these three gallant partisans were now anxiously employed in arranging measures for that organized resistance to the Tory Dominion which fills so striking a chapter in the history of the Southern war, and which it had been the special object of Butler's mission to promote. Horse Shoe was enabled to communicate to Williams and his confederates the general purpose of this mission, and the disasters which had befallen Butler in his attempt to reach those with whom he was to co-operate. This intelligence created a lively interest in behalf of the captive, and it was instantly determined to make some strenuous effort for his deliverance. Whilst these matters were brought into consultation by the leaders, Horse Shoe and John Ramsay mingled amongst the soldiers, in the enjoyment of that fellowship which forms the most agreeable feature in the associations of the camp.

SKETCHES OF LIFE IN OLD VIRGINIA.

From Swallow Barn· or, A Sojourn in the Old Dominion. Revised Edition (1852.)

SWALLOW BARN.

SWALLOW BARN is an aristocratical old edifice which sits, like a brooding hen, on the southern bank of the James River. It looks down upon a shady

pocket or nook, formed by an indentation of the
shore, from a gentle acclivity thinly sprinkled with
oaks whose magnificent branches afford habitation to
sundry friendly colonies of squirrels and wood-
peckers.

This time-honored mansion was the residence of
the family of Hazards. But in the present generation, the spells of love and mortgage have translated
the possession to Frank Meriwether, who having
married Lucretia, the eldest daughter of my late
Uncle Walter Hazard, and lifted some gentlemanlike
incumbrances which had been sleeping for years upon
the domain, was thus inducted into the proprietary
rights. The adjacency of his own estate gave a ter-
ritorial feature to this alliance, of which the fruits
were no less discernible in the multiplication of negroes, cattle, and poultry, than in a flourishing clan
of Meriwethers.

The main building is more than a century old. It
is built with thick brick walls, but one story in height,
and surmounted by a double-faced or hipped roof,
which gives the idea of a ship bottom upwards.
Later buildings have been added to this, as the wants
or ambition of the family have expanded. These are
all constructed of wood, and seem to have been built
in defiance of all laws of congruity, just as conven-
ience required. But they form altogether an agreeable picture of habitation, suggesting the idea of
comfort in the ample space they fill, and in their conspicuous adaptation to domestic uses.

The hall door is an ancient piece of walnut, which
has grown too heavy for its hinges, and by its daily
travel has furrowed the floor in a quadrant, over
which it has an uneasy journey. It is shaded by a
narrow porch, with a carved pediment upheld by
massive columns of wood, somewhat split by the sun.
An ample court-yard, inclosed by a semi-circular pa-

ling, extends in front of the whole pile, and is traversed by a gravel road leading from a rather ostentatious iron gate, which is swung between two pillars of brick surmounted by globes of cut stone. Between the gate and the house a large willow spreads its arched and pendent drapery over the grass. A bridle rack stands within the inclosure, and near it a ragged horse-nibbled plum-tree—the current belief being that a plum-tree thrives on ill usage—casts its skeleton shadow on the dust.

Some Lombardy poplars, springing above a mass of shrubbery, partially screen various supernumerary buildings at a short distance in the rear of the mansion. Amongst these is to be seen the gable end of a stable, with the date of its erection stiffly emblazoned in black bricks near the upper angle, in figures set in after the fashion of the work on a girl's sampler. In the same quarter a pigeon-box, reared on a post and resembling a huge tee-totum, is visible, and about its several doors and windows a family of pragmatical pigeons are generally strutting, bridling, and bragging at each other from sunrise until dark.

Appendant to this homestead is an extensive tract of land which stretches some three or four miles along the river, presenting alternately abrupt promontories mantled with pine and dwarf oak and small inlets terminating in swamps. Some sparse portions of forest vary the landscape, which, for the most part, exhibits a succession of fields clothed with Indian corn, some small patches of cotton or tobacco plants, with the usual varieties of stubble and fallow grounds. These are inclosed by worm fences of shrunken chestnut, where lizards and ground-squirrels are perpetually running races along the rails.

A few hundred steps from the mansion, a brook glides at a snail's pace towards the river, holding its course through a wilderness of laurel and alder,

and creeping around islets covered with green
mosses. Across this stream is thrown a rough
bridge, which it would delight a painter to see; and
not far below it an aged sycamore twists its roots
into a grotesque framework to the pure mirror of a
spring, which wells up its cool waters from a bed of
gravel and runs gurgling to the brook. There it aids
in furnishing a cruising ground to a squadron of
ducks who, in defiance of all nautical propriety, are
incessantly turning up their sterns to the skies. On
the grass which skirts the margin of the spring, I
observe the family linen is usually spread out by
some three or four negro women, who chant shrill
music over their wash-tubs, and seem to live in ceaseless warfare with sundry little besmirched and bow-
legged blacks, who are never tired of making somer-
sets, and mischievously pushing each other on the
clothes laid down to dry.

Beyond the bridge, at some distance, stands a
prominent object in the perspective of this picture,—
the most venerable appendage to the establishment,
—a huge barn with an immense roof hanging almost
to the ground, and thatched a foot thick with sun
burnt straw, which reaches below the eaves in ragged
flakes. It has a singularly drowsy and decrepit aspect. The yard around it is strewed knee-deep with
litter, from the midst of which arises a long rack
resembling a *chevaux de frise,* which is ordinarily
filled with fodder. This is the customary lounge of
half a score of oxen and as many cows, who sustain
an imperturbable companionship with a sickly
wagon, whose parched tongue and drooping swingle-
trees, as it stands in the sun, give it a most forlorn
and invalid character; whilst some sociable carts
under the sheds, with their shafts perched against
the walls, suggest the idea of a set of gossiping cronies taking their ease in a tavern porch. Now and

then a clownish hobble-de-hoy colt, with long fet-
locks and disordered mane, and a thousand burs in
his tail, stalks through this company. But as it is
forbidden ground to all his tribe, he is likely very
soon to encounter a shower of corn-cobs from some
of the negro men; upon which contingency he makes
a rapid retreat across the bars which imperfectly
guard the entrance to the yard, and with an uncouth
display of his heels bounds away towards the brook,
where he stops and looks back with a saucy defiance;
and after affecting to drink for a moment, gallops
away with a braggart whinny to the fields.

A COUNTRY GENTLEMAN.

THE master of this lordly domain is Frank Meriwether. He is now in the meridian of life—somewhere about forty-five. Good cheer and an easy temper tell well upon him. The first has given him a
comfortable, portly figure, and the latter a contemplative turn of mind, which inclines him to be lazy
and philosophical.

He has some right to pride himself on his personal
appearance, for he has a handsome face, with a dark
blue eye and a fine intellectual brow. His head is
growing scant of hair on the crown, which induces
him to be somewhat particular in the management of
his locks in that locality, and these are assuming a
decided silvery hue.

It is pleasant to see him when he is going to ride
to the Court House on business occasions. He is then
apt to make his appearance in a coat of blue broad-
cloth, astonishingly glossy, and with an unusual
amount of plaited ruffle strutting through the folds
of a Marseilles waistcoat. A worshipful finish is
given to this costume by a large straw hat, lined with
green silk. There is a magisterial fulness in his gar-

ments which betokens condition in the world, and a
heavy bunch of seals, suspended by a chain of gold,
jingles as he moves, pronouncing him a man of su-
perfluities.

It is considered rather extraordinary that he has
never set up for Congress: but the truth is, he is an
unambitoious man, and has a great dislike for curry-
ing favor—as he calls it. And, besides, he is thoroughly convinced that there will always be men
enough in Virginia willing to serve the people, and
therefore does not see why he should trouble his head
about it. Some years ago, however, there was really
an impression that he meant to come out. By some
sudden whim, he took it into his head to visit Washington during the session of Congress, and returned,
after a fortnight, very seriously distempered with
politics. He told curious anecdotes of certain secret
intrigues which had been discovered in the affairs of
the capital, gave a clear insight into the views of
some deep-laid combinations, and became, all at once,
painfully florid in his discourse, and dogmatical to a
degree that made his wife stare. Fortunately, this
orgasm soon subsided, and Frank relapsed into an
indolent gentleman of the opposition; but it had the
effect to give a much more decided cast to his studies, for he forthwith discarded the *Richmond Whig*
from his newspaper subscription, and took to *The
Enquirer*, like a man who was not to be disturbed by
doubts. And as it was morally impossible to believe
all that was written on both sides, to prevent his mind
from being abused, he from this time forward took a
stand against the re-election of Mr. Adams to the
Presidency, and resolved to give an implicit faith to
all alleged facts which set against his administration.
The consequence of this straight-forward and confiding deportment was an unexpected complimentary
notice of him by the Executive of the State. He was

put into the commission of the peace, and having thus
become a public man against his will, his opinions
were observed to undergo some essential changes.
He now thinks that a good citizen ought neither to
solicit nor decline office; that the magistracy of Virginia is the sturdiest pillar which supports the fabric of the Constitution; and that the people, "though
in their opinions they may be mistaken, in their sentiments they are never wrong";—with some such
other dogmas as, a few years ago, he did not hold
in very good repute. In this temper, he has of late
embarked on the millpond of county affairs, and notwithstanding his amiable character and his doctrin-
ary republicanism, I am told he keeps the peace as
if he commanded a garrison, and administers justice
like a Cadi.

He has some claim to supremacy in this last department; for during three years he smoked segars
in a lawyer's office in Richmond, which enabled him
to obtain a bird's-eye view of Blackstone and Revised Code. Besides this, he was a member of a Law
Debating Society, which ate oysters once a week in
a cellar; and he wore, in accordance with the usage
of the most promising law students of that day, six
cravats, one over the other, and yellow-topped boots,
by which he was recognized as a blood of the metropolis. Having in this way qualified himself to assert
and maintain his rights, he came to his estate, upon
his arrival at age, a very model of landed gentlemen.
Since that time his avocations have had a certain literary tincture; for having settled himself down as
a married man, and got rid of his superfluous foppery, he rambled with wonderful assiduity through
a wilderness of romances, poems, and dissertations,
which are now collected in his library, and, with their
battered blue covers, present a lively type of an army
of continentals at the close of the war, or a hospital

Vol. 8—9

of invalids. These have all, at last, given away to
the newspapers—a miscellaneous study very attractive and engrossing to country gentlemen. This line
of study has rendered Meriwether a most perilous
antagonist in the matter of legislative proceedings.

A landed proprietor, with a good house and a host
of servants, is naturally a hospitable man. A guest
is one of his daily wants. A friendly face is a necessary of life, without which the heart is apt to starve,
or a luxury without which it grows parsimonious.
Men who are isolated from society by distance, feel
these wants by an instinct, and are grateful for the
opportunity to relieve them. In Meriwether, the
sentiment goes beyond this. It has, besides, something dialectic in it. His house is open to everybody,
as freely almost as an inn. But to see him when he
has the good fortune to pick up an intelligent, educated gentleman,—and particularly one who listens
well!—a respectable, assentatious stranger!—All
the better if he has been in the Legislature, or better
still, if in Congress. Such a person caught within
the purlieus of Swallow Barn, may set down one
week's entertainment as certain—inevitable, and as
many more as he likes—the more the merrier. He
will know something of the quality of Meriwether's
rhetoric before he is gone.

Then again, it is very pleasant to see Frank's kind
and considerate bearing towards his servants and
dependents. His slaves appreciate this, and hold
him in most affectionate reverence, and, therefore,
are not only contented, but happy under his dominion.

Meriwether is not much of a traveler. He has
never been in New England, and very seldom beyond
the confines of Virginia. He makes now and then a
winter excursion to Richmond, which, I rather think,
he considers as the centre of civilization; and to-

wards autumn, it is his custom to journey over the
mountain to the Springs, which he is obliged to do to
avoid the unhealthy season in the tide-water region.
But the upper country is not much to his taste, and
would not be endured by him if it were not for the
crowds that resort there for the same reason which
operates upon him; and I may add,—though he
would not confess it—for the opportunity this con-
course affords him for discussion of opinions.

He thinks lightly of the mercantile interest, and,
in fact, undervalues the manners of the large cities
generally. He believes that those who live in them
are hollow-hearted and insincere, and wanting in that
substantial intelligence and virtue, which he affirms
to be characteristic of the country. He is an ardent admirer of the genius of Virginia, and is frequent in his commendation of a toast in which the
state is compared to the mother of the Gracchi:—
indeed, it is a familiar thing with him to speak of
the aristocracy of talent as only inferior to that of
the landed interest,—the idea of a freeholder inferring to his mind a certain constitutional pre-emi-
nence in all the virtues of citizenship, as a matter
of course.

The solitary elevation of a country gentleman,
well to do in the world, begets some magnificent notions. He becomes as infallible as the Pope; gradually acquires a habit of making long speeches; is apt
to be impatient of contradiction, and is always very
touchy on the point of honor. There is nothing more
conclusive than a rich man's logic anywhere, but in
the country, amongst his dependents, it flows with
the smooth and unresisted course of a full stream ir-
rigating a meadow, and depositing its mud in fertilizing luxuriance. Meriwether's sayings, about
Swallow Barn, import absolute verity. But I have
discovered that they are not so current out of his

jurisdiction. Indeed, every now and then, we have quite obstinate discussions when some of the neighboring potentates, who stand in the same sphere with Frank, come to the house; for these worthies have opinions of their own, and nothing can be more dogged than the conflict between them. They sometimes fire away at each other with a most amiable and unconvinceable hardihood for a whole evening, bandying interjections, and making bows, and saying shrewd things with all the courtesy imaginable. But for unextinguishable pertinacity in argument, and utter impregnability of belief, there is no disputant like your country gentleman who reads the newspapers. When one of these discussions fairly gets under weigh, it never comes to an anchor again of its own accord;—it is either blown out so far to sea as to be given up for lost, or puts into port in distress for want of documents,—or is upset by a call for the boot-jack and slippers—which is something like the previous question in Congress.

If my worthy cousin be somewhat over-argumentative as a politician, he restores the equilibrium of his character by a considerate coolness in religious matters. He piques himself upon being a high-churchman, but is not the most diligent frequenter of places of worship, and very seldom permits himself to get into a dispute upon points of faith. If Mr. Chub, the Presbyterian tutor in the family, ever succeeds in drawing him into this field, as he occasionally has the address to do, Meriwether is sure to fly the course; he gets puzzled with scripture names, and makes some odd mistakes between Peter and Paul, and then generally turns the parson over to his wife, who, he says, has an astonishing memory.

He is somewhat distinguished as a breeder of blooded horses; and, ever since the celebrated race between Eclipse and Henry, has taken to this occu-

pation with a renewed zeal, as a matter affecting
the reputation of the state. It is delightful to hear
him expatiate upon the value, importance, and patriotic bearing of this employment, and to listen to
all his technical lore touching the mystery of horse-
craft. He has some fine colts in training, which are
committed to the care of a pragmatical old negro,
named Carey, who, in his reverence for the occupation, is the perfect shadow of his master. He and
Frank hold grave and momentous consultations
upon the affairs of the stable, in such a sagacious
strain of equal debate, that it would puzzle a spectator to tell which was the leading member in the
council. Carey thinks he knows a great deal more
upon the subject than his master, and their frequent
intercourse has begot a familiarity in the old negro
which is almost fatal to Meriwether's supremacy.
The old man feels himself authorized to maintain his
positions according to the freest parliamentary form,
and sometimes with a violence of asseveration that
compels his master to abandon his ground, purely
out of faint-heartedness. Meriwether gets a little
nettled by Carey's doggedness, but generally turns
it off in a laugh. I was in the stable with him, a few
mornings after my arrival, when he ventured to ex-
postulate with the venerable groom upon a professional point, but the controversy terminated in its
customary way. "Who sot you up, Master Frank,
to tell me how to fodder that 'ere cretur, when I as
good as nursed you on my knee?"

"Well, tie up your tongue, you old mastiff," replied Frank, as he walked out of the stable, "and
cease growling, since you will have it your own
way";—and then, as we left the old man's presence,
he added, with an affectionate chuckle—"a faithful
old cur, too, that snaps at me out of pure honesty;

he has not many years left, and it does no harm to humor him!''

———

THE MISTRESS OF SWALLOW BARN.

WHILST Frank Meriwether amuses himself with his quiddities, and floats through life upon the current of his humor, his dame, my excellent cousin Lucretia, takes charge of the household affairs, as one who has a reputation to stake upon her administration. She has made it a perfect science, and great is her fame in the dispensation thereof!

Those who have visited Swallow Barn will long remember the morning stir, of which the murmurs arose even unto the chambers, and fell upon the ears of the sleepers;—the dry rubbing of floors, and even the waxing of the same until they were like ice;— and the grinding of coffee-mills;—and the gibber of ducks, and chickens, and turkeys; and all the multitudinous concert of homely sounds. And then, her breakfasts! I do not wish to be counted extravagant, but a small regiment might march in upon her without disappointment; and I would put them for excellence and variety against anything that ever was served upon platter. Moreover, all things go like clock-work. She rises with the lark, and infuses an early vigor into the whole household. And yet she is a thin woman to look upon, and a feeble; with a sallow complexion, and a pair of animated black eyes which impart a portion of fire to a countenance otherwise demure from the paths worn across it, in the frequent travel of a low-country ague. But, although her life has been somewhat saddened by such visitations, my cousin is too spirited a woman to give up to them; for she is therapeutical in her constitution, and considers herself a full match for any reasonable tertian in the world. Indeed, I have sometimes thought that she took more pride in her leech-craft than becomes a Christian woman: she is even a little vainglorious. For, to say nothing of her skill in compounding simples, she has occasionally brought down upon her head the sober remonstrances of her husband, by her pertinacious faith in the efficacy of certain spells in cases of intermittent. But there is no reasoning against her experience. She can enumerate the cases—"and men may say what they choose about its being contrary to reason, and all that:—it is their way! But seeing is believing—nine scoops of water in the hollow of the hand, from the sycamore spring, for three mornings, before sunrise, and a cup of strong coffee with lemon-juice, will break an ague, try it when you will." In short, as Frank says, "Lucretia will die in that creed."

I am occasionally up early enough to be witness to her morning regimen, which, to my mind, is rather tyrannically enforced against the youngsters of her numerous family, both white and black. She is in the habit of preparing some death-routing decoction for them, in a small pitcher, and administering it to the whole squadron in succession, who severally swallow the dose with a most ineffectual effort at repudiation, and gallop off, with faces all rue and wormwood.

Everything at Swallow Barn, that falls within the superintendence of my cousin Lucretia is a pattern of industry. In fact, I consider her the very priestess of the American system, for, with her, the protection of manufactures is even more of a passion than a principle. Every here and there, over the estate, may be seen, rising in humble guise above the shrubbery, the rude chimney of a log cabin, where all the livelong day the plaintive moaning of the spinning-wheel rises fitfully upon the breeze, like

the fancied notes of a hobgoblin, as they are sometimes imitated in the stories with which we frighten
children. In these laboratories the negro women are
employed in preparing yarn for the loom, from
which is produced not only a comfortable supply of
winter clothing for the working people, but some excellent carpets for the house.

It is refreshing to behold how affectionately vain
our good hostess is of Frank, and what deference
she shows to his judgment in all matters, except
those that belong to the home department;—for
there she is confessedly and without appeal, the par-
amount power. It seems to be a dogma with her,
that he is the very "first man in Virginia," an expression which in this region has grown into an emphatic provincialism. Frank, in return, is a devout
admirer of her accomplishments, and although he
does not pretend to an ear for music, he is in raptures at her skill on the harpsichord, when she plays
at night for the children to dance; and he sometimes
sets her to singing 'The Twins of Latona,' and 'Old
Towler,' and 'The Rose-Tree in Full Bearing' (she
does not study the modern music), for the entertainment of his company. On these occasions he stands
by the instrument, and nods his head as if he comprehended the airs.

She is a fruitful vessel, and seldom fails in her
annual tribute to the honors of the family; and,
sooth to say, Frank is reputed to be somewhat restiff
under these multiplying blessings. They have two
lovely girls, just verging towards womanhood, who
attract a supreme regard in the household, and to
whom Frank is perfectly devoted. Next to these is
a boy,—a shrewd, mischievous imp, who curvets
about the house, 'a chartered libertine.' He is a
little wiry fellow near thirteen, known altogether
by the nickname of Rip, and has a scapegrace coun-

tenance, full of freckles and devilry; the eyes are somewhat greenish, and the mouth opens alarmingly wide upon a tumultuous array of discolored teeth. His whole air is that of an untrimmed colt torn down and disorderly; and I most usually find him with the bosom of his shirt bagged out, so as to form a great pocket, where he carries apples or green walnuts, and sometimes pebbles, with which he is famous for pelting the fowls.

A SPINSTER

Prudence Meriwether is an only sister of Frank's, and holds a station somewhat eminent amongst the household idols. She is rather comely to look upon —very neat in person, and is considered high authority in matter of dress. But Time, who notches mortal shapes with as little mercy as the baker, in his morning circuit, notches his tally-stick, has calendared his visits even upon this goodly form. A shrewd observer may note in sundry evidences of a fastidious choice of colors, and of what,—to coin a word,—I might call a scrupulous *toiletry*, that the lapse of human seasons has not passed unheeded by this lady. He may detect, sometimes, an overdone vivacity in her accost, and an exaggerated thoughtlessness; sometimes, in her tone of conversation, a little too much girlishness, which betrays a suspicion of its opposite: and there are certain sober lines journeying from the mouth cheekward, which are ruminative, in spite of her light-heartedness. These are quite pleasant signs to an astute, experienced, perspicacious bachelor, like myself, who can read them with a learned skill; they speak of that mellow time when a woman captivates by complaisance, and overcomes her adversary rather by marching out of her fort to challenge attack, than by standing a siege within it.

There is a dash of the picturesque in the character of this lady. Towards sunset she is apt to stray forth amongst the old oaks, and to gather small bouquets of wild flowers, in the pursuit of which she contrives to get into very pretty attitudes; or she falls into raptures at the shifting tints of the clouds on the western sky, and produces quite a striking pictorial effect by the skilful choice of a position which shows her figure in strong relief against the evening light. And then in her boudoir may be found exquisite sketches from her pencil, of forms of love and beauty, belted and buckled knights, old castles and pensive ladies, Madonnas and cloistered nuns,—the offspring of an artistic imagination heated with romance and devotion. Her attire is, sometimes, studiously simple and plain, and her bearing is demure and contemplative; but this is never long continued, for, in spite of her discipline, she does not wish to be accounted as one inclined to be serious in her turn of mind. I have seen her break out into quite a riotous vivacity. This is very likely to ensue when she is brought into fellowship with a flaunting mad-cap belle who is carrying all before her: she then "overbears her continents," and becomes as flaunting a madcap as the other.

If Prudence has a fault—which proposition I prudently put with an *if*, as a doubtful question—it is in setting the domestic virtues at too high a value. One may, perhaps, be too inveterately charitable. I think the establishment of three Sunday schools, a colonization society membership, a management in a tract association, and an outward and visible patronage of the cause of temperance, by the actual enrolment of her name amongst those who have taken the pledge, smack a little of supererogation, though

I don't wish to set up my judgment too peremptorily
on this point. And I think, also, one may carry the
praise of the purity of country life, and of the bene-
fits of solitude and self-constraint, to an extent
which might appear merciless towards those whose
misfortune it is to live in a sphere where these virtues cannot be so fully cultivated. If a tendency in
this direction be a blemish in the composition of our
lady, it is a very slight one, and is amply compen-
sated by the many pleasant aberrations she makes
from this phase of her character. She converses
with great ease upon all subjects—even with a dangerous facility, I may say, which sometimes leads
her into hyperbole: her diction occasionally becomes
high-flown, and expands into the incomprehensible—
but that is only when she is excited. Her manner, at
times, might be called oratorical, particularly when,
in imitation of her brother, she bewails the departure of the golden age, or declaims upon the prospect
of its revival among the rejuvenescent glories of the
Old Dominion. She has an awful idea of the perfect
respectability, I might almost say splendor, of her
lineage, and this is one of the few points upon which
I know her to be touchy.

Apart from these peculiarities, which are but
fleecy clouds upon a summer sky, even enhancing its
beauty, or mites upon a snow-drift, she is a capti-
vating specimen of a ripened maiden, just standing
on that sunshiny verge from which the prospect beyond presents a sedate autumnal landscape gently
subsiding into undistinguishable and misty confusion of hill and dale arrayed in golden-tinted gray.
It is no wonder, therefore, that with her varied perfections, and the advantages of her position, the
James River world should insensibly have elevated
Prudence Meriwether to the poetical altitude of the
"cynosure of neighboring eyes."

WITHOUT much reverence for the profession of the law itself, I have a great regard for its votaries, and especially for that part of the tribe which comprehends the old and thorough-paced stagers of the bar. The feelings, habits and associations of the bar in general, have a happy influence upon character. It abounds with good fellows: and, take it altogether, there may be collected from it a greater mass of shrewd, observant, droll, playful and generous spirits, than from any other equal numbers of society. They live in each other's presence, like a set of players; congregate in the courts, as the former in the green-room; and break their unpremeditated jests, in the intervals of business, with that sort of undress freedom which contrasts amusingly with the solemn and even tragic seriousness with which they appear, in turn, upon the boards. They have one face for the public rife with the gravity of the profession, and another for themselves, replete with mirth and enjoyment. The toil and fatigue of business give them a peculiar relish for their hours of relaxation, and, in the same degree, incapacitate them for that frugal attention to their private concerns which their limited means usually require. They have, in consequence, a prevailing air of unthriftiness in personal matters, which, however it may operate to the prejudice of the pocket of the individual, has a mellow and kindly effect upon his disposition.

In an old member of the profession,—one who has grown gray in the service,—there is a rich unction of originality, which brings him out from the ranks of his fellow-men in strong relief. His habitual conversancy with the world in its strangest varieties, and with the secret history of character, gives him a shrewd estimate of the human heart. He is quiet and unapt to be struck with wonder at any of the actions of men. There is a deep current of observation running calmly through his thoughts, and seldom gushing out in words: the confidence which has been placed in him, in the thousand relations of his profession, renders him constitutionally cautious. His acquaintance with the vicissitudes of fortune, as they have been exemplified in the lives of individuals, and with the severe afflictions that have "tried the reins" of many, known only to himself, makes him an indulgent and charitable apologist of the aberrations of others. He has an impregnable good humor that never falls below the level of thoughtfulness into melancholy. He is a creature of habits; rising early for exercise; generally temperate from necessity, and studious against his will. His face is accustomed to take the ply of his pursuits with great facility, grave and even severe in business, and readily rising into smiles at a pleasant conceit. He works hard when at his task; and goes at it with the reluctance of an old horse in a bark-mill. His common-places are quaint and professional: they are made up of law maxims, and first occur to him in Latin. He measures all the sciences out of his proper line of study (and with these he is but scantily acquainted), by the rules of law. He thinks a steam engine should be worked with *due diligence*, and without *laches:* a thing little likely to happen, he considers as *potentia remotissima;* and what is not yet in existence, or *in esse,* as he would say, is *in nubibus.* He apprehends that wit best, which is connected with the affairs of the term; is particularly curious in his anecdotes of old lawyers, and inclined to be talkative concerning the amusing passages of his own professional life. He is, sometimes, not altogether free of outward foppery; is apt to be an especial good liver, and he keeps the best company. His literature is not much diversified; and he prefers books that are bound in plain calf, to those that are much lettered or gilded. He garners up his papers with a wonderful appearance of care; ties them in bundles with red tape; and usually has great difficulty to find them when he wants them. Too much particularity has perplexed him; and just so it is with his cases: they are well assorted, packed and laid away, in his mind, but are not easily to be brought forth again without labor. This makes him something of a procrastinator, and rather to delight in new business than finish his old. He is, however, much beloved, and affectionately considered by the people.

Philpot Wart belongs to the class whose characterestics I have here sketched. He is a practitioner of some thirty or forty years' standing; during the greater part of which time he has resided in this district. He is now verging upon sixty years of age, and may be said to have spent the larger portion of his life on horseback. His figure is short and thick-set, with a hard, muscular outline; his legs slightly bowed, his shoulders broad, and his hands and feet uncommonly large. His head is of extraordinary size, inclining to be cubical in shape, and clothed with a shock of wiry, dark hair. A brown and dry complexion; eyes small, keen, and undefined in color, furnished with thick brows; a large mouth, conspicuous for a range of teeth worn nearly to their sockets; and ample protruding ears, constitute the most remarkable points in his appearance. The predominant expression of his features is a sly, quick good nature, susceptible, however, of great severity.

His dress is that of a man who does not trouble himself with the change of fashions; careless, and, to a certain degree, quaint. It consists of a plain, dark coat, not of the finest cloth, and rather the worse for wear; dingy and faded nankeen small clothes, and a pair of half boots, such as were worn at the beginning of this century. His hat is old, and worn until the rim has become too pliable to keep its original form; and his cravat is sometimes, by accident, tied in such a manner, as not to include one side of his shirt collar;—this departure from established usage, and others like it, happen from Mr. Wart's never using a looking-glass when he makes his toilet.

His circuit takes in four or five adjoining counties, and, as he is a regular attendant upon the courts, he is an indefatigable traveler. His habit of being so much upon the road, causes his clients to make their appointments with him at the several stages of his journeyings; and it generally happens that he is intercepted, when he stops, by some one waiting to see him. Being obliged to pass a great deal of his time in small taverns, he has grown to be contented with scant accommodation, and never complains of his fare. But he is extremely particular in exacting the utmost attention to his horse.

He has an insinuating address that takes wonderfully with the people; and especially with the older and graver sorts. This has brought him into a close acquaintance with a great many persons, and has rendered Philly Wart,—as he is universally called, —a kind of cabinet-counsellor and private adviser with most of those who are likely to be perplexed with their affairs. He has a singularly retentive memory as to facts, dates, and names; and by his intimate knowledge of land titles, courses and distances, patents, surveys and locations, he has become a formidable champion in all ejectment cases. In addition to this, Philly has such a brotherly and companionable relation to the greater number of the

freeholders who serve upon the juries, and has such
a confiding, friendly way of talking to them when he
tries a cause, that it is generally supposed he can
persuade them to believe anything he chooses.

His acquirements as a lawyer are held in high respect by the bar, although it is reported that he reads
but little law of later date than Coke Littleton, to
which book he manifests a remarkable affection, having perused it, as he boasts, some eight or ten times;
but the truth is, he has not much time for other reading, being very much engrossed by written documents, in which he is painfully studious. He takes
a great deal of authority upon himself, nevertheless,
in regard to the Virginia decisions, inasmuch as he
has been contemporary with most of the cases, and
heard them, generally, from the courts themselves.
Besides this, he practised in the times of old Chan-
cellor Wythe, and President Pendleton, and must
necessarily have absorbed a great deal of that spirit
of law-learning which has evaporated in the hands of
the reporters. As Philly himself says, he under-
stands the currents of the law, and knows where
they must run; and, therefore, has no need of looking into the cases.

Philly has an excellent knack in telling a story,
which consists in a caustic, dry manner, that is well
adapted to give it point; and sometimes he indulges
this talent with signal success before the juries.
When he is at home,—which is not often above a
week or ten days at a time,—he devotes himself almost entirely to his farm. He is celebrated there for
a fine breed of hounds; and fox-hunting is quite a
passion with him. This is the only sport in which
he indulges to any excess; and so far does he carry
it, that he often takes his dogs with him upon the
circuit, when his duty calls him, in the hunting season, to certain parts of the country where one or

two gentlemen reside who are fond of this pastime.
On these occasions he billets the hounds upon his
landlord, and waits patiently until he dispatches his
business and then he turns into the field with all the
spirit and zest of Nimrod. He has some lingering
recollections of the classics, and is a little given to
quoting them, without much regard to the appropriateness of the occasion. It is told of him, that one
fine morning, in December, he happened to be with
a party of brother sportsmen in full chase for a gray
fox, under circumstances of unusual animation. The
weather was cool, a white frost sparkled upon the
fields, the sun had just risen and flung a beautiful
light over the landscape, the fox was a-foot, the dogs
in full cry, the huntsmen shouting with exuberant
mirth, the woods re-echoing to the clamor, and every
one at high speed in hot pursuit. Philly was in an
ecstasy, spurring forward his horse with uncommon
ardor, and standing in his stirrups, as if impatient
of his speed, when he was joined in the chase by two
or three others as much delighted as himself. In
this situation he cried out to one of the party, 'Isn't
this fine; don't it put you in mind of Virgil? Ti-
tyre tu patulæ recubans sub tegmine fagi.'' Philly
denies the fact; but some well authenticated flour-
ishes of his at the bar, of a similar nature, give
great semblance of truth to the story.

It sometimes happens that a pair of his hounds
will steal after him, and follow him through the circuit, without his intending it; and when this occurs,
he has not the heart to drive them back. This was
the case at the present court: accordingly, he was
followed by his dogs to Swallow Barn. They slink
close behind his horse, and trot together as if they
were coupled.

Philly's universal acquaintance through the country and his pre-eminent popularity have, long since,

brought him into public life. He has been elected
to the Assembly for twenty years past, without opposition; and, indeed, the voters will not permit him
to decline. It is, therefore, a regular part of his
business to attend to all political matters affecting
the county. His influence in this department is wonderful. He is consulted in reference to all plans,
and his advice seems to have the force of law. He
is extremely secret in his operations, and appears to
carry his point by his calm, quiet, and unresisting
manner. He has the reputation of being a dexterous
debater, and of making some sharp and heavy hits
when roused into opposition; though many odd stories are told, at Richmond, of his strenuous efforts,
at times, to be oratorical. He is, however, very much
in the confidence of the political managers of all parties, and seldom fails to carry a point when he sets
about it in earnest.

During the war, Philly commanded a troop of vol-
unteer light-horse, and was frequently employed in
active service, in guarding the hen-roosts along the
river from the attacks of the enemy. The occasions have furnished him with some agreeable episodes in the history of his life. He gives a faithful
narrative of his exploits at this period, and does not
fail to throw a dash of comic humor into his account
of his campaigns.

In our ride to Swallow Barn, he and Meriwether
were principally engrossed with the subject of the
expected arbitration. Meriwether particularly en-
joined it upon him so to manage the matter as to
make up a case in favor of Mr. Tracy, and to give
such a decision as would leave the old gentleman in
possession of the contested territory.

Philly revolved the subject carefully in his mind,
and assured Frank that he would have no difficulty

in putting Swansdown upon such a train as could not fail to accomplish their ends.

"But it seems strange to me," said the counsellor, "that the old man would not be content to take the land without all this circuity."

"We must accommodate ourselves to the peculiarities of our neighbors," replied Meriwether, "and, pray be careful that you give no offence to his pride, by the course you pursue."

"I have never before been engaged in a case with such instructions," said Philly. "This looks marvellously like an Irish donkey race, where each man cudgels his neighbor's ass. Well, I suppose Singleton Swansdown will take the beating without being more restive under it than others of the tribe!"

"I beseech you, use him gently," said Meriwether. "He will be as proud of his victory as ourselves."

Philly laughed the more heartily as he thought of this novel case. Now and then he relapsed into perfect silence, and then again and again broke forth into a chuckle at his own meditations upon the subject.

"You are like a king who surrenders by negotiation, all that he has won by fighting," said he, laughing again; "we shall capitulate, at least, with the honors of war,—drums beating and colors flying!"

"It is the interest of the commonwealth that there should be an end of strife; I believe so the maxim runs," said Meriwether, smiling.

"Concordia parvæ res crescunt; discordiâ maximæ dilabuntur," added the counsellor. "But it seems to me to be something of a wild-goose chase notwithstanding."

Philly repeated these last words as he dismounted at the gate at Swallow Barn, and, throwing his saddle-bags across his arm, he walked into the house with the rest of the party.

A DINNER PARTY.

THE day that followed our adventure in the Goblin Swamp was a busy one. We were to have our dinner party at Swallow Barn.

At an early hour before breakfast a servant waited at the front door for Hazard's orders. This was a negro boy equipped for service on horseback. He was rather more trig in his appearance than I was accustomed to see the servants. From his jockey air, and the conceited slant he had given to an old dark-colored cap with a yellow band, which stuck upon one side of his head, I was not wrong in my conjecture that he had something to do with the race-horses. He was mounted upon one of this stock, a tall, full-blooded bay, just ready to start, when Hazard came to instruct him in the purpose of his errand.

"Ganymede," said Ned, "you will go to the Court House, and give my compliments—"

"Yes, sir," said the messenger, with a joyful countenance.

—"To Mister Toll Hedges and the doctor, and tell them that we expect some friends here at dinner to day."

"Yes, sir," shouted the negro, and striking his heels into his horse's sides at the same instant, plunged forward some paces.

"Come back," cried Ned; "what are you going after?"

"To ax Mas Toll Hedges and the doctor to come here to dinner to-day," returned the impatient boy.

"Wait until you hear what I have to tell you," continued Ned. "Say to them that your Master Frank will be glad to see them; and that I wish them to bring anybody along with them they choose."

"That's all!" exclaimed the negro again, and once more bounded off towards the high road.

"You black rascal!" cried Ned at the top of his voice, and laughing, "come back again. You are in a monstrous hurry. I wish you would show something of this activity when it is more wanting. Now, hear me out. Tell them, if they see the 'squire, to bring him along."

"Yes, sir."

"And as you pass by Mr. Braxton Beverly's, stop there, and ask him if he will favor us with his company. And if he cannot come himself, tell him to send us some of the family. Tell him to send them, at any rate. Let me see; is there anybody else? If you meet any of the gentlemen about, give them my compliments, and tell them to come over."

"Yes, sir."

"Now can you remember it all?"

"Never fear me, Mas Ned," said the negro, with his low-country, broad pronunciation, that entirely discards the letter R.

"Then be off," cried Hazard, "and let me hear of no loitering on the road."

"That's me!" shouted Ganymede, in the same tone of excessive spirits he evinced on his first appearance. "I'll be bound I make tracks!" and, saying this, the negro flourished his hand above his head, struck his heels again on the horse's ribs, hallooed with a wild scream, and shot forward like an arrow from a bow.

Soon after breakfast the visitors from The Brakes began to appear. First came Prudence Meriwether, with Catharine, in Mr. Tracy's carriage. About an hour afterwards, Swansdown's glittering curricle arrived, bringing Bel Tracy under the convoy of the gentleman himself. After another interval, Harvey Riggs and Ralph followed on horseback. Mr. Tracy

had not accompanied either of these parties; but
Harvey brought an assurance from him that he
would be punctual to the engagement.

A dinner party in the country is not the premedi-
tated, anxious affair it is in town. It has nothing
of that long, awful interval between the arrival of
the guests and the serving up of the dishes, when
men look in each other's faces with empty stom-
achs, and utter inane common-places with an obvious
air of insincerity, if not of actual suffering. On the
contrary, it is understood to be a regular spending
of the day, in which the guests assume all the privileges of inmates, sleep on the sofas, lounge through
the halls, read the newspapers, stroll over the
grounds, and, if pinched by appetite, stay their stom-
achs with bread and butter, and toddy made of
choice old spirits.

*   *   *   *   *   *

I must not forget to mention, that before we had
taken our chairs, Mistress Winkle, decked out in all
the pomp of silk and muslin, sailed, as it were, with
muffled oars into the room from a side door; and,
with a prim and stealthy motion, deposited her time-
worn person near to my cousin Lucretia. It is a custom of affectionate courtesy in the family, to accord
to this venerable relic of the past generation the ci-
vility of a place at table. Mr. Tracy was aware of
Meriwether's feelings towards the aged dame; and,
prompted by his overflowing zeal on the present occasion to manifest his deference to his host, he no
sooner observed her than he broke out into a jocose
and gallant recognition:—

"Mistress Winkle! what, my old friend! It re-
joices me to see you looking so well—and so youthful! The world goes merrily with you. Gad's-my
life! if Colonel Tarleton were only alive again to
make another visit to the James River, it would be

hard to persuade him that time had gained so small
a victory over the romping girl whom he had the im-
pertinence to chuckle under the chin so boldly. A
saucy and stark trooper he was in those days, Mistress Winkle! But the gout, the gout, I warrant,
did the business for him long ago! Ha, ha! You
haven't forgot old times, Mistress Winkle, although
they have well nigh forgotten you.''

The housekeeper, during this outbreak, courtesied,
hemmed and smiled; and, with much confusion, rustled her silken folds in her chair, with somewhat
of the motion of a motherly hen in the process of in-
cubation. Mr. Tracy had touched upon an incident
which, for nearly half a century, had been a theme
that warmed up all her self-complacency, and which
owed its origin to one of the English partisan's fo-
rays upon the river side during the Revolution, in
which he was said to have made himself very much
at home at Swallow Barn, and to have bestowed
some complimental notice upon the then buxom and
blooming dependant of the family.

The table was furnished with a profusion of the
delicacies afforded by the country; and, notwithstanding it was much more ample than the accommodation of the guests required, it seemed to be
stored rather with a reference to its own dimensions
than to the number of wants of those who were collected around it. At the head, immediately under
the eye of our hostess, in the customary pride of
place, was deposited a goodly ham of bacon, rich in
its own perfections, as well as in the endemic honors
that belong to it in the Old Dominion. According
to a usage worthy of imitation, it was clothed in its
own dark skin, which the imaginative mistress of
the kitchen had embellished by carving into some
fanciful figures. The opposite end of the table smoked
with a huge roasted saddle of mutton, which seemed,

from its trim and spruce air, ready to gallop off the
dish. Between these two extremes was scattered an
enticing diversity of poultry, prepared with many
savory adjuncts, and especially that topical luxury,
which yet so slowly finds its way northward,—fried
chicken,—sworn brother to the ham, and old Virginia's standard dish. The intervening spaces displayed a profusion of the products of the garden;
nor were oysters and crabs wanting where room allowed; and, where nothing else could be deposited, as
if scrupulous of showing a bare spot of the table-
cloth, the bountiful forethought of Mistress Winkle
had provided a choice selection of pickles of every
color and kind. From the whole array of the board
it was obvious, that abundance and variety were
deemed no less essential to the entertainment, than
the excellence of the viands.

A bevy of domestics, in every stage of training,
attended upon the table, presenting a lively type of
the progress of civilization, or the march of intellect;
the veteran waitingman being well-contrasted with
the rude half-monkey, half-boy, who seemed to have
been for the first time admitted to the parlor; whilst,
between these two, were exhibited the successive degrees that mark the advance from the young savage
to the sedate and sophisticated image of the old-fashioned negro nobility. It was equal to a gallery of
caricatures, a sort of scenic satire upon man in his
various stages, with his odd imitativeness illustrated
in the broadest lines. Each had added some article
of coxcombry to his dress; a pewter buckle fastened
to the shirt for a breast-pin; a dingy parti-colored
ribbon, ostentatiously displayed across the breast,
with one end lodged in the waistcoat pocket; or a
preposterous cravat girding up an exorbitantly
starched shirt collar that rivalled the driven snow,
as it traversed cheeks as black as midnight, and

fretted the lower cartilage of a pair of refractory, raven-hued ears. One, more conceited than the rest, had platted his wool (after a fashion common amongst the negroes) into five or six short cues both before and behind; whilst the visages of the whole group wore that grave, momentous elongation which is peculiar to the African face, and which is eminently adapted to express the official care and personal importance of the wearer.

As the more immediate, and what is universally conceded to be the more important, business of the dinner was discussed, to wit, the process of dulling the edge of appetite, the merriment of the company rose in proportion to the leisure afforded to its exercise; and the elder portion of the guests gently slid into the vivacity of the younger. Mr. Tracy did not lose for an instant that antiquated cavalier air which he had assumed on entering the room. As Harvey Riggs expressed it, "he was painfully polite and very precisely gay." The ladies, for a time, gave their tone to the table; and, under this influence, we found ourselves falling into detached circles, where each pursued its separate theme, sometimes in loud and rapid converse, mingled with frequent bursts of laughter that spread an undistinguishable din through the room; and sometimes in low and confidential murmurings, of which it was impossible to say whether they were grave or gay. Swansdown's voice was poured into Bel's ear in gentle and unremitting whispers, of which Ned Hazard alone, of all the guests—to judge by his intense and abstracted gaze—was able to unriddle the import. Prudence, equally abstracted, was unnaturally merry, and laughed much more than was necessary at Harvey's jokes. Catharine talked with singular sagacity, and listened, with still more singular earnestness, to Mr. Beverley, who was instructing her, with equal interest and eloquence, upon the wholesome effects he had found in the abundant use of flannel—which he described with unnecessary amplitude of details—in repelling the assaults of an ancient enemy, the rheumatism. Now and then a loud and rather obstreperous laugh, not altogether suited to the region he inhabited, and which some such consciousness seemed abruptly to arrest, was set up by Taliaferro Hedges. This worthy had already begun to occupy that questionable ground which a gentleman of loose habits and decaying reputation is pretty sure to arrive at in his descending career. Dissipation had lowered him somewhat in the world, and had already introduced him to a class of associates who had made a visible impression on his manners, a circumstance which very few men have so little shrewdness as not to perceive, nor so much hardihood as not to be ashamed of. In truth, Toll had imbibed some of the slang, and much of the boisterousness of the bar-room; but he had not yet given such unequivocal indications of the incurableness of his infirmity, as to induce his acquaintances (who for the most part upheld him on some family consideration) to exclude him from their houses. On the contrary, a certain strain of disorderly but generous companionship, breaking out and shining above the vices to which it was akin, still recommended him to the favor of those who were unwilling to desert him as long as his case was not absolutely hopeless. The course of intemperance, however, gravitates by a fatal law downwards: it is unfortunately of the most rare occurrence, that the mind which has once been debauched by a habit of intoxication, ever regains that poise of self-respect which preserves the purity of the individual. It was easy to perceive that Hedges labored under a perpetual struggle to constrain his deportment within even the broader boundaries that limit the indulgence of the class of gentlemen.

Amidst these diversified exhibitions, Mr. Wart ate like a man with a good appetite, and gave himself no trouble to talk, except in the intervals of serving his plate; for he remarked, "that he was not accustomed to these late hours, and thought them apt to make one surcharge his stomach"; whilst the parson, who sat opposite to him, wore a perpetual smile during the repast; sometimes looking as if he intended to say something, but more generally watching every word that fell from Mr. Wart's lips.

The courses disappeared; a rich dessert came and went: the spirits of the company rose still higher. The wine, iced almost to the freezing point, moved in a busy sphere; for the intense heat of the weather gave it an additional zest. We had made the usual libations to the ladies, and exchanged the frequent healths, according to the hackneyed and unmeaning custom which prevails unquestioned, I suppose, over Christendom, when the epoch arrived at which, by the arbitrary law of the feast, the womankind are expected to withdraw; that time which, if I were a sovereign in this dinner-party realm, should be blotted from the festive calendar. I should shame me to acknowledge that there was any moment in the social day when it was unseemly for the temperate sex to look upon or listen to the lord of creation in his pastimes; but I was neither monarch nor magician, and so we were left alone to pursue unreproved the frolic current upon which we had been lifted. Before us glittered the dark sea of the table, studded over with "carracks," "argosies," and "barks" freighted with the wealth of the Azores, Spain, Portugal and France; and with the lighters by which these precious bulks were unladen, and deposited in their proper receptacles. In sooth, the wine was very good.

Almost the first words that were spoken, after we had readjusted ourselves from the stir occasioned by the retreat of the ladies, came from Mr. Tracy. He had been waiting for a suitable opportunity to acquit himself of a grave and formal duty. The occasion of the dinner, he conceived, demanded of him a peculiar compliment to the host. His strict and refined sensitiveness to the requirements of gentle breeding would have forbidden him to sleep quietly in his bed with this task unperformed; and therefore, with a tremulous and fluttered motion, like that of a young orator awe-struck at the thought of making a speech, he rose to command the attention of the table. A faint-hearted smile sat rigidly upon his visage, "like moonlight on a marble statue,"—his eye glassy, his cheek pale, and his gesture contrived to a faint and feeble counterfeit of mirth. It was evident the old gentleman was not accustomed to public speaking: and so he remarked, as he turned towards Meriwether, and continued an address somewhat in the following terms:—

"Since we have, my dear sir, so fortunately succeeded in putting an end to a vexatious question,—which, although it has resulted in throwing upon my hands a few barren and unprofitable acres, has given all the glory of the settlement to you;—(here his voice quavered considerably), for it was indubitably, my very worthy and excellent friend, at your instance and suggestion, that we struck out the happy thought of leaving it to the arbitrement of our kind friends:—and to tell the truth (at this point the old gentleman brightened up a little and looked jocular, although he still had the quaver), I don't know but I would as lief have the lawsuit as the land,—seeing that it has been the occasion of many merry meetings:—I will take upon myself to propose to this good company of neighbors and friends, that we

shall drink,—ha, ha! (continued the veteran, waving
his hand above his head, and inclining towards the
table with a gay gesticulation), that we shall drink,
gentlemen, a bumper; (here he took the decanter in
his hand, and filled his glass). "Fill your glasses all
around,—no flinching!"

"Fill up! fill up!" cried every one, anxious to
help the old gentleman out of his difficulties, "Mr.
Tracy's toast in a bumper!"

"Here," continued Mr. Tracy, holding his glass
on high with a trembling hand, "here is to our admirable host, Mister Francis Meriwether of Swallow
Barn!—a sensible and enlightened gentleman,—a
considerate landlord,—a kind neighbor, an independent, upright, sensible,—enlightened—(here he became sadly puzzled for a word, and paused for a
full half minute), reasonable defender of right and
justice; a man that is not headstrong (his perplexity
still increasing) on the score of landmarks, or indeed on any score!—I say, gentlemen, here's wishing him success in all his aims, and long life to enjoy a great many such joyous meetings as the present; besides—"

"Health of our host, and many such meetings!"
exclaimed Mr. Wart, interrupting the speaker, and
thus cutting short a toast of which it was evident
Mr. Tracy could not find the end.

"Health to our host,—joyous meetings!" cried
out half a dozen voices.

And thus relieved from his floundering progress,
the old gentleman took his seat in great glee, re-
marking to the person next to him, "that he was not
much practised in making dinner speeches, but that
he could get through very well when he was once
pushed to it."

Meriwether sat out this adulatory and unexpected
assault with painful emotions, sinking under the

weight of his natural diffidence. The rest of the
company awaited in silence, the slow, drawling and
distinct elocution of the speaker, with an amused and
ludicrous suspense, until Mr. Wart's interruption,
which was the signal for a shout of approbation;
and in the uproar that ensued, the wine was quaffed;
while Mr. Tracy chuckled at the eminent success of
his essay, and Meriwether stood bowing and blushing with the bashfulness of a girl.

* * * * * * *

As the feast drew to a close, the graver members
of the party stole off to the drawing-room, leaving
behind them that happy remnant which may be
called the sifted wheat of the stack. There sat Harvey Riggs, with his broad, laughing face mellowed
by wine and good cheer, and with an eye rendered
kindly by long shining on merry meetings, lolling
over two chairs, whilst he urged the potations like
a seasoned man, and a thirsty. And there sat Meriwether, abstemious but mirthful, with a face and
heart brimful of benevolence; beside him, the inimitable original Philly Wart. And there, too, was
seen the jolly parson, priestlike even over his cups,
filled with wonder and joy to see the tide of mirth
run so in the flood; ever and anon turning with bewildered eagerness, from one to another of his com-
potators, in doubt as to which pleased him most.
And there, too, above all, was Ned Hazard, an imp
of laughter, with his left arm dangling over the back
of his chair, and his right lifting up his replenished
glass on high, to catch its sparkling beams in the
light; his head tossed negligently back upon his
shoulder; and from his mouth forth issuing, in
elongated puff, that richer essence than incense of
Araby; his dog Wilful, too, privileged as himself,
with his faithful face recumbent between his master's knees.

JOHN ESTEN COOKE.

AN INTERIOR WITH PORTRAITS.*

From The Virginia Comedians, or Old Days in the Old Dominion. Edition of 1883.

On a splendid October afternoon, in the year of our Lord 1763, two persons who will appear frequently in this history were seated in the great dining-room of Effingham Hall.

But let us first say a few words of this old mansion. Effingham Hall was a stately edifice not far from Williamsburg, which, as everybody knows, was at that period the capital city of the colony of Virginia. The hall was constructed of elegant brick brought over from England: and from the great portico in front of the building a beautiful rolling country of hills and valleys, field and forest, spread itself pleasant before the eye, bounded far off along the circling belt of woods by the bright waters of the noble river.

Entering the large hall of the old house, you had before you, walls covered with deer's antlers, fishing-rods, and guns: portraits of cavaliers, and dames and children: even carefully painted pictures of celebrated race-horses, on whose speed and bottom many thousands of pounds had been staked and lost and won in their day and generation.

On one side of the hall a broad staircase with oaken balustrade led to the numerous apartments above: and on the opposite side, a door gave entrance into the great dining-room.

On the wall hung a dozen pictures of gay gallants, brave warriors, and dames, whose eyes outshone their diamonds:—and more than one ancestor looked grimly down, clad in a cuirass and armlet, and holding in his mailed hand the sword which had done bloody service in its time. The lady portraits, as an invariable rule, were decorated with sunset clouds of yellow lace—the bright locks were powdered, and many little black patches set off the dazzling fairness of the rounded chins. Lapdogs nestled on the satin laps; and not one of the gay dames but seemed to be smiling, with her head bent sidewise fascinatingly on the courtly or warlike figures ranged with them in a long glittering line.

These portraits are worth looking up to, but those which we promised the reader are real.

In one of the carved chairs, if anything more uncomfortable than all the rest, sits, or rather lounges, a young man of about twenty-five. He is very richly clad, and in a costume which would be apt to attract a large share of attention in our own day, when dress seems to have become a mere covering, and the prosaic tendencies of the age are to despise everything but what ministers to actual material pleasure.

The dining-room was decorated with great elegance:—the carved oak wainscot extending above the mantelpiece in an unbroken expanse of fruits and flowers, hideous laughing faces, and long foamy surges to the cornice. The furniture was in the Louis Quatorze style, which the reader is familar with, from its reproduction in our own day; and the chairs were the same low-seated affairs, with high carved backs, which are now seen. There were Chelsea figures, and a sideboard full of plate, and a Japan cabinet, and a Kidderminster carpet, and huge andirons. On the andirons crackled a few twigs lost in the great country fireplace.

The gentleman before us lives fortunately one hundred years before our day: and suffers from an

opposite tendency in costume. His head is covered
with a long flowing peruke, heavy with powder, and
the drop curls hang down on his cheeks ambrosially:
his cheeks are delicately rouged, and two patches,
arranged with matchless art, complete the distinguished *tout ensemble* of the handsome face. At the
breast, a cloud of lace reposes on the rich embroidery
of his figured satin waistcoat, reaching to his knees;
—this lace is *point de Venise** and white, that fashion having come in just one month since. The sleeves
of his rich doublet are turned back to his elbows, and
are as large as a bushel—the opening being filled
up, however, with long ruffles, which reach down
over the delicate jewelled hand. He wears silk stockings of spotless white, and his feet are cased in slippers of Spanish leather, adorned with diamond
buckles. Add velvet garters below the knee:—a little muff of leopard-skin reposing near at hand upon
a chair—not omitting a snuff-box peeping from the
pocket, and Mr. Champ Effingham, just from Oxford
and his grand tour, is before you with his various
surroundings.

He is reading the work which some time since attained to such extreme popularity, Mr. Joseph Addison's serial, "The Spectator,"—collected now for
its great merits, into bound volumes. Mr. Effingham
reads with a languid air, just as he sits, and turns
over the leaves with an ivory paper cutter, which he
brought from Venice with the plate glass yonder on
the sideboard near the silver baskets and pitchers.
This languor is too perfect to be wholly affected,
and when he yawns, as he does frequently, Mr. Effingham applies himself to that task very earnestly.

In one of these paroxysms of weariness the volume slips from his hand to the floor.

"My book," he says to a negro boy, who had just

---

* *I. e.* Venetian point lace.

brought in some dishes. The boy hastens respect-
fully to obey—crossing the whole width of the room
for that purpose. Mr. Effingham then continues
reading.

Now for the other occupant of the apartment. She
sits near the open window, looking out upon the
lawn and breathing the pure delicious air of October as she works. She is clad in the usual child's
costume of the period (she is only eleven or twelve),
namely, a sort of half coat, half frock, reaching
scarcely below the knees; an embroidered under-
vest; scarlet silk stockings with golden clocks, and
little rosetted shoes with high red heels. Her hair
is unpowdered, and hangs in curls upon her neck and
bare shoulders. Her little fingers are busily at work
upon a piece of embroidery which represents or is
to represent a white water dog upon an intensely
emerald background, and she addresses herself to
this occupation with a business air which is irresistibly amusing, and no less pleasant to behold.
There is about the child, in her movements, attitude,
expression, everything, a freshness and innocence
which is only possessed by children. This is Miss
Kate Effingham, whose parents died in her infancy,
for which reason the little sunbeam was taken by
the squire, her father's brother.

Kate seems delighted with the progress she has
made in delineating Carlo, as she calls him, and
pauses a moment to survey her brilliant handiwork.
She then opens her ivory decorated work-box to se-
lect another shade of silk, holding it on her lap by
the low-silled open window.

But disastrous event! Just as she had found
what she wanted, just as she had procured the exact
shade for Carlo's ears, just as she closed the pretty
box, full of all manner of little elegant instruments
of needle-work—she heard an impatient exclama-

tion of weariness and disdain, something fluttered
through the air, and this something striking the
handsome box delicately balanced on Kate's knee,
precipitated it, with its whole contents, through the
window to the lawn beneath.

The explanation of this sudden event is, that Mr.
Effingham has become tired of ''The Spectator,''
hurled it sidewise .from him without looking; and
thus the volume has, after its habit, produced a decided sensation, throwing the work-box upon the
lawn, and Kate into utter despair.

THE OLD THEATRE NEAR THE CAPITOL.*

From the Same.

THE ''old Theatre near the Capitol,'' discoursed
of in the manifesto issued by Mr. Manager Hallam,
was so far *old* that the walls were well browned by
time, and the shutters to the windows of a pleasant
neutral tint between rust and dust color. The building had no doubt been used for the present purpose
in bygone times, before the days of the *Virginia Ga-
zette,* which is our authority for many of the facts
here stated, and in relation to the ''Virginia Company of Comedians''—but of the former companies
of ''players,'' as my lord Hamlet calls them, and
their successes or misfortunes, printed words tell
us nothing, as far as the researches of the present
chronicle extend. That there had been such companies before, however, we repeat, there is some
reason to believe; else why that addition ''old'' applied to the ''Theatre near the Capitol''? The question is submitted to the future social historians of
the Old Dominion.

Within, the playhouse presented a somewhat more attractive appearance. There was "box," "pit," and "gallery," as in our own day; and the relative prices were arranged in much the same manner. The common mortals—gentlemen and ladies—were forced to occupy the boxes raised slightly above the level of the stage, and hemmed in by velvet-cushioned railings,—in front, a flower-decorated panel, extending all around the house,—and for this position were moreover compelled to pay an admission fee of seven shillings and sixpence. The demigods—so to speak—occupied a more eligible position in the "pit," from which they could procure a highly excellent view of the actors' feet and ankles, just on a level with their noses: to conciliate the demigods, this superior advantage had been offered, and the price for them was, further still, reduced to five shillings. But "the gods" in truth were the real favorites of the manager. To attract them, he arranged the high upper "gallery"—and left it untouched, unincumbered by railing or velvet cushions, or any other device: all was free space, and liberal as the air: there were no troublesome seats for "the gods," and three shillings and nine pence was all that the managers would demand. The honor of their presence was enough.

From the boxes a stairway led down to the stage, and some rude scenes, visible at the edges of the green curtain, completed the outline.

When Mr. Lee and his daughters entered the box which had been reserved for them, next to the stage, the house was nearly full, and the neatness of the edifice was lost sight of in the sea of brilliant ladies' faces, and strong forms of cavaliers, which extended —like a line of glistening foam—around the semicircle of the boxes. The pit was occupied by well-dressed men of the lower class, as the times had it,

and from the gallery proceeded hoarse murmurs and
the unforgotten slang of London.

Many smiles and bows were interchanged between
the parties in the different boxes; and the young
gallants, following the fashion of the day, gathered
at each end of the stage, and often walked across, to
exchange some polite speech with the smiling dames
in the boxes nearest.

Mr. Champ Effingham was, upon the whole, much
the most notable fop present; and his elegant, languid, *petit maitre* air, as he strolled across the stage,
attracted many remarks, not invariably favorable.
It was observed, however, that when the Virginia-
bred youths, with honest plainness, called him "ridiculous," the young ladies, their companions, took
Mr. Effingham's part, and defended him with great
enthusiasm. Only when they returned home, Mr.
Effingham was more unmercifully criticised than he
would otherwise have been.

A little bell rang, and the orchestra, represented
by three or four foreign-looking gentlemen, bearded
and moustached, entered with trumpet and violin.
The trumpets made the roof shake, indifferently, in
honor of the Prince of Morocco, or King Richard, or
any other worthy whose entrance was marked in the
play-book "with a flourish." But before the orchestra ravished the ears of everyone, the manager came
forward, in the costume of Bassanio, and made a
low bow. Mr. Hallam was a fat little man, of fifty
or fifty-five, with a rubicund and somewhat sensual
face, and he expressed extraordinary delight at
meeting so many of the "noble aristocracy of the
great and noble colony of Virginia," assembled to
witness his very humble representation. It would
be the chief end and sole ambition of his life, he said,
to please the gentry, who so kindly patronized their
servants—himself and his associates—and then the

smiling worthy concluded by bowing lower than before. Much applause from the pit and gallery, and
murmurs of approbation from the well-bred boxes,
greeted his address, and, the orchestra having
struck up, the curtain slowly rolled aloft. The young
gallants scattered to the corners of the stage—seating themselves on stools or chairs, or standing, and
the "Merchant of Venice" commenced. *Bassanio*
having assumed a dignified and lofty port, criticised
Gratanio with courteous and lordly wit; his friend
Antonio offered him his fortune with grand magnan-
imity, in a loud singing voice, worthy the utmost
commendation, and the first act proceeded on its way
in triumph.

AUGUSTUS BALDWIN LONGSTREET.

GEORGIA THEATRICALS.

From Georgia Scenes, Characters, Incidents, etc., in the First Half Century of the Republic. Second Edition (1840).

IF my memory fail me not, the 10th of June, 1809, found me, at about eleven o'clock in the forenoon, ascending a long and gentle slope in what was called "the Dark Corner" of Lincoln. I believe it took its name from the moral darkness which reigned over that portion of the county at the time of which I am speaking. If, in this point of view, it was but a shade darker than the rest of the county, it was inconceivably dark. If any man can name a trick of sin which had not been committed at the time of which I am speaking, in the very focus of the county's illumination (Lincolnton), he must himself be the most inventive of the tricky, and the very Judas of sinners. Since that time, however (all humor aside), Lincoln has become a living proof "that light shineth in darkness." Could I venture to mingle the solemn with the ludicrous, even for the purposes of honorable contrast, I could adduce from this county instances of the most numerous and wonderful transitions from vice and folly to virtue and holiness which have ever, perhaps, been witnessed since the days of the apostolic ministry. So much, lest it should be thought by some that what I am about to relate was characteristic of the county in which it occurred.

Whatever may be said of the *moral* condition of the Dark Corner at the time just mentioned, its *natural* condition was anything but dark. It smiled in all the charms of spring; and spring borrowed a new charm from its undulating grounds, its luxuri-

167

ant woodlands, its sportive streams, its vocal birds, and its blushing flowers.

Rapt with the enchantment of the season and the scenery around me, I was slowly rising the slope, when I was startled by loud, profane, and boisterous voices, which seemed to proceed from a thick covert of undergrowth about two hundred yards in advance of me, and about one hundred to the right of my road.

"You kin—kin you?"

"Yes, I kin, and I'm able to do it! Boo-oo-oo! Oh wake snakes and walk your chalks! Brimstone and fire! Don't hold me, Nick Stoval! The fight's made up, and let's go to it. My soul, if I don't jump down his throat, and gallop every chitterling out of him before you can say 'quit'!"

"Now, Nick, don't hold him! Jist let the wild-cat come, and I'll tame him. Ned'll see me a fair fight; won't you, Ned?"

"Oh, yes; I'll see you a fair fight, blast my old shoes if I don't!"

"That's sufficient, as Tom Haynes said when he saw the elephant. Now let him come."

Thus they went on, with countless oaths interspersed, which I dare not even hint at, and with much that I could not distinctly hear.

In mercy's name, thought I, what band of ruffians has selected this holy season and this heavenly retreat for such Pandemonium riots? I quickened my gait, and had come nearly opposite to the trick grove whence the noise proceeded, when my eye caught at intervals, through the foliage of the dwarf oaks and hickories which intervened, glimpses of a man or men, who seemed to be in a violent struggle; and I could occasionally catch those deep-drawn, emphatic oaths which men in conflict utter when they deal blows. I dismounted, and hurried to the

spot with all speed. I had overcome about half the
space which separated it from me, when I saw the
combatants come to the ground, and after a short
struggle I saw the uppermost one (for I could not
see the other) make a heavy plunge with both his
thumbs, and at the same instant heard a cry in the
accent of keenest torture, "Nuff! My eye's out!"

I was so completely horror-struck that I stood
transfixed for a moment to the spot where the cry
met me. The accomplices in the hellish deed which
had been perpetrated had all fled at my approach;
at least I supposed so, for they were not to be seen.

"Now, blast your corn-shuckling soul," said the
victor (a youth about eighteen years old) as he rose
from the ground, " come cutt'n your shines 'bout
me agin, next time I come to the Courthouse, will
you! Get your owl-eye in agin, if you can!"

At this moment he saw me for the first time. He
looked excessively embarrassed, and was moving off,
when I called to him, in a tone emboldened by the
sacredness of my office and the iniquity of his crime,
"Come back, you brute, and assist me in relieving
your fellow-mortal, whom you have ruined forever!"

My rudeness subdued his embarrassment in an
instant; and, with a taunting curl of the nose, he
replied, "You needn't kick before you're spurr'd.
There ain't nobody there, nor hain't been, nother. I
was jist seein' how I could 'a' *fout*." So saying, he
bounded to his plow, which stood in the corner of
the fence, about fifty yards beyond the battle-ground.

And would you believe it, gentle reader, his report was true! All that I had heard and seen was
nothing more nor less than a Lincoln rehearsal, in
which the youth who had just left me had played all
the parts of all the characters in a Courthouse fight.

I went to the ground from which he had arisen,
and there were the prints of his two thumbs, plunged

up to the balls in the mellow earth, about the distance of a man's eyes apart; and the ground around was broken up as if two stags had been engaged upon it.

THE HORSE-SWAP.

During the session of the Supreme Court in the village of ——, about three weeks ago, when a number of people were collected in the principal street of the village, I observed a young man riding up and down the street, as I supposed, in a violent passion. He galloped this way, then that, and then the other; spurred his horse to one group of citizens, then to another; then dashed off at half speed, as if fleeing from danger; and, suddenly checking his horse, returned first in a pace, then in a trot, and then in a canter. While he was performing these various evolutions, he cursed, swore, whooped, screamed, and tossed himself in every attitude which man could assume on horseback. In short, he *cavorted* most magnanimously (a term which, in our tongue, expresses all that I have described, and a little more), and seemed to be setting all creation at defiance. As I like to see all that is passing, I determined to take a position a little nearer to him, and to ascertain, if possible, what it was that affected him so sensibly. Accordingly, I approached a crowd before which he had stopped for a moment, and examined it with the strictest scrutiny. But I could see nothing in it that seemed to have anything to do with the cavorter. Every man appeared to be in good humor, and all minding their own business. Not one so much as noticed the principal figure. Still he went on. After a semicolon pause, which my appearance seemed to produce (for he eyed me closely as I approached), he fetched a whoop, and swore that "he could out-swap any live man, woman, or child that ever walked these hills, or that ever straddled horseflesh since the days of old daddy Adam." "Stranger," said he to me, "did you ever see the *Yellow Blossom* from Jasper?"

"No," said I, "but I have often heard of him."

"I'm the boy," continued he; "perhaps a *leetle* —jist a *leetle*—of the best man at a horse-swap that ever trod shoe-leather."

I began to feel my situation a little awkward, when I was relieved by a man somewhat advanced in years, who stepped up and began to survey the "Yellow Blossom's" horse with much apparent interest. This drew the rider's attention, and he turned the conversation from me to the stranger.

"Well, my old coon," said he, "do you want to swap *hosses?*"

"Why, I don't know," replied the stranger. "I believe I've got a beast I'd trade with you for that one, if you like him."

"Well, fetch up your nag, my old cock; you're jist the lark I wanted to get hold of. I am perhaps a *leetle*—jist a *leetle*—of the best man at a horse-swap that ever stole cracklins out of his mammy's fat gourd. Where's your hoss?"

"I'll bring him presently; but I want to examine your horse a little."

"Oh, look at him!" said the Blossom, alighting and hitting him a cut; "look at him! He's the best piece of hossflesh in the thirteen united univarsal worlds. There's no sort o' mistake in little Bullet. He can pick up miles on his feet, and fling 'em behind him as fast as the next man's hoss, I don't care where he comes from. And he can keep at it as long as the sun can shine without resting."

During this harangue, little Bullet looked as if he understood it all, believed it, and was ready at any

moment to verify it. He was a horse of goodly
countenance, rather expressive of vigilance than fire;
though an unnatural appearance of fierceness was
thrown into it by the loss of his ears, which had been
cropped pretty close to his head. Nature had done
but little for Bullet's head and neck; but he managed, in a great measure, to hide their defects by
bowing perpetually. He had obviously suffered se-
verely for corn, but if his ribs and hip-bones had
not disclosed the fact, *he* never would have done it;
for he was in all respects as cheerful and happy as
if he commanded all the corn-cribs and fodder-stacks
in Georgia. His height was about twelve hands;
but as his shape partook somewhat of that of the
giraffe, his haunches stood much lower. They were
short, straight, peaker, and concave. Bullet's tail,
however, made amends for all his defects. All that
the artist could do to beautify it had been done; and
all that horse could do to compliment the artist Bullet did. His tail was nicked in superior style, and exhibited the line of beauty in so many directions that
it could not fail to hit the most fastidious taste in
some of them. From the root it dropped into a
graceful festoon; then rose in a handsome curve;
then resumed its first direction; and then mounted
suddenly upward like a cypress knee, to a perpendic-
ular of about two and a half inches. The whole had
a careless and bewitching inclination to the right.
Bullet obviously knew where his beauty lay, and
took all occasions to display it to the best advantage.
If a stick cracked, or if any one moved suddenly
about him, or coughed, or hawked, or spake a little
louder than common, up went Bullet's tail like lightning; and if the *going up* did not please, the *coming
down* must of necessity, for it was as different from
the other movement as was its direction. The first
was a bold and rapid flight upward, usually to an

angle of forty-five degrees. In this position he kept
his interesting appendage until he satisfied himself
that nothing in particular was to be done; when he
commenced dropping it by half inches, in second
beats, then in triple times, then faster and shorter,
and faster and shorter still, until it finally died away
imperceptibly into its natural position. If I might
compare sights to sound, I should say its *settling*
was more like the note of a locust than anything
else in nature.

Either from native sprightliness of disposition,
from uncontrollable activity, or from an unconquer-
able habit of removing flies by the stamping of the
feet, Bullet never stood still; but always kept up a
gentle fly-scaring movement of his limbs, which was
peculiarly interesting.

"I tell you, man," proceeded the Yellow Blossom,
"he's the best live hoss that ever trod the grit of
Georgia. Bob Smart knows the hoss. Come here,
Bob, and mount this hoss, and show Bullet's motions." Here Bullet bristled up, and looked as if he
had been hunting for Bob all day long, and had just
found him. Bob sprang on his back. "Boo-oo-oo!"
said Bob, with a fluttering noise of the lips; and
away went Bullet, as if in a quarter race, with all
his beauties spread in handsome style.

"Now fetch him back," said Blossom. Bullet
turned, and came in pretty much as he went out.

"Now trot him by." Bullet reduced his tail to
"*customary*," sidled to the right and left airily, and
exhibited at least three varieties of trot in the short
space of fifty yards.

"Make him pace!" Bob commenced twitching
the bridle, and kicking at the same time. These
inconsistent movements obviously (and most naturally) disconcerted Bullet; for it was impossible for
him to learn from them whether he was to proceed

or stand still. He started to trot, and was told that
wouldn't do. He attempted a canter, and was
checked again. He stopped, and was urged to go
on. Bullet now rushed into the wide field of experiment, and struck out a gait of his own, that completely turned the tables upon his rider, and certainly deserved a patent. It seemed to have derived its
elements from the jig, the minuet, and the cotillion.
If it was not a pace, it certainly had *pace* in it, and
no man would venture to call it anything else; so it
passed off to the satisfaction of the owner.

"Walk him!" Bullet was now at home again,
and he walked as if money was staked on him.

The stranger,—whose name, I afterward learned,
was Peter Ketch,—having examined Bullet to his
heart's content, ordered his son Neddy to go and
bring up Kit. Neddy soon appeared upon Kit,
a well-formed sorrel of the middle size, and in good
order. His *tout ensemble* threw Bullet entirely in
the shade, though a glance was sufficient to satisfy
any one that Bullet had the decided advantage of
him in point of intellect.

"Why, man," said Blossom, "do you bring such
a hoss as that to trade for Bullet? Oh, I see you're
no notion of trading."

"Ride him off, Neddy!" said Peter. Kit put off
at a handsome lope.

"Trot him back!" Kit came in at a long, sweeping trot, and stopped suddenly at the crowd.

"Well," said Blossom, "let me look at him; may
be he'll do to plow."

"Examine him!" said Peter, taking hold of the
bridle close to the mouth; "he's nothing but a
tacky. He ain't as *pretty* a horse as Bullet, I know;
but he'll do. Start 'em together for a hundred and
fifty *mile,* and if Kit ain't twenty mile ahead of him
at the coming out, any man may take Kit for noth-

ing. But he's a monstrous mean horse, gentlemen; any man may see that. He's the scariest horse, too, you ever saw. He won't do to hunt on, nohow. Stranger, will you let Neddy have your rifle to shoot off him? Lay the rifle between his ears, Neddy, and shoot at the blaze in that stump. Tell me when his head is high enough.

Ned fired and hit the blaze; and Kit did not move a hair's breadth.

"Neddy, take a couple of sticks, and beat on that hogshead at Kit's tail."

Ned made a tremendous rattling, at which Bullet took fright, broke his bridle, and dashed off in grand style, and would have stopped all further negotiations by going home in disgust, had not a traveler arrested him and brought him back; but Kit did not move.

"I tell you, gentlemen," continued Peter, "he's the scariest horse you ever saw. He ain't as gentle as Bullet, but he won't do any harm if you watch him. Shall I put him in a cart, gig, or wagon for you, stranger? He'll cut the same capers there he does here. He's a monstrous mean horse."

During all this time Blossom was examining him with the nicest scrutiny. Having examined his frame and limbs, he now looked at his eyes.

"He's got a curious look out of his eyes," said Blossom.

"Oh, yes, sir," said Peter; "just as blind as a bat. Blind horses always have clear eyes. Make a motion at his eyes, if you please, sir?"

Blossom did so, and Kit threw up his head rather as if something pricked him under the chin than as if fearing a blow. Blossom repeated the experiment, and Kit jerked back in considerable astonishment.

"Stone blind, you see, gentlemen," proceeded

Peter; "but he's just as good to travel of a dark night as if he had eyes."

"Blame my buttons," said Blossom, "if I like them eyes."

"No," said Peter, "nor I neither. I'd rather have 'em made of diamonds; but they'll do, if they don't show as much white as Bullet's."

"Well," said Blossom, "make a pass at me."

"No," said Peter. "You made the banter; now make your pass."

"Well, I'm never afraid to price my hosses. You must give me twenty-five dollars boot."

"Oh, certainly; say fifty, and my saddle and bridle in. Here, Neddy, my son, take away daddy's horse."

"Well," said Blossom, "I've made my pass; now you make yours "

"I'm for short talk in a horse-swap, and therefore always tell a gentleman at once what I mean to do. You must give me ten dollars."

Blossom swore absolutely, roundly, and profanely, that he never would give boot.

"Well," said Peter, "I didn't care about trading; but you cut such high shines that I thought I'd like to back you out, and I've done it. Gentlemen, you see I've brought him to a back."

"Come, old man," said Blossom, "I've been joking with you. I begin to think you do want to trade; therefore, give me five dollars, and take Bullet. I'd rather lose ten dollars any time than not make a trade, though I hate to fling away a good hoss."

"Well," said Peter, "I'll be as clever as you are. Just put the five dollars on Bullet's back, and hand him over; it's a trade."

Blossom swore again, as roundly as before, that he would not give boot; and, said he, "Bullet wouldn't hold five dollars on his back, nohow. But, as I bantered you, if you say an even swap, here's at you."

"I told you," said Peter, "I'd be as clever as you. Therefore, here goes two dollars more, just for trade' sake. Give me three dollars, and it's a bargain."

Blossom repeated his former assertion; and here the parties stood for a long time, and the by-standers (for many were now collected) began to taunt both parties. After some time, however, it was pretty unanimously decided that the old man had backed Blossom out.

At length Blossom swore he "never would be backed out for three dollars after bantering a man;" and, accordingly, they closed the trade.

"Now," said Blossom, as he handed Peter the three dollars, "I'm a man that, when he makes a bad trade, makes the most of it until he can make a better. I'm for no rues and after-claps."

"That's just my way," said Peter. "I never goes to law to mend my bargains."

"Ah, you're the kind of boy I love to trade with. Here's your hoss, old man. Take the saddle and bridle off him, and I'll strip yours; but lift up the blanket easy from Bullet's back, for he's a mighty tender-backed hoss."

The old man removed the saddle, but the blanket stuck fast. He attempted to raise it, and Bullet bowed himself, switched his tail, danced a little, and gave signs of biting.

"Don't hurt him, old man," said Blossom, archly; "take it off easy. I am, perhaps, a lettle of the best man at a horse-swap that ever catched a coon."

Peter continued to pull at the blanket more and more roughly, and Bullet became more and more *cavortish;* insomuch that, when the blanket came off, he had reached the *kicking* point in good earnest.

The removal of the blanket disclosed a sore on Bullet's backbone that seemed to have defied all medical skill. It measured six full inches in length and four in breadth, and had as many features as Bullet had motions. My heart sickened at the sight; and I felt that the brute who had been riding him in that situation deserved the halter.

The prevailing feeling, however, was that of mirth. The laugh became loud and general at the old man's expense, and rustic witticisms were liberally bestowed upon him and his late purchase. These Blossom continued to provide by various remarks. He asked the old man "if he thought Bullet would let five dollars lies on his back." He declared most seriously that he had owned that horse three months, and had never discovered before that he had a sore back, "or he never should have thought of trading him," etc., etc.

The old man bore it all with the most philosophic composure. He evinced no astonishment at his late discovery, and made no replies. But his son Neddy had not disciplined his feelings quite so well. His eyes opened wider and wider from the first to the last pull of the blanket; and, when the whole sore burst upon his view, astonishment and fright seemed to contend for the mastery of his countenance. As the blanket disappeared, he stuck his hands in his breeches pockets, heaved a deep sigh, and lapsed into a profound reverie, from which he was only roused by the cuts at his father. He bore them as long as he could; and, when he could contain himself no longer, he began, with a certain wildness of expression which gave a peculiar interest to what he uttered: "His back 's mighty bad off; but dod trot my soul if he's put it to daddy as bad as he thinks he has, for old Kit's both blind and *deef,* I'll be dod drot if he eint.''

"The devil he is!" said Blossom.

"Yes, dod drot my soul if he *eint.* You walk him, and see if he eint. His eyes don't look like it; but he'd *jist as leve go agin* the house with you, or in a ditch, as anyhow. Now you go try him.'' The laugh was now turned on Blossom, and many rushed to test the fidelity of the little boy's report. A few experiments established its truth beyond controversy.

"Neddy," said the old man, "you ought n't to try and make people discontented with their things. Stranger, don't mind what the little boy says. If you can only get Kit rid of them little failings, you'll find him all sorts of a horse. You are a *leetle* the best man at a horse-swap that ever I got hold of; but don't fool away Kit. Come, Neddy, my son, let's be moving; the stranger seems to be getting snappish.''

WILLIAM TAPPAN THOMPSON.

A NOVEL COURTSHIP.

From Major Jones's Courtship: Detailed with Other Scenes, Incidents, and Adventures, in a Series of Letters, by Himself. Second Edition (1844).

PINEVILLE, *December* 27, 1842.

To MR. THOMPSON: *Dear Sir*—Crismus is over, and the thing is ded. You know I told you in my last letter I was gwine to bring Miss Mary up to the chalk a Crismus. Well, I done it, slick as a whistle, though it come mighty nigh bein a serious undertakin. But I'll tell you all about the whole circumstance.

The fact is, I's made my mind up more'n twenty times to jest go and come rite out with the whole bisness; but whenever I got whar she was, and whenever she looked at me with her witchin eyes, and kind o' blushed at me, I always felt sort o' skeered and fainty, and all what I made up to tell her was forgot, so I couldn't think of it to save me. But you's a married man, Mr. Thompson, so I couldn't tell you nothin about popin the question, as they call it. It's a mighty grate favor to ax of a rite pretty gall, and to people as ain't used to it, goes monstrous hard, don't it? They say widders don't mind it no more'n nothin. But I'm makin a trangression, as the preacher ses.

Crismus eve I put on my new suit, and shaved my face as slick as a smoothin iron, and after tea went over to old Miss Stallinses. As soon as I went into the parler whar they was all settin round the fire, Miss Carline and Miss Kesiah both laughed rite out.

"There, there," ses they, "I told you so, I knew it would be Joseph."

180

"What's I done, Miss Carline?" ses I.

"You come under little sister's chicken bone, and I do believe she knew you was comin when she put it over the dore."

"No I didn't—I didn't no such thing, now," ses Miss Mary, and her face blushed red all over.

"Oh, you needn't deny it," ses Miss Kesiah; "you b'long to Joseph now, jest as sure as ther's any charm in chicken bones."

I knowd that was a first rate chance to say something, but the dear little creater looked so sorry and kep blushin so, I couldn't say nothin zactly to the pint, so I tuck a chair and reached up and tuck down the bone and put it in my pocket.

"What are you gwine to do with that old bone now, Majer?" ses Miss Mary.

"I'm gwine to keep it as long as I live," ses I, "as a Crismus present from the handsomest gall in Georgia."

When I sed that, she blushed worse and worse.

"Ain't you shamed, Majer?" ses she.

"Now you ought to give *her* a Crismus gife, Joseph, to keep all *her* life," sed Miss Carline.

"Ah," ses old Miss Stallins, "when I was a gall we used to hang up our stockins——"

"Why, mother!" ses all of 'em, "to say stockins rite afore——"

Then I felt a little streaked too, cause they was all blushin as hard as they could.

"Highty-tity!" ses the old lady—"what monstrous 'finement. I'd like to know what harm ther is in stockins. People nowadays is gitten so mealy-mouthed they can't call nothing by its rite name, and I don't see as they's any better than the old-time people was. When I was a gall like you, child, I used to hang up my stockins and git 'em full of presents."

The galls kep laughin.

"Never mind," ses Miss Mary, "Majer's got to give me a Crismus gift,—won't you, Majer?"

"Oh, yes," ses I; "you know I promised you one."

"But I didn't mean *that*," ses she.

"I've got one for you, what I want you to keep all your life, but it would take a two-bushel bag to hold it," ses I.

"Oh, that's the kind," ses she.

"But will you keep it as long as you live?" ses I.

"Certainly I will, Majer."

"Monstrous 'finement nowadays — old people don't know nothin bout perliteness," said old Miss Stallins, jest gwine to sleep with her nittin in her hand.

"Now you hear that, Miss Carline," ses I. "She ses she'll keep it all her life."

"Yes, I will," ses Miss Mary—"but what is it?"

"Never mind," ses I, "you hang up a bag big enuff to hold it and you'll find out what it is, when you see it in the mornin."

Miss Carline winked at Miss Kesiah, and then whispered to her—then they both laughed and looked at me as mischievous as they could. They spicioned something.

"You'll be sure to give it to me now, if I hang up a bag?" ses Miss Mary.

"And promise to keep it," ses I.

"Well, I will, cause I know that you wouldn't give me nothin that wasn't worth keepin."

They all agreed they would hang up a bag for me to put Miss Mary's Crismus present in, in the back porch; and bout nine o'clock I told 'em good evenin and went home.

I sot up till midnight, and when they was all gone to bed I went softly into the back gate, and went up to the porch, and thar, shore enuff, was a grate big

meal-bag hangin to the jice. It was monstrous un-
handy to git to it, but I was tarmined not to back out.
So I sot some chairs on top of a bench and got hold
of the rope and let myself into the bag; but jest as
I was gittin in, the bag swung agin the chairs, and
down they went with a terrible racket. But nobody
didn't wake up but old Miss Stallinses grate big cur
dog, and here he cum rippin and tearing through the
yard like rath, and round and round he went tryin
to find what was the matter. I sot down in the bag
and didn't breathe louder nor a kitten, for fear he'd
find me out, and after a while he quit barkin. The
wind begun to blow bominable cold, and the old bag
kep turning round and swinging so it made me sea-
sick as the mischief. I was fraid to move for fear
the rope would break and let me fall, and thar I
sot with my teeth rattlin like I had a ager. It
seemed like it would never come daylight, and I do
blieve if I didn't love Miss Mary so powerful I
would froze to death; for my hart was the only spot
that felt warm, and it didn't beat more'n two licks a
minit, only when I thought how she would be sprised
in the mornin, and then it went in a canter. Bimeby
the cussed old dog come up on the porch and began
to smell about the bag, and then he barked like he
thought he'd treed something. "Bow! wow! wow!"
ses he. Then he'd smell agin, and try to git up to
the bag. "Git out!" ses I, very low, for fear they
would hear me. "Bow! wow! wow!" ses he. "Be
gone! you bominable fool!" ses I, and I felt all over
in spots, for I spected every minit he'd nip me, and
what made it worse, I didn't know wharabouts he'd
take hold. "Bow! wow! wow!" Then I tried coax-
in—"Come here, good feller," ses I, and whistled
a little to him, but it wasn't no use. Thar he stood
and kep up his eternal whinin and barkin, all night.
I couldn't tell when daylight was breakin, only by the

chickens crowin, and I was monstrous glad to hear 'em, for if I'd had to stay thar one hour more, I don't believe I'd ever got out of that bag alive.

Old Miss Stallins come out fust, and as soon as she saw the bag; ses she:

"What upon yeath has Joseph went and put in that bag for Mary? I'll lay it's a yearlin or some live animal, or Bruin wouldn't bark at it so."

She went in to call the galls, and I sot thar, shiverin all over so I couldn't hardly speak if I tried to, —but I didn't say nothin. Bimeby they all come runnin out.

"My Lord, what is it?" ses Miss Mary.

"Oh, it's alive!" ses Miss Kesiah. "I seed it move."

"Call Cato, and make him cut the rope," ses Miss Carline, "and let's see what it is. Come here, Cato, and git this bag down."

"Don't hurt it for the world," ses Miss Mary.

Cato untied the rope that was round the jice, and let the bag down easy on the floor, and I tumbled out all covered with corn-meal, from head to foot.

"Goodness gracious!" ses Miss Mary, "if it ain't the Majer himself!"

"Yes," ses I, "and you know you promised to keep my Crismus present as long as you lived."

The galls laughed themselves almost to deth, and went to brushin off the meal as fast as they could, sayin they was gwine to hang that bag up every Crismus till they got husbands too. Miss Mary— bless her bright eyes—she blushed as butiful as a morninglory, and sed she's stick to her word. She was rite out of bed, and her hair wasn't komed, and her dress wasn't fix't at all, but the way she looked pretty was rale distractin. I do blieve if I was froze stiff, one look at her charmin face, as she stood lookin down to the floor with her rogish eyes, and her bright curls fallin all over her snowy neck, would fotch'd me too. I tell you what, it was worth hangin in a meal bag from one Crismus to another to feel as happy as I have ever sense.

I went home after we had the laugh out, and set by the fire till I got thawed. In the forenoon all the Stallinses come over to our house and we had one of the greatest Crismus dinners that ever was seed in Georgia, and I don't blieve a happier company ever sot down to the same table. Old Miss Stallins and mother settled the match, and talked over everything that ever happened in ther families, and laughed at me and Mary, and cried bout ther ded husbands, cause they wasn't alive to see ther children married.

It's all settled now, 'cept we hain't sot the weddin day. I'd like to have it all over at once, but young galls always like to be engaged a while, you know, so I spose I must wait a month or so. Mary (she ses I mustn't call her Miss Mary now) has been a good deal of trouble and botheration to me; but if you could see her you wouldn't think I ought to grudge a little sufferin to git sich a sweet little wife.

You must come to the weddin if you possibly kin. I'll let you know when. No more from

Your frend, till deth,

JOS. JONES.

JOHNSON JONES HOOPER.

CAPTAIN SUGGS ATTENDS A CAMP-MEETING.

From Some Adventures of Captain Simon Suggs, Late of the Talla-
poosa Volunteers (1846). New Edition, with Alabama
Sketches (1881).

CAPTAIN SUGGS found himself as poor at the conclusion of the Creek war as he had been at its commencement. Although no "arbitrary," "despotic,"
"corrupt," and "unprincipled" judge had fined him
a thousand dollars for his proclamation of martial
law at Fort Suggs, or the enforcement of its rules in
the case of Mrs. Haycock, yet somehow—the thing is
alike inexplicable to him and to us — the money
which he had contrived, by various shifts, to obtain
melted away, and was gone forever. To a man like
the Captain, of intense domestic affections, this state
of destitution was most distressing. "He could
stand it himself,—did n't care a d—n for it, no
way," he observed; "but the woman and the children,—*that* bothered him!"

As he sat, one day, ruminating upon the unpleasant condition of his "financial concerns," Mrs.
Suggs informed him that "the sugar and coffee was
nigh about out," and that there were not "a dozen
j'ints and middlins, *all put together,* in the smoke-
house." Suggs bounced up on the instant, exclaim-
ing, "D—n it! *somebody* must suffer!" But whether
this remark was intended to convey the idea that he
and his family were about to experience the want of
the necessaries of life, or that some other and as
yet unknown individual should "suffer" to prevent
that prospective exigency, must be left to the com-
mentators, if perchance any of that ingenious class
of persons should hereafter see proper to write notes

for this history. It is enough for us that we give all
the facts in this connection, so that ignorance of the
subsequent conduct of Captain Suggs may not lead
to an erroneous judgment in respect to his words.

Having uttered the exclamation we have repeated,
and perhaps hurriedly walked once or twice across
the room, Captain Suggs drew on his famous old
green-blanket overcoat, and ordered his horse, and
within five minutes was on his way to a camp-meeting, then in full blast on Sandy Creek, twenty miles
distant, where he hoped to find amusement, at least.
When he arrived there, he found the hollow square
of the encampment filled with people, listening to
the mid-day sermon and its dozen accompanying
"exhortations." A half dozen preachers were dispensing the word; the one in the pulpit a meek-
faced old man, of great simplicity and benevolence.
His voice was weak and cracked, notwithstanding
which, however, he contrived to make himself heard
occasionally, above the din of the exhorting, the
singing, and the shouting which were going on
around him. The rest were walking to and fro
(engaged in the other exercises we have indicated)
among the "mourners,"—a host of whom occupied
the seat set apart for their especial use,—or made
personal appeals to the mere spectators. The excitement was intense. Men and women rolled about
on the ground, or lay sobbing or shouting in promis-
cuous heaps. More than all, the negroes sang and
screamed and prayed. Several, under the influence
of what is technically called "the jerks," were plunging and pitching about with convulsive energy. The
great object of all seemed to be to see who could
make the greatest noise:

> "And each, for madness ruled the hour,
> Would try his own expressive power."

"Bless my poor old soul!" screamed the preacher

in the pulpit; "ef yonder ain't a squad in that corner that we ain't got one outen yet! It'll never do,"—raising his voice,—"you must come outen that! Brother Fant, fetch up that youngster in the blue coat! I see the Lord's a-workin' upon him! Fetch him along—glory—yes!—hold to him!"

"Keep the thing warm!" roared a sensual-seeming man, of stout mould and florid countenance, who was exhorting among a bevy of young women, upon whom he was lavishing caresses. "Keep the thing warm, breethring! Come to the Lord, honey!" he added, as he vigorously hugged one of the damsels he sought to save.

"Oh, I've got him!" said another in exulting tones, as he led up a gawky youth among the mourners,—"I've got him—he tried to git off, but—ha! Lord!"—shaking his head, as much as to say, it took a smart fellow to escape him—"ha! Lord!"— and he wiped the perspiration from his face with one hand, and with the other patted his neophyte on the shoulder—"he couldn't do it! No! Then he tried to argy wi' me—but bless the Lord! he couldn't do that nother! Ha! Lord! I tuk him, fust in the Old Testament—bless the Lord!—and I argyed him all thro' Kings—then I throwed him into Proverbs,—and from that, here we had it up and down, kleer down to the New Testament; and then I began to see it work him!—then we got into Matthy, and from Matthy right straight along to Acts; and *thar* I throwed him! Y-e-s L-o-r-d!" assuming the nasal twang and high pitch which are, in some parts, considered the perfection of rhetorical art, "Y-e-s L-o-r-d! and h-e-r-e he is! Now g-i-t down thar," addressing the subject, "and s-e-e ef the Lo-r-d won't do somethin' f-o-r you!" Having thus deposited his charge among the mourners, he started out summarily to convert another soul!

"Gl-o-*ree!*" yelled a huge, greasy negro woman, as in a fit of the jerks she threw herself convulsively from her feet, and fell, "like a thousand of brick," across a diminutive old man in a little round hat, who was squeaking consolation to one of the mourners.

"Good Lord, have mercy!" ejaculated the little man earnestly and unaffectedly, as he strove to crawl from under the sable mass which was crushing him.

In another part of the square a dozen old women were singing. They were in a state of absolute ecstasy, as their shrill pipes gave forth,—

> "I rode on the sky,
> Quite ondestified I,
> And the moon it was under my feet."

Near these last stood a delicate woman, in that hysterical condition in which the nerves are uncontrollable, and which is vulgarly—and almost blasphemously—termed the "holy laugh." A hideous grin distorted her mouth, and was accompanied with a maniac's chuckle; while every muscle and nerve of her face twitched and jerked in horrible spasms.*

Amid all this confusion and excitement Suggs stood unmoved. He viewed the whole affair as a grand deception, a sort of "opposition line" running against his own, and looked on with a sort of professional jealousy. Sometimes he would mutter running comments upon what passed before him.

"Well, now," said he, as he observed the full-faced brother who was "officiating" among the

---

*Mr. Hooper adds the following note in this place:—
"The reader is requested to bear in mind that the scenes described in this chapter are not *now* to be witnessed. Eight or ten years ago, all classes of population of the Creek country were very different from what they now are. Of course, no disrespect is intended to any denomination of Christians. We believe that camp-meetings are not peculiar to any church, though most usual in the Methodist,—a denomination whose respectability in Alabama is attested by the fact that *very many* of its worthy clergymen and lay members hold honorable and profitable offices in the gift of the state legislature; of which, indeed, almost a controlling portion are themselves Methodists."

women, "that ere feller takes *my* eye! Thar he's
been this half hour, a-fightin' amongst them galls,
and's never said the fust word to nobody else. Wonder what's the reason these here preachers never
hugs up the old, ugly women! Never seed one do it
in my life,—the sperrit never moves 'em that way!
It's nater tho'; and the women, *they* never flocks
round one o' the old dried-up breethring. Bet two to
one, old splinter-legs thar"—nodding at one of the
ministers—"won't git a chance to say turkey to a
good-lookin' gall to-day! Well! who blames 'em?
Nater will be nater, all the world over; and I judge
ef I was a preacher, I should save the purtiest souls
fust, myself!"

While the Captain was in the middle of this conversation with himself, he caught the attention of
the preacher in the pulpit, who, inferring from an
indescribable something about his appearance that
he was a person of some consequence, immediately
determined to add him at once to the church, if it
could be done; and to that end began a vigorous,
direct personal attack.

"Breethring," he exclaimed, "I see yonder a man
that's a sinner! I *know* he's a sinner! Thar he
stands," pointing at Simon, "a missuble old crittur,
with his head a-blossomin' for the grave! A few
more short years, and d-o-w-n he'll go to perdition,
lessen the Lord have mer-cy on him! Come up
here, you old hoary-headed sinner, a-n-d git down
upon your knees, a-n-d put up your cry for the Lord
to snatch you from the bottomless pit! You're ripe
for the devil! you're b-o-u-n-d for hell, and the Lord
only knows what'll become on you!"

"D—n it," thought Suggs, "*ef* I only had you
down in the krick swamp for a minit or so, *I'd* show
you who's *old!* I'd alter your tune *mighty* sudden,
you sassy, 'saitful old rascal!" But he judiciously

held his tongue, and gave no utterance to the thought.

The attention of many having been directed to the Captain by the preacher's remarks, he was soon surrounded by numerous well-meaning and doubtless very pious persons, each one of whom seemed bent on the application of his own particular recipe for the salvation of souls. For a long time the Captain stood silent, or answered the incessant stream of exhortation only with a sneer; but at length his countenance began to give token of inward emotion. First his eyelids twitched; then his upper lip quivered; next a transparent drop formed on one of his eyelashes, and a similar one on the tip of his nose; and at last a sudden bursting of air from nose and mouth told that Captain Suggs was overpowered by his emotions. At the moment of the explosion, he made a feint as if to rush for the crowd, but he was in experienced hands, who well knew that the battle was more than half won.

"Hold to him!" said one. "It's a-workin' in him as strong as a Dick horse!"

"Pour it into him," said another; "it'll all come right directly."

"That's the way I love to see 'em do," observed a third; "when you begin to draw the water from their eyes, 't ain't gwine to be long afore you'll have 'em on their knees!"

And so they clung to the Captain manfully, and half dragged, half led him to the mourner's bench; by which he threw himself down, altogether unmanned, and bathed in tears. Great was the rejoicing of the brethren, as they sang, shouted, and prayed around him; for by this time it had come to be generally known that the "convicted" old man was Captain Simon Suggs, the very "chief of sinners" in all that region.

The Captain remained groveling in the dust during the usual time, and gave vent to even more than the requisite number of sobs and groans and heart-piercing cries. At length, when the proper time had arrived, he bounced up, and with a face radiant with joy commenced a series of vaultings and tumblings, which "laid in the shade" all previous performances of the sort at that camp-meeting. The brethren were in ecstasies at this demonstrative evidence of completion of the work; and whenever Suggs shouted "Gloree!" at the top of his lungs, every one of them shouted it back, until the woods rang with echoes.

The effervescence having partially subsided, Suggs was put upon his pins to relate his experience, which he did somewhat in this style, first brushing the tear-drops from eyes, and giving the end of his nose a preparatory wring with his fingers, to free it of the superabundant moisture.

"Friends," he said, "it don't take long to curry a short horse, accordin' to the old sayin', and I'll give you the perticklers of the way I was 'brought to a knowledge' "—here the Captain wiped his eyes, brushed the tip of his nose, and snuffled a little—"in less'n no time."

"Praise the Lord!" ejaculated a by-stander.

"You see I come here full o' romancin' and devilment, and jist to make game of all the purceedins. Well, sure enough, I done so for some time, and was a-thinkin' how I should play some trick"—

"Dear soul alive! *don't* he talk sweet?" cried an old lady in black silk. "Whar's John Dobbs? You Sukey!" screaming at a negro woman on the other side of the square, "ef you don't hunt up your mass John in a minute, and have him here to listen to his 'sperience, I'll tuck you up when I git home and give you a hundred and fifty lashes, madam!

see ef I don't! Blessed Lord!'' referring again to
the Captain's relation, ''ain't it a *precious*
'scourse?''

''I was jist a-thinkin' how I should play some
trick to turn it all into redecule, when they began to
come round me and talk. Long at fust I did n't
mind it, but arter a little that brother,'' pointing to
the reverend gentleman who had so successfully
carried the unbeliever through the Old and New
Testaments, and who, Simon was convinced, was the
''big dog of the tan-yard,''—''that brother spoke a
word that struck me kleen to the heart, and run all
over me, like fire in dry grass''—

''*I-I-I* can bring 'em!'' cried the preacher alluded
to, in a tone of exultation. ''Lord, thou knows ef
thy servant can't stir 'em up, nobody else need n't
try; but the glory ain't mine. I'm a poor worrum
of the dust,'' he added, with ill-managed affectation.

''And so from that I felt somethin' a-pullin' me
inside''—

''Grace! grace! nothin' but grace!'' exclaimed
one; meaning that ''grace'' had been operating in
the Captain's gastric region.

''And then,'' continued Suggs, ''I wanted to git
off, but they hilt me, and bimeby I felt so missuble
I had to go yonder,'' pointing to the mourners' seat;
''and when I lay down thar it got wuss and wuss,
and 'peared like somethin' was a-mashin' down on
my back''—

''That was his load o' sin,'' said one of the brethren. ''Never mind; it'll tumble off presently, see ef
it don't,'' and he shook his head professionally and
knowingly.

''And it kept a-gittin heavier and heavier, ontwell
it looked like it might be a four-year-old steer, or a
big pine log, or somethin' of that sort''—

''Glory to my soul,'' shouted Mrs. Dobbs, ''it's

the sweetest talk I *ever* hearn! You Sukey! ain't you got John yit? Never mind, my lady, *I*'ll settle wi' you!" Sukey quailed before the finger which her mistress shook at her.

"And arter a while," Suggs went on, "'peared like I fell into a trance, like, and I seed"—

"Now we'll git the good on it!" cried one of the sanctified.

"And I seed the biggest, longest, rip-roarenest, blackest, scaliest"—Captain Suggs paused, wiped his brow, and ejaculated, "Ah, L-o-r-d!" so as to give full time for curiosity to become impatience to know what he saw.

"*Sarpent*, warn't it!" asked one of the preachers.

"No, not a sarpent," replied Suggs, blowing his nose.

"Do tell us *what* it war! Soul alive! Whar *is* John?" said Mrs. Dobbs.

"Alligator!" said the Captain.

"Alligator!" repeated every woman present, and screamed for very life.

Mrs. Dobbs's nerves were so shaken by the announcement that, after repeating the horrible word, she screamed to Sukey, "You Sukey, I say, you Su-u-ke-e-y! ef you let John come a-nigh this way, what the dreadful alliga—Shaw! what am I thinkin' 'bout! 'T warn't nothin' but a vishin!"

"Well," said the Captain in continuation, "the alligator kept a-comin' and a-comin' to'ards me, with his great long jaws a-gapin' open like a ten-foot pair o' tailors' shears"—

"Oh! oh! oh! Lord! gracious above!" cried the women.

"Satan!" was the laconic ejaculation of the oldest preacher present, who thus informed the congregation that it was the devil which had attacked Suggs in the shape of an alligator.

"And then I concluded the jig was up, 'thout I could block his game some way; for I seed his idee was to snap off my head"—

The women screamed again.

"So I fixed myself jist like I was purfectly willin' for him to take my head, and rather he'd do it as not,"—here the women shuddered perceptibly,—"and so I hilt my head straight out,"—the Captain illustrated by elongating his neck; "and when he come up, and was a-gwine to *shet down* on it, I jist pitched in a big rock, which choked him to death; and that minit I felt the weight slide off, and I had the best feelins—sorter like you'll have from *good* sperrits—anybody ever had!"

"Didn't I *tell* you so? Didn't I *tell* you so?" asked the brother who had predicted the off-tumbling of the load of sin. "Ha, Lord! fool *who!* I've been *all* along thar! yes, *all along thar!* and I know every inch of the way jist as good as I do the road home!", and then he turned round and round, and looked at all, to receive a silent tribute to his superior penetration.

Captain Suggs was now the "lion of the day." Nobody could pray so well, or exhort so movingly, as "brother Suggs." Nor did his natural modesty prevent the proper performance of appropriate exercises. With the Reverend Bela Bugg (him to whom, under providence, he ascribed his conversion) he was a most especial favorite. They walked, sang, and prayed together for hours.

"Come, come up; thar's room for all!" cried brother Bugg, in his evening exhortation. "Come to the 'seat,' and ef you won't pray yourselves let *me* pray for you!"

"Yes!" said Simon, by way of assisting his friend; "it's a game that all can win at; Ante up! ante up, boys—friends, I mean! Don't back out!"

"Thar ain't a sinner here," said Bugg, "no matter ef his soul's black as a nigger, but what thar's room for him!"

"No matter what sort of a hand you've got," added Simon, in the fullness of his benevolence; "take stock; Here am *I*, the wickedest and blindest of sinners; has spent my whole life in the sarvice of the devil; has now come in on *nary pair* and won a *pile!*", and the Captain's face beamed with holy pleasure.

"Do-n-'t be afeard!" cried the preacher; "come along! the meanest won't be turned away! humble yourselves, and come!"

"No!" said Simon, still indulging in his favorite style of metaphor; "the bluff game ain't played here! No runnin' of a body off! Everybody holds four aces, and when you bet you win!"

And thus the Captain continued, until the services were concluded, to assist in adding to the number at the mourners' seat; and up to the hour of retiring, he exhibited such enthusiasm in the cause that he was unanimously voted to be the most efficient addition the church had made during that meeting.

The next morning, when the preacher of the day first entered the pulpit, he announced that "brother Simon Suggs," mourning over his past iniquities, and desirous of going to work in the cause as speedily as possible, would take up a collection to found a church in his own neighborhood, at which he hoped to make himself useful as soon as he could prepare himself for the ministry, which, the preacher didn't doubt, would be in a very few weeks, as brother Suggs was "a man of mighty good judg-*ment*, and of *a great discorse.*" The funds were to be collected by "brother Suggs," and held in trust by brother Bela Bugg, who was the financial officer of the circuit, until some arrangement could be made to build a suitable house.

"Yes, breethring," said the Captain, rising to his feet; "I want to start a little 'sociation close to me, and I want you all to help. I'm mighty poor myself, as poor as any of you. Don't leave, breethring," observing that several of the well-to-do were about to go off,—"don't leave; ef you ain't able to afford anything, jist give us your blessin', and it'll be all the same!"

This insinuation did the business, and the sensitive individuals reseated themselves.

"It's mighty little of this world's goods I've got," resumed Suggs, pulling off his hat, and holding it before him; "but I'l bury *that* in the cause, anyhow," and he deposited his last five-dollar bill in the hat. There was a murmur of approbation at the Captain's liberality throughout the assembly.

Suggs now commenced collecting, and very prudently attacked first the gentlemen who had shown a disposition to escape. These, to exculpate themselves from anything like poverty, contributed handsomely.

"Look here, breethring," said the Captain, displaying the bank-notes thus received, "brother Snooks has drapt a five wi' me, and brother Snodgrass a ten! In course 't ain't expected that you *that aint as well off as them* will give *as much;* let every one give *accordin'* to ther means."

This was another chain-shot that raked as it went! "Who so low" as not to be able to contribute as much as Snooks and Snodgrass?

"Here's all the *small* money I've got about me," said a burly old fellow, ostentatiously handing to Suggs, over the heads of a half dozen, a ten-dollar bill.

"That's what I call maganimus!" exclaimed the Captain; "that the way *every* rich man ought to do!"

These examples were followed more or less closely by almost all present, for Simon had excited the pride of purse of the congregation, and a very handsome sum was collected in a very short time.

The Reverend Mr. Bugg, as soon as he observed that our hero had obtained all that was to be had at that time, went to him, and inquired what amount had been collected. The Captain replied that it was still uncounted, but that it couldn't be much under a hundred.

"Well, brother Suggs, you'd better count it, and turn it over to me now. I'm goin' to leave presently."

"No!" said Suggs; "can't do it!"

"Why? what's the matter?" inquired Bugg.

"It's got to be *prayed over*, fust!" said Simon, a heavenly smile illuminating his whole face.

"Well," replied Bugg, "less go one side and do it!"

"No!" said Simon, solemnly.

Mr. Bugg gave a look of inquiry.

"You see that krick swamp?" asked Suggs. "I'm gwine down in *thar*, and I'm gwine to lay this money down so,"—showing how he would place it on the ground,—"and I'm gwine to git on these here knees," slapping the right one, "and I'm n-e-v-e-r gwine to quit the grit ontwell I fell it's got the blessin'! And nobody ain't got to be thar but me!"

Mr. Bugg greatly admired the Captain's fervent piety, and, bidding him godspeed, turned off.

Captain Suggs "struck for" the swamp sure enough, where his horse was already hitched. "Ef them fellers ain't done to a cracklin'," he muttered to himself as he mounted, "*I*'ll never bet on two pair agin! They're peart at the snap game, they-selves; but they're badly lewed this hitch! Well! Live and let live is a good old motter, and it's my sentiments adzactly!" And giving the spur to his horse, off he cantered.

TAKING THE CENSUS.

From Some Adventures of Captain Simon Suggs, Late of the Talla-poosa Volunteers (1846). New Edition, with Alabama Sketches (1881).

We rode up one day to the residence of a widow rather past the prime of life—just that period at which nature supplies most abundantly the oil which lubricates the hinges of the female tongue—and hitching to the fence, walked into the house.

"Good morning, madam," said we, in our usual bland, and somewhat insinuating manner.

"Mornin'," said the widow gruffly.

Drawing our blanks from their case, we proceeded —"I am the man, madam, that takes the census, and—"

"The mischief you are!" said the old termagant. "Yes, I've hearn of you; Parson W. told me you was coming, and I told him jist what I tell you, that if you said 'cloth,' 'soap,' ur 'chickens,' to *me*, Id set the dogs on ye.—Here, Bull; here, Pomp!" Two wolfish curs responded to the call for Bull and Pomp, by coming to the door, smelling at our feet with a slight growl, and then laid [sic] down on the steps. "Now," continued the old she-savage, "them's the severest dogs in this country. Last week Bill Ston-ecker's two-year-old steer jumped my yard-fence, and Bull and Pomp tuk him by the throat, and they killed him afore my boys could break 'em loose, to save the world.''

"Yes, ma'am," said we, meekly; "Bull and Pomp seem to be very fine dogs.''

"You may well say that: what I tells them to do they do—and if I was to sick them on your old hoss yonder, they'd eat him up afore you could say Jack Roberson. And it's jist what I shall do, if you try to pry into my consarns. They are none of your business, nor Van Buren's nuther, I reckon. Oh, old Van BanBuren! I wish I had you here, you old rascal! *I*'d show you what—I'd—I'd make Bull and Pomp show you how to be sendin' out men to take down what little stuff people's got, jist to tax it, when it's taxed enough a'ready!''

All this time we were perspiring through fear of the fierce guardians of the old widow's portal. At length, when the widow paused, we remarked that as she was determined not to answer questions about the produce of the farm, we would just set down the age, sex, and complexion of each member of her family.

"No sich a thing—you'll do no sich a thing," said she; "I've got five in family, and that's all you'll git from me. Old Van Buren must have a heap to do, the dratted old villyan, to send you to take down how old my children is. I've got five in family, and they are all between five and a hundred years old; * * * and whether they are *he* or *she,* is none of your consarns.''

We told her we would report her to the marshal, and she would be fined: but it only augmented her wrath.

"Yes! send your marshal, or your Mr. Van Buren here, if you're bad off to—let 'em come—let Mr. Van Burean come"—looking as savage as a Bengal tigress—"Oh, I wish he *would* come"—and her nostrils dilated, and her eyes gleamed—"I'd cut his head off!"

"That might kill him," we ventured to remark, by way of a joke.

"Kill him! kill him—oh—if I had him here by the *years* I reckon I *would* kill him. A pretty fellow to be eating his vittils out'n gold spoons that poor people's taxed for, and raisin' an army to get him made king of Ameriky—the oudacious, nasty, stinking old scamp!" She paused a moment, and then resumed, "And now, mister, jist put down what I tell you on that paper, and don't be telling no lies to send to Washington city. Jist put down 'Judy Tompkins, ageable woman, and four children.'"

We objected to making any such entry, but the old hag vowed it should be done, to prevent any misrepresentation of her case. We, however, were pretty resolute, until she appealed to the couchant whelps, Bull and Pomp. At the first glimpse of their teeth, our courage gave way, and we made the entry in a bold hand across a blank schedule—"Judy Tompkins, *ageable* woman, and four children."

JOSEPH GLOVER BALDWIN.

VIRGINIANS IN A NEW COUNTRY.

*From Flush Times in Alabama and Mississippi. A Series of Sketches
(1853). Seventh Edition (1854).*

THE disposition to be proud and vain of one's
country, and to boast of it, is a natural feeling, indulged or not in respect to the pride, vanity, and
boasting, according to the character of the native;
but with a Virginian it is a passion. It inheres in
him, even as the flavor of a York River oyster in
that bivalve; and no distance of deportation, and no
trimmings of a gracious prosperity, and no pickling
in the sharp acids of adversity can destroy it. It is
a part of the Virginia character, just as the flavor
is a distinctive part of the oyster, "which cannot,
save by annihilating, die." It is no use talking about
it; the thing may be right, or wrong: like Falstaff's victims at Gadshill, it is past praying for: it
is a sort of cocoa grass that has got into the soil,
and has so matted over it, and so *fibred* through
it, as to have become a part of it; at least, there is
no telling which is the grass and which is the soil;
and certainly it is useless labor to try to root it out.
You may destroy the soil, but you can't root out the
grass.

Patriotism with a Virginian is a noun personal.
It is the Virginian himself, and something over. He
loves Virginia *per se* and *propter se;* he loves her for
herself and for himself; because *she is* Virginia
and — everything else beside. He loves to talk
about her: out of the abundance of the heart the
mouth speaketh. It makes no odds where he goes,
he carries Virginia with him; not in the entirety,
always, but the little spot he came from in Virginia;

as Swedenborg says, the smallest part of the brain is an abridgment of all of it. *"Cœlum, non animum, mutant qui trans mare currunt,"* was made for a Virginian. He never gets acclimated elsewhere; he never loses citizenship to the old home. The right of expatriation is a pure abstraction to him. He may breathe in Alabama, but he lives in Virginia. His treasure is there, and his heart also. If he looks at the Delta of the Mississippi, it reminds him of James River "low grounds;" if he sees the vast prairies of Texas, it is a memorial of the meadows of the Valley. Richmond is the centre of attraction, the *dépot* of all that is grand, great, good and glorious. "It is the Kentucky of a place" which the preacher described heaven to be to the Kentucky congregation.

Those who came many years ago from the borough towns, especially from the vicinity of Williamsburg, exceed, in attachment to their birthplace, if possible, the *émigrés* from the metropolis. It is refreshing, in these costermonger times, to hear them speak of it: they remember it when the old burg was the seat of fashion, taste, refinement, hospitality, wealth, wit, and all social graces; when genius threw its spell over the public assemblages and illumined the halls of justice, and when beauty brightened the social hour with her unmatched and matchless brilliancy. Then the spirited and gifted youths of the College of old William and Mary, some of them just giving out the first scintillations of the genius that afterwards shone refulgent in the forum and the Senate, added to the attractions of a society gay, cultivated, and refined beyond example, *even* in the Old Dominion. A hallowed charm seems to rest upon the venerable city, clothing its very dilapidation in a drapery of romance and of serene and classic interest, as if all the sweet and softened splendor which invests the "Midsummer Night's Dream" were poured in a flood of mellow and poetic radiance over the now quiet and half "deserted village." There is something in the shadow from the old college walls, cast by the moon upon the grass and sleeping on the sward, that throws a like shadow, soft, sad, and melancholy, upon the heart of the returning pilgrim who saunters out to view again, by moonlight, his old *Alma Mater*, the nursing mother of such a list and such a line of statesmen and heroes.

There is nothing presumptuously froward in this Virginianism. The Virginian does not make broad his phylacteries, and crow over the poor Carolinian and Tennesseeian. He does not reproach him with his misfortune of birthplace. No, he thinks the affliction is enough without the triumph. The franchise of having been born in Virginia and the prerogative founded thereon are too patent of honor and distinction to be arrogantly pretended. The bare mention is enough. He finds occasion to let the fact be known, and then the fact is fully able to protect and take care of itself. Like a ducal title, there is no need of saying more than to name it; modesty then is a becoming and expected virtue; forbearance to boast is true dignity.

The Virginian is a magnanimous man. He never throws up to a Yankee the fact of his birthplace. He feels on the subject as a man of delicacy feels in alluding to a rope in the presence of a person one of whose brothers "stood upon nothing and kicked at the United States," or to a female indiscretion where there had been scandal concerning the family. So far do they carry this refinement, that I have known one of my countrymen, on occasion of a Bostonian owning where he was born, generously protest that he had never heard of it before. As if honest confession half obliterated the shame of the fact. Yet he does not lack the grace to acknowledge worth or merit in another, wherever the native place of that other: for it is a common thing to hear them say of a neighbor: "He is a clever fellow, *though* he *did* come from New Jersey, or even Connecticut."

In politics the Virginian is learned much beyond what is written, for they have heard a great deal of speaking on that prolific subject, especially by one or two Randolphs and any number of Barbours. They read the same papers here they read in Virginia, the "Richmond Enquirer" and the "Richmond Whig." The democrat stoutly asseverates a fact, and gives "The Enquirer" as his authority with an air that means to say, *that* settles it; while the whig quoted Hampden Pleasants with the same confidence. But the faculty of personalizing everything, which the exceeding social turn of a Virginian gives him, rarely allowed a reference to the paper, *eo nomine;* but made him refer to the editor, as "Ritchie" said so and so, or "Hampden Pleasants" said this or that. When two of opposite politics got together, it was amusing, if you had nothing else to do that day, to hear the discussion. I never knew a debate that did not start *ab urbe condita.* They not only went back to first principles, but also to first times; nor did I ever hear a discussion in which old John Adams and Thomas Jefferson did not figure—as if an interminable dispute had been going on for so many generations between those disputatious personages; as if the quarrel had begun before time, but was not to end with it. But the strangest part of it to me was, that the dispute seemed to be going on without poor Adams having any defence or champion; and never waxed hotter than when both parties agreed in denouncing the man of Braintree as the worst of public sinners and the vilest of political heretics. They both agreed on one thing, and that was to refer the matter to the Resolutions of 1798-99; which said resolutions, like Goldsmith's "Good-Natured Man," arbitrating between Mr. and Mrs. Croaker, seemed so impartial that they agreed with both parties on every occasion.

Nor do I recollect of hearing any question debated that did not resolve itself into a question of constitution, strict construction, etc., — the constitution being a thing of that curious virtue that its chief excellency consisted in not allowing the government to do anything; or in being a regular prize-fighter that knocked all laws and legislators into a cocked hat, except those of the objector's party.

Frequent reference was reciprocally made to "gorgons, hydras, and chimeras dire," to black cockades, blue lights, Essex juntos, the Reign of Terror, and some other mystic entities; but who or what these monsters were, I never could distinctly learn; and was surprised, on looking into the history of the country, to find that, by some strange oversight, no allusion was made to them.

Great is the Virginian's reverence of great men, that is to say, of great Virginians. This reverence is not Unitarian. He is a Polytheist. He believes in a multitude of Virginia gods. As the Romans of every province and village had their tutelary or other divinities, besides having divers national gods, so the Virginian of every county has his great man, the like of whom cannot be found in the new country he has exiled himself to. This sentiment of veneration for talent, especially for speaking talent; this amiable propensity to lionize men, is not peculiar to any class of Virginians among us: it abides in all. I was amused to hear "old Culpepper," as we call him (by nickname derived from the county he came from), declaiming in favor of the Union. "What,

gentlemen,'' said the old man, with a sonorous swell
—''what, burst up this glorious Union! and who, if
this Union is torn up, could write another? Nobody except Henry Clay and J. S. B. of Culpepper
—and may be *they* wouldn't—and what then would
you do for another?''

The greatest compliment a Virginian can ever pay
to a speaker is to say that he reminds him of a Colonel Broadhorn or a Captain Smith, who represented
some royal-named county some forty years or less
in the Virginia House of Delegates; and of whom
the auditor of course has heard, as he made several
speeches in the capitol at Richmond. But the force
of the compliment is somewhat broken by a long
narrative, in which the personal reminiscences of the
speaker go back to sundry sketches of the Virginia
statesman's efforts, and recapitulations of his sayings interspersed, *par parenthèse,* with many valu-
able notes illustrative of his pedigree and performances; the whole of which, given with great historical fidelity of detail, leaves nothing to be wished
for except the point, or rather two points,—the gist
and the period.

It is not to be denied that Virginia is the land of
orators, heroes, and statesmen; and that, directly or
indirectly, she has exerted an influence upon the
national councils nearly as great as all the rest of
the States combined. It is wonderful that a State
of its size and population should have turned out
such an unprecedented quantum of talent, and of
talent as various in kind as prodigious in amount.
She has reason to be proud; and the other States
so largely in her debt (for, from Cape May to Puget's
Sound she has colonized the other States and the
Territories with her surplus talent), ought to allow
her the harmless privilege of a little bragging. In
the showy talent of oratory has she especially shone.

To accomplish her in this art the State has been turned into a debating society, and while she has been *talking* for the benefit of the nation, as she thought, the other, and by nature less favored States, have been *doing* for their own. Consequently, what she has gained in reputation, she has lost in wealth and *material aids*. Certainly the Virginia character has been less distinguished for its practical than its ornamental traits, and for its business qualities than for its speculative temper. *Cui bono* and utilitarianism, at least until latterly, were not favorite or congenial inquiries and subjects of attention to the Virginia politician. What the Virginian was upon his native soil, that he was abroad; indeed, it may be said that the *amor patriæ,* strengthened by absence, made him more of a conservative abroad than he would have been if he had stayed at home, for most of them here would not, had they been consulted, have changed either of the old Constitutions.

It is far, however, from my purpose to treat of such themes. I only glance at them to show their influence on the character as it was developed on a new theatre.

Eminently social and hospitable, kind, humane, and generous, is a Virginian, at home or abroad. They are so by nature and habit. These qualities and their exercise develop and strengthen other virtues. By reason of these social traits, they necessarily become well mannered, honorable, spirited, and careful of reputation, desirous of pleasing, and skilled in the accomplishments which please. Their insular position and sparse population, mostly rural, and easy but not affluent fortunes, kept them from the artificial refinements and the strong temptation which corrupt so much of the society of the Old World and some portions of the New. There was no character more attractive than that of a young

Virginian, fifteen years ago, of intelligence, of good family, education, and breeding.

It was of the instinct of a Virginian to seek society; he belongs to the gregarious, not to the solitary division of animals; and society can only be kept up by grub and gab—something to eat, and, if not something to talk about, talk. Accordingly they came accomplished already in the knowledge and the talent for these important duties.

A Virginian could always get up a good dinner. He could also do his share—a full hand's work—in disposing of one after it was got up. The qualifications for hostmanship were signal—the old Udaller himself, assisted by Claud Halrco, could not do up the thing in better style, or with a heartier relish, or a more cordial hospitality. In *petite* manners— the little attentions of the table, the filling up of the chinks of the conversation with small fugitive observations, the supplying the hooks and eyes that *kept* the discourse together, the genial good humor, which, like that of the family of the good Vicar, made up in laughter what was wanting in wit,—in these, and in the science of getting up and in getting through a picnic, or chowder party, or fish fry, the Virginian, like Eclipse, was first, and there was no second. Great was he, too, at mixing an apple toddy or mint julep, where ice could not be got for love or money; and not deficient, by any means, when it came to his turn to do honor to his own fabrics. It was in this department that he not only shone, but *out*shone, not merely all others, but himself. Here he was at home indeed. His elocution, his matter, his learning, his education, were of the first order. He could discourse of everything around him with an accuracy and a fullness which would have put Coleridge's or Mrs. Ellis's table talk to the blush. Every dish was a text, horticulture, hunting, poultry, fishing (Isaak Walton or Daniel Webster would have been charmed and instructed to hear him discourse piscatory-wise), a slight divergence in favor of fox-chasing and a detour towards a horse-race now and then, and continual parentheses of recommendation of patricular dishes or glasses—Oh! I tell you, if ever there was an interesting man, it was he. Others might be agreeable, but he was fascinating, irresistible, not-to-be-done-without.

In the fullness of time the new era had set in, the era of the second great experiment of independence,—the experiment, namely, of credit without capital, and enterprise without honesty. The Age of Brass had succeeded the Arcadian period, when men got rich by saving a part of their earnings, and lived at their own cost and in ignorance of the new plan of making fortunes on the profits of what they owed. A new theory, not found in the works on poltical economy, was broached. It was found out that the prejudice in favor of the metals (brass excluded) was an absurd superstition, and that, in reality, anything else which the parties interested in giving in currency chose might serve as a representative of value and medium for exchange of property; and as gold and silver had served for a great number of years as representatives, the republican doctrine of rotation in office required they should give way. Accordingly, it was decided that Rags, a very familiar character, and very popular and easy of access, should take their place. Rags belonged to the school of progress. He was representative of the then Young America. His administration was not tame. It was *very* spirited. It was based on the Bonapartist idea of keeping the imagination of the people excited. The leading fiscal idea of his system was to *democratize* capital, and to make, for all purposes of trade, credit, and enjoyment of wealth, the man that had *no* money a little richer, if anything, than the man that had a million. The principle of success and basis of operation, though inexplicable in the hurry of the time, is plain enough now: it was faith. Let the public believe that a smutted rag is money, it is money: in other words, it was a sort of financial biology, which made, at night, the thing conjured for the thing that was seen, so far as the patient was concerned, while the fit was on him—except that now a man does not do his trading when under the mesmeric influence: in the flush times he did.

This country was just settling up. Marvelous accounts had gone forth of the fertility of its virgin lands; and the productions of the soil were commanding a price remunerating to slave labor as it had never been remunerated before. Emigrants came flocking in from all quarters of the Union, especially from the slave-holding States. The new country seemed to be a reservoir, and every road leading to it a vagrant stream of enterprise and adventure. Money, or what passed for money, was the only cheap thing to be had. Every cross-road and every avocation presented an opening, through which a fortune was seen by the adventurer in near perspective. Credit was a thing of course. To refuse it—if the thing was ever done—were an insult for which a bowie-knife were not a too summary or exemplary a means of redress. The state banks were issuing their bills by the sheet, like a patent steam printing-press *its* issues; and no other showing was asked of the applicant for the loan than an authentication of his great distress for money. Finance, even in its most exclusive quarter, had thus already got, in this wonderful revolution, to work upon the principles of the charity hospital.

If an overseer grew tired of supervising a plantation, and felt a call to the mercantile life, even if he omitted the compendious method of buying out a merchant wholesale, stock, house, and good-will, and laying down, at once, his bull-whip for the yard-stick, all he had to do was to go on to New York, and present himself in Pearl Street with a letter avouching his citizenship and a clean shirt, and he was regularly given a through ticket to speedy bankruptcy.

Under this stimulating process prices rose like smoke. Lots in obscure villages were held at city prices; lands, bought at the minimum cost of government, were sold at from thirty to forty dollars per acre, and considered dirt cheap at that. In short, the country had got to be a full antetype of California, in all except the gold. Society was wholly unorganized, there was no restraining public opinion, the law was well-nigh powerless, and religion scarcely was heard of except as furnishing the oaths and *technics* of profanity. The world saw a fair experiment of what it would have been if the fiat had never been pronounced which decreed subsistence as the price of labor.

Money got without work, by those unaccustomed to it, turned the heads of its possessors, and they spent it with a recklessness like that with which they gained it. The pursuits of industry neglected, riot and coarse debauchery filled up the vacant hours. "Where the carcass is, there will the eagles be gathered together;" and the eagles that flocked to the Southwest were of the same sort as the *black eagles* the Duke of Saxe-Weimar saw on his celebrated journey to the Natural Bridge. "The cankers of a long peace and a calm world"—there were no Mexican wars and filibuster expeditions in those days —gathered in the villages and cities by scores.

Even the little boys caught the taint of the general infection of morals; and I knew one of them— Jim Ellett by name—to give a man ten dollars to hold him up to bet at the table of a faro-bank. James was a fast youth; and I sincerely hope he may not fulfill his early promise, and some day be *assisted up still higher.*

The groceries—*vulgice* doggeries—were in full blast in those days, no village having less than a half dozen all busy all the time: gaming and horse-racing were polite and well-patronized amusements. I knew of a judge to adjourn two courts (or court twice) to attend a horse-race, at which he officiated judicially and ministerially, and with more appropriateness than in the judicial chair. Occasionally the scene was diversified by a murder or two, which, though perpetrated from behind a corner, or behind the back of the deceased, whenever he accused *chose* to stand his trial, was always found to be committed in self-defense, securing the homicide an honorable acquittal *at the hands of his peers.*

The old rules of business and the calculations of prudence were alike disregarded, and profligacy, in all the departments of the *crimen falsi,* held riotous carnival. Larceny grew not only respectable, but genteel, and ruffled it in all the pomp of purple and fine linen. Swindling was raised to the dignity of the fine arts. Felony came forth from its covert, put on more seemly habiliments, and took its seat with unabashed front in the upper places of the synagogue. Before the first circles of the patrons of this brilliant and dashing villainy, Blunt Honesty felt as abashed as poor Halbert Glendinning by the courtly refinement and supercilious airs of Sir Piercie Shafton.

Public office represented, by its incumbents, the state of public morals with some approach to accuracy. Out of sixty-six receivers of public money in the new States, sixty-two were discovered to be defaulters; and the agent sent to look into the affairs of a peccant office-holder in the Southwest reported him *minus* some tens of thousands, but advised the government to retain him, for a reason one of Æsop's fables illustrates: the agent ingeniously surmising that the appointee succeeding would do his stealing without any regard to the proficiency already made by his predecessor, while the present incumbent would probably consider, in mercy to the treasury, that he *had* done *something* of the pious duty of providing for his household.

There was no petit larceny: there was all the difference between stealing by the small and the 'operations" manipulated that there is between a single assassination and an hundred thousand men killed in an opium war. The placeman robbed with the gorgeous magnificence of a Governor-General of Bengal.

The man of straw, not worth the buttons on his shirt, with a sublime audacity, bought lands and negroes, and provided times and terms of payment which a Wall Street capitalist would have to recast his arrangements to meet.

O Paul Clifford and Augustus Tomlinson, philosophers of the road, practical and theoretical! If ye had lived to see those times, how great an improvement on your ruder scheme of distribution would these gentle arts have seemed,—arts whereby, without risk, or loss of character, or the vulgar barbarism of personal violence, the same beneficial results flowed, with no greater injury to the superstitions of moral education!

With the change of times and the imagination of wealth easily acquired came a change in the thoughts and habits of the people. "Old times were changed,

old manners gone.'' Visions of affluence, such as
crowded Dr. Samuel Johnson's mind, when adver-
tising a sale of Thrale's Brewery, and casting a soft
sheep's eye toward Thrale's widow, thronged upon
the popular fancy. Avarice and hope joined part-
nership. It was strange how the reptile arts of humanity, as at a faro-table, warmed into life beneath
their heat. The *cacoethes accrescendi* became epidemic. It seized upon the universal community.
The pulpits even were not safe from its insidious
invasion. What men anxiously desire they willingly
believe; and all believed a good time was coming,—
nay, had come.

''Commerce was king,'' and Rags, Tag, and Bob-
tail his cabinet council. Rags was treasurer. Banks,
chartered on a specie basis, did a very flourishing
business on the promissory notes of the individual stockholders, ingeniously substituted in lieu of
cash. They issued ten for one, the *one* being fictitious. They generously loaned all the directors could
not use themselves, and were not choice whether
Bardolph was the indorser for Falstaff or Falstaff
borrowed on his own proper credit or the funds
advanced him by Shallow. The stampede towards
the golden temple became general; the delusion
prevailed far and wide that this thing was not a
burlesque on commerce and finance. Even the directors of the banks began to have their doubts
whether the intended swindle was not a failure.
Like Lord Clive, when reproached for extortion to
the extent of some millions in Bengal, they exclaimed, after the bubble burst, ''When they thought
of what they had got, and what they might have got,
they were astounded at their own moderation!''

The old capitalists for a while stood out. With
the Tory conservatism of cash in hand, worked for,
they could n't reconcile their old notions to the new

régime. They looked for the thing's ending, and *then* their time. But the stampede still kept on. Paper fortunes still multiplied; houses and lands changed hands; real estate see-sawed up as morals went down on the other end of the plank; men of straw, corpulent with bank bills, strutted past them on 'Change. They began, too, to think there might be something in this new thing. Peeping cautiously, like hedgehogs, out of their holes, they saw the stream of wealth and adventurers passing by; then, looking carefully around, they inched themselves half-way out; then, sallying forth and snatching up a morsel, ran back; until at last, grown more bold, *they* ran out too with their hoarded store, in full chase with the other unclean beasts of adventure. They never got back again. Jonah's gourd withered one night, and next morning the vermin that had nestled under its broad shade were left unprotected, a prey to the swift retribution that came upon them. They were left naked, or only clothed themselves with cursing (the Specie Circular on the United States Bank) as with a garment. To drop the figure, Shylock himself could n't live in those times, so reversed was everything. Shaving paper and loaning money at a usury of fifty per cent. was for the first time since the Jews left Jerusalem a breaking business to the operator.

The condition of society may be imagined: vulgarity, ignorance, fussy and arrogant pretension, unmitigated rowdyism, bullying insolence, if they did not rule the hour, *seemed* to wield unchecked dominion. The workings of these choice spirits were patent upon the face of society; and the modest, unobtrusive, retiring men of worth and character (for there were many, perhaps a large majority of such) were almost lost sight of in the hurly-burly of those strange and shifting scenes.

Even in the professions were the same character-

istics visible. Men dropped down into their places
as from the clouds. Nobody knew who or what they
were, except as they claimed, or as a surface view of
their characters indicated. Instead of taking to the
highway, and magnanimously calling upon the way-
farer to stand and deliver, or to the fashionable larceny of credit without prospect or design of paying,
some unscrupulous horse doctor would set up his
sign as "Physician and Surgeon," and draw his
lancet on you, or fire at random a box of his pills
into your bowels, with a vague chance of hitting
some disease unknown to him, but with a better
prospect of killing the patient, whom or whose ad-
ministrator he charged some ten dollars a trial for
his markmanship.

A superannuated justice or constable in one of
the old States was metamorphosed into a lawyer;
and though he knew not the distinction between a
fee tail and a *female* would undertake to construe,
off-hand, a will involving all the subtleties of *uses
and trusts*.

But this state of things could not last forever: society cannot always stand on its head, with its heels
in the air.

The Jupiter Tonans of the White House saw the
monster of a free credit prowling about like a beast
of apocalyptic vision, and marked him for his prey.
Gathering all his bolts in his sinewy grasp, and
standing back on his heels, and waving his wiry
arm, he let the mall fly, hard and swift, upon all the
hydra's heads. Then came a crash, as "if the ribs
of nature broke," and a scattering, like the bursting
of a thousand magazines, and a smell of brimstone,
as if Pandemonium had opened a window next to
earth for ventilation,—and all was silent. The
beast never stirred in his tracks. To get down from
the clouds to level ground, the Specie Circular was

issued without warning, and the splendid lie of a
false credit burst into fragments. It came in the
midst of the dance and the frolic, as Tam O'Shan-
ter came to disturb the infernal glee of the warlocks,
and to disperse the rioters. Its effect was like that
of a general creditor's bill in the chancery court, and
a marshaling of all the assets of the trades-people.
General Jackson was no fairy; but he did some very
pretty fairy work in converting the bank bills back
again into rags and oak-leaves. Men worth a million were insolvent for two millions; promising young
cities marched back again into the wilderness. The
ambitious town plat was re-annexed to the plantation, like a country girl taken home from the city.
The frolic was ended, and what headaches and feverish limbs the next morning! The retreat from
Moscow was performed over again, and "Devil take
the hindmost" was the tune to which the soldiers of
fortune marched. The only question was as to the
means of escape, and the nearest and best route to
Texas. The sheriff was as busy as a militia adjutant
on review day; and the lawyers were mere wreckers,
earning salvage. Where are ye now, my ruffling gallants? Where now the braw cloths and watch-chains
and rings and fine horses? Alas for ye! they are
glimmering among the things that were, the wonder
of an hour! They live only in memory, as unsub-
stantial as the promissory notes ye gave for them.
When it came to be tested, the whole matter was
found to be hollow and fallacious. Like a sum
ciphered out through a long column, the first figure
an error, the whole and all the parts were wrong,
throughout the entire calculation.

Such is a charcoal sketch of the interesting region
—now inferior to none in resources and the character of its population—during the FLUSH TIMES;
a period constituting an episode in the commercial

history of the world,—the reign of humbug and wholesale insanity, just overthrown in time to save the whole country from ruin. But while it lasted, many of our countrymen came into the Southwest in time to get "a benefit." The *auri sacra fames* is a catching disease. Many Virginians had lived too fast for their fortunes, and naturally desired to recuperate; many others, with a competency, longed for wealth; and others, again, with wealth, yearned — the common frailty — for still more. Perhaps some friend or relative, who had come out, wrote back flattering accounts of the El Dorado, and fired with dissatisfaction those who were doing well enough at home, by the report of his real or imagined success; for who that ever moved off was not "doing well" in the new country, himself or friends being chroniclers?

Superior to many of the settlers in elegance of manners and general intelligence, it was the weakness of the Virginian to imagine he was superior too in the essential art of being able to hold his hand and make his way in a new country, and especially *such* a country, and at *such* a time. What a mistake that was! The times were out of joint. It was hard to say whether it were more dangerous to stand still or to move. If the emigrant stood still, he was consumed, by no slow degrees, by expenses; if he moved, ten to one he went off in a galloping consumption, by a ruinous investment. Expenses then — necessary articles about three times as high, and extra articles still more extra-priced—were a different thing in the new country from what they were in the old. In the old country, a jolly Virginian, starting the business of free living on a capital of a plantation and fifty or sixty negroes, might reasonably calculate, if no ill luck befell him, by the aid of a usurer and the occasional sale of a negro or two, to hold out without declared insolvency until a green old age. His estate melted like an estate in chancery, under the gradual thaw of expenses; but in this fast country it went by the sheer cost of living,—some *poker* losses included,—like the fortune of the confectioner in California, who failed for one hundred thousand dollars in the six months' keeping of a candy-shop. But all the habits of his life, his taste, his associations, his education,—everything; the trustingness of his disposition, his want of business qualifications, his sanguine temper all that was Virginian in him, made him the prey, if not of imposture, at least of unfortunate speculations. Where the keenest jockey often was bit, what chance had *he?* About the same that the verdant Moses had with the venerable old gentleman, his father's friend, at the fair, when he traded the Vicar's pony for the green spectacles. But how could he believe it? How *could* he believe that that shuttering, grammarless Georgian, who had never heard of the resolutions of '98, could beat him in a land trade? "Have no money dealings with my father," said the friendly Martha to Lord Nigel; "for, idiot though he seems, he will make an ass of thee." What a pity some monitor, equally wise and equally successful with old Trapbois' daughter, had not been at the elbow of every Virginian! "Twad frae monie a blunder free'd him, an' foolish notion."

If he made a bad bargain, how could he expect to get rid of it? *He* knew nothing of the elaborate machinery of ingenious chicane, such as feigning bankruptcy, fraudulent conveyances, making over to his wife, running property; and had never heard of such tricks of trade as sending out coffins to the graveyard, with negroes inside, carried off by sudden spells of imaginary disease, to be "resurrected" in due time, grinning, on the banks of the Brazos.

The new philosophy, too, had commended itself to his speculative temper. He readily caught at the idea of a new spirit of the age having set in, which rejected the saws of Poor Richard as being as much out of date as his almanacs. He was already, by the great rise of property, compared to his condition under the old-time prices, rich; and what were a few thousands of debt, which two or three crops would pay off, compared to the value of his estate? (He never thought that the value of property might come down, while the debt was a fixed fact). He lived freely, for it was a liberal time, and liberal fashions were in vogue, and it was not for a Virginian to be behind others in hospitality and liberality. He required credit and security, and of course had to stand security in return. When the crash came, and no "accommodations" could be had, except in a few instances, and in those on the most ruinous terms, he fell an easy victim. They broke up neighborhoods. They usually indorsed for each other, and when one fell—like the child's play of putting bricks on end at equal distances, and dropping the first in the line against the second, which fell against the third, and so on to the last—all fell; each got broke as security, and yet few or none were able to pay their own debts! So powerless of protection were they in those times that the witty H. G. used to say they reminded him of an oyster, both shells torn off, lying on the beach, with the sea-gulls screaming over them; the only question being *which* should "gobble them up."

There was one consolation: if the Virginian involved himself like a fool, he suffered himself to be sold out like a gentleman. When his card house of visionary projects came tumbling about his ears, the next question was the one Webster plagiarized, "Where am I to go?" Those who had fathers, uncles, aunts, or other like *dernier resorts* in Virginia limped back, with feathers moulted and crestfallen, to the old stamping ground, carrying the returned Californian's fortune of ten thousand dollars,—six bits in money, and the balance in experience. Those who were in the condition of the prodigal (barring the father, the calf,—the fatted one I mean,—and the fiddle) had to turn their accomplishments to account; and many of them, having lost all by eating and drinking, sought the retributive justice from meat and drink, which might, at least, support them in poverty. Accordingly, they kept tavern, and made a barter of hospitality a business, the only disagreeable part of which was receiving the money, and the only one I know of for which a man can eat and drink himself into qualification. And while I confess I never knew a Virginian, out of the State, to keep a bad tavern, I never knew one to draw a solvent breath from the time he opened house until death or the sheriff closed it.

Others, again, got to be not exactly overseers, but some nameless thing, the duties of which were nearly analogous, for some more fortunate Virginian, who had escaped the wreck, and who had got his former boon companion to live with him on board, or other wages, in some such relation that the friend was not often found at table at the dinings given to the neighbors, and had got to be called Mr. Flournoy instead of Bob, and slept in an out-house in the yard, and only read the "Enquirer" of nights and Sundays.

Some of the younger scions, that had been transplanted early, and stripped of their foliage at a tender age, had been turned into birches for the corrective discipline of youth. Yes; many who had received academical or collegiate educations, disregarding the allurements of the highway, turning from the gala-day exercise of ditching, scorning the effeminate relaxation of splitting rails, heroically led the Forlorn Hope of the battle of life, the corps of pedagogues of country schools, *academies,* I beg pardon for *not* saying; for, under the Virginia economy, every cross-road log-cabin, where boys were flogged from B-a-k-e-r to Constantinople, grew into the dignity of a sort of runt college; and the teacher vainly endeavored to hide the meanness of the calling beneath the sonorous *sobriquet* of Professor. "Were there no wars?" Had *all* the oysters been opened? Where was the regular army? Could not interest procure service as a deck-hand on a steamboat? Did no stage-driver, with a contract for running at night through the prairies in mid-winter, want help, at board wages, and sweet lying in the loft, when off duty, thrown in? What right had the Dutch Jews to monopolize *all* the peddling? "To such vile uses may we come at last, Horatio." The subject grows melancholy. I had a friend on whom this catastrophe descended. Tom Edmundson was a buck of the first head,—gay, witty, dashing, vain, proud, handsome, and volatile, and, withal, a dandy and lady's man to the last intent in particular. He had graduated at the University, and had just settled with his guardian, and received his patrimony of ten thousand dollars in money. Being a young gentleman of enterprise, he sought the alluring fields of Southwestern adventure, and found them in this State. Before he well knew the condition of his exchequer, he had made a permanent investment of one half his fortune in cigars, champagne, trinkets, buggies, horses, and current expenses, including some small losses at poker, which game he patronized merely for amusement; and found that it diverted him a good deal, but diverted his cash much more. He invested the balance, on private information kindly given him, in *"Choctaw Floats."* A most lucrative investment it would have turned out, but for the facts: (1) that the Indians never had any title; (2) the white men who kindly interposed to act as guardians for the Indians did not have the Indian title; and (3) the land, left subject to entry, if the "Floats" had been good, was not worth entering. "These imperfections off its head," I know of no fancy stock I would prefer to a "Choctaw Float." "Brief, brave, and glorious" was "Tom's young career." When Thomas found, as he did shortly, that he had bought five thousand dollars' worth of moonshine, and had no title to it, he honestly informed his landlord of the state of his "fiscality," and that worthy kindly consented to take a new buggy, at half price, in payment of the old balance. The horse, a nick-tailed trotter, Tom had raffled off; but omitting to require cash, the process of collection resulted in his getting the price of one chance, —the winner of the horse magnanimously paying his subscription. The rest either had gambling offsets, or else were not prepared just as any one particular given moment to pay up, though always ready generally and in a general way.

Unlike his namesake, Tom and his landlady were not—for a sufficient reason—very gracious; and so, the only common bond, Tom's money, being gone, Tom received "notice to quit" in regular form.

In the hurly-burly of the times, I had lost sight of Tom for a considerable period. One day, as I was traveling over the hills in Greene, by a cross-road, leading me near a country mill, I stopped to get water at a spring at the bottom of a hill. Clambering up the hill, after remounting, on the other side, the summit of it brought me to a view, through the bushes, of a log country school-house, the door being wide open; and who did I see but Tom Edmundson, dressed as fine as ever, sitting back in an armchair, one thumb in his waistcoat armhole, the other hand brandishing a long switch, or rather pole. As I approached a little nearer, I heard him speak out: "Sir, Thomas Jefferson, of Virginia, was the author of the Declaration of Independence,—mind that. I thought everybody knew that, even the Georgians." Just then he saw me coming through the bushes and entering the path that led by the door. Suddenly he broke from the chair of state, and the door was slammed to, and I heard some one of the boys, as I passed the door, say, "Tell him he can't come in; the master's sick." This is the last I ever saw of Tom. I understand he afterwards moved to Louisiana, where he married a rich French widow, having first, however, to fight a duel with one of her sons, whose opposition could n't be appeased until some such expiatory sacrifice to the manes of his worthy father was attempted; which failing, he made rather a *lame* apology for his zealous indiscretion,—the poor fellow could make no other, for Tom had unfortunately fixed him for visiting his mother on crutches the balance of his life.

One thing I will say for the Virginians: I never knew one of them, under any pressure, extemporize a profession. The sentiment of reverence for the mysteries of medicine and law was too large for a deliberate quackery; as to the pulpit, a man might as well do his starving with the hypocrisy.

But others were not so nice. I have known them to rush, when the wolf was after them, from the counting-house or the plantation into a doctor's shop or a law office, as if those places were the sanctuaries from the avenger; some pretending to be doctors that did not know a liver from a gizzard, administering medicine by the guess, without knowing enough of pharmacy to tell whether the stuff exhibited in the big-bellied blue, red, and green bottles at the show-windows of the apothecaries' shops was given by the drop or the half pint.

Divers others left, but what became of them I never knew, any more than they know what becomes of the sora after frost.

Many were the instances of suffering; of pitiable misfortune, involving and crushing whole families; of pride abased; of honorable sensibilities wounded; of the provision for old age destroyed; of the hopes of manhod overcast; of independence dissipated, and the poor victim, without help, or hope, or sympathy, forced to petty shifts for a bare subsistence, and a ground-scuffle for what in happier days he threw away. But there were too many examples of this sort for the expenditure of a useless compassion; just as the surgeon, after a battle, grows case-hardened, from an excess of objects of pity.

My memory, however, fixes itself on one honored exception, the noblest of the noble, the best of the good. Old Major Willis Wormley had come in long before the *new era*. He belonged to the old school of Virginians. Nothing could have torn him from the Virginia he loved, as Jacopi Foscari, Venice, but the marrying of his eldest daughter, Mary, to a gentleman of Alabama. The Major was something between, or made of about equal parts of, Uncle Toby and Mr. Pickwick, with a slight flavor of Mr. Micawber. He was the soul of kindness, disinterestedness, and hospitality. Love to everything that had life in it burned like a flame in his large and benignant soul; it flowed over in his countenance, and glowed through every feature, and moved every muscle in the frame it animated. The Major lived freely, was rather corpulent, and had not a lean thing on his plantations; the negroes, the dogs, the horses, the cattle, the very chickens, wore an air of corpulent complacency, and bustled about with a good-humored rotundity. There was more laughing, singing, and whistling at "Hollywood" than would have set up a dozen Irish fairs. The Major's wife had, from a long life of affection, and the practice of the same pursuits, and the indulgence of the same feelings and tastes, got so much like him that she seemed a feminine and modest edition of himself. Four daughters were all that remained in the family,—two had been married off,—and they had no son. The girls ranged from sixteen to twenty-two,—fine, hearty, whole-souled, wholesome, cheerful lasses, with constitutions to last, and a flow of spirits like mountain springs; not beauties, but good housewife girls, whose open countenances and neat figures and rosy cheeks and laughing eyes and frank and cordial manners made them, at home, abroad, on horseback or on foot, at the piano or discoursing on the old English books or Washington Irving's Sketch Book, —a favorite in the family ever since it was written,— as entertaining and as well calculated to fix solid impressions on the heart as any four girls in the country. The only difficulty was they were so much alike that you were put to fault which to fall in love with. They were all good housewives, or women, rather. But Mrs. Wormley, or Aunt Wormley, as we called her, was as far ahead of any other woman in that way, as could be found this side of the Virginia border. If there was anything good in the culinary line that she couldn't make, I should like to know it. The Major lived on the main stage-road, and if any decently dressed man ever passed the house after sundown he escaped by sheer accident.

The house was greatly visited. The Major knew everybody, and everybody near him knew the Major. The stage-coach could n't stop long, but in the hot summer days, about noon, as the driver tooted his horn at the top of the red hill, two negro boys stood opposite the door, with trays of the finest fruit and a pitcher of cider for the refreshment of the wayfarers; the Major himself being on the lookout, with his hands over his eyes, bowing—as he only could bow—vaguely into the coach, and looking wistfully to find among the passengers an acquaintance whom he could prevail upon to get out and stay a week with him. There was n't a poor neighbor to whom the Major had not been as good as an insurer, without premium, for his stock, or for his crop; and from the way he rendered the service, you would think he was the party obliged,—as he was.

This is not, in any country I have ever been in, a money-making business; and the Major, though he always made good crops, must have broke at it long ago, but for the fortunate death of a few aunts, after whom the girls were named, who, paying their several debts of nature, left the Major the means to pay his less serious but still weighty obligations.

The Major, for a wonder, being a Virginian, had no partisan politics. He could not have. His heart could not hold anything that implied a warfare upon the thoughts or feelings of others. He voted all the time for his friend, that is, the candidate living nearest to him; regretting, generally, that he did not have another vote for the other man.

It would have done a Comanche Indian's heart good to see all the family together—grandchildren and all—of a winter evening, with a guest or two to excite sociability a little; not company enough to embarrass the manifestations of affection. Such a concordance, as if all hearts were attuned to the same feeling: the old lady knitting in the corner, the old man smoking his pipe opposite; both of their fine faces radiating, in the pauses of the laugh, the jest, or the caress, the infinite satisfaction within.

It was enough to convert an abolitionist to see the old Major, when he came home from a long journey of two days to the county town,—the negroes running in a string to the buggy, this one to hold the horse, that one to help the old man out, and the others to inquire how he was; and to observe the benignity with which—the kissing of the girls and the old lady hardly over—he distributed a piece of calico here, a plug of tobacco there, or a card of *town* gingerbread to the little snow-balls that grinned around him: what was given being but a small part of the gift, divested of the kind, cheerful, rollicking way the old fellow had of giving it.

The Major had given out his autograph (as had almost everybody else) as indorser on three several bills of exchange, of even tenor and date, and all maturing at or about the same time. His friend's friend failed to pay as he or his firm agreed, the friend himself did no better, and the Major, before he knew anything at all of his danger, found a writ served upon him, and was told by his friend that he was dead broke, and all he could give him was his sympathy; the which the Major as gratefully received as if it was a legal tender, and would pay the debt. The Major's friends advised him he could get clear of it; that notice of protest not having been sent to the Major's post-office released him. But the Major would n't hear of such a defense; he said *his* understanding was that he was to pay the debt, if his friend did n't; and to slip out of it by a quibble was little better than pleading the gambling act. Besides, what would the lawyers say? And what would be said by his old friends in Virginia, when it reached their ears that he had plead want of notice to get clear of a debt, when everybody knew it was the same thing as if he had got notice? And if this defense were good at law, it would not be in equity; and if they took it into chancery, it mattered not what became of the case; the property would all go, and he never could expect to see the last of it. No, no; he would pay it, and had as well set about it at once.

The rumor of the Major's condition spread far and wide. It reached old N. D., "an angel," whom the Major had "entertained," and one of the few that ever traveled that road. He came, post haste, to see into the affair; saw the creditor; made him, upon threat of defense, agree to take half the amount, and discharge the Major; advanced the money, and took the Major's negroes, except the house servants, and put them on the Mississippi plantation to work out the debt.

The Major's heart pained him at the thought of the negroes going off; he could n't witness it, though he consoled himself with the idea of the discipline and exercise being good for the health of sundry of them who had contracted sedentary diseases.

The Major turned his house into a tavern,—that is, changed its name,—put up a sign, and three weeks afterwards you could n't have told that anything had happened. The family were as happy as ever: the Major, never having put on airs of arrogance in prosperity, felt no humiliation in adversity; the girls were as cheerful, as bustling, and as lighthearted as ever, and seemed to think of the duties of hostesses as mere bagatelles, to enliven the time. The old Major was as profluent of anecdotes as ever, and never grew tired of telling the same ones to every new guests; and yet the Major's anecdotes

were all of Virginia growth, and not one of them
under the legal age of twenty-one. If the Major
had worked his negroes as he had those anecdotes,
he would have been able to pay off the bills of exchange without any difficulty.

The old lady and the girls laughed at the anecdotes, though they must have heard them at least a
thousand times, and knew them by heart, for the
Major told them without the variations; and the
other friends of the Major laughed, too. Indeed, with
such an air of thorough benevolence, and in such a
truly social spirit, did the old fellow proceed "the
tale to unfold," that a Cassius-like rascal that
wouldn't laugh, whether he saw anything to laugh
at or not, ought to have been sent to the penitentiary for life,—half of the time to be spent in solitary confinement.

JOEL CHANDLER HARRIS.

BROTHER WOLF SAYS GRACE.*

From Nights with Uncle Remus (1883).

'TILDY, the house-girl, made such a terrible report of the carryings on of Daddy Jack that the little boy's mother thought it prudent not to allow him to visit Uncle Remus so often. The child amused himself as best he could for several nights, but his playthings and picture-books finally lost their interest. He cried so hard to be allowed to go to see Uncle Remus that his mother placed him under the care of Aunt Tempy,—a woman of large authority on the place, and who stood next to Uncle Remus in the confidence of her mistress. Aunt Tempy was a fat, middle-aged woman, who always wore a head-handkerchief, and kept her sleeves rolled up, displaying her plump, black arms, winter and summer. She never hesitated to exercise her authority, and the younger negroes on the place regarded her as a tyrant; but in spite of her loud voice and brusque manners she was thoroughly good-natured, usually good-humored, and always trustworthy. Aunt Tempy and Uncle Remus were secretly jealous of each other, but they were careful never to come in conflict, and, to all appearances, the most cordial relations existed between them.

"Well de goodness knows!" exclaimed Uncle Remus, as Aunt Tempy went in with the little boy. "How you come on, Sis Tempy? De rainy season aint so mighty fur off w'en you come a-sojourneyin' in dis house. Ef I'd a-know'd you'd a-bin a-comin' I'd a-sorter steered 'roun' en bresh'd de cobwebs out'n de cornders."

"Don't min' me, Brer Remus. Luck in de house whar de cobwebs hangs low. I 'uz des a-passin'—a-passin' 'long—en Miss Sally ax me ef I kin come fur ez de do' wid dat chile dar, but bless you, 't aint in my manners ter tu'n back at de do'. How you come on, Brer Remus?"

"Po'ly, Sis Tempy; en yit I aint complainin'. Pain yer, en a ketch yander, wid de cramps th'ow'd in, aint no mo' dan ole folks kin 'speck. How you is, Sis Tempy?"

"I thank de Lord I'm able to crawl, Brer Remus, en dat's 'bout all. Ef I wa'nt so sot in my ways, deze yer niggers would er run me 'stracted d'rectly."

Daddy Jack was sitting in the corner laughing and talking to himself, and the little boy watched him not without a feeling of awe. After a while he said:

"Uncle Remus, won't Daddy Jack tell us a story to-night?"

"Now, den, honey," responded the old man, "we aint got ter push Brer Jack too closte; we ull des hatter creep up on 'im en ketch 'im fer er tale wence he in de humors. Sometime hoss pull, sometime he aint pull. You aint bin down yer so long, hit sorter look lak it my tu'n; 'kaze it done come 'cross my 'membunce dat dey wuz one time w'en Brer Wolf kotch Brer Rabbit, w'ich I aint never gun it out ter you yit."

"Brother Wolf caught Brother Rabbit, Uncle Remus?" exclaimed the little boy, incredulously.

"Yasser! dat's de up en down un it, sho'," responded the old man with emphasis, "en I be mighty glad ef Sis Tempy yer will 'scuze me w'iles I runs over de tale 'long wid you."

"Bless yo' soul, Brer Remus, don't pay no 'tention ter me," said Aunt Tempy, folding her fat arms upon her ample bosom, and assuming an attitude of rest and contentment. "I'm bad ez de chillun 'bout dem ole tales, 'kase I kin des set up yer un lissen at um de whole blessid night, un a good part er de day. Yass, Lord!"

"Well, den," said Uncle Remus, "we ull des huddle up yer en see w'at 'come er Brer Rabbit w'en ole Brer Wolf kotch 'im. In dem days," he continued, looking at Daddy Jack and smiling broadly, "de creeturs wuz constant gwine a-courtin'. Ef 'twa'n't Miss Meadows en de gals dey wuz flyin' 'roun', hit 'uz Miss Motts. Dey wuz constant a-courtin'. En 'twa'n't none er dish yer 'Howdy-do-ma'm-I-'speck-I-better-be-gwine,' ne'r. Hit 'uz go atter brekkus en stay twel atter supper. Brer Rabbit, he got tuk wid a-likin' fer Miss Motts, en soon one mawnin', he tuck'n slick hisse'f up, he did, en put out ter call on 'er. W'en Brer Rabbit git ter whar Miss Motts live, she done gone off some'rs.

"Some folks 'ud er sot down en wait twel Miss Motts come back, en den ag'in some folks 'ud er tuck der foot in der han' en went back; but ole Brer Rabbit, he aint de man fer ter be outdone, en he des tuck'n go in de kitchen en light he seegyar, en den he put out fer ter pay a call on Miss Meadows en de gals.

"W'en he git dar, lo en beholes, he fine Miss Motts dar, en he tipped in, ole Brer Rabbit did, en he galanted 'roun' 'mungs um, same lak one er dese yer town chaps, w'at you see come out ter Harmony Grove meetin'-house. Dey talk en dey laff; dey laff en dey giggle. Bimeby, 'long todes night, Brer Rabbit 'low he better be gwine. De wimmen folks dey all ax 'im fer ter stay twel atter supper, 'kaze he sech lively comp'ny, but Brer Rabbit fear'd some er de yuther creeturs be hidin' out fer 'im; so he tuck'n pay his 'specks, he did, en start fer home.

"He aint git fur twel he come up with a great big

basket settin' down by de side er de big road. He
look up de road; he aint see nobody. He looks down
de road; he aint see nobody. He look befo', he look
behime, he look all 'round'; he aint see nobody. He
lissen, en lissen; he aint year nothin'. He wait, en
he wait; nobody aint come.

"Den, bimeby Brer Rabbit go en peep in de basket, en it seem lak it half full er green truck. He
retch he han' in, he did, en git some en put it in he
mouf. Den he shet he eyes en do lak he studyin'
'bout sump'n'. Atter w'ile, he 'low ter hisse'f, 'Hit
look lak sparrer-grass, hit feel like sparrer-grass, hit
tas-e lak sparrer-grass, en I be bless ef 't aint sparrer-grass.'

"Wid dat Brer Rabbit jump up, he did, en crack
he heel tergedder, en he fetch one leap en lan' in
de basket, right spang in 'mungs de sparrer-grass.
Dar whar he miss he footin'," continued Uncle
Remus, rubbing his beard meditatively, "'kaze w'en
he jump in 'mungs de sparrer-grass, right den en
dar he jump in 'mungs ole Brer Wolf, w'ich he wer'
quile up at de bottom."

"Dar now!" exclaimed Aunt Tempy, enthusias-
tically. "W'at I tell you? W'at make him pester
t'er folks doin's? I boun' Brer Wolf nail't 'im."

"Time Brer Wolf grab 'im," continued Uncle
Remus, "Brer Rabbit knowed he 'uz a gone case;
yit he sing out, he did:

"I des tryin' ter skeer you, Brer Wolf; I des
tryin' ter skeer you. I know'd you 'uz in dar, Brer
Wolf. I know'd you by de smell!' sez Brer Rabbit,
sezee.

"Ole Brer Wolf grin, he did, en lick he chops, en
up'n say:

" 'Mighty glad you know'd me, Brer Rabbit, 'kaze
I know'd you des time you drapt in on me. I tuck'n
tell Brer Fox yistiddy dat I 'uz gwine take a nap

'longside er de road, en I boun' you 'ud come 'long
en wake me up, en sho' nuff, yer you come en yer
you is,' sez Brer Wolf, sezee.''

"Oh-ho, Mr. Rabbit! How you feel now?" exclaimed Aunt Tempy, her sympathies evidently with
Brother Wolf.

"W'en Brer Rabbit year dis," said Uncle Remus,
payin no attention to the interruption, "he 'gun ter
git mighty skeer'd, en he whirl in en beg Brer Wolf
fer ter place tu'n 'im loose; but dis make Brer Wolf
grin wusser, en he toof look so long en shine so
w'ite, en he gum look so red, dat Brer Rabbit hush
up en stay still. He so skeer'd dat he bref come
quick, en he heart go lak flutter-mill. He chune up
lak he gwine cry:

" 'Whar you gwine kyar me, Brer Wolf?'

" 'Down by de branch, Brer Rabbit.'

" 'W'at you gwine down dar fer, Brer Wolf?'

" 'So I kin git some water ter clean you wid atter
I done skunt you, Brer Rabbit.'

" 'Please, sir, lemme go, Brer Wolf.'

" 'You talk so young you make me laff, Brer Rabbit.'

" 'Dat sparrer-grass done make me sick, Brer
Wolf.'

" 'You ull be sicker'n dat 'fo' I git done wid you,
Brer Rabbit.'

" 'Whar I come fum nobody dast ter eat sick
folks, Brer Wolf.'

" 'Whar I come fum dey aint dast ter eat no
yuther kin', Brer Rabbit.' "

"Ole Mr. Rabbit wuz a-talkin', mon," said Aunt
Tempy, with a chuckle that caused her to shake like
a piece of jelly.

"Dey went on dis a-way," continued Uncle
Remus, "plum twel dey git ter de branch. Brer
Rabbit, he beg en cry, en cry en beg, en Brer Wolf,

he 'fuse en grin, en grin en 'fuse. W'en dey come
ter de branch, Brer Wolf lay Brer Rabbit down on
de groun' en hilt 'im dar, en den he study how he
gwine make way wid 'im. He study en he study, en
w'iles he studyin' Brer Rabbit, he tuck'n study some
on he own hook.

"Den w'en it seem lak Brer Wolf done fix all de
'rangerments, Brer Rabbit, he make lak he cryin'
wusser en wusser; he des fa'rly blubber."

Uncle Remus gave a ludicrous imitation of
Brother Rabbit's wailings.

" 'Ber—ber—Brer Wooly—ooly—oolf! Is you
gwine—is you gwine ter sakerfice-t me right now—
ow—ow?'

" 'Dat I is, Brer Rabbit; dat I is.'

" 'Well, ef I blee-eedz ter be kilt, Brer Wooly—
ooly—oolf, I wants ter be kilt right, en ef I blee-eedz
ter be e't, I wants ter be e't ri—ight, too, now!'

" 'How dat, Brer Rabbit?' "

" 'I want you ter show yo' p'liteness, Brer Wooly
—ooly—oolf!'

" 'How I gwine do dat, Brer Rabbit?'

" 'I want you ter say grace, Brer Wolf, en say
it quick, 'kaze I gittin' mighty weak.'

" 'How I gwine say grace, Brer Rabbit?'

" 'Fol' yo' han's und' yo' chin, Brer Wolf, en
shet yo' eyes, en say; "Bless us en bine us, en put
us in crack whar de Ole Boy can't fine us." Say it
quick, Brer Wolf, 'kaze I failin' mighty fas'.' "

"Now aint dat des too much!" exclaimed Aunt
Tempy, as delighted as the little boy. Uncle Remus
laughed knowingly and went on:

"Brer Wolf, he put up he han's, he did, en shot
he eyes, en 'low, 'Bless us en bine us;' but he aint
git no furder, 'kaze des time he take up he han's,
Brer Rabbit fotch a wiggle, he did, en lit on he foots,
en he does nat'ally lef' a blue streak behime 'im."

"Ay-yi-ee!" exclaimed Daddy Jack, while Aunt Tempy allowed her arms to drop helplessly from her lap as she cried "Dar now!" and the little boy clasped his hands in an ectasy of admiration.

"Oh, I just knew Brother Rabbit would get away," the child declared.

"Dat's right, honey," said Uncle Remus. "You put yo' pennunce in Brer Rabbit en yo' won't be fur out er de way."

There was some further conversation among the negroes, but it was mostly plantation gossip. When Aunt Tempy rose to go, she said:

"Goodness knows, Brer Remus ef dis de way you all runs on, I'm gwine ter pester you some mo.' Hit come 'cross me like ole times, dat it do."

"Do so, Sis Tempy, do so," said Uncle Remus, with dignified hospitality. "You allers fine a place at my h'a'th. Ole Times is about all we got lef'."

"Trufe, too!" exclaimed Aunt Tempy; and with that she took the child by the hand and went out into the darkness.

BROTHER RABBIT AND THE LITTLE GIRL.*

From Nights with Uncle Remus (1883).

"What did Brother Rabbit do after that?" the little boy asked presently.

"Now, den, you don't wanter push ole Brer Rabbit too close," replied Uncle Remus significantly. "He mighty tender-footed creetur, en de mo' w'at you push 'im, de furder he lef' you."

There was prolonged silence in the old man's cabin, until, seeing that the little boy was growing

restless enough to cast several curious glances in
the direction of the tool-chest in the corner, Uncle
Remus lifted one leg over the other, scratched his
head reflectively, and began:

"One time, atter Brer Rabbit done bin trompin'
'roun' huntin' up some sallid fer ter make out he
dinner wid, he fine hisse'f in de neighborhoods er
Mr. Man house, en he pass 'long twel he come ter
de gyardin-gate, en nigh de gyardin-gate he see Little Gal playin' roun' in de san'. W'en Brer Rabbit
look 'twix' de gyardin-palin's en see de colluds, en
de sparrer-grass, en de yuther gyardin truck grow-
in' dar, hit make he mouf water. Den he take en
walk up ter de Little Gal, Brer Rabbit did, en pull
he roach,* en bow, en scrape he foot, en talk mighty
nice en slick.

" 'Howdy, Little Gal', sez Brer Rabbit, sezee;
'how you come on?' sezee.

"Den de Little Gal, she 'spon' howdy, she did, en
she ax Brer Rabbit how he come on, en Brer Rabbit,
he 'low he mighty po'ly, en den he ax ef dis de Little Gal w'at 'er pa live up dar in de big w'ite house,
w'ich de Little Gal, she up'n say 'twer'. Brer Rabbit, he say he mighty glad, kaze he des bin up dar
fer to see 'er pa, en he say dat 'er pa, he sont 'im out
dar fer ter tell de Little Gal dat she mus' open de
gyardin-gate so Brer Rabbit kin go in en git some
truck. Den de Little Gal, she jump 'roun', she did,
en she open de gate, en wid dat, Brer Rabbit, he hop
in, he did, en got 'im a mess er greens, en hop out
ag'in, en w'en he gwine off he make a bow, he did,
en tell de Little Gal dat he much 'blije', en den atter
dat he put out fer home.

"Nex' day, Brer Rabbit, he hide out, he did, twel
he see de Little Gal come out ter play, en den he put
up de same tale, en walk off wid a n'er mess er

---

*Topknot, foretop.

truck, en hit keep on dis a-way, twel bimeby Mr. Man, he 'gun ter miss his greens, en he keep on a-missin' un um, twel he got ter excusin' eve'ybody on de place er 'stroyin' un um, en w'en dat come ter pass, de Little Gal, she up'n say:

" 'My goodness, pa!' sez she, 'you done tole Mr. Rabbit fer ter come and make me let 'im in de gyardin atter some greens, en aint he done come en ax me, en aint I done gone en let 'im in?' sez she.

"Mr. Man aint hatter study long 'fo' he see how de lan' lay, en den he laff, en tell de Little Gal dat he done gone en disremember all 'bout Mr. Rabbit, en den he up'n say, sezee:

" 'Nex' time Mr. Rabbit come, you tak'n tu'n 'im in, en den you run des ez fas' ez you kin en come en tell me, kase I got some bizness wid dat young chap dat's bleedze ter be 'ten' ter,' sezee.

"Sho' nuff, nex' mawnin' dar wuz de Little Gal playin' 'roun', en yer come Brer Rabbit atter he 'lowance er greens. He wuz ready wid de same tale, en den de Little Gal, she tu'n 'im in, she did, en den she run up ter de house en holler:

" 'O pa! pa! O pa! Yer Brer Rabbit in de gyardin now! Yer he is, pa!'

"Den Mr. Man, he rush out, en grab up a fishin'-line w'at bin hangin' in de back po'ch, en mak fer de gyardin, en w'en he git dar, dar wuz Brer Rabbit tromplin' 'roun' on de strawbe'y-bed en mashin' down de termartusses. W'en Brer Rabbit see Mr. Man, he squot behime a collud leaf, but 't wa'n't no use. Mr. Man done seed him, en 'fo' you kin count 'lev'm, he done got ole Brer Rabbit tie hard en fas' wid de fishin'-line. Atter he got him tie good, Mr. Man step back, he did, en say, sezee:

" 'You done bin fool me lots er time, but dis time you er mine. I'm gwine ter take you en gin you a larrupin',' seezee, 'en den I'm gwine ter skin you

en nail yo' hide on de stable do',' sezee; en den ter
make sho dat you git de right kinder larrupin', I'll
des step up ter de house,' sezee, 'en fetch de little
red cowhide, en den I'll take en gin you brinjer',
sezee.

"Den Mr. Man call to der Little Gal ter watch
Brer Rabbit w'iles he gone.

"Brer Rabbit aint sayin' nothin', but Mr. Man
aint mo'n out de gate 'fo' he 'gun ter sing; en in
dem days Brer Rabbit wuz a singer, mon," continued Uncle Remus, with unusual emphasis, "en w'en
he chuned up fer ter sing he make dem yuther creeturs hol' der bref."

"What did he sing, Uncle Remus?" asked the
little boy.

"Ef I aint fergit dat song off'n my min'," said
Uncle Remus, looking over his spectacles at the fire,
with a curious air of attempting to remember some-
thing, "hit run sorter dish yer way:
" 'De jay-bird hunt de sparrer-nes',
De bee-martin sail all 'roun';
De squer'l, he holler from de top er de tree,
Mr. Mole, he stay in de groun';
He hide en he stay twel de dark drap down—
Mr. Mole, he hide in de groun'.'

"W'en de Little Gal year dat, she laugh, she did,
and she up'n ax Brer Rabbit fer ter sing some mo',
but Brer Rabbit, he sorter cough, he did, en 'low
dat he got a mighty bad ho'seness down into he win'-
pipe some'rs. De Little Gal, she swade,* en swade,
en bimeby Brer Rabbit, he up'n 'low dat he kin
dance mo' samer dan w'at he kin sing. Den de Little
Gal, she ax 'im won't he dance, en Brer Rabbit, he
'spon' how in de name er goodness kin a man dance
w'iles he all tie up dis a-way, en den de Little Gal,
she say she kin ontie 'im, en Brer Rabbit, he say he

*Persuaded.
Vol. 8—16

aint keerin' ef she do. Wid dat de Little Gal, she
retch down en onloose de fish-line, en Brer Rabbit,
he sorter stretch hisse'f en look 'roun'."

Here Uncle Remus paused and sighed, as though
he had relieved his mind of a great burden. The little boy waited a few minutes for the old man to resume, and finally he asked:

"Did the Rabbit dance, Uncle Remus?"

"Who? Him?" exclaimed the old man, with a
queer affectation of elation. "Bless yo' soul, honey!
Brer Rabbit gedder up his foots und' 'im, en he
dance outer dat gyardin, en he dance home. He did
dat! Sho'ly you don't 'speck dat a ole-timer w'at
done had 'spe'unce like Brer Rabbit gwine ter stay
dar en let dat ar Mr. Man sackyfice 'im? *Shoo!*
Brer Rabbit dance, but he dance home. You year
me!"

FREE JOE AND THE REST OF THE WORLD.*

From Free Joe and Other Georgia Sketches (1887).

THE name of Free Joe strikes humorously upon
the ear of memory. It is impossible to say why, for
he was the humblest, the simplest, and the most serious of all God's living creatures, sadly lacking in all
those elements that suggest the humorous. It is certain, moreover, that in 1850 the sober-minded citizens of the little Georgian village of Hillsborough
were inclined to take a humorous view of Free Joe,
and neither his name nor his presence provoked a
smile. He was a black atom, drifting hither and
thither without an owner, blown about by all the

winds of circumstances and given over to shiftlessness.

The problems of one generation are the paradoxes
of a succeeding one, particularly if war, or some such
incident, intervenes to clarify the atmosphere and
strengthen the understanding. Thus, in 1850, Free
Joe represented not only a problem of large concern,
but, in the watchful eyes of Hillsborough, he was the
embodiment of that vague and mysterious danger
that seemed to be forever lurking on the outskirts
of slavery, ready to sound a shrill and ghostly signal
in the impenetrable swamps, and steal forth under
the midnight stars to murder, rapine, and pillage,—
a danger always threatening, and yet never assuming shape; intangible, and yet real; impossible, and
yet not improbable. Across the serene and smiling
front of safety, the pale outlines of the awful shadow
of insurrection sometimes fell. With this invisible
panorama as background, it was natural that the
figure of Free Joe, simple and humble as it was,
should assume undue proportions. Go where he
would, do what he might, he could not escape the
finger of observation and the kindling eye of suspicion. His lightest words were noted, his slightest
actions marked.

Under all the circumstances it was natural that
his peculiar condition should reflect itself in his
habits and manners. The slaves laughed loudly day
by day, but Free Joe rarely laughed. The slaves
sang at their work and danced at their frolics, but
no one ever heard Free Joe sing or saw him dance.
There was something painfully plaintive and appealing in his attitude, something touching in his
anxiety to please. He was of the friendliest nature,
and seemed to be delighted when he could amuse the
little children who had made a playground of the
public square. At times he would please them by

making his little dog Dan perform all sorts of curious tricks, or he would tell them quaint stories of the beast of the field and birds of the air; and frequently he was coaxed into relating the story of his own freedom. That story was brief, but tragical.

In the year of our Lord 1840, when a negro speculator of a sportive turn of mind reached the little village of Hillsborough on his way to the Mississippi region, with a caravan of likely negroes of both sexes, he found much to interest him. In that day and at that time there were a number of young men in the village who had not bound themselves over to repentance for the various misdeeds of the flesh. To these young men the negro-speculator (Major Frampton was his name) proceeded to address himself. He was a Virginian, he declared; and, to prove the statement, he referred all the festively inclined young men of Hillsborough to a barrel of peach-brandy in one of his covered wagons. In the minds of these young men there was less doubt in regard to the age and quality of the brandy than there was in regard to the negro-trader's birthplace. Major Frampton might or might not have been born in the Old Dominion,—that was a matter for consideration and inquiry,—but there could be no question as to the mellow pungency of the peach-brandy.

In his own estimation, Major Frampton was one of the most accomplished of men. He had summered at the Virginia Springs; he had been to Philadelphia, to Washington, to Richmond, to Lynchburg, and to Charleston, and had accumulated a great deal of experience which he found useful. Hillsborough was hid in the woods of Middle Georgia, and its general aspect of innocence impressed him. He looked on the young men who had shown their readiness to test his peach-brandy, as overgrown country boys who needed to be introduced to some of the arts and sciences he had at his command. Thereupon the Major pitched his tents, figuratively speaking, and became, for the time being, a part and parcel of the innocence that characterized Hillsborough. A wiser man would doubtless have made the same mistake.

The little village possessed advantages and seemed to be providentially arranged to fit the various enterprises that Major Frampton had in view. There was the auction-block in front of the stuccoed courthouse, if he desired to dispose of a few of his negroes; there was a quarter-track, laid out to his hand and in excellent order, if he chose to enjoy the pleasures of horse-racing; there were secluded pine thickets within easy reach, if he desired to indulge in the exciting pastime of cock-fighting; and various lonely and unoccupied rooms in the second story of the tavern, if he cared to challenge the chances of dice or cards.

Major Frampton tried them all with varying luck, until he began his famous game of poker with Judge Alfred Wellington, a stately gentleman with a flowing white beard and mild blue eyes that gave him the appearance of a benevolent patriarch. The history of the game in which Major Frampton and Judge Alfred Wellington took part is sometime more than a tradition in Hillsborough, for there are still living three or four men who sat around the table and watched its progress. It is said that at various stages of the game Major Frampton would destroy the cards with which they were playing, and send for a new pack, but the result was always the same. The mild blue eyes of Judge Wellington, with few exceptions, continued to overlook "hands" that were invincible—a habit they had acquired during a long and arduous course of training from Saratoga to New Orleans. Major Frampton lost

his money, his horses, his wagons, and all his negroes but one, his body-servant. When his misfortune had reached this limit, the major adjourned
the game. The sun was shining brightly, and all
nature was cheerful. It is said that the major also
seemed to be cheerful. However this may be, he
visited the court-house, and executed the papers that
gave his body-servant his freedom. This being done,
Major Frampton sauntered into a convenient pine
thicket, and blew out his brains.

The negro thus freed came to be known as Free
Joe. Compelled, under the law, to choose a guardian, he chose Judge Wellington, chiefly because his
wife Lucinda was among the negroes won from
Major Frampton. For several years Free Joe had
what may be called a jovial time. His wife Lucinda
was well provided for, and he found it a comparatively easy matter to provide for himself; so that,
taking all the circumstances into consideration, it
is not matter for astonishment that he became somewhat shiftless.

When Judge Wellington died, Free Joe's troubles
began. The judge's negroes, including Lucinda,
went to his half-brother, a man named Calderwood,
who was a hard master and a rough customer generally,—a man of many eccentricities of mind and
character. His neighbors had a habit of alluding
to him as "Old Spite;" and the name seemed to fit
him so completely that he was known far and near
as "Spite" Calderwood. He probably enjoyed the
distinction the name gave him, at any rate, he never
resented it, and it was not often that he missed an
opportunity to show that he deserved it. Calderwood's place was two or three miles from the village of Hillsborough, and Free Joe visited his wife
twice a week, Wednesday and Saturday nights.

One Sunday morning he was sitting in front of

Lucinda's cabin, when Calderwood happened to pass that way.

"Howdy, marster?" said Free Joe, taking off his hat.

"Who are you?" exclaimed Calderwood abruptly, halting and staring at the negro.

"I'm name' Joe, marster, I'm Lucindy's ole man."

"Who do you belong to?"

"Marse John Evans is my gyardeen, marster."

"Big name—gyardeen. Show your pass."

Free Joe produced the document, and Calderwood read it aloud slowly, as if he found it difficult to get at the meaning:

"To whom it may concern: This is to certify that the boy Joe Frampton has my permission to visit his wife Lucinda."

This was dated at Hillsborough, and signed *"John W. Evans."*

Calderwood read it twice, and then looked at Free Joe, elevating his eyebrows, and showing his discolored teeth.

"Some might big words in that there. Evans owns his place, I reckon. When's he comin' down to take hold?"

Free Joe fumbled with his hat. He was badly frightened.

"Lucindy say she speck you wouldn't min' my comin', long ez I behave, Marster."

Calderwood tore the pass in pieces and flung it away.

"Don't want no free niggers 'round here," he exclaimed. "There's the big road. It'll carry you to town. Don't let me catch you here no more. Now, mind what I tell you."

Free Joe presented a shabby spectacle as he moved off with his little dog Dan slinking at his heels. It should be said in behalf of Dan, however, that his bristles were up, and that he looked back and growled. It may be that the dog had the advantage of insignificance, but it is difficult to conceive how a dog bold enough to raise his bristles under Calderwood's very eyes could be as insignificant as Free Joe. But both the negro and his little dog seemed to give a new and more dismal aspect to forlornness as they turned into the road and went toward Hillsborough.

After this incident Free Joe seemed to have clear ideas concerning his peculiar condition. He realized the fact that though he was free he was more helpless than any slave. Having no owner, every man was his master. He knew that he was the object of suspicion, and therefore all his slender resources (ah! how pitifully slender they were!) were devoted to winning, not kindness and appreciation, but toleration; all his efforts were in the direction of mitigating the circumstances that tended to make his condition so much worse than that of the negroes around him,—negroes who had friends because they had masters.

So far as his own race was concerned, Free Joe was an exile. If the slaves secretly envied him his freedom (which is to be doubted, considering his miserable condition), they openly despised him, and lost no opportunity to treat him with contumely. Perhaps this was in some measure the result of the attitude which Free Joe chose to maintain toward them. No doubt his instinct taught him that to hold himself aloof from the slaves would be to invite from the whites the toleration which he coveted, and without which even his miserable condition would be rendered more miserable still.

His greatest trouble was the fact that he was not allowed to visit his wife; but he soon found a way

out of this difficulty. After he had been ordered
away from the Calderwood place, he was in the
habit of wandering as far in that direction as prudence would permit. Near the Calderwood place,
but not on Calderwood's land, lived an old man
named Micajah Staley and his sister Becky Staley.
These people were old and very poor. Old Micajah
had a palsied arm and hand; but, in spite of this, he
managed to earn a precarious living with his turn-
ing-lathe.

When he was a slave Free Joe would have scorned
these representatives of a class known as poor white
trash, but now he found them sympathetic and help-
ful in various ways. From the back door of the
cabin he could hear the Calderwood negroes singing at night, and he fancied he could distinguish
Lucinda's shrill treble rising above the other voices.
A large poplar grew in the woods some distance from
the Staley cabin, and at the foot of this tree Free
Joe would sit for hours with his face turned toward
Calderwood's. His little dog Dan would curl up
in the leaves near by, and the two seemed to be as
comfortable as possible.

One Saturday afternoon Free Joe, sitting at the
foot of this friendly poplar, fell asleep. How long
he slept, he could not tell; but when he awoke little
Dan was licking his face, the moon was shining
brightly, and Lucinda his wife stood before him
laughing. The dog seeing that Free Joe was asleep,
had grown somewhat impatient, and he concluded
to make an excursion to the Calderwood place on his
own account. Lucinda was inclined to give the incident a twist in the direction of superstition.

"I'z settin' down front er de fireplace," she said,
"cookin' me some meat, w'en all of a sudden I year
sumpin at de do'—scratch, scratch. I tuck'n tu'n
de meat over, en make out I aint year it. Bimeby it

come dar 'gin—scratch, scratch. I up en open de
do', I did, en, bless de Lord! dar wuz little Dan, en
it look like ter me dat his ribs done grown tergeer.
I gin 'im some bread, en den, w'en he start out, I
tuck'n foller 'im, kaze, I say ter myse'f, maybe my
nigger man mought be some'rs 'roun'. Dat are little
dog got sense, mon.''

Free Joe laughed and dropped his hand lightly on
Dan's head. For a long time after that he had no
difficulty in seeing his wife. He had only to sit by
the poplar tree until little Dan could run and fetch
her. But after a while the other negroes discovered
that Lucinda was meeting Free Joe in the woods, and
information of the fact soon reached Calderwood's
ears. He said nothing; but one day he put Lucinda
in his buggy, and carried her to Macon, sixty miles
away. He carried her to Macon, and came back
without her; and nobody in or around Hillsborough,
or in that section, ever saw her again.

For many a night after that Free Joe sat in the
woods and waited. Little Dan would run merrily off
and be gone a long time, but he always came back
without Lucinda. This happened over and over
again. The ''willis-whistlers'' would call and call,
like phantom hunstmen wandering on a far-off
shore; the screech-owl would shake and shiver in
the depths of the woods; the night-hawks, sweeping
by on noiseless wings, would snap their beaks as
though they enjoyed the huge joke of which Free
Joe and little Dan were the victims; and the whip-
poor-wills would cry to each other through the
gloom. Each night seemed to be lonelier than the
preceding, but Free Joe's patience was proof against
loneliness. Then came a time, however, when little
Dan refused to go after Lucinda. When Free Joe
motioned him in the direction of the Calderwood
place, he would simply move about uneasily and

whine; then he would curl up in the leaves and make himself comfortable.

One night, instead of going to the poplar-tree to wait for Lucinda, Free Joe went to the Staley cabin, and, in order to make his welcome good, as he expressed it, he carried with him an armful of fat-pine splinters. Miss Becky Staley had a great reputation in those parts as a fortune-teller, and the school-girls, as well as older people, often tested her powers in that direction, some in jest and some in earnest. Free Joe placed his humble offering of light-wood in the chimney-corner, and then seated himself on the steps, dropping his hat on the ground outside.

"Miss Becky," he said presently, "whar in de name er gracious you reckon Lucindy is?"

"Well, the Lord he'p the nigger!" exclaimed Miss Becky, in a tone that seemed to reproduce, by some curious agreement of sight with sound, her general aspect of peakedness. "Well, the Lord he'p the nigger! haint you been a-seein' her all this blessed time? She's over at old Spite Calderwood's, if she's anywhere, I reckon."

"No'm, dat I aint, Miss Becky. I aint seen Lucindy in now gwine on mighty nigh a mont'."

"Well, it haint a-gwine to hurt you," said Miss Becky, somewhat sharply. "In my day an' time it wuz allers took to be a bad sign when niggers got to honeyin' 'roun' an' gwine on."

"Yessum," said Free Joe, cheerfully assenting to the proposition—"yessum, dat's so, but me an' my ole 'oman, we 'uz raise tergeer, en dey aint bin many days w'en we 'uz 'way fum one 'n'er like we is now."

"Maybe she's up an' took up wi' some un else," said Micajah Staley from the corner. "You know what the sayin' is, 'New master, new nigger.'"

"Dat's so, dat's de sayin', but tain't wid my ole

'oman like 'tis wid yuther niggers. Me en her wuz
des natally raise up tergeer. Dey's lots likelier niggers dan w'as I is," said Free Joe, viewing his shab-
biness with a critical eye, "but I know Lucindy mos'
good ez I does little Dan dar—dat I does."

There was no reply to this, and Free Joe continued,—

"Miss Becky, I wish you please, ma'am, take en
run yo' kyards en see sump'n n'er 'bout Lucindy;
kaze ef she sick, I'm gwine dar. Dey ken take en
take me up en gimme a stroppin', but I'm gwine
dar."

Miss Becky got her cards, but first she picked up a
cup, in the bottom of which were some coffee
grounds. These she whirled slowly round and round,
ending finally by turning the cup upside down on
the hearth and allowing it to remain in that position.

"I'll turn the cup first," said Miss Becky, "and
then I'll run the cards and see what they say."

As she shuffled the cards the fire on the hearth
burned slow, and in its fitful light the gray-haired,
thin-featured woman seemed to deserve the weird
reputation which rumor and gossip had given her.
She shuffled the cards for some moments, gazing in-
tently in the dying fire; then, throwing a piece of
pine on the coals, she made three divisions of the
pack, disposing them about in her lap. Then she
took the first pile, ran the cards slowly through her
fingers, and studied them carefully. To the first
she added the second pile. The study of these were
evidently not satisfactory. She said nothing, but
frowned heavily; and the frown deepened as she
added the rest of the cards until the entire fifty-two
had passed in review before her. Though she
frowned, she seemed to be deeply interested. Without changing the relative position of the cards, she

ran them over again. Then she threw a larger piece
of pine on the fire, shuffled the cards afresh, divided
them into three piles, and subjected them to the same
careful and critical examination.

"I can't tell the day when I've seed the cards run
this a-way," she said after a while. "What is an'
what aint, I'll never tell you; but I know what the
cards sez."

"W'at does dey say, Miss Becky?" the negro inquired, in a tone the solemnity of which was heightened by its eagerness.

"They er runnin' quare. These here that I'm
a-lookin' at," said Miss Becky, "they stan' for the
past. Them there, they er the present; and the
t'others, they er the future. Here's a bundle,"—
tapping the ace of clubs with her thumb,—"an'
here's a journey as plain as the nose on a man's
face. Here's Lucinda"—

"Whar she, Miss Becky?"

"Here she is—the queen of spades."

Free Joe grinned. The idea seemed to please him
immensely.

"Well, well, well!" he exclaimed. "Ef dat don't
beat my time! De queen er spades! W'en Lucindy
year dat hit'll tickle 'er, sho'!"

Miss Becky continued to run the cards back and
forth through her fingers.

"Here's a bundle an' a journey, and here's Lucinda. An' here's ole Spite Calderwood."

She held the cards toward the negro and touched
the king of clubs.

"De Lord he'p my soul!" exclaimed Free Joe
with a chuckle. "De fever's dar. Yesser, dat's him!
W'at de matter 'long wid all un um, Miss Becky?"

The old woman added the second pile of cards to
the first, and then the third, still running them
through her fingers slowly and critically. By this

time the piece of pine in the fireplace had wrapped
itself in a mantle of flame, illuminating the cabin
and throwing into strange relief the figure of Miss
Becky as she sat studying the cards. She frowned
ominously at the cards and mumbled a few words to
herself. Then she dropped her hands in her lap and
gazed once more into the fire. Her shadow danced
and capered on the wall and floor behind her, as if,
looking over her shoulder into the future, it could
behold a rare spectacle. After a while she picked
up the cup that had been turned on the hearth. The
coffee grounds, shaken around, presented what
seemed to be a most intricate map.

"Here's the journey," said Miss Becky, presently;
"here's the big road, here's rivers to cross, here's
the bundle to tote." She paused and sighed. "They
haint no names writ here, an' what it all means I'll
never tell you. Cajy, I wish you'd be so good as to
han' me my pipe."

"I haint no hand wi' the kyards," said Cajy, and
he handed the pipe, "but I reckon I can patch out
your misinformation, Becky, bekaze the other day,
whiles I was a-fishin' up Mizzer Perdue's rolling-
pin, I hearn a rattlin' in the road. I looked out, an'
Spite Calderwood was a-drivin' by in his buggy,
an' thar sot Lucinda by him. It'd in-about drapt
out er my min'."

Free Joe sat on the door-sill and fumbled at his
hat, flinging it from one hand to the other.

"You haint see um gwine back, is you, Marse
Cajy?" he asked after awhile.

"Ef they went back by this road,"said Mr. Staley,
with the air of one who is accustomed to weigh
well his words, "It must 'a' bin endurin' of the
time whiles I was asleep, bekaze I haint bin no furder from my shop than to yon bed."

"Well, sir!" exclaimed Free Joe in an awed tone,

which Mr. Staley seemed to regard as a tribute to his extraordinary power of statement.

"Ef its my beliefs you want," continued the old man, "I'll pitch 'em at you fair and free. My beliefs is that Spite Calderwood is gone an' took Lucindy outen the country. Bless your heart and soul! when Spite Calderwood meets the Old Boy in the road they'll be a turrible scuffle. You mark what I tell you."

Free Joe still fumbling with his hat, rose and leaned against the door-facing. He seemed to be embarrassed. Presently he said—

"I speck I better be gittin' 'long. Nex' time I see Lucindy, I'm gwine tell 'er w'at Miss Becky say 'bout de queen er spades—dat I is. If dat don't tickle 'er, dey ain't no nigger 'oman never bin tickle'."

He paused a moment, as though waiting for some remark or comment, some confirmation of misfortune, or, at the very least, some indorsement of his suggestion that Lucinda would be greatly pleased to know that she had figured as the queen of spades; but neither Miss Becky nor her brother said anything.

"One minnit ridin' in the buggy 'longside er Mars Spite, en de nex' highfalutin' 'roun' playin' de queen er spades. Mon, deze yer nigger gals gittin' up in de pictur's; dey sholy is."

With a brief "Good-night, Miss Becky, Mars Cajy," Free Joe went out into the darkness, followed by little Dan. He made his way to the poplar, where Lucinda had been in the habit of meeting him, and sat down. He sat there a long time; he sat there until little Dan, growing restless, trotted off in the direction of the Calderwood place. Dozing against the poplar in the gray dawn of the morning, Free Joe heard Spite Calderwood's fox-hounds in full cry a mile away.

"Shoo!" he exclaimed, scratching his head, and laughing to himself, "dem ar dogs is des a-warmin' dat old fox up."

But it was Dan the hounds were after, and the little dog came back no more. Free Joe waited and waited, until he grew tired of waiting. He went back the next night and waited, and for many nights thereafter. His waiting was in vain, and yet he never regarded it as in vain. Careless and shabby as he was, Free Joe was thoughtful enough to have his theory. He was convinced that little Dan had found Lucinda, and that at some night when the moon was shining brightly through the trees, the dog would rouse him from his dreams as he sat sleeping at the foot of the poplar-tree, and he would open his eyes and behold Lucinda standing over him, laughing merrily as of old; and then he thought what fun they would have about the queen of spades.

How many long nights Free Joe waited at the foot of the poplar-tree for Lucinda and little Dan, no one can ever know. He kept no account of them, and they were not recorded by Micajah Staley or by Miss Becky. The season ran into summer and then into fall. One night he went to the Staley cabin, cut the two old people an arm-full of wood, and seated himself on the door-steps, where he rested. He was always thankful—and proud, as it seemed—when Miss Becky gave him a cup of coffee, which she was sometime thoughtful enough to do. He was especially thankful on this particular night.

"You er still layin' off for to strike up wi Lucindy out thar in the woods, I reckon," said Micajah Staley, smiling grimly. The situation was not without its humorous aspects.

"Oh, dey er comin', Mars Cajy, dey er comin', sho," Free Joe replied, "I boun' you dey'll come; en w'en dey does come, I'll des takes en fetch um yer, whar you kin see um wid you own eyes, you en Miss Becky."

"No," said Mr. Staley, with a quick and emphatic gesture of disapproval. "Don't, don't fetch 'em anywheres. Stay right wi' 'em as long as may be."

Free Joe chuckled, and slipped away into the night, while the two old people sat gazing in the fire. Finally Micajah spoke.

"Look at that nigger; look at 'im. He's pine-blank as happy now as a killdee by a mill-race. You can't 'feze 'em. I'd in-about give up my t'other hand ef I could stan' flat-footed, an' grin at trouble like that there nigger."

"Niggers is niggers," said Miss Becky, smiling grimly, "an' you can't rub it out; yet I lay I've seed a heap of white people lots meaner'n Free Joe. He grins,—an' that's nigger,—but I've ketched his under jaw a-trimblin' when Lucindy's name uz brung up. An' I tell you," she went on bridling up a little, and speaking with almost fierce emphasis, "the Old Boy's done sharpened his claws for Spite Calderwood. You'll see it."

"Me, Rebecca?" said Mr. Staley, hugging his palsied arm; "me? I hope not."

"Well, you'll know it then," said Miss Becky, laughing heartily at her brother's look of alarm.

The next morning Micajah Staley had occasion to go into the woods after a piece of timber. He saw Free Joe sitting at the foot of the poplar, and the sight vexed him somewhat.

"Git up from there," he cried, "an' go an' arn your livin'. A mighty purty pass it's come to, when great big buck niggers can lie a-snorin' in the woods

all day, when t'other folks is got to be up an' a-
gwine. Git up from there!''

Receiving no response, Mr. Staley went to Free
Joe, and shook him by the shoulder; but the negro
made no response. He was dead. His hat was off,
his head was bent, and a smile was on his face. It
was as if he had bowed and smiled when death stood
before him, humble to the last. His clothes were
ragged; his hands were rough and callous; his shoes
were literally tied together with strings; he was
shabby in the extreme. A passer-by, glacing at him,
could have no idea that such a humble creature had
been summoned as a witness before the Lord God
of Hosts.

GEORGE W. CABLE.

GEORGE WASHINGTON CABLE.

MADAME DELICIEUSE.*

From Old Creole Days (1879).

JUST adjoining the old Café de Poésie on the corner, stood the little one-story, yellow-washed tenement of Dr. Mossy, with its two glass doors protected by batten shutters, and its low, weed-grown tile roof sloping out over the sidewalk. You were very likely to find the Doctor in, for he was a great student and rather negligent of his business—as business. He was a small, sedate, Creole gentleman of thirty or more, with a young-old face and manner that provoked instant admiration. He would receive you—be you who you may—in a mild, candid manner, looking into your face with his deep blue eyes, and re-assuring you with a modest, amiable smile, very sweet and rare on a man's mouth.

To be frank, the Doctor's little establishment was dusty and disorderly—very. It was curious to see the jars, and jars, and jars. In them were serpents and hideous fishes and precious specimens of many sorts. There were stuffed birds on broken perches; and dried lizards, and eels, and little alligators, and old skulls with their crowns sawed off, and ten thousand odd scraps of writing-paper strewn with crumbs of lonely lunches, and interspersed with long-lost spatulas and rust-eaten lancets.

All New Orleans, at least all Creole New Orleans, knew, and yet did not know, the dear little Doctor. So gentle, so kind, so skilful, so patient, so lenient; so careless of the rich and attentive to the poor; a man, all in all, such as, should you once love him, you would love him forever. So very learned, too, but

with apparently no idea of how to *show himself* to
his social profit,—two features much more smiled at
than respected, not to say admired, by a people remote from the seats of learning, and spending most
of their esteem upon animal heroisms and exterior
display.

"Alas!" said his wealthy acquaintances, "what a
pity; when he might as well be rich."

"Yes, his father has plenty."

"Certainly, and gives it freely. But intends his
son shall see none of it."

"His son? You dare not so much as mention
him."

"Well, well, how strange! But they can never
agree—not even upon their name. Is not that droll?
—a man named General Villivicencio, and his son,
Dr. Mossy?"

"Oh, that is nothing; it is only that the Doctor
drops the *de Villivicencio*."

"Drops the *de Villivicencio?* but I think the *de
Villivicencio* drops him, ho, ho, ho,—*diable!*"

Next to the residence of good Dr. Mossy towered
the narrow, red-brick-front mansion of young Madame Délicieuse, firm friend at once and always of
those two antipodes, General Villivicencio and Dr.
Mossy. Its dark, covered carriage-way was ever
rumbling, and, with nightfall, its drawing-rooms always sent forth a luxurious light from the lace-cur-
tained windows of the second-story balconies.

It was one of the sights of the Rue Royale to see
by night its tall, narrow outline reaching high up toward the stars, with all its windows aglow.

The Madame had had some tastes of human experience; had been betrothed at sixteen (to a man she
did not love, "being at that time a fool," as she
said); one summer day at noon had been a bride, and
at sundown—a widow. Accidental discharge of the

tipsy bridegroom's own pistol. Pass it by! It left but one lasting effect on her, a special detestation of quarrels and weapons.

The little maidens whom poor parentage has doomed to sit upon street door-sills and nurse their infant brothers have a game of "choosing" the beautiful ladies who sweep by along the pavement; but in Rue Royale there was no choosing; every little damsel must own Madame Délicieuse or nobody, and as that richly adorned and regal favorite of old General Villivicencio came along they would lift their big, bold eyes away up to her face and pour forth their admiration in a universal—"Ah-h-h-h!"

But, mark you, she was good Madame Délicieuse as well as fair Madame Délicieuse: her principles, however, not constructed in the austere Anglo-Saxon style, exactly (what need, with the lattice of the Confessional not a stone's-throw off?). Her kind offices and beneficent schemes were almost as famous as General Villivicencio's splendid alms; if she could at times do what the infantile Washington said he could not, why, no doubt she and her friends generally looked upon it as a mere question of enterprise.

She had charms, too, of intellect—albeit not such a sinner against time and place as to be an "educated woman"—charms that, even in a plainer person, would have brought down the half of New Orleans upon one knee, with both hands on the left side. *She* had the *whole* city at her feet, and, with the fine tact which was the perfection of her character, kept it there contented. Madame was, in short, one of the kind that gracefully wrest from society the prerogative of doing as they please, and had gone even to such extravagant lengths as driving out in the *Américain* faubourg, learning the English tongue, talking national politics, and similar

freaks whereby she provoked the unbounded worship
of her less audacious lady friends. In the centre of
the cluster of Creole beauties which everywhere
gathered about her, and, most of all, in those incom-
parable companies which assembled in her own
splendid drawing-rooms, she was always queen lily.
Her house, *her* drawing-rooms, etc.; for the little
brown aunt who lived with her was a mere piece of
curious furniture.

There was this notable charm about Madame Délicieuse, she improved by comparison. She never
looked so grand as when, hanging on General Villivicencio's arm at some gorgeous ball, these two bore
down on you like a royal barge lashed to a ship-of-
the-line. She never looked so like her sweet name,
as when she seated her prettiest lady adorers close
around her, and got them all a-laughing.

Of the two balconies which overhung the *banquette* on the front of the Délicieuse house, one was
a small affair, and the other a deeper and broader
one, from which Madame and her ladies were wont
upon gala days to wave handkerchiefs and cast
flowers to the friends in the processions. There they
gathered one Eighth of January morning to see the
military display. It was a bright blue day, and the
group that quite filled the balcony had laid wrap-
pings aside, as all flower-buds are apt to do on such
Creole January days, and shone resplendent in
spring attire.

The sight-seers passing below looked up by hundreds and smiled at the ladies' eager twitter, as,
flitting in humming-bird fashion from one subject
to another, they laughed away the half-hours waiting
for the pageant. By and by they fell a-listening, for
Madame Délicieuse had begun a narrative concerning Dr. Mossy. She sat somewhat above her listeners, her elbow on the arm of her chair, and her plump

white hand waving now and then in graceful gesture, they silently attending with eyes full of laughter and lips starting apart.

"*Vous savez*," she said (they conversed in French of course), "you know it is now long that Dr. Mossy and his father have been in disaccord. Indeed, when have they not differed? For, when Mossy was but a little boy, his father thought it hard that he was not a rowdy. He switched him once because he would not play with his toy gun and drum. He was not *so* high when his father wished to send him to Paris to enter the French army; but he would not go. We used to play often together on the *banquette* —for I am not so very many years younger than he, no indeed—and, if I wanted some fun, I had only to pull his hair and run into the house; he would cry, and monsieur papa would come out with his hand spread open and"—

Madame gave her hand a malicious little sweep, and joined heartily in the laugh which followed.

"That was when they lived over the way. But wait! you shall see; I have something. This evening the General"—

The houses of Rue Royale gave a start and rattled their windows. In the long, irregular line of balconies the beauty of the city rose up. Then the houses jumped again and the windows rattled; Madame steps inside the window and gives a message which the housemaid smiles at in receiving. As she turns the houses shake again, and now again; and now there comes a distant strain of trumpets, and by and by the drums and bayonets and clattering hoofs, and plumes and dancing banners; far down the long street stretch out the shining ranks of gallant men, and the fluttering, over-leaning swarms of ladies shower down their sweet favors and wave their countless welcomes.

In the front, towering above his captains, rides General Villivicencio, veteran of 1814-15, and, with the gracious pomp of the old-time gentleman, lifts his cocked hat, and bows, and bows.

Madame Délicieuse's balcony was a perfect maze of waving kerchiefs. The General looked up for the woman of all women; she was not there. But he remembered the other balcony, the smaller one, and cast his glance onward to it. There he saw Madame and one other person only. A small blue-eyed, broad-browed, scholarly-looking man whom the arch lady had lured from his pen by means of a mock professional summons, and who now stood beside her, a smile of pleasure playing on his lips and about his eyes.

"Vite!" said Madame, as the father's eyes met the son's. Dr. Mossy lifted his arm and cast a bouquet of roses. A girl in the crowd bounded forward, caught it in the air, and, blushing, handed it to the plumed giant. He bowed low, first to the girl, then to the balcony above; and then, with a responsive smile, tossed up two splendid kisses, one to Madame, and one, it seemed—

"For what was that cheer?"

"Why, did you not see? General Villivicencio cast a kiss to his son."

CAFÉ DES EXILÉS.*

From Old Creole Days (1879).

THAT which in 1835—I think he said thirty-five —was a reality in the Rue Burgundy—I think he said Burgundy—is now but a reminiscence. Yet so vividly was its story told me, that at this moment the old Café des Exilés appears before my eye, floating in the clouds of revery, and I doubt not I see it just as it was in the old times.

An antiquated story-and-a-half Creole cottage sitting right down on the banquette, as do the Choctaw squaws who sell bay and sassafras and life-everlasting, with a high, close board-fence shutting out of view the diminutive garden on the southern side. An ancient willow droops over the roof of round tiles, and partly hides the discolored stucco, which keeps dropping off into the garden as though the old café was stripping for the plunge into oblivion— disrobing for its execution. I see, well up in the angle of the broad side gable, shaded by its rude awning of clapboards, as the eyes of an old dame are shaded by her wrinkled hand, the window of Pauline. Oh for the image of the maiden, were it but for one moment, leaning out of the casement to hang her mocking-bird and looking down into the garden,— where, above the barrier of old boards, I see the top of the fig-tree, the pale green clump of bananas, the tall palmetto with its jagged crown, Pauline's own two orange-trees holding up their hands toward the window, heavy with the promises of autumn; the broad, crimson mass of the many-stemmed oleander, and the crisp boughs of the pomegranate loaded with freckled apples, and with here and there a lingering scarlet blossom.

The Café des Exilés, to use a figure, flowered, bore fruit, and dropped it long ago—or rather Time and Fate, like some uncursed Adam and Eve, came side by side and cut away its clusters, as we sever the golden burden of the banana from its stem; then, like a banana which has borne its fruit, it was razed to the ground and made way for a newer, brighter growth. I believe it would set every tooth on edge should I go by there now,—now that I have heard the story,—and see the old site covered by the "Shoofly Coffee-house." Pleasanter far to close my eyes and call to view the unpretentious portals of the old café, with her children—for such those exiles seem to me—dragging their rocking-chairs out, and sitting in their wonted group under the long, out-reaching eaves which shaded the banquette of the Rue Burgundy.

It was in 1835 that the Café des Exilés was, as one might say, in full blossom. Old M. D'Hemecourt, father of Pauline and host of the café, himself a refugee from San Domingo, was the cause—at least the human cause—of its opening. As its white-cur-tained, glazed doors expanded, emitting a little puff of his own cigarette smoke, it was like the bursting of catalpa blossoms, and the exiles came like bees, pushing into the tiny room to sip its rich variety of tropical sirups, its lemonades, its orangeades, its orgeats, its barley-waters, and its outlandish wines, while they talked of dear home—that is to say, of Barbadoes, of Martinique, of San Domingo, and of Cuba.

There were Pedro and Benigno, and Fernandez and Francisco, and Benito. Benito was a tall, swarthy man, with immense gray moustachios, and hair as harsh as tropical grass and gray as ashes. When he could spare his cigarette from his lips, he would tell you in a cavernous voice, and with a wrinkled smile, that he was "a-t-thorty-seveng."

There was Martinez of San Domingo, yellow as a canary, always sitting with one leg curled under him, and holding the back of his head in his knitted fingers against the back of his rocking-chair. Father, mother, brothers, sisters, all, had been massacred in the struggle of '21 and '22; he alone was left to tell the tale, and told it often, with that strange, infantile insensibility to the solemnity of his bereavement so peculiar to Latin people.

But, besides these, and many who need no mention, there were two in particular, around whom all the story of the Café des Exilés, of old M. D'Hemecourt and of Pauline, turns as on a double centre. First, Manuel Mazaro, whose small, restless eyes were as black and bright as those of a mouse, whose light talk became his dark girlish face, and whose redundant locks curled so prettily and so wonderfully black under the fine white brim of his jaunty Panama. He had the hands of a woman, save that the nails were stained with the smoke of cigarettes. He could play the guitar delightfully, and wore his knife down behind his coat-collar.

The second was "Major" Galahad Shaughnessy. I imagine I can see him, in his white duck, brass-buttoned roundabout, with his sabreless belt peeping out beneath, all his boyishness in his sea-blue eyes, leaning lightly against the door-post of the Café des Exilés as a child leans against his mother, running his fingers over a basketful of fragrant limes, and watching his chance to strike some solemn Creole under the fifth rib with a good old Irish joke.

Old D'Hemecourt drew him close to his bosom. The Spanish Creoles were, as the old man termed it, both cold and hot, but never warm. Major Shaughnessy was warm, and it was no uncommon thing to find those two apart from the others, talking in an undertone, and playing at *confidantes* like two schoolgirls. The kind old man was at this time drifting close up to his sixtieth year. There was much he could tell of San Domingo, whither he had been carried from Martinique in his childhood, whence he had become a refugee to Cuba, and thence to New Orleans in the flight of 1809.

It fell one day to Manuel Mazaro's lot to discover,

by sauntering within earshot, that to Galahad
Shaughnessy only, of all the children of the Café des
Exilés, the good host spoke long and confidentially
concerning his daughter. The words, half heard and
magnified like objects seem in a fog, meaning Manuel
Mazaro knew not what, but made portentous by his
suspicious nature, were but the old man's recital of
the grinding he had got between the millstones of
his poverty and his pride, in trying so long to sustain, for little Pauline's sake, that attitude before
society which earns respect from a surface-viewing
world. It was while he was telling this that Manuel
Mazaro drew near; the old man paused in an embarrassed way; the Major, sitting sidewise in his
chair, lifted his cheek from its resting-place on his
elbow; and Mazaro, after standing an awkward moment, turned away with such an inward feeling as
one may guess would arise in a heart full of Cuban
blood, not unmixed with Indian.

As he moved off, M. D'Hemecourt resumed: that
in a last extremity he had opened, partly from dire
want, partly for very love to homeless souls, the
Café des Exilés. He had hoped that, as strong drink
and high words were to be alike unknown to it, it
might not prejudice sensible people; but it had. He
had no doubt they said among themselves, "She is
an excellent and beautiful girl and deserving all respect;" and respect they accorded, but their *respects*
they never came to pay.

"A café is a café," said the old gentleman. "It is
nod possib' to ezcape him, aldough de Café des
Exilés is differen' from de rez."

"It's different from the Café des Réfugiés," suggested the Irishman.

"Differen' as possib'," replied M. D'Hemecourt.
He looked about upon the walls. The shelves were
luscious with ranks of cooling sirups which he alone

know how to make. The expression of his face changed from sadness to a gentle pride, which spoke without words, saying—and let our story pause a moment to hear it say:

"If any poor exile, from any island where guavas or mangoes or plantains grow, wants a draught which will make him see his home among the cocoa-palms, behold the Café des Exilés ready to take the poor child up and give him the breast! And if gold or silver he has them not, why Heaven and Santa Maria and Saint Christopher bless him! It makes no difference. Here is a rocking-chair, here a cigarette, and here a light from the host's own tinder. He will pay when he can."

As this easily pardoned pride said, so it often occurred; and if the newly come exile said his father was a Spaniard—"Come!" old M. D'Hemecourt would cry; "another glass; it is an innocent drink; my mother was a Castilian." But, if the exile said his mother was a Frenchwoman, the glasses would be forthcoming all the same, for "My father," the old man would say, "was a Frenchman of Martinique, with blood as pure as that wine and a heart as sweet as this honey; come, a glass of orgeat;' and he would bring it himself in a quart tumbler.

Now, there are jealousies and jealousies. There are people who rise up quickly and kill, and there are others who turn their hot thoughts over silently in their minds as a brooding bird turns her eggs in the nest. Thus did Manuel Mazaro, and took it ill that Galahad should see a vision in the temple while he and all the brethren tarried without. Pauline had been to the Café des Exilés in some degree what the image of the Virgin was to their churches at home; and for her father to whisper her name to one and not to another was, it seemed to Mazaro, as if the old man, were he a sacristan, should say to

some single worshipper, "Here, you have this ma-
donna; I make it a present to you." Or, if such was
not the handsome young Cuban's feeling, such, at
least, was the disguise his jealousy put on. If Pauline was to be handed down from her niche, why,
then, farewell Café des Exilés. She was its preserving influence, she made the place holy; she was the
burning candles on the altar. Surely the reader will
pardon the pen that lingers in the mention of her.

And yet I know not how to describe the forbear-
ing, unspoken tenderness with which all these exiles
regarded the maiden. In the balmy afternoons, as I
have said, they gathered about their mother's knee,
this is to say, upon the banquette outside the door.
There, lolling back in their rocking-chairs, they
would pass the evening hours with oft-repeated tales
of home; and the moon would come out and glide
among the clouds like a silver barge among islands
wrapped in mist, and they loved the silently gliding
orb with a sort of worship, because from her soaring
height she looked down at the same moment upon
them and upon their homes in the far Antilles. It
was somewhat thus that they looked upon Pauline
as she seemed to them held up half way to heaven,
they knew not how. Ah! those who have been pilgrims; who have wandered out beyond harbor and
light; whom fate hath led in lonely paths strewn
with thorns and briers not of their own sowing; who,
homeless in a land of homes, see windows gleaming
and doors ajar, but not for them,—it is they who
well understand what the worship is that cries to
any daughter of our dear mother Eve whose footsteps chance may draw across the path, the silent,
beseeching cry, "Stay a little instant that I may
look upon you. Oh, woman, beautifier of the earth!
Stay till I recall the face of my sister; stay yet a moment while I look from afar, with helpless-hanging

hands, upon the softness of thy cheek, upon the folded coils of thy shining hair; and my spirit shall fall down and say those prayers which I may never again—God knoweth—say at home.''

She was seldom seen; but sometimes, when the lounging exiles would be sitting in their afternoon circle under the eaves, and some old man would tell his tale of fire and blood and capture and escape, and the heads would lean forward from the chair-backs and a great stillness would follow the ending of the story, old M. D'Hemecourt would all at once speak up and say, laying his hands upon the nar-rator's knee, ''Comrade, your throat is dry, here are fresh limes; let my dear child herself come and mix you a lemonade.'' Then the neighbors over the way, sitting about their doors, would by and by softly say, ''See, see! there is Pauline!'' and all the exiles would rise from their rocking-chairs, take off their hats and stand as men stand in church, while Paul-ine came out like the moon from a cloud, descended the three steps of the café door, and stood with waiter and glass, a new Rebecca with her pitcher, before the swarthy wanderer.

What tales that would have been tear-compelling, nay, heart-rending, had they not been palpable in-ventions, the pretty, womanish Mazaro from time to time poured forth, in the ever ungratified hope that the goddess might come down with a draught of nectar for him, it profiteth not to recount; but I should fail to show a family feature of the Café des Exilés did I omit to say that these make-believe ad-ventures were heard with every mark of respect and credence; while, on the other hand, they were never attempted in the presence of the Irishman. He would have moved an eyebrow, or made some barely audible sound, or dropped some seemingly innocent word, and the whole company, spite of themselves, would have smiled. Wherefore, it may be doubted whether at any time the curly-haired young Cuban had that playful affection for his Celtic comrade, which a habit of giving little velvet taps to Galahad's cheek made a show of.

Such was the Café des Exilés, such its inmates, such its guests, when certain apparently trivial events began to fall around it as germs of blight fall upon corn, and to bring about that end which cometh to all things.

ALL'S WELL THAT ENDS WELL.*

From The Grandissimes (1880).

LATER on they parted at the *porte-cochère*. Honoré and Aurora had got there before them, and were passing on up the stairs. Clotilde, catching, a moment before, a glimpse of her face, had seen that there was something wrong; weather-wise as to its indications she perceived an impending shower of tears. A faint shade of anxiety rested an instant on her own face. Frowenfeld could not go in. They paused a little within the obscurity of the corridor, and just to reassure themselves that everything *was* "all right," they——

God be praised for love's young dream.

The slippered feet of the happy girl, as she slowly mounted the stair alone, overburdened with the weight of her blissful reverie, made no sound. As she turned its mid-angle she remembered Aurora. She could guess pretty well the source of her trouble; Honoré was trying to treat that hand-clasping at the bedside of Agricola as a binding compact;

"which, of course, was not fair." She supposed they would have gone into the front drawing-room; she would go into the back. But she miscalculated; as she silently entered the door she saw Aurora standing a little way beyond her, close before Honoré, her eyes cast down, and the trembling fan hanging from her two hands like a broken pinion. He seemed to be reiterating, in a tender undertone, some question intended to bring her to a decision. She lifted up her eyes toward his with a mute, frightened glance.

The intruder, with an involuntary murmur of apology, drew back; but, as she turned, she was suddenly and unspeakably saddened to see Aurora drop her glance, and, with a solemn slowness whose momentous significance was not to be mistaken, silently shake her head.

"Alas!" cried the tender heart of Clotilde. "Alas! M. Grandissime!"

If M. Grandissime had believed that he was prepared for the supreme bitterness of that moment, he had sadly erred. He could not speak. He extended his hand in a dumb farewell, when, all unsanctioned by his will, the voice of despair escaped him in a low groan. At the same moment, a tinkling sound drew near, and the room, which had grown dark with the fall of night, began to brighten with the softly widening light of an evening lamp, as a servant approached to place it in the front drawing-room.

Aurora gave her hand and withdrew it. In the act the two somewhat changed position, and the rays of the lamp, as the maid passed the door, falling upon Aurora's face, betrayed the again upturned eyes.

"'Sieur Grandissime——"

They fell.

The lover paused.

"You thing I'm crool."

She was the statue of meekness.

"Hope has been cruel to me," replied M. Grandissime, "not you; that I cannot say. Adieu."

He was turning.

"'Sieur Grandissime——"

She seemed to tremble.

He stood still.

"'Sieur Grandissime,"—her voice was very tender,—"wad you' horry?"

There was a great silence.

"'Sieur Grandissime, you know—teg a chair."

He hesitated a moment and then both sat down. The servant repassed the door; yet when Aurora broke the silence, she spoke in English—having such hazardous things to say. It would conceal possible stammerings.

"'Sieur Grandissime—you know dad riz'n I——"

She slightly opened her fan, looking down upon it, and was still.

"I have no right to ask the reason," said M. Grandissime. "It is yours—not mine."

Her head went lower.

"Well, you know,"—she drooped it meditatively to one side, with her eyes on the floor,—"'tis bick-ause—'tis bick-ause I thing in a few days I'm goin' to die."

M. Grandissime said never a word. He was not alarmed.

She looked up suddenly and took a quick breath, as if to resume, but her eyes fell before his, and she said, in a tone of half-soliloquy:

"I 'ave so mudge troub' wit dad hawt."

She lifted one little hand feebly to the cardiac region, and sighed softly, with a dying languor.

M. Grandissime gave no response. A vehicle

rumbled by in the street below, and passed away. At the bottom of the room, where a gilded Mars was driving into battle, a soft note told the half-hour. The lady spoke again.

"Id mague" — she sighed once more — "so strange,—sometime' I thing I'm git'n' crezzy."

Still he to whom these fearful disclosures were being made remained as silent and motionless as an Indian captive, and, after another pause, with its painful accompaniment of small sounds, the fair speaker resumed with more energy, as befitting the approach to an incredible climax:

"Some day', 'Sieur Grandissime,—id mague me fo'gid my hage! I thing I'm young!"

She lifted her eyes with the evident determination to meet his own squarely, but it was too much; they fell as before; yet she went on speaking:

"An' w'en someboddie git'n' ti'ed livin' wid 'imsev an' big'n' to fill ole, an' wan' someboddie to teg de care of 'im an' wan' me to gid marri'd wid 'im—I thing 'e's in love to me." Her fingers kept up a little shuffling with the fan. "I thing I'm crezzy. I thing I muz be go'n' to die torecklie." She looked up to the ceiling with large eyes, and then again at the fan in her lap, which continued its spreading and shutting. "An' daz de riz'n, 'Sieur Grandissime." She waited until it was certain he was about to answer, and then interrupted him nervously: "You know 'Sieur Grandissime, id woon be righd! Id woon be de juztiz to *you!* An' you de bez man I evva know in my life, 'Sieur Grandissime!" Her hands shook. "A man w'at nevva wan' to gid marri'd wid noboddie in 'is life, and now trine to gid marri'd juz only to rip-ose de sould of 's oncl'——"

M. Grandissime uttered an exclamation of protest, and she ceased.

"I asked you," continued he, with low-toned emphasis, "for the single and only reason that I want you for my wife."

"Yez," she quickly replied; "daz all. Daz wad I thing. An' I thing daz de rad weh to say, 'Sieur Grandissime. Bick-ause, you know, you an' me is too hole to talg aboud dad *lovin'*, you know. An' you godd dad grade *rizpeg* fo' me, an' me I godd dad 'ighez rispeg fo' you; bud——" she clutched the fan and her face sunk lower still—"bud——" she swallowed—shook her head—"bud——" She bit her lip; she could not go on.

"Aurora," said her lover, bending forward and taking one of her hands. "I *do* love you with all my soul."

She made a poor attempt to withdraw her hand, abandoned the effort, and looked savagely through a pair of overflowing eyes, demanding:

"*Mais*, fo' w'y you di'n' wan' to sesso?"

M. Grandissime smiled argumentatively.

"I have said so a hundred times, in every way but in words."

She lifted her head proudly, and bowed like a queen.

"*Mais*, you see, 'Sieur Grandissime, you bin meg one mizteg."

"Bud 'tis corrected in time," exclaimed he, with suppressed but eager joyousness.

"'Sieur Grandissime," she said with tremendous solemnity, "I'm verrie sawrie, *mais*—you spogue too lade."

"No, no!" he cried, "the correction comes in time. Say that, lady; say that!"

His ardent gaze beat hers once more down; but she shook her head. He ignored the motion.

"And you will correct your answer; ah! say that,

too!" he insisted, covering the captive hand with both his own, and leaning forward from his seat.

"*Mais,* 'Sieur Grandissime, you know, dad is so verrie unegspeg'."

"Oh! unexpected!"

"*Mais,* I was thing all dad time id was Clotilde wad you——"

She turned her face away and buried her mouth in her handkerchief.

"Ah!" he cried, "mock me no more, Aurore Nancanou!"

He rose erect and held the hand firmly which she strove to draw away:

"Say the word, sweet lady; say the word!"

She turned upon him suddenly, rose to her feet, was speechless an instant while her eyes flashed into his, and crying out:

"No!" burst into tears, laughed through them, and let him clasp her to his bosom.

MARY NOAILLES MURFREE.

("CHARLES EGBERT CRADDOCK.")

A PROPHET OF THE MOUNTAINS.*

From The Prophet of the Great Smoky Mountains (1885).

KELSEY had forgotten the gander-pulling, the impending election, the excitement of the escape, before he had ridden five miles from the Settlement. He jogged along the valley road, the reins on the horse's neck, his eyes lifted to the heights. The fullness of day was on their unpeopled summits. Infinity was expressed before the eye. On and on the chain of mountains stretched, with every illusion of mist and color, with every differing grace of distance, with inconceivable measures of vastness. The grave delight in which their presence steeped the senses stirred his heart. They breathed solemnities. They lent wings to the thoughts. They lifted the soul. Could he look at them and doubt that one day he should see God? He had been near,—oh, surely, He had been near.

Kelsey was comforted as he rode on. Somehow, the mountains had for his ignorant mind some coercive internal evidence of the great truths. In their exalted suggestiveness were congruities: so far from the world were they,—so high above it; so interlinked with the history of all that makes the races of men more than the beasts that perish, that conserves the values of that noble idea,—an immortal soul. On a

*Copyright by Houghton, Mifflin Company. Reprinted with the kind permission of the publishers.

CHARLES EGBERT CRADDOCK.
(Miss Murfree)

mountain the ark rested; on a mountain the cross was planted; the steeps beheld the glories of the transfiguration; the lofty solitudes heard the prayers of the Christ; and from the heights issued the great sermon instinct with all the moralities of every creed. How often He went up into the mountain!

The thought uplifted Kelsey. The flush of strong feeling touched his cheek. His eyes were fired with that sudden gleam of enthusiasm as remote from earthly impulses as the lightnings of Sinai.

"An' I will preach his name!" the parson exclaimed, in a tense and thrilling voice. He checked his horse, drew out of his pocket a thumbed old Bible, clumsily turned the leaves and sought for his text.

No other book had he ever read: only that sublime epic, with its deep tendernesses and its mighty portents; with its subtleties of prophecy in wide and splendid phrase, and their fulfillment in the barren record of the simplest life; with all the throbbing presentment of martyrdom and doom and death, dominated by the miracle of resurrection and the potency of divinity. Every detail was as clearly pictured to his mind as if, instead of the vast, unstoried stretches of the Great Smoky Mountains, he looked upon the sanctities of the hills of Judæa.

He read as he rode along,—slowly, slowly. A bird's shadow would flit across the holy page, and then away to the mountain; the winds of heaven caressed it. Sometimes the pollen of flowering weeds fell upon it; for in the midst of the unfrequented road they often stood in tall rank rows, with a narrow path on either side, trodden by the oxen of the occasional team, while the growth bent elastically under the passing bed of the wagon.

He was almost happy. The clamors of his insistent heart were still. His conscience, his memory, his self-reproach, had loosed their hold. His keen and subtile native intellect stretched its unconscious powers and discriminated the workings of character, and reviewed the deploying of events, and measured results. He was far away, walking with the disciples.

Suddenly, like an aerolite, he was whirled from high ethereal spaces by the attraction of the earth. A man was peering from between the rails of a fence by the wayside.

"Kin ye read yer book, pa'son, an' ride yer beastis all ter wunst?" he cried out, with the fervor of admiration.

That tree of knowledge,—ah, the wily serpent! Galilee,—it was thousands of miles away across the deep salt seas.

The parson closed his book with a smile of exultation.

"The beast don't hender me none. I kin read ennywhar," he said, proud of the attainment.

"Waal, sir!" exclaimed the other, one of that class, too numerous in Tennessee, who can neither read nor write. "Air it the Good Book?" he demanded, with a sudden thought.

"It air the Holy Bible," said the parson, handing him the book.

The man eyed it with reverence. Then, with a gingerly gesture, he gave it back. The parson was looking down at him, all softened and humanized by this unconscious flattery.

"Waal, pa'son," said the illiterate admirer of knowledge, with a respectful and subordinate air, "I hearn ez ye war a-goin' ter hold fo'th up yander at the meet'n-house at the Notch nex' Sunday. Air that a true word?"

"I 'lows ter preach thar on the nex' Lord's day,"
replied the parson.

* * * * * * * * *

The little log meeting-house at the Notch stood
high on a rugged spur of the Great Smoky. Dense
forests encompassed it on every hand, obscuring
that familiar picture of mountain and cloud and
cove. From its rude, glassless windows one could
look out on no distant vista, save perhaps in the
visionary glories of heaven or the climatic discom-
forts of hell, according to the state of the conscience,
or perchance the liver. The sky was aloof and
limited. The laurel tangled the aisles of the woods.
Sometimes from the hard benches a weary tow-
headed brat might rejoice to mark in the monotony
the frisking of a squirrel on a bough hard by, or a
woodpecker solemnly tapping. The acorns would
rattle on the roof, if the wind stirred, as if in punctu-
ation of the discourse. The pines, mustering strong
among the oaks, joined their mystic threnody to the
sad-voiced quiring within. The firs stretched down
long, pendulous, darkling boughs, and filled the air
with their balsamic fragrance. Within the house
the dull light fell over a few rude benches and a
platform with a chair and table, which was used as
pulpit. Shadows of many deep, rich tones of brown
lurked among the rafters. Here and there a cob-
web, woven to the consistence of a fabric, swung in
the air. The drone of a blue-bottle, fluttering in and
out of the window in a slant of sunshine, might in-
vade the reverent silence, as Brother Jake Tobin
turned the leaves to read the chapter. Sometimes
there would sound, too, a commotion among the
horses without, unharnessed from the wagons and
hitched to the trees; then in more than one of the

solemn faces might be described an anxious perturbation,—not fear because of equine perversities,
but because of the idiosyncrasies of callow human
nature in the urchins left in charge of the teams. No
one ventured to investigate, however, and, with that
worldly discomfort contending with the spiritual ex-
altations they sought to foster, the rows of religion-
ists swayed backward and forward in rhythm to the
reader's voice, rising and falling in long, billowy
sweeps of sound, like the ground swell of ocean
waves.

It was strange, looking upon their faces, and with
a knowledge of the limited phases of their existence,
their similarity of experience here, where a century
might come and go, working no change save that,
like the leaves, they fluttered awhile in the outer air
with the spurious animation called life, and fell in
death, and made way for new bourgeonings like unto
themselves,—strange to mark how they differed.
Here was a man of a stern, darkly religious conviction, who might either have writhed at the stake
or stooped to kindle the flames; and here was an ac-
countant soul that knew only those keen mercantile
motives,—the hope of reward and the fear of hell;
and here was an enthusiast's eye, touched by the
love of God; and here was an unfinished, hardly
humanized face, that it seemed as presumptuous to
claim as the exponent of a soul as the faces of the
stupid oxen out-of-doors. All were earnest; many
wore an expression of excited interest, as the details
of the chapter waxed to a climax, like the tense stillness of a metropolitan audience before an unimag-
ined *coup de théâtre*. The men all sat on one side,
chewing their quids; the women on the other, almost
masked by their limp sun-bonnets. The ubiquitous
baby—several of him—was there, and more than
once babbled aloud and cried out peevishly. Only

one, becoming uproarious, was made a public example; being quietly borne out and deposited in
the ox-wagon, at the mercy of the urchins who pre-
sided over the teams, while his mother creaked in
again on the tips of deprecating, anxious toes, to
hear the Word.

Brother Jake Tobin might be accounted in some
sort a dramatic reader. He was a tall, burly man,
inclining to fatness, with grizzled hair roached back
from his face. He cast his light gray eyes upward
at the end of every phrase, with a long, resonant
"Ah!" He smote the table with his hands at emphatic passages; he rolled out denunciatory clauses
with a freshened relish which intimated that he considered one of the choicest pleasures of the saved
might be to gloat over the unhappy predicament of
the damned. He chose for his reading paragraphs
that, applied to aught but spiritual enemies and per-
sonified sins, might make a civilized man quake for
his dearest foe. He paused often and interpolated
his own observations, standing a little to the side of
the table, and speaking in a conversational tone.
"Ain't that so, my brethren an' sisters! But *we* air
saved in the covenant—ah!" Then, clapping his
hands with an ecstatic upward look,—"I'm so
happy, I'm so happy!"—he would go on to read
with the unction of immediate intention, "Let death
seize them! Let them go down quick into hell!"

He wore a brown jeans suit, the vest much creased
in the regions of the enhanced portliness, its maker's
philosophy not having taken into due account his
susceptibility to "chicken fixin's." After concluding
the reading he wiped the perspiration from his brow
with his red bandana handkerchief, and placed it
around the collar of his unbleached cotton shirt, as
he proceeded to the further exertion of "lining out"
the hymn.

The voices broke forth in those long, lingering cadences that have a melancholy, spiritual, yearning effect, in which the more tutored church music utterly fails. The hymn rose with a solemn jubilance, filling the little house, and surging out into the woods; sounding far across unseen chasms and gorges, and rousing in the unsentient crags an echo with a testimony so sweet, charged with so devout a sentiment, that it seemed as if with this voice the very stones would have cried out, had there been dearth of human homage when Christ rode into Jerusalem.

Then the sudden pause, the failing echo, the sylvan stillness, and the chanting voice lined out another couplet. It was well, perhaps, that this part of the service was so long; the soul might rest on its solemnity, might rise on its aspiration.

It came to an end at last. Another long pause ensued. Kelsey, sitting on the opposite side of the table, his elbow on the back of his chair, his hand shading his eyes, made no movement. Brother Jake Tobin looked hard at him, with an expression which in a worldly man we should pronounce exasperation. He hesitated for a moment in perplexity. There was a faint commotion, implying suppressed excitement in the congregation. Parson Kelsey's idosyncrasies were known by more than one to be a thorn in the side of the frankly confiding Brother Jake Tobin.

"Whenst I hev got him in the pul*pit* alongside o' me," he would say to his cronies, "I feel ez onlucky an' weighted ez ef I war a-lookin' over my lef' shoulder at the new moon on a November Friday. I feel ez oncommon ez ef he war a deer, or suthin', ez hev got no salvation in him. An' ef he don't feel the sperit ter pray, he *won't* pray, an' I hev got ter surroun' the throne o' grace by myself. He *kin* pray ef he hev a mind ter, an' he *do* seem ter hev hed a

outpourin' o' the sperit o' prophecy; but he hev
made me 'pear mighty comical 'fore the Lord a-many
a time, when I hev axed him ter open his mouth an'
he hev kep' it shut.''

Brother Jake did not venture to address him now.
An alternative was open to him. "Brother Reuben
Bates, will ye lead us in prayer?'' he said to one of
the congregation.

They all knelt down, huddled like sheep in the narrow spaces between the benches, and from among
them went up the voice of supplication, that anywhere and anyhow has the commanding dignity of
spiritual communion, the fervor of exaltation, and
all the moving humility of the finite leaning upon
the infinite. Ignorance was annihilated, so far as
Brother Reuben Bates's prayer was concerned. It
grasped the fact of immortality,—all worth knowing!—and humble humanity was presented as pos-
sessing the intimate inherent principle of the splendid fruitions of eternity.

He had few words, Brother Reuben, and the as-
pirated "Ah!'' was long drawn often, while he
swiftly thought of something else to say. Brother
Jake Tobin, after the manner in vogue among them,
broke out from time to time with a fervor of assent.
"Yes, my Master!'' he would exclaim in a wild,
ecstatic tone. "Bless the Lord!'' "That's a true
word!'' "I'm so happy!''

Always these interpolations came opportunely
when Brother Reuben seemed entangled in his
primitive rhetoric, and gave him a moment for improvisation. It was doubtless Hi Kelsey's miserable misfortune that his acute intuition should detect in the reverend tones a vainglorious self-satis-
faction, known to no one else, not even to the
speaker; that he should accurately gauge how Brother Jake Tobin secretly piqued himself upon his

own gift in prayer, never having experienced these
stuttering halts, never having needed these pious
boosts; that he should be aware, ignorant as he was,
of that duality of cerebration by which Brother
Jake's mind was divided between the effect on God,
bending down a gracious ear, and the impression of
these ecstatic outbursts on the congregation; that
the petty contemptibleness of it should depress him;
that its dissimulations angered him. With the rigor
of an upright man, he upbraided himself. He was
on his knees: was he praying? Were these the sin-
cerities of faith. Was this lukewarm inattention the
guerdon of the sacrifice of the cross? His ideal and
himself, himself and what he sought to be,—oh, the
gulf! the deep divisions!

He gave his intentions no grace. He conceded
naught to human nature. His conscience revolted
at a sham. And he was a living, breathing sham—
upon his knees.

Ah, let us have a little mercy on ourselves! Most
of us do. For there was Brother Jake Tobin, with
a conscience free of offense, happily unobservant of
his own complicated mental processes and of the
motives of his own human heart, becoming more and
more actively assistant as Brother Reuben Bates
grew panicky, hesitant, and involved, and kept convulsively on through sheer inability to stop, suggesting epilepsy rather than piety.

It was over at last; exhausted nature prevailed,
and Brother Bates resumed his seat, wiping the perspiration from his brow and raucously clearing his
rasped throat.

There was a great scraping of the rough shoes and
boots on the floor as the congregation rose, and one
or two of the benches were moved backward with a
harsh, grating sound. A small boy had gone to
sleep during the petition, and remained in his

prayerful attitude. Brother Jake Tobin settled
himself in his chair as comfortably as might be,
tilted it back on its hindlegs against the wall, and
wore the air of having fairly exploited his share of
the services and cast off responsibility. The congregation composed itself to listen to the sermon.

There was an expectant pause. Kelsey remembered ever after the tumult of emotion with which
he stepped forward to the table and opened the book.
He turned to the New Testament for his text,—
turned the leaves with a familiar hand. Some ennobling phase of that wonderful story which would
touch the tender, true affinity of human nature for
the higher things,—from this he would preach to-
day. And yet, at the same moment, with a contra-
riety of feeling from which he shrank aghast, there
was skulking into his mind all that grewsome company of doubts. In double file they came: fate and
free agency, free will and foreordination, infinite
mercy and infinite justice, God's loving kindness and
man's intolerable misery, redemption and damna-
tion. He had evolved them all from his own unconscious logical faculty, and they pursued him as if he
had, in some spiritual necromancy, conjured up a
devil,—nay, legions of devils. Perhaps if he had
known how they have assaulted the hearts of men
in times gone past; how they have been combated and
baffled, and yet have risen and pursued again; how,
in the scrutiny of science and research, men have
paused before their awful presence, analyzed them,
philosophized about them, and found them interesting; how others, in the levity of the world, having
heard of them, grudge the time to think upon them,
—if he had known all this, he might have felt some
courage in numbers.

As it was, there was no fight left in him. He
closed the book with a sudden impulse. "My

frien's," he said, "I stan' not hyar ter preach ter-day, but fur confession."

There was a galvanic start among the congregation, then intense silence.

"I hev los' my faith!" he cried out, with a poignant despair. "God ez gin it—ef thar is a God—hev tuk it away. You-uns kin go on. You-uns kin b'lieve. Yer paster b'lieves, an' he'll lead ye ter grace,—leastwise ter a better life. But fur me thar's the nethermost depths of hell, ef"—how his faith and his unfaith tried him!—"ef thar be enny hell. Leastwise— Stop, brother,"—he held up his hand in deprecation, for Parson Tobin had risen at last, with a white, scared face; nothing like this had ever been heard in all the length and breadth of the Great Smoky Mountains,—"bear with me a little; ye'll see me hyar no more. Fur me thar is shame, ah! an' trial, ah! an' doubt, ah! an' despair, ah! The good things o' life hev not fallen ter me. The good things o' heaven air denied. My name is ter be a by-word an' a reproach 'mongst ye. Ye'll grieve ez ye hev ever hearn the Word from me, ah! Ye'll be held in derision! An' I hev hed trials,—none like them ez air comin', comin', down the wind. I hev been a man marked fur sorrow, an' now fur shame."

He stood erect; he looked bold, youthful. The weight of his secret, lifted now, had been heavier than he knew. In his eyes shone that strange light which was frenzy, or prophecy, or inspiration; in his voice rang a vibration they had never before heard.

"I will go forth from 'mongst ye,—I that am not of ye. Another shall gird me an' carry me where I would not. Hell an' the devil hev prevailed agin me. Pray fur me, brethren, ez I cannot pray fur myself. Pray that God may yet speak ter me,—speak from out o' the whurlwind."

There was a sound upon the air. Was it the rising of the wind? A thrill ran through the congregation. The wild emotion, evoked and suspended in this abrupt pause, showed in pallid excitement on every face. Several of the men rose aimlessly, then turned and sat down again. Brought from the calm monotony of their inner life into this supreme crisis of his, they were struck aghast by the hardly comprehended situations of his spiritual drama enacted before them. And what was that sound on the air? In the plentitude of their ignorant faith, were they listening for the invoked voice of God?

Kelsey, too, was listening, in anguished suspense.

It was not the voice of God, that man was wont to hear when the earth was young; not the rising of the wind. The peace of the golden sunshine was supreme. Even a tiny cloudlet, anchored in the limited sky, would not sail to-day.

On and on it came. It was the galloping of horse, —the beat of hoofs, individualized presently to the ear,—with that thunderous, swift, impetuous advance that so domineers over the imagination, quickens the pulse, shakes the courage.

It might seem that all the ingenuity of malignity could not have compassed so complete a revenge. The fulfillment of his prophecy entered at the door. All its spiritual significance was annihilated; it was merged into a prosaic material degradation when the sheriff of the county strode, with jingling spurs, up the aisle, and laid his hand upon the preacher's shoulder. He wore his impassive official aspect. But his deputy, following hard at his heels, had a grin of facetious triumph upon his thin lips. He had been caught by the nape of the neck, and in a helpless, roden-like attitude had been slung out of the door by the stalwart man of God, when he and Amos

Vol. 8—19.

James had ventured to the meeting-house in liquor; and neither he nor the congregation had forgotten the sensation. It was improbable that such high-handed proceedings could be instituted to-day, but the sheriff had taken the precaution to summon the aid of five or six burly fellows, all armed to the teeth. They too came tramping heavily up the aisle. Several wore the reflection of the deputy's grin; they were the "bold, bad men," the prophet's early associates before "he got religion, a' sot hisself ter consortin' with the saints." The others were sheepish and doubtful, serving on the posse with a protest under the constraining penalties of the law.

The congregation was still with a stunned astonishment. The preacher stood as one petrified, his eyes fixed upon the sheriff's face. The officer, with a slow, magisterial gesture, took a paper from his breast-pocket, and laid it upon the Bible.

"Ye kin read, pa'son," he said. "Ye kin read the warrant fur yer arrest.

THE STAR IN THE VALLEY.*

From In the Tennessee Mountains (1884).

HE first saw it in the twilight of a clear October evening. As the earliest planet sprang into the sky, an answering gleam shone red amid the glooms in the valley. A star too it seemed. And later, when the myriads of the fairer, whiter lights of a moonless night were all athrob in the great concave vault bending to the hills, there was something very im-

---

pressive in that solitary star of earth, changeless and motionless beneath the ever-changing skies.

Chevis never tired of looking at it. Somehow it broke the spell that draws all eyes heavenward on starry nights. He often strolled with his cigar at dusk down to the verge of the crag, and sat for hours gazing at it and vaguely speculating about it. That spark seemed to have kindled all the soul and imagination within him, although he knew well enough its prosaic source, for he had once questioned the gawky mountaineer whose services he had secured as guide through the forest solitudes during this hunting expedition.

"That thar spark in the valley?" Hi Bates had replied, removing the pipe from his lips and emitting a cloud of strong tobacco smoke. "'Tain't nuthin' but the light in Jerry Shaw's house, 'bout haffen mile from the foot of the mounting. Ye pass that thar house when ye goes on the Christel road, what leads down the mounting off the Back-bone. That's Jerry Shaw's house,—that's what it is. He's a blacksmith, an' he kin shoe a horse toler'ble well when he ain't drunk, ez he mos'ly is."

"Perhaps that is the light from the forge," suggested Chevis.

"That thar forge ain't run more'n half the day, let 'lone o' nights. I hev never hearn tell on Jerry Shaw a-workin' o' nights,—nor in the daytime nuther, ef he kin get shet of it. No sech no 'count critter 'twixt hyar an' the Settlemint."

So spake Chevis's astronomer. Seeing the star even through the prosaic lens of stern reality did not detract from its poetic aspect. Chevis never failed to watch for it. The first faint glinting in the azure evening sky sent his eyes to that red reflection suddenly aglow in the valley; even when the mists rose above it and hid it from him, he gazed at

the spot where it had disappeared, feeling a calm
satisfaction to know that it was still shining beneath
the cloud-curtain. He encouraged himself in this
bit of sentimentality. These unique eventide effects
seemed a fitting sequel to the picturesque day, passed
in hunting deer, with horn and hounds, through the
gorgeous autumnal forest; or perchance in the more
exciting sport in some rocky gorge with a bear at
bay and the frenzied pack around him; or in the
idyllic pleasures of bird-shooting with a thoroughly-
trained dog; and coming back in the crimson sunset
to a well-appointed tent and a smoking supper of
venison or wild turkey,—the trophies of his skill.
The vague dreaminess of his cigar and the charm
of that bright bit of color in the night-shrouded valley added a sort of romantic zest to these primitive
enjoyments, and ministered to that keen susceptibility of impressions which Reginald Chevis considered eminently characteristic of a highly wrought
mind and nature.

He said nothing to his fancies, however, to his
fellow sportsman, Ned Varney, nor to the mountaineer. Infinite as was the difference between these
two in mind and cultivation, his observation of both
had convinced him that they were alike incapable
of appreciating and comprehending his delicate and
dainty musings. Varney was essentially a man of
this world; his mental and moral conclusions had
been adopted in a calm, mercantile spirit, as giving
the best return for the outlay, and the market was
not liable to fluctuations. And the mountaineer could
go no further than the prosaic fact of the light in
Jerry Shaw's house. Thus Reginald Chevis was
wont to sit in contemplative silence on the crag until his cigar was burnt out, and afterwards to lie
awake deep in the night, listening to the majestic

lyric welling up from the thousand nocturnal voices
of these mountain wilds.

During the day, in place of the red light a gauzy
little curl of smoke was barely visible, the only sign
or suggestion of human habitation to be seen from
the crag in all the many miles of long, narrow valley and parallel tiers of ranges. Sometimes Chevis
and Varney caught sight of it from lower down on
the mountain side, whence was faintly distinguish-
able the little log-house and certain vague lines
marking a rectangular inclosure; near at hand, too,
the forge, silent and smokeless. But it did not
immediately occur to either of them to theorize concerning its inmates and their lives in this lonely
place; for a time, not even to the speculative Chevis.
As to Varney, he gave his whole mind to the matter
in hand,—his gun, his dog, his game,—and his note-
book was as systematic and as romantic as the ledger
at home.

It might be accounted an event in the history of
that log-hut when Reginald Chevis, after riding past
it eighty yards or so, chanced one day to meet a
country girl walking toward the house. She did not
look up, and he caught only an indistinct glimpse of
her face. She spoke to him, however, as she went
by, which is the invariable custom with the inhabitants of the sequestered nooks among the encom-
passing mountains, whether meeting stranger or
acquaintance. He lifted his hat in return, with that
punctilious courtesy which he made a point of according to persons of low degree. In another moment she had passed down the narrow sandy road,
overhung with gigantic trees, and, at a deft, even
pace, hardly slackened as she traversed the great log
extending across the rushing stream, she made her
way up the opposite hill, and disappeared gradually
over its brow.

The expression of her face, half-seen though it was, had attracted his attention. He rode slowly along, meditating. "Did she go into Shaw's house, just around the curve of the road?" he wondered. "Is she Shaw's daughter, or some visiting neighbor?"

That night he looked with a new interest at the red star, set like a jewel in the floating mists of the valley.

"Do you know," he asked of Hi Bates, when the three men were seated, after supper, around the camp-fire, which sent lurid tongues of flame and a thousand bright sparks leaping high in the darkness, and illumined the vistas of the woods on every side, save where the sudden crag jutted over the valley,—"Do you know whether Jerry Shaw has a daughter,—a young girl?"

"Ye-es," drawled Hi Bates, disparagingly, "he hev."

A pause ensued. The star in the valley was blotted from sight; the rising mists had crept to the verge of the crag; nay, in the undergrowth fringing the mountain's brink, there were softly clinging white wreaths.

"Is she pretty?" asked Chevis.

"Waal, no, she ain't," said Hi Bates, decisively. "She's a pore, no 'count critter." Then he added, as if he were afraid of being misapprehended, "Not ez thar is any harm in the gal, ye onderstand. She's a mighty good, saft-spoken, quiet sort o' gal, but she's a pore, white-faced, slim little critter. She looks like she hain't got no sort'n grit in her. She makes me think o' one o' them slim little slips o' willow every time nor I sees her. She hain't got long ter live, I reckon," he concluded, dismally.

Reginald Chevis asked him no more questions about Jerry Shaw's daughter.

Not long afterwards, when Chevis was hunting through the deep woods about the base of the mountain near the Christel road, his horse happened to cast a shoe. He congratulated himself upon his proximity to the forge, for there was a possibility that the blacksmith might be at work; according to the account which Hi Bates had given of Jerry Shaw's habits, there were half a dozen chances against it. But the shop was at no great distance, and he set out to find his way back to the Christel road, guided by sundry well-known landmarks on the mountain side: certain great crags hanging above the tree-tops, showing in grander sublimity through the thinning foliage, or beetling bare and grim; a dismantled and deserted hovel, the red-berried vines twining amongst the rotting logs; the full flow of a tumultuous stream making its last leap down a precipice eighty feet high, with yeasty, maddening waves below and a rainbow-crowned crystal sheet above. And here again the curves of the woodland road. As the sound of the falling water grew softer and softer in the distance, till it was hardly more than a drowsy murmur, the faint vibrations of a far-off anvil rang upon the air. Welcome indeed to Chevis, for, however enticing might be the long rambles through the redolent October woods with dog and gun, he had no mind to tramp up the mountain to his tent, five miles distant, leading the resisting horse all the way. The afternoon was so clear and so still that the metallic sound penetrated far through the quiet forest. At every curve of the road he expected to see the log-cabin with its rail fence, and beyond the low-hanging chestnut-tree, half its branches resting upon the roof of the little shanty of a blacksmith's shop. After many windings a sharp turn brought him in full upon the humble dwelling, with its background of primeval

woods and the purpling splendors of the western
hills. The chickens were going to roost in a stunted
cedar-tree just without the door; an incredibly old
man, feeble and bent, sat dozing in the lingering
sunshine on the porch; a girl, with a pail on her
head, was crossing the road and going down a declivity toward a spring which bubbled up in a cleft
of the gigantic rocks that were piled one above another, rising to a great height. A mingled breath of
cool, dripping water, sweet-scented fern, and pungent mint greeted him as he passed it. He did not
see the girl's face, for she had left the road before
he went by, but he recognized the slight figure, with
that graceful poise acquired by the prosaic habit of
carrying weights upon the head, and its lithe, swaying beauty reminded him of the mountaineer's comparison,—a slip of willow.

And now, under the chestnut-tree, in anxious converse with Jerry Shaw, who came out hammer in
hand from the anvil, concerning the shoe to be put
on Strathspey's left fore-foot, and the problematic
damage sustained since the accident. Chevis's own
theory occupied some minutes in expounding, and
so absorbed his attention that he did not observe,
until the horse was fairly under the blacksmith's
hands, that, despite Jerry Shaw's unaccustomed industry, this was by no means a red-letter day in his
habitual dissipation. He trembled for Strathspey,
but it was too late now to interfere. Jerry Shaw
was in that stage of drunkenness which is greatly
accented by an elaborate affectation of sobriety. His
desire that Chevis should consider him perfectly
sober was abundantly manifest in his rigidly steady
gait, the preternatural gravity in his bloodshot eyes,
his sparingness of speech, and the earnestness with
which he enunciated the acquiescent formulæ which
had constituted his share of the conversation. Now

and then, controlling his faculties by a great effort, he looked hard at Chevis to discover what doubts might be expressed in his face concerning the genuineness of this staid deportment; and Chevis presently found it best to affect too. Believing that the blacksmith's histrionic attempts in the *rôle* of sober artisan were occupying his attention more than the paring of Strathspey's hoof, which he held between his knees on his leather apron, while the horse danced an animated measure on the other three feet, Chevis assumed an appearance of indifference, and strolled away into the shop. He looked about him, carelessly, at the horseshoes hanging on a rod in the rude aperture that served as window, at the wagon-tires, the plowshares, the glowing fire of the forge. The air within was unpleasantly close, and he soon found himself again in the doorway.

"Can I get some water here?" he asked, as Jerry Shaw reëntered, and began hammering vigorously at the shoe destined for Strathspey.

The resonant music ceased for a moment. The solemn, drunken eyes were slowly turned upon the visitor, and the elaborate affectation of sobriety was again obtrusively apparent in the blacksmith's manner. He rolled up more closely the blue-checked homespun sleeve from his corded hammer-arm, twitched nervously at the single suspender that supported his copper-colored jeans trousers, readjusted his leather apron hanging about his neck, and, casting upon Chevis another glance, replete with a challenging gravity, fell to work upon the anvil, every heavy and well-directed blow telling with the precision of machinery.

The question had hardly been heard before forgotten. At the next interval, when he was going out to fit the horse, Chevis repeated his request.

"Water, did ye say?" asked Jerry Shaw, looking

at him with narrowing eyelids, as if to shut out all other contemplation that he might grapple with this problem. ''Thar's no fraish water hyar, but ye kin go yander ter the house and ax fur some; or,'' he added, shading his eyes from the sunlight with his broad blackened hand, and looking at the huge wall of stone beyond the road, ''ye kin go down yander ter the spring, an' ax that thar gal fur a drink.''

Chevis took his way, in the last rays of sunshine, across the road and down the declivity in the direction indicated by the blacksmith. A cool gray shadow fell upon him from the heights of the great rocks, as he neared them; the narrow path leading from the road grew dank and moist, and presently his feet were sunk in the still green and odorous water-loving weeds, the clumps of fern, and the pungent mint. He did not notice the soft verdure; he did not even see the beautiful vines that hung from earth-filled niches among the rocks, and lent to their forbidding aspect something of a smiling grace; their picturesque grouping, where they had fallen apart to show this sparkling fountain of bright up-springing water, was all lost upon his artistic perceptions. His eyes were fixed on the girl standing beside the spring, her pail filled, but waiting, with a calm, expectant look on her face, as she saw him approaching.

No creature could have been more coarsely habited: a green cotton dress, faded to the faintest hue; rough shoes, just visible beneath her skirts; a dappled gray and brown calico sun-bonnet, thrown aside on a moss-grown bowlder near at hand. But it seemed as if the wild nature about her had been generous to this being toward whom life and fortune had played the niggard. There were opaline lights in her dreamy eyes which one sees nowhere save in sunset clouds that brood above dark hills;

the golden sunbeams, all faded from the landscape, had left a perpetual reflection in her bronze hair; there was a subtle affinity between her and other pliant, swaying, graceful young things, waving in the mountain breezes, fed by the rain and the dew. She was hardly more human to Chevis than certain lissome little woodland flowers, the very names of which he did not know,—pure white, star-shaped, with a faint green line threading its way through each of the five delicate petals; he had seen them embellishing the banks of lonely pools, or growing in dank, marshy places in the middle of the unfrequented road, where perhaps it had been mended in a primitive way with a few rotting rails.

"May I trouble you to give me some water?" asked Chevis, prosaically enough. She neither smiled nor replied. She took the gourd from the pail, dipped it into the lucent depths of the spring, handed it to him, and stood awaiting its return when he should have finished. The cool, delicious water was drained, and he gave the gourd back. "I am much obliged," he said.

"Ye're welcome," she replied, in a slow, singing monotone. Had the autumn winds taught her voice that melancholy cadence?

Chevis would have liked to hear her speak again, but the gulf between his station and hers—so undreamed of by her (for the differences of caste are absolutely unknown to the independent mountaineers), so patent to him—could be bridged by few ideas. They had so little in common that for a moment he could think of nothing to say. His cogitation suggested only the inquiry, "Do you live here?" indicating the little house on the other side of the road.

"Yes," she chanted in the same monotone, "I live hyar."

She turned to lift the brimming pail. Chevis
spoke again: "Do you always stay at home? Do you
never go anywhere?"

Her eyes rested upon him, with a slight surprise
looking out from among their changing lights. "No,"
she said, after a pause; "I hev no call to go nowhar
ez I knows on."

She placed the pail on her head, took the dappled
sun-bonnet in her hand, and went along the path with
the assured, steady gait and the graceful backward
poise of the figure that precluded the possibility of
spilling a drop from the vessel.

He had been touched in a highly romantic way by
the sweet beauty of this little woodland flower. It
seemed hard that so perfect a thing of its kind
should be wasted here, unseen by more appreciative
eyes than those of bird, or rabbit, or the equally un-
cultured human beings about her; and it gave him a
baffling sense of the mysterious injustice of life to
reflect upon the difference in her lot and that of
others of her age in higher spheres. He went thoughtfully through the closing shadows to the shop,
mounted the re-shod Strathspey, and rode along the
rugged ascent of the mountain, gravely pondering
on worldly inequalities.

He saw her often afterward, although he spoke
to her again but once. He sometimes stopped as he
came and went on the Christel road, and sat chatting
with the old man, her grandfather, on the porch, sunshiny days, or lounged in the barn-like door of Jerry
Shaw's shop talking to the half-drunken blacksmith.
He piqued himself on the readiness with which he
became interested in these people, entered into their
thoughts and feelings, obtained a comprehensive
idea of the machinery of life in this wilderness,—
more complicated than one could ready believe, looking upon the changeless face of the wide un-

populated expanse of mountain ranges stretching so
far beneath that infinite sky. They appealed to him
from the basis of their common humanity, he
thought, and the pleasure of watching the development of the common human attributes in this peculiar and primitive state of society never palled upon
him. He regarded with contempt Varney's frivolous
displeasure and annoyance because of Hi Bates's
utter insensibility to the difference in their social
position, and the necessity of either acquiescing in
the supposititious equality or dispensing with the
invaluable services of the proud and independent
mountaineer; because of the *patois* of the untutored
people, to hear which, Varney was wont to declare,
set his teeth on edge; because of their narrow prejudices, their mental poverty, their idle shiftlessness,
their uncouth dress and appearance. Chevis flat-
tered himself that he entertained a broader view.
He had not even a subacute idea that he looked upon
these people and their inner life only as picturesque
bits of the mental and moral landscape; that it was
an æsthetic and theoretical pleasure their contemplation afforded him; that he was as far as ever from
the basis of common humanity.

Sometimes, while he talked to the old man on the
sunlit porch, the "slip o' willow" sat in the doorway, listening too, but never speaking. Sometimes
he would find her with her father at the forge, her
fair, ethereal face illumined with an alien and fluctu-
ating brilliancy, shining and fading as the breath
of the fire rose and fell. He came to remember that
face so well that in a sorry sketch-book, where nothing else was finished, there were several laborious
pages lighted up with a faint reflection of its beauty.
But he was as much interested perhaps, though less
poetically, in that massive figure, the idle blacksmith. He looked at it all from an ideal point of

view. The star in the valley was only a brilliant, set in the night landscape, and suggested a unique and pleasing experience.

How should he imagine what luminous and wistful eyes were turned upward to where another star burned,—the light of his camp-fire on the crag; what pathetic, beautiful eyes had learned to watch and wait for that red gleam high on the mountain's brow, —hardly below the stars in heaven it seemed! How could he dream of the strange, vague, unreasoning trouble with which his idle comings and goings had clouded that young life, a trouble as strange, as vague, as vast, as the limitless sky above her.

She understood him as little. As she sat in the open doorway, with the flare of the fire behind her, and gazed at the red light shining on the crag, she had no idea of the heights of worldly differences that divided them, more insurmountable than precipices and flying chutes of mountain torrents, and chasms and fissures of the wild ravine: she knew nothing of the life he had left, and of its rigorous artificialities and gradations of wealth and estimation. And with a heart full of pitiable unrealities she looked up at the glittering simulacrum of a star on the crag, while he gazed down on the ideal star in the valley.

The weeks had worn deep into November. Chevis and Varney were thinking of going home; indeed, they talked of breaking camp day after-tomorrow, and saying a long adieu to wood and mountain and stream. They had had an abundance of good sport and a surfeit of roughing it. They would go back to town and town avocations invigorated by their holiday, and taking with them a fresh and exhilarating recollection of the forest life left so far behind.

It was near dusk, on a dull, cold evening, when Chevis dismounted before the door of the blacksmith's little log-cabin.   The chestnut-tree hung desolate and bare on the eaves of the forge; the stream rushed by in swift gray whirlpools under a sullen gray sky; the gigantic wall of broken rocks loomed gloomy and sinister on the opposite side of the road,—not so much as a withered leaf of all their vines clung to their rugged surfaces. The mountains had changed color: the nearest ranges were black with the myriads of the grim black branches of the denuded forest; far away they stretched in parallel lines, rising tier above tier, and showing numberless gradations of a dreary, neutral tint, which grew ever fainter in the distance, till merged in the uniform tone of the sombre sky.

Indoors it was certainly more cheerful. A hickory fire dispensed alike warmth and light. The musical whir of a spinning-wheel added its unique charm. From the rafters depended numberless strings of bright red pepper-pods and ears of pop-corn; hanks of woolen and cotton yarn; bunches of medicinal herbs; brown gourds and little bags of seeds.   On rude shelves against the wall were ranged cooking utensils, drinking vessels, etc., all distinguished by that scrupulous cleanliness which is a marked feature of the poor hovels of these mountaineers, and in striking contrast to the poor hovels of lowlanders. The rush-bottomed chairs, drawn in a semicircle before the rough, ill-adjusted stones which did duty as hearth, were occupied by several men, who seemed to be making the blacksmith a prolonged visit; various members of the family were humbly seated on sundry inverted domestic articles, such as wash-tubs, and splint-baskets made of white oak. There was circulating among Jerry Shaw's friends a flat bottle, facetiously denominated "tickler," readily emptied, but as readily replenished from a keg in the corner. Like the widow's cruse of oil,

that keg was miraculously never empty. The fact of
a still near by in the wild ravine might suggest a reason for its perennial flow. It was a good strong article of apple-brandy, and its effects were beginning to
be distinctly visible.

Truly the ethereal woodland flower seemed
strangely incongruous with these brutal and uncouth conditions of her life, as she stood at a little
distance from this group, spinning at her wheel.
Chevis felt a sudden sharp pang of pity for her when
he glanced toward her; the next instant he had forgotten it in his interest in her work. It was altogether at variance with the ideas which he had hitherto entertained concerning that humble handicraft.
There came across him a vague recollection from his
city life that the peasant girls of art galleries and
of the lyric stage were wont to sit at the wheel.
"But perhaps they were spinning flax," he reflected.
This spinning was a matter of walking back and
forth with smooth, measured steps and graceful, un-
dulatory motion; a matter, too, of much pretty gesticulation,—the thread in one hand, the other regu-
lating the whirl of the wheel. He thought he had
never seen attitudes so charming.

Jerry Shaw hastened to abdicate and offer one
of the rush-bottomed chairs with the eager hospitality characteristic of these mountaineers,—a hospitality that meets a stranger on the threshold of every
hut, presses upon him, ungrudgingly, its best, and
follows him on his departure with protestations of
regret out to the rickety fence. Chevis was more or
less known to all of the visitors, and after a little,
under the sense of familiarity and the impetus of
the apple-brandy, the talk flowed on as freely as before his entrance. It was wilder and more antago-
istic to his principles and prejudices than anything
he had hitherto heard among these people, and he

looked on and listened, interested in this new development of a phase of life which he had thought he had sounded from its lowest note to the top of its compass. He was glad to remain; the scene had impressed his cultivated perceptions as an interior by Teniers might have done, and the vehemence and lawlessness of the conversation and the threats of violence had little reality for him; if he thought about the subject under discussion at all, it was with a reassuring conviction that before the plans could be carried out the already intoxicated mountaineers would be helplessly drunk. Nevertheless, he glanced ever and anon at the young girl, loath that she should hear it, lest its virulent, angry bitterness should startle her. She was evidently listening, too, but her fair face was as calm and untroubled as one of the pure white faces of those flower-stars of his early stay in the mountains.

"Them Peels ought n't ter be let live!" exclaimed Elijah Burr, a gigantic fellow, arrayed in brown jeans, with the accompaniments of knife, powder-horn, etc., usual with the hunters of the range; his gun stood, with those of the other guests, against the wall in a corner of the room. "They ought n't ter be let live, an' I'd top off all three of 'em fur the skin an' horns of a deer."

"That thar is a true word," assented Jerry Shaw. "They oughter be run down an' kilt,—all three o' them Peels."

Chevis could not forbear a question. Always on the alert to add to his stock of knowledge of men and minds, always analyzing his own inner life and the inner life of those about him, he said, turning to his intoxicated host, "Who are the Peels, Mr. Shaw,—if I may ask?"

"Who air the Peels?" repeated Jerry Shaw, making a point of seizing the question. "They air the

meanest men in these hyar mountings. Ye might
hunt from Copperhead Ridge ter Clinch River, an'
the whole spread o' the valley, an' never hear tell o'
no sech no 'count critters.''

"They ought n't ter be let live!" again urged
Elijah Burr. "No man ez treats his wife like that
dad-burned scoundrel Ike Peel do oughter be let live.
That thar woman is my sister an' Jerry Shaw's
cousin,—an' I shot him down in his own door year
afore las'. I shot him ter kill; but somehow 'nother
I war that shaky, an' the cussed gun hung fire a-fust,
an' that thar pore wife o' his'n screamed an' hol-
ered so, that I never done nuthin' arter all but lay
him up for four month an' better for that thar pore
critter ter nuss. He'll see a mighty differ nex' time
I gits my chance. An' 't ain't fur off," he added
threateningly.

"Would n't it be better to persuade her to leave
him?" suggested Chevis pacifically, without, however, any wild idea of playing peace-maker between
fire and tow.

Burr growled a fierce oath, and then was silent.

A slow fellow on the opposite side of the fireplace
explained: "Thar's whar all the trouble kem from.
She would n't leave him, fur all he treated her awful.
She said ez how he war mighty good ter her when
he war n't drunk. So 'Lijah shot him."

This way of cutting the Gordian knot of domestic
difficulties might have proved efficacious but for the
shakiness induced by the thrill of fraternal sentiment, the infusion of apple-brandy, the protest of
the bone of contention, and the hanging fire of the
treacherous gun. Elijah Burr could remember no
other failure of aim for twenty years.

"He won't git shet of me that easy again!" Burr
declared, with another pull at the flat tickler. "But
ef it hed n't hev been fur what happened las' week,

I mought hev let him off fur awhile,'' he continued, evidently actuated by some curiously distorted sense of duty in the premises. "I oughter hev kilt him afore. But now the cussed critter is a gone coon. Dad-burn the whole tribe!''

Chevis was desirous of knowing what had happened last week. He did not, however, feel justified in asking more questions. But apple-brandy is a potent tongue-loosener, and the unwonted communicativeness of the stolid and silent mountaineers attested its strength in this regard. Jerry Shaw, without inquiry, enlightened him.

"Ye see,'' he said, turning to Chevis, '' 'Lijah he thought ez how ef he could git that fool woman ter come ter his house, he could shoot Ike fur his meanness 'thout botherin' of her, an' things would all git easy again. Waal, he went thar one day when all them Peels, the whole lay-out, war gone down ter the Settlemint ter hear the rider preach, an' he jes' run away with two of the brats,—the littlest ones, ye onderstand,—a-thinkin' he moght tole her off from Ike that thar way. We hearn ez how the pore critter war nigh on ter distracted 'bout 'em, but Ike never let her come arter 'em. Leastways, she never kem. Las' week Ike kem fur 'em hisself,—him an' them two cussed brothers o' his'n. All 'Lijah's folks war out'n the way; him an' his boys war off a-hunting', an' his wife hed gone down ter the spring, a haffen mile an' better, a-washin' clothes; nobody war ter the house 'ceptin' them two chillen o' Ike's. An' Ike an' his brothers jes' tuk the chillen away, an' set fire ter the house; an' time 'Lijah's wife got thar, 't war nuthin' but a pile o' ashes. So we've determinated ter go up yander ter Laurel Notch, twenty mile along the ridge of the mounting, ter-night, an' wipe out them Peels,—'kase they air a-goin' ter move away. That thar wife o' Ike's, what made all the

trouble, hev fretted an' fretted at Ike till he hev determinated ter break up an' wagon across the range
ter Kaintucky, whar his uncle lives in the hills thar.
Ike hev gin his cornsent ter go jes' ter pleasure her,
'kaze she air mos' crazed ter git Ike away what 'Lijah can't kill him. Ike's brothers is a-goin', too. I
hearn ez how they'll make a start at noon ter-morrer.''

"They'll never start ter Kaintucky ter-morrer,''
said Burr, grimly. "They'll git off, afore that, fur
hell, stiddier Kaintucky. I hev been a-tryin' ter
make out ter shoot that thar man ever since that
thar gal was married ter him, seven years ago,—
seven years an' better. But what with her a-foolin'
round, an' a-talking', an' a-goin' on like she war distracted—she run right 'twixt him an' the muzzle
of my gun wunst, or I would hev hed him that time
for sure—an' somehow 'nother that critter makes
me so shaky with her ways of goin' on that I feel
like I hain't got good sense, an' can't git no good
aim at nuthin'. Nex' time, though, thar'll be a differ. She ain't a-going' ter Kaintucky along of him
ter be beat fur nuthin' when he's drunk.''

It was a pitiable picture presented to Chevis's
open-eyed imagination,—this woman standing for
years between the two men she loved: holding back
her brother from his vengeance of her wrongs by
that subtle influence that shook his aim; and going
into exile with her brute of a husband when that influence had waned and failed, and her wrongs were
supplemented by deep and irreparable injuries to
her brother. And the curious moral attitude of the
man: the strong fraternal feeling that alternately
nerved and weakened his revengeful hand.

"We air goin' thar 'bout two o'clock ter-night,''
said Jerry Shaw, "and wipe out all three o' them
Peels,—Ike an' his two brothers.''

"They ought n't ter be let live," reiterated Elijah Burr, moodily. Did he speak to his faintly stirring conscience, or to a woful premonition of his sister's grief?

"They'll all three be stiff an' stark afore day-break," resumed Jerry Shaw. "We air all kin ter 'Lijah, an' we air goin' ter holp him top off them Peels. Thar's ten of us an' three o' them, an' we won't hev no trouble 'bout it. An' we'll bring that pore critter, Ike's wife, an' her children hyar ter stay. She's welcome ter live along of us till 'Lijah kin fix some sort'n place fur her an' the little chillen. Thar won't be no trouble a-gittin' rid of the men folks, ez thar is ten of us an' three o' them, an' we air goin' ter take 'em in the night."

There was a protest from an unexpected quarter. The whir of the spinning-wheel was abruptly silenced. "I don't see no sense," said Celia Shaw, her singing monotone vibrating in the sudden lull,—"I don't see no sense in shootin' folks down like they war nuthin' better nor bear, nor deer, nor suthin' wild. I don't see no sense in it. An' I never did see none."

There was an astonished pause.

"Shet up, Cely! Shet up!" exclaimed Jerry Shaw, in mingled anger and surprise. "Them folks ain't no better nor bear, nor sech. They hain't got no right ter live,—them Peels."

"No, that they hain't!" said Burr.

"They is powerful no 'count critters, I know," replied the little woodland flower, the firelight bright in her opaline eyes and on the flakes of burnished gold gleaming in the dark masses of her hair. "They is always a-hanging' round the still an' a-gittin' drunk; but I don't see no sense in a-huntin' 'em down an' a-killin' 'em off. 'Pears ter me like

they air better nor the dumb ones. I don't see no
sense in shootin' 'em.''

"Shet up, Cely! Shet up!" reiterated Shaw.

Celia said no more. Reginald Chevis was pleased
with this indication of her sensibility; the other
women—her mother and grandmother—had heard
the whole recital with the utmost indifference, as
they sat by the fire monotonously carding cotton.
She was beyond her station in sentiment, he thought.
However, he was disposed to recant this favorable
estimate of her higher nature when, twice afterward,
she stopped her work, and, filling the bottle from
the keg, pressed it upon her father, despite her un-
favorable criticism of the hangers-on of stills. Nay,
she insisted. "Drink some more," she said. "Ye
hain't got half enough yit." Had the girl no pity
for the already drunken creature? She seemed sys-
tematically trying to make him even more helpless
than he was.

He had fallen into a deep sleep before Chevis left
the house, and the bottle was circulating among the
other men with a rapidity that boded little harm to
the unconscious Ike Peel and his brothers at Laurel
Notch, twenty miles away. As Chevis mounted
Strathspey he saw the horses of Jerry Shaw's
friends standing partly within and party without
the blacksmith's shop. They would stand there all
night, he thought. It was darker when he commenced the ascent of the mountain than he had anticipated. And what was this driving against his
face,—rain? No, it was snow. He had not started
a moment too soon. But Strethspey, by reason of
frequent travel, knew every foot of the way, and perhaps there would only be a flurry. And so he went
on steadily up and up the wild, winding road among
the great, bare, black trees and the grim heights
and chasms. The snow fell fast,—so fast and so

silently, before he was half-way to the summit he
had lost the vague companionship of the sound of
his horse's hoofs, now muffled in the thick carpet so
suddenly flung upon the ground. Still the snow fell,
and when he had reached the mountain's brow the
ground was deeply covered, and the whole aspect
of the scene was strange. But though obscured by
the fast-flying flakes, he knew that down in the bosom
of the white valley there glittered still that changeless star.

"Still spinning, I suppose," he said to himself, as
he looked toward it and thought of the interior of
the log-cabin below. And then he turned into the
tent to enjoy his cigar, his æsthetic reveries, and a
bottle of wine.

But the wheel was no longer awhirl. Both music
and musician were gone. Toiling along the snow-
filled mountain ways, struggling with the fierce gusts
of wind as they buffeted and hindered her, and fluttered derisively among her thin, worn, old garments;
shivering as the driving flakes came full into the
pale, calm face, and fell in heavier and heavier
wreaths upon the dappled calico sun-bonnet; threading her way through unfrequented woodland paths,
that she might shorten the distance; now deftly on
the verge of a precipice, whence a false step of those
coarse, rough shoes would fling her into unimagin-
able abysses below; now on the sides of steep
ravines, falling sometimes with the treacherous,
sliding snow, but never faltering; tearing her hands
on the shrubs and vines she clutched to help her
forward, and bruised and bleeding, but still going
on; trembling more than with the cold, but never
turning back, when a sudden noise in the terrible
loneliness of the sheeted woods suggested the
close proximity of a wild beast, or perhaps, to her
ignorant, superstitious mind, a supernatural pres-

ence,—thus she journeyed on her errand of deliverance.

Her fluttering breath came and went in quick gasps; her failing limbs wearily dragged through the deep drifts; the cruel winds untiringly lashed her; the snow soaked through the faded green cotton dress to the chilled white skin,—it seemed even to the dull blood coursing feebly through her freezing veins. But she had small thought for herself during those long, slow hours of endurance and painful effort. Her pale lips moved now and then with muttered speculations: how the time went by; whether they had discovered her absence at home; and whether the fleeter horsemen were even now ploughing their way through the longer, winding mountain road. Her only hope was to outstrip their speed. Her prayer—this untaught being!—she had no prayer, except perhaps her life, the life she was so ready to imperil. She had no high, cultured sensibilities to sustain her. There was no instinct stirring within her that might have nerved her to save her father's, or her brother's, or a benefactor's life. She held the creatures that she would have died to warn in low estimation, and spoke of them with reprobation and contempt. She had known no religious training, holding up forever the sublimest ideal. The measureless mountain wilds were not more infinite to her than that great mystery. Perhaps, without any philosophy, she stood upon the basis of a common humanity.

When the silent horsemen, sobered by the chill night air and the cold snow, made their cautious approach to the little porch of Ike Peel's log-hut at Laurel Notch, there was a thrill of dismayed surprise among them to discover the door standing half open, the house empty of its scanty furniture and goods, its owners fled, and the very dogs disappeared; only, on the rough stones before the dying fire, Celia Shaw, falling asleep and waking by fitful starts.

"Jerry Shaw swore ez how he would hev shot that thar gal o' his'n,—that thar Cely," Hi Bates said to Chevis and Varney the next day, when he recounted the incident, "only he did n't think she hed her right mind; a-walkin' through this hyar deep snow full fifteen mile,—it's fifteen mile by the short cut ter Laurel Notch,—ter git Ike Peel's folks off 'fore 'Lijah an' her dad could come up an' settle Ike an' his brothers. Leastways, 'Lijah an' the t'others, fur Jerry hed got so drunk he could n't go; he war dead asleep till ter-day, when they kem back a-fotchin' the gal with 'em. That thar Cely Shaw never did look ter me like she had good sense, nohow. Always looked like she war queer an' teched in the head."

There was a furtive gleam of speculation on the dull face of the mountaineer when his two listeners broke into enthusiastic commendation of the girl's high heroism and courage. The man of ledgers swore that he had never heard of anything so fine, and that he himself would walk through fifteen miles of snow and midnight wilderness for the honor of shaking hands with her. There was that keen thrill about their hearts sometimes felt in crowded theatres, responsive to the cleverly simulated heroism of the boards; or in listening to a poet's mid-air song; or in looking upon some grand and ennobling phase of life translated on a great painter's canvas.

Hi Bates thought that perhaps they too were a little "teched in the head."

There had fallen upon Chevis a sense of deep humiliation. Celia Shaw had heard no more of that momentous conversation than he; a wide contrast was suggested. He began to have a glimmering perception that despite all his culture, his sensibil-

ity, his yearnings toward humanity, he was not so
high a thing in the scale of being; that he had placed
a false estimate upon himself. He had looked down
on her with a mingled pity for her dense ignorance,
her coarse surroundings, her low station, and a
dilettante's delight in picturesque effects, and with
no recognition of the moral splendors of that star
in the valley. A realization, too, was upon him that
fine feelings are of most avail as the motive power of
fine deeds.

He and his friend went down together to the little log-cabin. There had been only jeers and taunts
and reproaches for Celia Shaw from her own people. These she had expected, and she had stolidly
borne them. But she listened to the fine speeches
of the city-bred men with a vague wonderment on
her flower-like face,—whiter than ever to-day.

"It was a splendid—a noble thing to do," said
Varney, warmly.

"I shall never forget it," said Chevis, "it will always be like a sermon to me."

There was something more that Reginald Chevis
never forgot: the look on her face as he turned and
left her forever; for he was on his way back to his
former life, so far removed from her and all her
ideas and imaginings. He pondered long upon that
look in her inscrutable eyes,—was it suffering, some
keen pang of despair?—as he rode down and down
the valley, all unconscious of the heart-break he left
behind him. He thought of it often afterward; he
never penetrated its mystery.

He heard of her only once again. On the eve of a
famous day, when visiting the outposts of a gallant
corps, Reginald Chevis happened to recognize in
one of the pickets the gawky mountaineer who had
been his guide through those autumnal woods so far
away. Hi Bates was afterward sought out and hon-

ored with an interview in the general's tent; for the accidental encounter had evoked many pleasant reminiscences in Chevis's mind, and among other questions he wished to ask was what had become of Jerry Shaw's daughter.

"She's dead,—long ago," answered Hi Bates. "She died afore the winter war over the year ez ye war a-huntin' thar. She never hed good sense ter my way o' thinkin', nohow, an' one night she run away, an' walked 'bout fifteen mile through a big snow-storm. Some say it settled on her chist. Anyhow, she jes' sorter fell away like afterward, an' never held up her head good no more. She always war a slim little critter, an' looked like she war teched in the head."

There are many things that suffer unheeded in those mountains: the birds that freeze on the trees; the wounded deer that leaves its cruel kind to die alone; the despairing, flying fox with its pursuing train of savage dogs and men. And the jutting crag whence had shone the camp-fire she had so often watched—her star, set forever—looked far over the valley beneath, where in one of those sad little rural graveyards she had been laid so long ago.

But Reginald Chevis has never forgotten her. Whenever he sees the earliest star spring into the evening sky, he remembers the answering red gleam of that star in the valley.

THOMAS NELSON PAGE.

CHRISTMAS BEFORE THE WAR.*

From In Ole Virginia (1887).

"WELL, twuz de next Christmas we meet Miss
Charlotte an' Nancy. Mr. Braxton invite we all to
go down to spen' Christmas wid him at he home.
An' sich a time as we had!

"We got dyah Christmas Eve night—dis very
night—jes befo' supper, an' jes natchelly froze to
death," he pursued, dealing in his wonted hyperbole, "an' we jes had time to git a apple toddy or
two when supper was ready, an' wud come dat dee
wuz waitin' in de hall. I had done fix Marse
George up gorgeousome, I tell you; and when he
walk down dem stairs in dat swaller-tail coat, an'
dem paten'-leather pumps on, dee warn nay one
dyah could tetch him; he looked like he own 'em
all. I jes rest my mind. I seen him when he shake
hands wid 'em all roun', an' I say, 'Um-m-m! he
got 'em.'

"But he ain' teck noticement o' none much tell
Miss Charlotte come. She didn' live dyah, had jes
come over de river dat evenin' from her home, 'bout
ten miles off, to spen' Christmas like we all, an' she
come down de stairs jes as Marse George finish
shakin' hands. I seen he eye light on her as she
come down de steps smilin', wid her dim blue dress
trainin' behind her, an' her little blue foots peepin'

THOMAS NELSON PAGE.

out so pretty, an' holdin' a little handcher, lookin'
like a spider-web, in one hand, an' a gret blue fan in
turr, spread out like a peacock tail, an' jest her
roun' arms an' th'oat white, an' her gret dark eyes
lightin' up her face. I say, 'Dyah 'tis!' and when
de ole Cun'l stan' aside an' interduce 'em, an' Marse
George step for'ard an' meck he grand bow, an' she
sort o' swing back an' gin her curtchy, wid her dress
sort o' dammed up 'ginst her, an' her arms so white,
an' her face sort o' sunsetty, I say, 'Yes, Lord! Edin-
burg, dyah you mistis.' Marse George look like he
think she done come down right from de top o' de
blue sky an' bring piece on it wid her. He ain'
nuver took he eyes from her dat night. Dee glued
to her, mun! an' she—well, do' she mighty rosy, an'
look mighty unconsarned, she sutney ain' hender
him. Hit look like kyarn nobody else tote dat fan
an' pick up dat hankcher skusin' o' him; an' after
supper, when dee all playin' blindman's-buff in de
hall—I don' know how twuz—but do' she jes as
nimble as a filly, an' her ankle jes as clean, an' she
kin git up her dress an' dodge out de way o' ev'y-
body else, somehow or nurr she kyarn help him
ketchin' her to save her life; he al'ays got her corn-
dered; an' when dee'd git fur apart, dat ain' nuttin,
dee jes as sure to come togerr agin as water is whar
you done run you hand thoo. An' do' he kiss ev'y-
body else under de mistletow, 'cause dee be sort o'
cousins, he ain' nuver kiss her, nor nobody else
nurr, 'cep' de ole Cun'l. I was standin' down at
de een de hall wid de black folks, an' I notice it
'tic'lar 'cause I done meck de 'quaintance o' Nancy;
she wuz Miss Charlotte's maid; a mighty likely
young gal she wuz den, an' jes as impident as a fly.
She see it too, do' she ain' 'low it.

"Fust thing I know I seen a mighty likely light-
skinned gal standin' dyah by me, wid her hyah mos'

straight as white folks, an' a mighty good frock on,
an' a clean apron, an' her hand mos' like a lady, only
it brown, an' she keep on 'vidin' her eyes twix me
an' Miss Charlotte; when I watchin' Miss Charlotte
she watchin' me, an' when I steal my eye 'roun' on
her she noticin' Miss Charlotte; an' presney I sort
o' sidle 'longside her, an' I say, 'Lady, you mighty
sprightly to-night.' An' she say she 'bleeged to be
sprightly, her mistis look so good; an' I ax her
which one twuz, an' she tell me, 'Dat queen one
over dyah,' an' I tell her dee's a king dyah too, she
got her eye set for; an' when I say her mistis tryin'
to set her cap for Marse George, she fly up, an' say
she an' her mistis don' have to set dee cap for nobody; *dee* got to set dee cap an' all dee clo'es for
dem, an' den dee ain' gwine cotch 'em, 'cause dee
ain' studyin' 'bout no up-country folks whar dee
ain' nobody know nuttin 'bout.

"Well, dat oudaciousness so aggrivate me, I lite
into dat nigger right dyah. I tell her she ain' been
nowhar 'tall ef she don' know we all; dat we wuz
de bes' of quality, de ve'y top de pot; an' den I tell
her 'bout how gret we wuz; how de ker'idges wuz
al'ays hitched up night an' day, an' niggers jes thick
as weeds; an' how Unc' Torm he wared he swaller-
tail ev'y day when he wait on de table; and Marse
George he won' wyah a coat mo'n once or twice
anyways, to save you life. Oh! I sutney 'stonish
dat nigger, 'cause I wuz teckin up for de fambly, an'
I meck out like dee use gold up home like urr folks
use wood, an' sow silver like urr folks sow wheat;
an' when I got thoo dee wuz all on 'em listenin,' an'
she 'lowed dat Marse George he were ve'y good,
sho 'nough, ef twarn for he nigger; but I ain' tarri-
fyin' myself none ' bout dat, 'cause I know she jes
projickin, an' she couldn' help bein' impident ef you
wuz to whup de frock off her back.

"Jes den dee struck up de dance. Dee had wheel de pianer out in de hall, and somebody say Jack Forester had come cross de river, an' all on 'em say dee mus' git Jack; an' presney he come in wid he fiddle, grinnin' and scrapin', 'cause he wuz a notable fiddler, do' I don' think he wuz equal to we all's Tubal, an' I know he couldn' tech Marse George, 'cause Marse George wuz a natchel fiddler, jes like 'coons is natchel pacers, an' mules is natchel kickers. Howsomever, he sutney jucked a jig sweet, an' when he shake dot bow you couldn' help you foot switchin' a leetle—not ef you wuz a member of de chutch. He was a mighty sinful man, Jack wuz, an' dat fiddle had done drawed many souls to torment.

"Well, in a minute dee wuz all flyin', an' Jack he wuz rockin' like boat rockin' on de water, an' he face right shiny, an' he teef look like ear o' corn he got in he mouf, an' he big foot set 'way out keepin' time, an' Marse George he was in de lead row dyah too; ev'y chance he git he tunned Miss Charlotte— 'petchel motion, right hand across, an' cauliflower, an' croquette—dee croquette plenty o' urrs, but I notice dee ain' nuver fail to tun one nurr, an' ev'y tun he gin she wrappin' de chain roun' him; once when de wuz 'prominadin-all' down we all's een o' de hall, as he tunned her somebody step on her dress an' to' it. I heah de screech o' de silk, an' Nancy say, 'O Lord!' den she say, 'Nem mine! now I'll get it!' an' dee stop for a minute for Marse George to pin it up, while turrers went on, an' Marse George wuz down on he knee, an' she look down on him mighty sweet out her eyes, an' say, 'Hit don' meck no difference,' an' he glance up an' cotch her eye, an', jes 'dout a wud, he tyah a gret piece right out de silk an' slipt it in he bosom, an' when he got up, he say, right low, lookin' in her eyes right deep, 'I gwine wyah dis at my weddin',' an' she jes look sweet as candy; an ef Nancy ever wyah dat frock I ain' see it.

"Den presney dee wuz talkin' 'bout stoppin'. De ole Cun'l say hit time to have prars, an' dee wuz beggin' him to wait a leetle while; an' Jask Forester lay he fiddle down nigh Marse George, an' he picked 't up an' drawed de bow 'cross it jes to try it, an' den jes projickin' he struck dat chune 'bout 'You'll ermember me.' He hadn' mo'n tech de string when you could heah a pin drap. Marse George he warn noticin', an' he jes lay he face on de fiddle, wid he eyes sort o' half shet, an' drawed her out like he'd do some nights at home in dee moonlight on de gret porch, tell on a sudden he looked up an' cotch Miss Charlotte eye leanin' for'ards so earnest, an' all on 'em list'nin', an' he stopt, an' dee all clapt dee hands, an' he sudney drapt into a jig. Jack Forester ain' had to play no mo' dat night; even de ole Cun'l ketched de fever, an' he stept out in de flo', in he long-tail coat an' high collar, an' knocked 'em off de 'Snow-bud on de Ash-bank,' an' 'Chicken in de Bread-tray,' right natchel.

"Oh, he could jes plank 'em down!

"Oh, dat wuz a Christmas like you been read 'bout! An' twuz hard to tell which gittin cotch most, Marse George or me; 'cause dat nigger she jes as confusin' as Miss Charlotte. An' she sutney wuz sp'ilt dem days; ev'y nigger on dat place got he eye on her, an' she jes az oudacious an' aggrivatin as jes womens kin be.

"Dees monsus 'ceivin' critters, womens is, jes as onreliable as de hind-leg of a mule; a man got to watch 'em all de time; you kyarn break 'em like you kin horses.

"Now dat off mule dyah" (indicating, by a lazy but not light lash of his whip the one selected for his illustration), "dee ain' no countin' on her at all; she go 'long all day, or maybe a week, jes dat easy an' sociable, an' fust thing you know you ain' know nuttin, she done knock you brains out; dee ain' no 'pendence to be placed in 'em 'tall, suh; she jes as sweet as a kiss one minute, an' next time she comes out de house she got her head up in de air, an' her ears backed, an' goin' 'long switchin' herself like I ain' good 'nough for her to walk on.

" 'Fox-huntin's?' oh, yes, suh, ev'y day mos'; an' when Marse George didn' git de tail, twuz 'cause twuz a bob-tail fox—you heah me! He play de fiddle for he pastime, but he fotched up in de saddle —dat he cradle!

"De fust day dee went out I heah Nancy quoilin 'bout de tail layin' on Miss Charlotte dressin'-table gittin' hyahs over ev'ything.

"One day de ladies went out too, Miss Charlotte 'mongst 'em, on Miss Lucy gray myah Switchity, an' Marse George he rid Mr. Braxton's chestnut Willful.

"Well, suh, he stick so close to dat gray myah, he leetle mo' los' dat fox; but, Lord! he know what he 'bout—he monsus 'ceivin' 'bout dat—he know de way de fox gwine jes as well as he know heself; an' all de time he leadin' Miss Charlotte whar she kin heah de music, but he watchin' him too, jes as narrow as a ole hound. So, when de fox tun de head o' de creek, Marse George had Miss Charlotte on de aidge o' de flat, an' he de fust man see de fox tun down on turr side wid de hounds right rank after him. Dat sort o' set him back, 'cause by rights de fox ought to 'a double an' come back dis side: he kyarn git out dat way; an' two or three gent'mens dee had see it too, an' wuz jes layin de horses to de groun' to git roun' fust, 'cause de creek wuz heap too wide to jump, an' wuz 'way over you head, an hit cold as Christmas, sho 'nough; well, suh, when dee tunned, Mr. Clarke he wuz in de lead (he wuz ridin' for Miss Charlotte too), an' hit fyah set Marse George on fire; he ain' said but one wud, 'Wait,' an' jes set de chestnut's head straight for de creek, whar he fox comin' wid he hyah up on he back, an' de dogs ravlin mos' on him.

"De ladies screamed, an' some de gent'mens hollered for him to come back, but he ain' mind; he went 'cross dat flat like a wild-duck; an' when he retch de water he horse try to flinch, but dat hand on de bridle, an' dem rowels in he side, an' he 'bleeged to teck it.

"Lord! suh, sich a screech as dee set up! But he wuz swimmin' for life, an' he wuz up de bank an' in de middle o' de dogs time dee tetched ole Gray Jacket; an' when Mr. Clarke got dyah Marse George wuz stan'in' holdin' up de tail for Miss Charlotte to see, turr side de creek, an' de hounds wuz wallerin' all over de body, an' I don' think Mr. Clarke don got up wid 'em yit.

"He cotch de fox, an' he cotch some'n' else besides, in my 'pinion, 'cause when de ladies went upstairs dat night Miss Charlotte had to wait on de steps for a glass o' water, an' couldn' nobody git it but Marse George; an' den when she tell him goodnight over de banisters, he couldn' say it good enough; he got to kiss her hand; an' she ain' do nuttin but jes peep upstairs ef anybody dyah lookin'; an' when I come thoo de do' she juck her hand 'way an' ran upstairs jes as farst as she could. Marse George look at me sort o' loughin', and' say: 'Confound you! Nancy couldn' been very good to you.' An' I say, 'She le' me squench my thrist kissin' her hand;' an' he sort o' laugh an' tell me to keep my mouf shet.

MARSE CHAN.*

From the Same.

"WE didn't know nuthin' 'bout dis den. We wuz a-fightin' an' a-fightin' all dat time; an' come one day a letter to Marse Chan, an' I see 'im start to read it in his tent, an' he face hit look so cu'ious, an' he han's trembled so I couldn' mek out what wuz de matter wid 'im. An' he fol' de letter up an' wen' out an' wen' away down 'hine de camp, an' stayed dyah 'bout nigh an hour. Well, seh, I wuz on de lookout for 'im when he come back, an', fo' Gord, ef he face didn' shine like a angel's! I say to myse'f, 'Um'm! ef de glory o' Gord ain' done shine on 'im!' An' what you' 'spose 'twuz?

"He tuk me wid 'im dat evenin', an' he tell me he hed done git a letter from Miss Anne, an' Marse Chan he eyes look like gre't big stars, an' he face wuz jes' like 'twuz dat mawnin' when de sun riz up over de low groun', an' I see 'im stan'in' dyah wid de pistil in he han', lookin' at it, an' not knowin' but what it mout be de lars' time, an' he done mek up he mine not to shoot ole Cun'l Chahmb'lin fur Miss Anne's sake, what writ 'im de letter.

"He fol' de letter wha' was in his han' up, an' put it in he inside pocket—right dyar on de lef' side; an' den he tole me he tho't mebbe we wuz gwine hev some warm wuk in de nex' two or th'ee days, an' arfter dat ef Gord speared 'im he'd git a leave o' absence fur a few days, an' we'd go home.

"Well, dat night de orders come, an' we all hed to git over to'ds Romney; an' we rid all night till 'bout light; an' we halted right on a little creek, an'

---

* Copyright by Charles Scribner's Sons. Reprinted with the kind permission of the publishers. The extract is taken from the story of the same name.

we stayed dyah till mos' breakfas' time, an' I see
Marse Chan set down on de groun' 'hine a bush an'
read dat letter over an' over. I watch 'im, an' de
battle waz a-goin' on, but we had orders to stay
'hine de hill, an' ev'y now an' den de bullets would
cut de limbs o' de trees right over us, an' one o' dem
big shells what goes *'Awhar—awhar—awhar!'*
would fall right 'mong us; but Marse Chan he didn'
mine it no mo'n nuthin'! Den it 'peared to git
closer an' thicker, and Marse Chan he calls me, an'
I crep' up, an' he sez:

"'Sam, we'se goin' to win in dis battle, an' den
we'll go home an' git married; an' I'se goin' home
wid a star on my collar.' An' den he sez, 'Ef I'm
wounded' kyar me home, yo' hear?' An' I sez,
'Yes, Marse Chan.'

"Well, jes' den dey blowed boots an' saddles, 'an
we mounted; an' de orders come to ride 'roun' de
slope, an' Marse Chan's comp'ny wuz de secon', an'
when we got 'roun' dyah, we wuz right in it. Hit
wuz de wust place ever dis nigger got in. An' dey
said, 'Charge 'em!'' an' my king! ef ever you see
bullets fly, dey did dat day. Hit wuz jes' like hail;
an' we wen' down de slope (I long wid de res') an'
up de hill right to'ds de cannons, an' de fire wuz so
strong dyar (dey hed a whole rigiment o' infintrys
layin' down dyar onder de cannons) our lines sort o'
broke an' stop; de cun'l was kilt, an' I b'lieve dey
wuz jes' 'bout to bre'k all to pieces, when Marse
Chan rid up an' cotch hol' de fleg an' hollers, 'Foller me!' an' rid strainin' up de hill 'mong de cannons. I seen 'im when he went, de sorrel four good
lengths ahead o' ev'y urr hoss, jes' like he use' to
be in a fox-hunt, an' de whole rigiment right arfter
'im. Yo' ain' nuver hear thunder! Fust thing I
knowed, de roan roll' head over heels an' flung me
up 'g'inst de bank, like yo' chuck a nubbin over

'g'inst de foot o' de corn pile. An dat's what kep'
me from bein' kilt, I 'spects. Judy she say she
think 'twuz Providence, but I think 'twuz de bank.
O' co'se, Providence put de bank dyah, but how
come Providence nuver saved Marse Chan? When
I look' 'roun', de roan wuz layin' dyah by me, stone
dead, with a cannon-ball gone 'mos' th'oo him an'
our men hed done swep' dem on t'urr side from
de top o' de hill. 'Twan' mo'n a minit, de sorrel
come gallupin' back wid his mane flyin', an' de rein
hangin' down on one side to his knee. 'Dyar!'
says I, 'fo' Gord! I 'specks dey done kill Marse
Chan, an' I promised to tek care on him.'

"I jumped up an' run over de bank, an, dyar, wid
a whole lot o' dead men, an' some not dead yit,
onder one o' de guns wid de fleg still in he han', an'
a bullet right th'oo he body, lay Marse Chan. I
tu'n 'im over an' call 'im, 'Marse Chan!' but 'twan'
no use, he wuz done gone home, sho' 'nuff. I pick'
'im up in my arms wid de fleg still in he han's, an'
toted 'im back jes' like I did dat day when he wuz
a baby, an' ole marster gin 'im to me in my arms,
an' sez he could trus' me, an' tell me to tek keer on
'im long ez he lived. I kyar'd 'im 'way off de bat-
tlefiel' out de way o' de balls, an' I laid 'im down
onder a big tree till I could git somebody to ketch
de sorrel for me. He wuz cotched arfter a while,
an' I hed some money, so I got some pine plank
an' made a coffin dat evenin', an' wrapt Marse
Chan's body up in de fleg, an' put 'im in de coffin;
but I didn' nail de top on strong, 'cause I knowed
ole missis wan' see 'im; an' I got a' ambulance an'
set out for home dat night. We reached dyar de
nex' evenin', arfter travellin' all dat night an' all
nex' day.

"Hit 'peared like somethin' hed tole ole misses we wuz comin' so; for when we got home she wuz waitin' for us—done drest up in her best Sunday-clo'es, an' stan'n' at de head o' de big steps, an' ole marster settin' in his big cheer—ez we druv up de hill to'ds de house, I drivin' de ambulance an' de sorrel leadin' 'long behine wid de stirrups crost over de saddle.

"She come down to de gate to meet us. We took de coffin out de ambulance an' kyar'd it right into de big parlor wid de pictures in it, whar dey use' to dance in ole times when Marse Chan wuz a school-boy, an' Miss Anne Chahmb'lin use' to come over, an' go wid ole misses into her chamber an' tek her things off. In dyar we laid de coffin on two o' de cheers, an' ole misses nuver said a wud; she jes' looked so ole an' white.

"When I had tell 'em all 'bout it, I tu'ned right 'roun' an' rid over to Cun'l Chahmb'lin's, 'cause I knowed dat wuz what Marse Chan he'd 'a' wanted me to do. I didn' tell nobody whar I wuz gwine, 'cause yo' know none on 'em hadn' nuver speak to Miss Anne, not sence de duil, an' dey didn' know 'bout de letter.

"When I rid up in de yard, dyar wuz Miss Anne a-stan'in' on de poach watchin' me ez I rid up. I tied my hoss to de fence, an' walked up de parf. She knowed by de way I walked dyar wuz some-thin' de motter, an' she wuz mighty pale. I drapt my cap down on de een' o' de steps an' went up. She nuver opened her mouf; jes' stan' right still an' keep her eyes on my face. Fust, I couldn' speak; den I cotch my voice, an' I say, 'Marse Chan, he done got he furlough.'

THE MARRIAGE OF MEH LADY.*

From the Same.

"DEN we come on home, I ridin' a horse de Cun'l done hire to rest de mule, an' I mos' tired as he, but de Cun'l he ridin' jes' as fresh as ef he jes' start; an' he bring me a nigh way whar he learnt in de war, he say, when he used to slip th'oo de lines an' come at night forty miles jes' to look at de house an' see de light shine in Meh Lady's winder.

"De preacher an' he wife wuz dyah when we git home; but you know Meh Lady ain' satisfied in her mine yit. She say she do love him, but she don' know wherr she ought to marry him, 'cause she ain' got nobody to 'vise her. But he says he gwine be her 'viser from dis time, an' he lead her to de do' an' kiss her; an' she went to git ready, an' de turr lady wid her, an' her mammy wait on her, while I wait on de Cun'l, an' be he body-servant, an' git he warm water to shave, an' he cut off all he beard 'sep' he mustache, 'cause Meh Lady jes' say de man she knew didn' hed no beard on he face. An' Hannah she sut'n'y wuz comical, she ironin' an' sewin' dyah so induschus she oon' le' me come in meh own house.

"Well, pres'n'y we wuz ready, an' we come out in de hall, an' de Cun'l went in de parlor whar dee wuz gwine be married, an' de preacher he wuz in dyah, an' dee chattin' while we waitin' fur Meh Lady; an' I jes' slip out an' got up in de j'ice an' git out dem little rocks whar Mistis gin' me an' blow de dust off 'em good, and good Gord! ef dee didn' shine! I put 'em in meh pocket an' put on meh clean shu't an' come 'long back to de house. Hit right late now,

* Copyright by Charles Scribner's Sons. Reprinted with the kind permission of the publishers. The extract is the conclusion of the story entitled *Meh Lady: A Story of the War.* The "Cun'l" had been in the Northern army.

todes evenin', an' de sun wuz shinin' all 'cross de
yard an' th'oo de house, an' de Cun'l he so impatient he cyarn' set still, he jes' champin' he bit; so
he git up an' walk 'bout in de hall, an' he sut'n'y
look handsome an' young, jes' like he did dat day
he stand dyah wid he cap in he hand, an' Meh Lady
say she ain' claim no kin wid him, an' he say he
cyarn' intrude on ladies, an' back out de front do',
wid he head straight up, an' ride to git her de letter,
an' now he walkin' in de hall waitin' to marry her.
An' all on a sudden Hannah fling de do' wide open,
an' Meh Lady walk out!

"Gord! ef I didn' think 'twuz a angel.

"She stan dyah jes' white as snow fum her head to
way back' down on de flo' behine her, an' her veil
done fall roun' her like white mist, an' some roses in
her han'. Ef it didn' look like de sun done come th'oo
de chahmber do' wid her, an' blaze all over de styars,
an' de Cun'l he look like she bline him. An' 'twuz
Hannah an' she, while we wuz 'way dat day, done
fine Mistis' weddin' dress an' veil an' all, down to de
fan an' little slippers 'bout big as two little white
ears o' pop-corn; an' de dress had sort o' cobwebs
all over it, whar Hannah say was lace, an' hit jes'
fit Meh Lady like Gord put it dyah in de trunk for
her.

"Well, when de Cun'l done tell her how beautiful
she is, an' done meck her walk 'bout de hall showin'
her train, an' she lookin' over her shoulder at it an'
den at de Cun'l to see ef he proud o' her, he gin her
he arm; an' jes' den I walk up beto' her an' teck
dem things out meh pocket, an' de Cun'l drap her
arm an' stan' back, an' I put 'em 'roun' her thote
an' on her arms, an' gin her de res', an' Hannah put
'em on her ears, an' dee shine like stars, but her face
shine wus'n dem, an' she leetle mo' put bofe arms
'roun' meh neck, wid her eyes jes' runnin' over. An'

de Cun'l gi' her he arm, an' dee went in de parlor, an' Hannah an' me behine 'em. An' dyah,
facin' Mistis' picture an' Marse Phil's (tooken when
he wuz a little boy), lookin' down at 'em bofe, dee
wuz married.

"An' when de preacher git to dat part whar ax
who give dis woman to de man, he sort o' wait an'
he eye sort o' rove to me disconfused like he ax me
ef I know; an' I don' know huccome 'twuz, but I
think 'bout Marse Jeems an' Mistis when he ax me
dat, an' Marse Phil, whar all dead, an' all de scufflin'
we done been th'oo, an' how de chile ain' got nobody to teck her part now 'sep' jes' me; an' now,
when he wait an' look at me dat way, an' ax me dat,
I 'bleeged to speak up, I jes' step for'ard an' say:

" 'Ole Billy.'

"An' jes' den de sun crawl roun' de winder
shetter an' res' on her like it pourin' light all over
her.

"An' dat night when de preacher was gone wid
he wife, an' Hannah done drapt off to sleep, I wuz
settin' in de do' wid meh pipe, an' I heah 'em settin' dyah on de front steps, dee voices soun'in' low
like bees, an' de moon sort o' meltin' over de yard,
an' I sort o' got to studyin', an' hit 'pear like de
plantation 'live once mo', an' de ain' no mo' scufflin',
an' de ole times done come back ag'in, an' I heah
meh kerridge-horses stompin' in de stalls, an' de
place all cleared up ag'in, an' fence all roun' de
pahsture, an' I smell de wet clover-blossoms right
good, an' Marse Phil an' Meh Lady done come back,
an' runnin' all roun' me, climbin' up on meh knees,
callin' me 'Unc' Billy,' an' pesterin' me to go fishin',
while somehow Meh Lady an' de Cun'l, settin' dyah
on de steps wid dee voice hummin' low like water
runnin' in de' dark—.

JAMES LANE ALLEN: A STUDY.*

By John Bell Henneman.

Late Professor of English, University of the South.

Mr. James Lane Allen is an interesting case of evolution in literature. He himself, who has become in his latest story, *The Reign of Law*, an acknowledged student of the influence of the doctrine of evolution upon the thought of the age, represents in the changes and development of his work these same principles. He derives from Southern literature, and began as a portrayer of simple Kentucky landscape and local life; he has attained to the point of view of world literature in the significance of his themes. He has dealt only with the native Kentucky soil, a soil and race from which he sprung and which he knows well; but his treatment and his art instinct have carried him from the particular to the universal. Thus it comes that no two of his volumes are alike or represent the same ideas and grade of development. Each has been an added experiment in a new field, a new effort in a different sphere of thought, a new success with fresh material. In this variety and growth and in his close touch with the literary and intellectual movements and achievements of his day, Mr. Allen's position among Southern writers, so called by accident of birth and environment, is unique.

---

* In their inability to secure from the publishers of Mr. Allen's works the right to include selections from his writings, the publishers deem themselves fortunate in using selections from this full and admirable study by Professor Henneman. For permission to do so we are grateful to Messrs. Smith and Lamar, the publishers of *Southern Writers* (Vol. II).

JAMES LANE ALLEN.

No doubt the qualities derived from his birth and environment determined his career. In the heart of the rich limestone soil and beautiful blue grass region of Kentucky lay the scenes of his early life. Here came the blight of war, which befell his youth somewhat like the description of Gabriella's volume of life in *The Reign of Law*—the struggle with poverty, and then the still bitterer heart struggles for a literary career. Here lie the scenes of all his tales and stories. It is, therefore, what he has lived and been bred in and what he knows that he has written about; and in describing the phases of this life there is no faltering and no uncertainty. It is a country worthy of the noble expression it has found in Mr. Allen's writings, and the final biography and criticism of Mr. Allen and his works will possibly come some day from one born and nurtured in the same meadows and fields along the same white turnpikes and lanes and stones and hedgerows. For the present, perhaps, one nearer home may fail to get the proper perspective; and so one not a Kentuckian may be permitted to express an opinion.

Some four or five divisions of Mr. Allen's work in fiction—omitting his earliest contributions and letters to various papers and an occasional poem or criticism—may be distinguished. First is that of the *Flute and Violin* volume and his sketches and descriptive pieces of Kentucky and Kentucky life. A second series begins with the *Kentucky Cardinal* and its conclusion, *Aftermath*, revealing his intimacy with the most secret moods of nature. This was followed by *Summer in Arcady*, in which the workings of nature profoundly affect the destinies of life. A fourth may be made of the remodeling of *John Gray* into *The Choir Invisible*, where the historical background, in part anticipatory of a current fashion, was freely used

for the human problem also brought out. And latest
of all, so far as his writings have been published,
and catching something of the freer use of the moods
and modes of nature revealed in *Summer in Arcady,* is the aggressively insistent *Reign of Law.*
Yet what is this but saying that each of Mr. Allen's
volumes is to be treated by itself? A strong and
sincere love for man and nature—"human life in
relation to nature," as he himself has phrased it in
a review of another's writings—is his most characteristic mark. A sympathetic portraiture of one
and a lover's description of the other we always expect, but we may not know what is to be the especial
phase of study and type development.

Here most of all, it seems to me, Mr. Allen's peculiar strength lies. He has a romantic background
to deal with, one that is historic as well as romantic,
which he always observes with the clear eye and
feels with the true heart; but he is also profoundly
and intimately interested in human life—the life
about him, life under many complex conditions, life
as wrought through the workings of elemental nature within us and controlled by the spiritual beyond us. It is a natural and rapid step from history
to the problems of contemporary life; therefore romantic and naturalistic tendencies alike combine in
him. He sees nature with the eye of the poet and
the love of the artist, yet scrutinizes her appearances and examines her laws with the apprehension
and insight of the student of science. Indeed, this
growth of the scientific interest within him best
accounts for obvious qualities in works of quite different spirit, as the *Kentucky Cardinal* and *Summer
in Arcady* or *The Reign of Law,* regarded by
many as contradictory. To the poet part of his
nature, the delicacy and pathos of a situation
appeal keenly. To the mind familiar with scientific

modes of thought comes the consciousness of these changes in conceptions of philosophy, theology and cosmology going on about it, into relation with which the particular conditions must be brought. Every man truly living and thinking at the close of the Nineteenth century has been conscious of these changes, has felt the throbbings of nature, has questioned the mystery of life, has experienced the power of an intellectual and spiritual stimulus. These themes run through every one of Mr. Allen's writings. Each is the evolution or development of a thesis or idea.

Even in the *Flute and Violin* stories there is an awakening to broader and higher conceptions and ideals. In *Flute and Violin* itself it takes the form of a more unselfish thought of duty. In the *Two Gentlemen of Kentucky* and in *King Solomon* it is broader charity and deeper human sympathies. In *The White Cowl* and *Sister Dolorosa* there is the contradiction between the free, natural life of the Kentuckian and the cramping of the cloistered abbey and convent having lodgment in its soil, until there comes, through the seed of love sown, the arousing from a restricted and artificial life and world to one more extended and more natural. In the *Kentucky Cardinal* and its sequel the changes wrought on both heart and mind belong to love and nature together. In *Summer in Arcady* the forces of nature are struggling with the human and spiritual elements, and both poet and scientist are there noting cause and effect, yet amid the warring of passions guiding to beneficent issues. No wonder there came a cry from the sentimentalists. Emotions were all; they could not think; they did not understand how things as sacred and holy as love and marriage should have their underlying conditions subjected to analysis, and by one who at the same time was supremely conscious of spiritual beauty in nature and life. *The Choir Invisible,* based on a former story by the same author, is somewhat of a return to an earlier method; but while its setting is drawn from pioneer conditions in Kentucky history, its interest centers in the development of human character and destiny. It was a temporary aberration to the historical and romantic type of story then winning in popular favor, yet it was ever psychological in spirit and descriptive of nature's appeals. It was of the play of spiritual forces in that early Western land that saved and gained a nation; but it did not go to the extravagant lengths of Mr. Churchill and Miss Johnston, and, as if dreading the infection, Mr. Allen returned at once to other paths. We can now see that the study and analysis steadily obtruding in *Aftermath* and in *Summer in Arcady* merely foretold the tendencies leading to far deeper issues in thought and life as undertaken in *The Reign of Law.*

These are movements of which we are forced to take heed. Many readers prefer Mr. Allen's earlier vein, just as many prefer Thackeray's *Henry Esmond* to his *Vanity Fair* and *Pendennis,* and some of the marvelous adventures of *Richard Carvel* and *To Have and to Hold* to studies of character and destiny. There is no quarrel here, for there is room and to spare for both; but the novel is bound to become more and not less subtle and delicate in its portrayal of motive and character. And it is this direction of manifest destiny that Mr. Allen has taken. Not only so, but he is a careful artist in style, and his speech, though prose, is often the utterance of a poet. His chief defect is that of his qualities: he takes his art consciously and seriously, and so is sometimes even too earnest in it. And yet, in a day when the lack of seriousness

in the domain of literature is as overwhelming as it
is, this constitutes high praise. It is not of so much
moment whether Mr. Allen believes this or that, or
is or is not right in all his conclusions—if, indeed,
he dogmatizes at all, though there seem to be traces
of this in his latest work. Mr. Allen *is* the consciously working artist, and the great fundamental
facts of human nature attract him in his study of
life and its conditions, and of the profound changes
in attitude and thought. The awakening of the soul
to life, sometimes to its own hurt, and to eternal
heartache, but always to fuller liberty, is his constant interest.

Would he be so true if he ended his stories just as
we would have them—ideally? Though some may
object from quite another point of view that with
given conditions he ends often too ideally. Certainly
he prefers a spiritual outcome to every struggle.
Apparently a realist by conviction, he is an idealist
by nature. The one lesson of both nature and life
is that they are inexorable. Many dear to us we may
love, and they may disappoint our love; and the
poetical nature, catching a part of divine love, treats
with greater charity the failures and misunder-
standings of mankind, and sees in them all only the
noble promise. The great-hearted Shakespeare sym-
pathizes with Falstaff's death; his villains are always dealt with gently at the close; he is great
enough to understand and feel pity.

Some of Mr. Allen's problems may be greater
than he can answer—perhaps than any one can
answer. But at least the sincerity of facing them,
the attempt to give them an artistic background, is
worth a good deal. The artist cannot be dictated to
even by himself. He cannot always please his own
ideals, let alone those of others. He must deal with
images and convictions that haunt the brain, and

deliver them and take his chance as to their being true. And the note of utter sincerity in his art, I think, can be claimed as a special distinction of Mr. Allen's work. His tendencies have thus followed logical directions, and both his personal and his historical position in American letters is already an interesting one. What the ultimate judgment may be must be left to fuller accomplishment—and to time.

We can well believe Mr. Allen reads, thinks, studies, observes, imagines. He has evidently studied Darwin, Huxley, Tyndall and the thinkers of an inexorably scientific age. He has read, too, Balzac and the moderns in fiction. His shrinking, even in his earliest sketches, from the extreme romantic, an obvious tendency in most Southern writers, shows the influence of other authors and of other forces than mere suggestions from Kentucky surroundings. His has been an inevitable development. The problems of the universe have allured him, and he sees them reflected in the landscape and history of his own state and in the contemporary life about him.

Thus he transcends other Southern writers in the planning of his work. No longer does he belong to a locality, even though all his scenes may be laid there; he becomes cosmopolitan in his appeal. And so he is read in England as in America, in the East as in the South—indeed, more so. He is a product of the soil, but his branches tower into the air and welcome all the winds of the heavens, the rain and the sunshine. Mr. Page is Virginian; Mr. Harris is Southern; Mr. Allen, whether he attains it or not, is striving toward the universal.

* * * * * * *

Mr. Allen's work belongs to the last fifteen years, and the appearance of his collected work in volumes essentially to the last ten. His first volume was made up of six pieces which had previously appeared in the magazines—one from *Harper's* and the remaining five from the *Century*. He had, therefore, been before the public some years when the Messrs. Harper published this volume in 1891. The exact title was *Flute and Violin, and Other Kentucky Tales and Romances,* and the volume was dedicated to his mother. The contents were: *Flute and Violin* (*The Parson's Magic Flute* and *A Boy's Violin*), *King Solomon of Kentucky, Two Gentlemen of Kentucky, The White Cowl, Sister Dolorosa* and *Posthumous Fame.* The story of the *Flute and Violin* had announced a master of very delicately humorous and pathetic effect; the *White Cowl* and *Sister Dolorosa* had wonderfully popularized him. Particularly the last made little less than a sensation among more emotional readers when it first came out in the *Century Magazine.*

The sub-title reveals the romantic character of the volume, and the author's interest in and consciousness of the past. The process of his development, as has been said, has been that of the romanticist in nature, changing to the realist in method. As the realities of life press about him and he gains in experience, he turns from the past to the present—from the past with its romance to the present full of its questionings. It is Kentucky's history that holds him, the past of his own state, filled with rich traditions and associations. The early history of Lexington and the beginnings of Transylvania University furnish the material for the first story in the figure of the Rev. James Moore, who had been brought up a Presbyterian but had become the first Episcopal minister in the Western settlements, with his weakness for flute-playing and his attractiveness for the female portion of his congregation. Both the Rev. James Moore and a phase of the history of this institution of learning reappear in Mr. Allen's later work. The wise and gentle counselor and friend of John Gray in the *Choir Invisible* is this same flute-loving parson at an earlier and more vigorous stage of his career; and it is in a department of Transylvania University, just after the war, that the scene of the major part of *The Reign of Law* is laid.

* * * * * * *

The order of composition of the stories in the *Flute and Violin* volume is really fortuitous. It seems to begin chronologicaly with the *Two Gentlemen of Kentucky,* written in exemplification of the author's theory that the glory of the new Southern fiction after the war was that it helped in uniting North and South by revealing to the world the tender relations which had existed between master and man. This is a story, with a blending of both humor and pathos, of the decay of a gentleman of the old school and his devoted negro attendant, another gentleman of the same school. Both, stranded on the shores of a new sort of world, pass down the slope of life together until at last they lie side by side in their graves. Mr. Allen is in this story in closest touch with Mr. Page of Virginia, and Mr. Harris of Georgia. But if he follows them in general theme, the treatment is still individual, and he soon passes away into definite paths of his own.

A darker picture of relations between white and black is touched on in *King Solomon of Kentucky.* The basis of the story is historic, a reminiscence from the cholera devastation in Kentucky in the thirties. The shiftless, run-down white man is sold at public outcry for service, and is bought in by a freed negro woman, who saves him and serves him and leaves him free. The terrible cholera epi-

demic overwhelms the town—it is a page out of the
life of Lexington that is portrayed—and King Solomon's redemption comes at last in his bravery in
resolutely digging graves for the scores of dead,
when all others had fled. The picture becomes more
than pathetic; it grows grimly tragical and heroic,
in the relation of slave and free, black and white, and
in the dawning of spiritual possibilities in the wreck
of a human soul.

That there was in the heart of Kentucky since the
pioneer days a colony of Trappist Monks and a
Convent of the Stricken Heart came with a surprise
to many unacquainted with these special facts of
local history. Mr. Allen had already called attention to the seeming incongruity of their presence in
his *Blue Grass Region of Kentucky,* and in them he
lays the scene of the next two stories. In the light
of his latter work, both have melodramatic elements
and are too highly colored. But this very use of
the imagination seized hold of the popular fancy.
Both have fundamentally the same subject: the re-
volt of the human heart when once stirred against
unnatural restraint. A "brother" of the order over-
hears a conversation which he cannot get out of his
head—he meets the woman—he is haunted with her
memory—the inherited Kentucky ancestral strain
asserts itself—he breaks his vows—he wooes and
wins her—losing all, he returns to die. A "sister"
of the convent meets a stranger—her heart is moved
and ensnares her—and there remains the unhappiness of her fate.

*   *   *   *   *   *   *

The gem of the collection, viewed from its growing insight into life and the portrayal of human
nature, is unquestionably the one which gives its
name to the series, *Flute and Violin.* It was suggested by a slab of marble to the memory of the

Rev. James Moore, in Christ Church, Lexington, and is a very real page from the romance of the past, delicately, naturally and humorously drawn. Its sympathy and interest, the humor and the pathos of its situations, the reaction of circumstance on life and the stiffening of the moral qualities are its traits; the dear flute-playing bachelor parson; the widow Spurlock and dame Furnace spying through the keyhole and the window, both of which have been made more spacious in order "to provide the parson unawares with a sufficiency of air and light"; the widow Babcock silently weeping behind her veil as she hears the parson's solemn warning on "The Kiss that Betrayeth"; the temptation of the crippled boy; the union of both flute and violin hung solemnly in memory on the wall, unconscious instruments, symbolical of the tragedy that resulted. It is a piece which takes hold of the heart —the reader both smiles and is touched, and he remembers.

*   *   *   *   *   *   *

Up to this time in Mr. Allen's work, as before remarked, we had had Nature as a background, always visible, but largely external; we had not been let into her secrets. This Mr. Allen suddenly does in the *Kentucky Cardinal,* which appeared first in *Harper's Magazine* in 1893-94. It denotes a new epoch in his artistic work and growth. To those of us reading each sketch of his as it had come out, it gave a thrill we had not dared anticipate. It is a pastoral poem in prose, noting the procession of the seasons. Here was the heart of Nature laid bare; here wrote a novelist who at the same time was a disciple of Thoreau and Audubon. Indeed, the spirit of Audubon hovers through the book, as his person had traversed these scenes in earlier days, and veneration of the master is the first bond of

union between Adam and Georgiana. Sylvia, as her
pastoral name suggests, is a little creature of the
sun and earth, and fits naturally into the landscape.
As we turn the pages, everything speaks of one
intimately present at Nature's processes: the freezing and the thawing, the depths of winter's cold and
the glistening in the sunlight. We feel Nature in
her moods. The very similes are taken from Nature's laws and appearances, which continues true
of all Mr. Allen's work henceforth. And this love
and close observation of Nature leads him into the
study of the laws underlying the physical universe.
Nature and humanity become united. There is the
poetry of the country in the prodigal gifts and appearances of Nature; there is the prose of town in
the communion with men. "The longer I live here,
the better satisfied I am in having pitched my
earthly camp fire, gypsy-like, on the edge of a town,
keeping it on one side, and the green fields, lanes
and woods on the other. Each in turn is to me as
a magnet to the needle. At times the needle of my
nature points toward the country. On that side
everything is poetry. I wander over field and forest, and through me runs a glad current of feeling
that is like a clear brook across the meadows of
May. At others the needle veers round and I go to
town—to the massed haunts of the highest animal
and cannibal. That way nearly everything is
prose." The old bachelor, "the rain crow," and
the widow, "the mocking bird," are neighbors.
Strawberries and *Lalla Rookh*, grapes and *The
Seasons*; the arbor and Sir Walter's novels; the
schoolgirl and apples and salt—all are commingled
in profusion, the brightness of the humorist uniting
with the tender and intimate knowledge of the world
not made with hands. The evergreens are "Nature's hostelries for the homeless ones." "Death,

lover of the peerless, strikes at him (the Cardinal)
from afar." "Is it this flight from the inescapable
just behind that makes the singing of the red bird
thoughtful and plaintive, and indeed all the wild
sounds of nature so like the outcry of the doomed?"
"This set flowing toward me for days a stream of
people, like a line of ants passing to and from the
scene of a terrific false alarm. I had nothing to do
but sit perfectly still and let each ant, as it ran up,
touch me with its antennæ, get the countersign and
turn back to the village ant-hill." "Mrs. Walters
does not get into our best society; so that the town
is to her like a pond to a crane; she wades round it,
going in as far as she can, and snatches up such
small fry as come shoreward from the middle. In
this way lately I have gotten hints of what is stirring
in the vasty deeps of village opinion." "The scent
of spring, is it not the first lyric of the nose—that
despised poet of the senses?"—which reminds one
curiously of Du Maurier's scenting of old Paris.
There is this swelling in the sights and sounds of
Nature, yet as one restrained and checked with a
sense of delicacy in speaking of his intimates and
friends—an effect heightened by the use of the
first person in autobiographic and reminiscential
manner.

It is again the "other nature" which persists in
this enthusiasm of a sense of appropriation: "They
are all mine—these Kentucky wheat fields. After
the owner has taken from them his last sheaf I come
in and gather my harvest also—one that he did not
see, and doubtless would not begrudge me—the harvest of beauty. Or I walk beside tufted aromatic
hemp-fields, as along the shores of softly foaming
emerald seas; or part the rank and file of fields of
Indian corn, which stand like armies that had gotten
ready to march, but been kept waiting for further

orders, until at last the soldiers had gotten tired, as the gayest will, of their yellow plumes and green ribbons, and let their big hands fall heavily down at their sides. There the white and the purple morning-glories hang their long festoons and open to the soft midnight winds their elfin trumpets.''

With the descriptions of nature there grows a tendency toward moralizing and comment, but it is in a vein the Anglo-Saxon has never objected to. It is Thackeray's manner of being confidential with his readers. One paragraph beginning, ''The birds are molting—if man could only molt also,'' recalls the latter's *Roundabout* on *De Finibus*.

In character portrayal a contrast is necessarily suggested between the two sisters, intended rather as symbols of widely differing types. Sylvia is a ''little half-fledged spirit to whom the yard is the earth and June eternity, but who peeps over the edge of the nest at the chivalry of the ages, and fancies that she knows the world.'' But the chief characterization, wherever the first person is used, lies in the revelation of the gentleness, firmness, sensitiveness and unconscious selfishness—all combined—in the creation, Adam Moss. Georgiana is pale beside him, though we catch here and there sincere glimpses of her, too, as in the merry twinkle and good humor of her words when she is growing stronger—words which playfully repeat the first ever passed between her and Adam: ''Old man, are you the gardener?''

The ''Cardinal'' naturally demanded a sequel, though there have been some to wish one had never been written. In the ''Cardinal'' the winter of bachelordom, thawed by the springtide of love and a consequent new life, was blossoming into the summer of joy. The conclusion is *Aftermath,* the autumn and winter of life come again, the fall of the leaves and of hopes, and the funeral dirge. The idyllic sweetness has passed away with the flowers. It tells of the dread winter of 1851-52, when all animals, unprepared for the season's unwonted severity, suffered intensely. The fate of the Cardinal but preceded their end and Georgiana's death. The sympathy with the suffering dumb ones of God's creation, fellow-beings, even if not human, prefigures the snow-storm and David's care for the cattle in *The Reign of Law.* In a book dedicated to Nature there is the struggle between Nature and love, and in the loss of the beloved comes the overpowering sense of *the eternity of Nature.* In *The Reign of Law* almost the converse is suggested: the cruelty and severity of Nature softened through love.

Like its predecessor, *Aftermath* is a story commingled with Nature's moods and seasons. It is also in the first person, and is again of Adam Moss. His own bereaved home and that of the birds furnish "the universal tragedy of the nests." Tenderness and delicacy of expression are occasionally crossed with boldness of utterance—the saying of things that are thought and are true, but are usually left unspoken. Where this is necessary and vital our author may be applauded for his frankness. That it is not always so is the ground upon which the severest attacks upon Mr. Allen have been made. Chief among Nature's mysteries sex questions manifestly interest him, poetically and scientifically. The Sylvia episode is a foreshadowing of what can easily become butterflies fluttering in *Summer in Arcady.*

* * * * * * *

Summer in Arcady is the later and more poetical name for what appeared in the numbers of the *Cosmopolitan* in the winter of 1895-96 as *Butterflies: A Tale of Nature.* This story marks the most distinct turning point in Mr. Allen's work. In its new objective method of treatment, that of detachment of the object for purposes of study and reflection, it is the logical forerunner of his latest tale, which, by a similar chance, has had two titles, one in America and the second in England: *The Reign of Law* and *The Increasing Purpose*. As the title indicates, *Butterflies,* or *Summer in Arcady,* is the more idyllic of the two productions, and besides possesses a sense of the satirical that connects it with *Aftermath.*

Summer in Arcady is a story of inheritance, of Nature's gifts and Nature's mysterious workings. *The Reign of Law* is more that of environment, the influence of a new era of thought awakening every mind at the close of the Nineteenth century and calling a challenge to old forms of belief. Both show Mr. Allen's paths leading him along the ways of scientific thought. Both heroes are in rebellion to old and worn-out phases of thought and attitudes in life; both are "expelled from Church"; both suffer and gain control and mastery in some measure over self. With both it is the struggle of spiritual with material forces. In the two tales immediately preceding Mr. Allen worshipped Nature subjectively, more like a poet of Wordsworth's school. In his later work, beginning with the *Summer in Arcady,* the poet still feels Nature, but the reasoning mind is now objective and holds calmly aloof as it studies the workings of Nature, where man is but one of its creatures and often its cruel sport. The great difference, though, with traces before, is at once discernible. It is the turning of the romanticist into scientific and realistic habits of thought.

For this reason the older title of *Butterflies,* with its sub-title, *A Tale of Nature,* is more indicative of the author's attitude than the later one. As "a tale of Nature'' it is the reign of Nature's universal and all-powerful law in ourselves as in all animal and physical creation, carefuly noted and studied. This work deals more with the physical forces of Nature. In the author's latest book, where the consciousness of this reign is asserted in the title, the subject is almost entirely transported to the intellectual and spiritual spheres. In *Summer in Arcady* man is again and again compared with the ''butterflies,'' and, as with butterflies, Nature is strong and the creature seems weak, whirled about by elemental forces, all powerful alike for beneficence and harm.

The hot summer's day is typical of the setting, the burning passion of Nature on all sides. ''Nature is lashing everything—grass, fruit, insects, cattle, human creatures—more fiercely onward to the fulfillment of her ends. She is the great, heartless haymaker, wasting not a ray of sunshine on a clod, but caring naught for the light that beats upon a throne, and holding man and woman, with their longing for immortality and their capacities for joy and pain, as of no more account than a couple of fertilizing nasturtiums.'' And the story is of the full summer tide also in its climax. ''A pair of butterflies out of their countless kind had met on the meadows of life and, forgetting all others, were beginning to cling. The time was not far off when Nature would demand her crisis—that ever-old, ever-new miracle of the dust through which the perishable becomes the enduring and the individual of a moment renews itself into a type for ages.

''The crisis came on in beauty. The noon of summer now was nigh. Each day the great, tawny sun became a more fierce and maddening lover of the earth, and flushed her more deeply, and awoke in her throes of responsive energy until the whole land

seemed to burn with color and to faint in its own
sweetness.

"And this high aërial miracle of two floating
spheres that swept all life along in the flow of its
tide caught the boy as a running sea catches a
weed."

*   *   *   *   *   *   *

Summer in Arcady is thus a story of the eternal
mystery of sex attraction—of the primary forces
and passions stirring in man, but becoming controlled and guided nevertheless by some physical
restraint toward higher purposes. This, therefore,
ought to be the complete answer to those who find in
the book only frank revelations of "natural," and
therefore depraved, tendencies, and hold up their
hands in consternation and horror. Such an attitude seems a perversion and a blindness to artistic
and real truth.

*   *   *   *   *   *   *

The Choir Invisible, which follows, is in one sense
out of its natural order in this thought evolution.
But not so in art. It can be better understood if it
be remembered that it is an old story of Mr. Allen's,
John Gray, which had appeared originally in *Lippin-
cott's Magazine* in 1893, built upon and altered and
enlarged. It is, therefore, not so much the fundamental conception of the story, which admittedly belongs to an earlier period, as the alterations and
changes in attitude that indicate Mr. Allen's growth
in artistic power.

Here it is Colonial and Revolutionary Kentucky
which has hold of him. The love story itself, the
chief thing which the original *John Gray* bequeathed
to the new form, has been made more delicate and
more human, though there again are those who complain of a departure from its original sweetness.
Such a departure was necessary in the growing

strength of the conception. The gain in subtlety is a sign of this change. But particularly pervading is the consciousness of historic evolution which has made Kentucky what she has been and is at her best. There are the feelings of more than a century's past and growth; the thought of Kentucky's lonely stand on the borderland of the great Western wilderness; the recognition that after the original thirteen colonies the first new territory and new state to be added to the westward was Kentucky, admitted to the Union in 1792; the emphasis that the Anglo-Saxon pioneer had pushed his way through the mountain fastnesses of the Alleghanies and was destined to occupy the great Mississippi basin, and thence pass from ocean to ocean; and that this was the beginning of the movement for expansion and for nationality. The additions to *John Gray* are chiefly in expression of this historical spirit and in subtilizing the characters of the story.

Mr. Allen's growing strength is seen by another circumstance. It is the author's first long story or complete novel. The contrast can be seen from the Table of Contents, where the ten chapters of *John Gray* with titles have grown in *The Choir Invisible* into twenty-three without. The volume also appeared in the year 1897, the year of Dr. Mitchell's *Hugh Wynne,* and at the beginning of the revival of the novel with historic setting in American fiction. Thus in a sense it might be considered as an anticipation. But Mr. Allen's work was far more than a mere historical novel, and was not at all a tale of adventure. There is not an adventure in it except the newly inserted struggle with the panther, "a clear contest between will and will, courage and courage, strength and strength, the love of prey and the love of life." But this is brought in not merely for itself, but to portray more faithfully the actual dangers of pioneer days and to help forward the development of the story, the gradual revelation of character and self-knowledge. It is a soul study and conflict, or rather that of two souls, in a faithfully presented historical environment. It is as if the author would say: There were high and noble souls then in the laying of Kentucky's foundations, and high and noble generations have sprung from them. From a local picture the story passes into general significance.

*   *   *   *   *   *   *

In its original the story was merely one of unrequited love, a true man's love for a lighter nature incapable of fully entering into and being made happy by the depths of his character, and the man's battle with self until he rose on the stepping-stones of his disappointment to better things. In the early volume Amy was all, and Mrs. Falconer, her aunt, only a lay figure. But the contrast between the two women is the central thought of the new volume, and the plot of the old story serves merely as an introduction to the new. In the deeper psychological spirit of the new setting the heart and soul of the movement centers around Mrs. Falconer. The direct influence of her personality and the indirect influence of the great book she lends to John Gray (Sir Thomas Malory's narrative of the conquest of others and of self by King Arthur and the Knights of the Round Table) become the great motive powers in building up his character and life. It is thus an entirely new work that we have, a book entering upon a wider world and passing into larger reaches of art and life. There is a nicer and finer sense of delicacy. Amy announces to Mrs. Falconer in the garden her engagement, and tells of John's struggle with the panther. The wound from the panther both conceals and emphasizes the infliction of the deeper spiritual wound. The parson's visit to John is refined and the historical undertone deepened and strengthened. Mrs. Falconer brings the patient the Book, and henceforth the principles of the Book take the place of the hitherto omnipresent historic feeling. The pastor's sermon and the teacher's address on the last day at school grow more earnest. Even more significant are the changes at the end. In *John Gray* there is feeling, but no love. John is married before Major Falconer's death, and the youth comes as a joy to a woman's old age. In the new version Major Falconer dies, Mrs. Falconer waits, and John writes—her feelings are not given, but it is the tragedy of life!

*   *   *   *   *   *   *

In her parting from John Gray she had held out to him all the ideals of manhood, for in having put into his hands the Book "out of her own purity she had judged him." Thus "it is the woman who bursts the whole grape of sorrow against the irrepressible palate at such a moment; to a man like him the same grape distills a vintage of yearning that will brim the cup of memory many a time beside his lamp in the final years." As time passed changes came into her life, and with those changes her final confession to herself of "her love of him, the belief that he had loved her," which "she, until this night, had never acknowledged to herself." "I shall understand everything when he comes," her first thought, shadowed into "I shall go softly all my years." "It was into the company of these quieter pilgrims that she had passed: she had missed happiness twice." "It was about this time also that there fell upon her hair the earliest rays of that light which is the dawn of the Eternal Morning." At last with the receding years came young John, and came the letter, and with it the revelation she had known was hers: "If I have kept unbroken faith with any of mine, thank you and thank God!"

The situation and the action have been objected to. Some have found them even immoral. The test of a book is its final impression. Are the ideals ennobling or debasing? Do they lift up or drag down? A right-minded man cannot but be awed into reverence as he feels the strugglings of human nature carried through tenderly and yet triumphantly, with truth of circumstance to the highest in self. It is the humanness and the humanity of the story which make the strongest appeal. Mr. Allen is striving to come nearer to the divination of the human soul, to apprehending man with his conflicts and contradictions and his truth. Much of the book is a poem in prose, pulsating with the sense of a nation's destiny and the spiritual testing of individual lives.

"Men and women could love together seven years, . . . and then was love truth and faithfulness."

"In the Country of the Spirit there is a certain high table-land that lies far on among the outposts toward Eternity. . . . But no man can write a description of this place for those who have never trodden it; by those who have, no description is desired: their fullest speech is Silence."

The two opening chapters of *The Reign of Law,* Mr. Allen's latest work, possess the same historic consciousness displayed in *The Choir Invisible.* There is the underlying recognition of the part the settlement of Kentucky has played in the development of the country and the part that hemp has had in Kentucky's history. There is also the keenest sense of Nature and the expression of her attributes as if in a tumultuous rush—in point of style, a profusion of epithets cast down often without the necessary predicate—the more benignant law of the sea-

sons and their changes portrayed preparatory to a
story wherein man obedient with Nature succumbs
to the Reign of Law. For "a round year of the
earth's changes enters into the creation of the
hemp." Far from being unnecessary, the opening
prelude on hemp is but the overture to the wells of
passion following like the processes of the tides and
suns, the strains of which are constantly heard
through the entire piece. And there is the same
apparent contradiction, yet twofold aspect, of
Nature in the book—the poet's combined with the
scientist's, the feminine correlated with the mascu-
line, Gabriella's at last united with David's. Nature
and Life, their union and their relation—these are
typified by the hemp. "Ah! type, too, of our life,
which also is earth-sown, earth-rooted; which must
struggle upward, be cut down, rotted and broken,
ere the separation take place between our dross and
our worth—poor, perishable, shard and immortal
fiber. O the mystery, the mystery of that growth
from the casting of the soul as a seed into the dark
earth, until the time when, led through all natural
changes and cleansed of weakness, it is borne from
the fields of its nativity for the long service!"

We are not done with heredity any more than in
Summer in Arcady. The opening chapter, catching
a note from its predecessor, is on religious toleration, wideness of appeal and openness to new
thought; and this note is held continuously throughout. The hero is the descendant of the pioneer who
built a church on the edge of a farm that there might
be therein freedom of worship forever. Sixty-five
years later, when the scientific and philosophical
conceptions of the latter half of the Nineteenth century furthered by Darwin and his followers had
burst upon the world, he, too, with his stubborn
honesty and pride, would have acted much the same

as David. The indignant turning of this progenitor
of David's upon the early congregation is of the
same spirit as, in *Summer in Arcady*, the turning
of Hilary upon Daphne's father, the elder who had
"expelled him from the Church." It must be
remembered that Middle Kentucky has always been
the scene of peculiarly fervent and often violent
religious excitement and altercations.

With the two preludes, one of Nature and the
other of History, the story opens with the big, raw-
boned boy of eighteen cutting hemp in 1865. The
date was the end of old and the beginning of new
things in Kentucky and everywhere in the Southern
states, among many signs being the opening of the
university at Lexington the following autumn. It
was the day of revolutions, of new expansions and
undertakings, new directions of activity and thought
in the South specifically and in the world generally.
These two movements, the local and the world-wide,
Mr. Allen seeks to bring together. "For some years
this particular lad, this obscure item in Nature's
plan which always passes understanding, had been
growing more unhappy in his place in creation."
A certain birth, a farm and its tasks, a country
neighborhood and its narrowness—what more are
these often than the starting point for a young life
groping for the world beyond, of which it is as yet
ignorant?

The introduction of the university and the Bible
college is again as the outcome of a century of tradition. It is unfortunate that time and place are
both so near; but they are as necessary for the
author's story as the breath for life. The educational ideals expressed and hoped for many have
held and none has been able wholly to achieve; a
position halfway between North and South, an institution of learning with no politics, based upon broad

ideas and at the same time religious. Ideals far
short of what has ever actually been realized! It
seems this must be the case and cannot be escaped.
The sensitiveness to the criticism is, therefore,
natural, but the failure has been unquestionable.

*   *   *   *   *   *   *

The pastor of his own Church preached "a series
of sermons on errors in the faith and practice of the
different Protestant sects," treading on very delicate ground for delicate souls. The result for one
of David's temper could have been foreseen. The
night after the first sermon this particular young
man had a seat at that other church which had been
riddled. It was a rift in the life of the human soul
which ultimately had to widen with his nature into
a great breach. The case of the Churches may be
exaggerated for the purposes of the story; there
were many wiser men than these preachers; and yet
it will readily be admitted that not so many years
ago sermons of the sort were rehearsed and sought
after, one body of Christians arraying itself sternly
against another. This could not fail to bewilder
impressionable hearts and repel thinking minds.
Naturally David's religious peace was disturbed.
"The constant discussion of *some* dogma and dis-
proof of *some* dogma inevitably begets in a certain
order of mind the temper to discuss and distrust *all*
dogma." The division into Northern and Southern
Churches within the same denomination, each intol-
erant of the other, while apparently slowly disap-
pearing in a new century, was directly after the war
more than usually acrimonious. The methods, too,
of analyzing the Bible hurt David. "The mysterious, untouched Christ-feeling was in him so
strong that he shrank from these critical analyses as
he would from dissecting the body of the crucified
Redeemer." In David's interview the pastor seems

rough, unsympathetic and blind; yet it could have
occurred, for there are such men in the Churches,
although we know all are by no means so.

The catechism scene is a strong one, and with the
growing knowledge and wider toleration of to-day
it almost seems that it could hardly be possible. But
we know such experiences were common with the
recreant in the days of the Church militant, if not so
still. The heartiest sympathies go out to the agoni-
zing soul of an honest man doubting. " 'I am in
trouble!' he cried, sitting down again. 'I don't
know what to believe. I don't know what I do believe. My God!' he cried again, burying his face in
his hands. 'I believe I am beginning to doubt the
Bible. Great God, what am I coming to? What is
my life coming to? *Me* doubt the Bible!' " Denom-
inationalism run mad! is what Mr. Allen sees,
although it be possibly in his own denomination and
college. But this has kept Kentucky and many
another state and section from achieving their due
educationally. For it must be essentially true.
"True learning always stands for peace. Letters
always stand for peace." This man could have been
saved. It was a worn-out form of belief and practice that he had fallen upon; and if he could have
been saved, then he still may be saved and is worth
the saving. This is suggested clearly, and is the
central thought of the second part of the volume, as
much as Faust's redemption is the subject of Part
II. of Goethe's great poem.

Fault may be found in the structure of the book
that the true story rests in the first half with the
catastrophe. There the book could have ended, and
would have ended, did Mr. Allen belong exclusively
to the realists. But there was the spiritual awakening of Hilary in *Summer in Arcady;* there was the
moral strengthening of John Gray in *The Choir*

Invisible, where also a new element enters and a new story begins; and there is the struggling for *any* light in David. An old creed was outworn; a new one to suit the age and the man, it is surely intimated, will be found for the struggler by means of the eternal feminine—Goethe's *das ewig weibliche.*

And yet, while all this seems true as to purpose, it is just as true, like Goethe's *Faust* again, that in point of construction of plot the human interest is the awful struggle of the human soul. The real book to most readers will still end with the climax and catastrophe, as the boy leaves college and goes to his father and mother and the home left two years before.

* * * * * * *

But Mr. Allen cannot be content with negation or destruction. He feels there is something positive beyond, more to be experienced and more to learn in the essay after truth. With the dramatic end of one story another immediately begins. Put upon the stage, the action would end here. But while dramatically the climax has been passed, yet for the removal of the sense of incompleteness a conclusion must be added. Out of the ashes of the old life and the old faith a new structure is to rise—a dwelling spot for love, which must bring forth ultimately the best sort of life and the highest, because rational, ideals of faith. The story fills three hundred and eighty-five pages, and the first reference to the second important character, who thenceforth dominates the book, is on page 225: "David's college experience had effected the first great change in him as he passed from youth to manhood; Gabriella had wrought the second." Absorbed with the soul struggle, not a word of Gabriella hitherto!

* * * * * * *

The bringing together of the lives of this man and

this woman is effected: the mutual influences of the elements and strength and weakness that have gone to make up both, the support each can offer, the demands each must make. The contrast is wrought between their different sorts of faith and their different natures and needs, and the conquering of neither one wholly, but a strengthening union of both, will be Nature's outcome.

There are many fine passages in this latter portion: the sleet and snow-storm, the care for the cattle, the life on the farm, the inborn sympathy between man and other animal creatures, a newer and wider interpretation of Nature's aspects and processes, not as of some direct intention toward man, but as "small incidents in the long history of the planet's atmosphere and changing surface." The love-making as inclined to become too didactic, a discussion of dogmas and of new beliefs and theories in place of old ones, and Gabriella is in some danger of being a "patient Griselda" to the demands of this unconscious but natural egotist. Many a weary hour she will have to pass before he tortuously works himself to an understanding with her. It is a pity that the exigencies of the development of the changes in belief must give space thus far to the discussion of many theories. Artistically it is a blemish, and is to be defended only on the ground that otherwise the actions of David might seem obscure or illogical. Like *Aftermath*, this part is an epilogue to a previous story, and will have its fine points, but cannot sustain the same interest. And yet the everlasting truth is gradually unrolled that it is the patience and tenderness and faith of woman whereby man at length finds spiritual regeneration and salvation.

If Mr. Allen's change of title in his English edition, "The Increasing Purpose," did not indicate this, it would be revealed in the last bit of conversation vouchsafed in the book. Surely the meaning is clear: "Ah, Gabriella, it is love that makes man believe in a God of Love!" "David! David!"— A way to a higher and purer faith and conduct of life is implied. Only a description and a reflection are added—of the hemp, the real pervasive element in the whole book, and the emblem of man's life directed toward beneficent ends:

"The south wind, warm with the first thrill of summer, blew from across the valley, from across the mighty rushing sea of the young hemp.

"O Mystery Immortal! which is in the hemp and in our souls, in its bloom and in our passions; by which our poor, brief lives are led upward out of the earth for a season, then cut down, rotted and broken —for Thy long service!"

ELLEN GLASGOW.

THE PEACEFUL SIDE OF WAR.*

From The Battle-Ground (1902).

On a sparkling January morning, when Lee's army had gone into winter quarters beside the Rappahannock, Dan stood in the doorway of his log hut smoking the pipe of peace, while he watched a messmate putting up a chimney of notched sticks across the little roadway through the pines.

"You'd better get Pinetop to daub your chinks for you," he suggested. "He can make a mixture of wet clay and sandstone that you couldn't tell from mortar."

"You jest wait till I git through these shoes an' I'll show you," remarked Pinetop, from the woodpile, where he was making moccasins of untanned beef hide laced with strips of willow. "I ain't goin' to set my bar' feet on this frozen groun' agin, if I can help it. 'Tain't so bad in summer, but, I d'clar it takes all the spirit out of a fight when you have to run bar-footed over the icy stubble."

"Jack Powell lost his shoes in the battle of Fredericksburg," said Baker, as he carefully fitted his notched sticks together. "That's why he got promoted, I reckon. He stepped into a mud puddle, and his feet came out but his shoes didn't."

"Well, I dare say, it was cheaper for the Government to give him a title than a pair of shoes," observed Dan, cynically. "Why, you are going in for luxury! Is that pile of oak shingles for your roof? We made ours of rails covered with pine tags."

"And the first storm that comes along sweeps them off—yes, I know. By the way, can anybody tell me if there's a farmer with a haystack in these parts?"

"Pinetop got a load about three miles up," replied Dan, emptying his pipe against the door sill. "I say, who is that cavalry peacock over yonder? By George, it's Champe!"

"Perhaps it's General Stuart," suggested Baker witheringly, as Champe came composedly between the rows of huts, pursued by the frantic jeers of the assembled infantry.

"Take them earrings off yo' heels—take 'em off! Take 'em off!" yelled the chorus, as his spurs rang on the stones. "My gal she wants 'em—take 'em off!"

"Take those tatters off your backs—take 'em off!" responded Champe, genial and undismayed, swinging easily along in his worn gray uniform, his black plume curling over his soft felt hat.

As Dan watched him, standing in the doorway, he felt, with a sudden melancholy, that a mental gulf had yawned between them. The last grim months which had aged him with experiences as with years, had left Champe apparently unchanged. All the deeper knowledge, which he had bought with his youth for the price, had passed over his cousin like the clouds, leaving him merely gay and kind as he had been of old.

"Hello, Beau!" called Champe, stretching out his hand as he drew near. "I just heard you were over here, so I thought I'd take a look. How goes the war?"

Dan refilled his pipe and borrowed a light from Pinetop.

"To tell the truth," he replied, "I have come to the conclusion that the fun and frolic of war consist in picket duty and guarding mule teams."

"Well, these excessive dissipations have taken up so much of your time that I've hardly laid eyes on you since you got routed by malaria. Any news from home?"

"Grandma sent me a Christmas box, which she smuggled through, heaven knows how. We had a jolly dinner that day, and Pinetop and I put on our first clean clothes for three months. Big Abel got a linsey suit made at Chericoke—I hope he'll come along in it."

"Oh, Beau, Beau!" lamented Champe. "How have the mighty fallen! You aren't so particular now about wearing only white or black ties, I reckon."

"Well, shoestrings are usually black, I believe," returned Dan, with a laugh, raising his hand to his throat.

Champe seated himself upon the end of an oak log, and taking off his hat, ran his hand through his curling hair. "I was at home last summer on a furlough," he remarked, "and I declare, I hardly knew the valley. If we ever come out of this war it will take an army with ploughshares to bring the soil up again. As for the woods—well, well, we'll never have them back in our day."

"Did you see Uplands?" asked Dan eagerly.

"For a moment. It was hardly safe, you know, so I was at home only a day. Grandpa told me that the place had lain under a shadow ever since Virginia's death. She was buried in Hollywood—it was impossible to bring her through the lines they said—and Betty and Mrs. Ambler have taken this very hardly."

"And the Governor," said Dan, with a tremor in his voice as he thought of Betty.

"And Jack Morson," added Champe, "he fell at Brandy Station when I was with him. At first he was wounded only slightly, and we tried to get him to the rear, but he laughed and went straight in again. It was a sabre cut that finished him at the last."

"He was a first-rate chap," commented Dan, "but I never knew exactly why Virginia fell in love with him."

"The other fellow never does. To be quite candid, it is beyond my comprehension how a certain lady can prefer the infantry to the cavalry—yet she does emphatically."

Dan colored.

"Was grandpa well?" he inquired lamely.

With a laugh Champe flung one leg over the other, and clasped his knee.

"It's an ill wind that blows nobody good," he responded. "Grandpa's thoughts are so much given to the Yankees that he has become actually angelic to the rest of us. By the way, do you know that Mr. Blake is in the army?"

"What?" cried Dan, aghast.

"Oh, I don't mean that he really carries a rifle—though he swears he would if he only had twenty years off his shoulders—but he has become our chaplain in young Chrysty's place, and the boys say there is more gun powder in his prayers than in our biggest battery."

"Well, I never!" exclaimed Dan.

"You ought to hear him—it's better than fighting on your own account. Last Sunday he gave us a prayer in which he said: 'O Lord, thou knowest that we are the greatest army thou hast ever seen; put forth thy hand then but a very little and we will whip the earth.' By Jove, you look cosey here," he added, glancing into the hut where Dan and Pinetop slept in bunks of straw. "I hope the roads won't dry before you've warmed your house." He shook hands again, and swung off amid the renewed jeers that issued from the open doorways.

Dan watched him until he vanished among the distant pines, and then, turning, went into the little hut where he found Pinetop sitting before a rude chimney, which he had constructed with much labor. A small book was open on his knee, over which his yellow head drooped like a child's, and Dan saw his calm face reddened by the glow of the great log fire.

"Hello! What's that?" he inquired lightly.

The mountaineer started from his abstraction, and the blood swept to his forehead as he rose from the half of a flour barrel upon which he had been sitting.

"'Tain't nothin'," he responded, and as he towered to his great height his fair curls brushed the ceiling of crossed rails. In his awkwardness the book fell to the floor, and before he could reach it, Dan had stooped, with a laugh, and picked it up.

"I say, there are no secrets in this shebang," he said smiling. Then the smile went out, and his face grew suddenly grave, for, as the book fell open in his hand, he saw that it was the first primer of a child, and on the thumbed and tattered page the word "RAT" stared at him in capital letters.

"By George, man!" he exclaimed beneath his breath, as he turned from Pinetop to the blazing logs.

For the first time in his life he was brought face to face with the tragedy of hopeless ignorance for

an inquiring mind, and the shock stunned him, at
the moment, past the power of speech. Until knowing Pinetop he had, in the lofty isolation of his
class, regarded the plebeian in the light of an alien
to the soil, not as a victim to the kindly society in
which he himself had moved—a society produced
by that free labor which had degraded the white
workman to the level of the serf. At the instant
the truth pierced home to him, and he recognized
it in all the grimness of its pathos. Beside that
genial plantation life which he had known he saw
rising the wistful figure of the poor man doomed
to conditions which he could not change—born, it
may be, like Pinetop, self-poised, yet with an untaught intellect, grasping, like him, after the primitive knowledge which should be the birthright of
every child. Even the spectre of slavery, which had
shadowed his thoughts, as it had those of many a
generous mind around him, faded abruptly before
the very majesty of the problem that faced him
now. In his sympathy for the slave, whose bond-
age he had and his race had striven to make easy, he
had overlooked the white sharer of the negro's
wrong. To men like Pinetop, slavery, stern or mild,
could be but an equal menace, and yet these were
the men who, when Virginia called, came from their
little cabins in the mountains, who tied the flint-
locks upon their muskets and fought uncomplain-
ingly until the end. Not the need to protect a decaying institution, but the instinct in every free man
to defend the soil, had brought Pinetop, as it had
brought Dan, into the army of the South.

"Look here, old man, you haven't been quite fair
to me," said Dan, after the long silence. "Why
didn't you ask me to help you with this stuff?"

"Wall, I thought you'd joke," replied Pinetop
blushing, "and I knew yo' nigger would."

"Joke? Good Lord!" exclaimed Dan. "Do you think I was born with so short a memory, you scamp? Where are those nights on the way to Romney when you covered me with your overcoat to keep me from freezing in the snow? Where, for that matter, is that march in Maryland when Big Abel and you carried me three miles in your arms after I had dropped delirious by the roadside? If you thought I'd joke you about this, Pinetop, all I can say is that you've turned into a confounded fool."

Pinetop came back to the fire and seated himself upon the flour barrel in the corner. "'Twas this way, you see," he said, breaking, for the first time, through his strong mountain reserve. "I al'ays thought I'd like to read a bit, 'specially on winter evenings at home, when the nights are long and you don't have to git up so powerful early in the mornings, but when I was leetle thar warn't nobody to teach me how to begin; maw she didn't know nothin' an' paw he was dead, though he never got beyond the first reader when he was 'live."

He looked up and Dan nodded gravely over his pipe.

"Then when I got bigger I had to work mighty hard to keep things goin'—an' it seemed to me every time I took out that thar leetle book at night I got so dead sleepy I couldn't tell one letter from another; A looked jest like Z."

"I see," said Dan quietly. "Well, there's time enough here anyhow. It will be a good way to pass the evenings." He opened the primer and laid it on his knee, running his fingers carelessly through its dog-eared pages. "Do you know your letters?" he inquired in a professional tone.

"Lordy, yes," responded Pinetop. "I've got about as fur as this here place." He crossed to where Dan sat and pointed with a long forefinger to the printed words his mild blue eyes beaming with excitement.

"I reckon I kin read that by myself," he added with an embarrassed laugh. "T-h-e c-a-t c-a-u-g-h-t t-h-e r-a-t. Ain't that right?"

"Perfectly. We'll pass on to the next." And they did so, sitting on the halves of a divided flour barrel before the blazing chimney.

From this time there were regular lessons in the little hut, Pinetop drawling over the soiled primer, or crouching, with his long legs twisted under him and his elbows awkwardly extended, while he filled a sheet of paper with sprawling letters.

"I'll be able to write to the old woman soon," he chuckled jubilantly, "an she'll have to walk all the way down the mounting to git it read."

"You'll be a scholar yet if this keeps up," replied Dan, slapping him upon the shoulder, as the mountaineer glanced up with a pleased and shining face. "Why, you mastered that first reader there in no time."

"A powerful heap of larnin' has to pass through yo' head to git a leetle to stick thar," commented Pinetop, wrinkling his brows. "Air we goin' to have the big book agin to-night?"

"The big book" was a garbled version of "Les Miserables," which, after running the blockade with a daring English sailor, had passed from regiment to regiment in the resting army. At first Dan had begun to read with only Pinetop for a listener, but gradually, as the tale unfolded, a group of eager privates filled the little hut and even hung breathlessly about the doorway in the winter nights. They were mostly gaunt, unwashed volunteers from the hills or the low countries, to whom literature was only a vast silence and life a courageous strug-

gle against greater odds. To Dan the picturesque-
ness of the scene lent itself with all the force of its
strong lights and shadows, and with the glow of the
pine torches on the open page, his eyes would sometimes wander from the words to rest upon the
kindling faces in the shaggy circle by the fire. Dirty,
hollow-eyed, unshaven, it sat spell-bound by the
magic of the tale it could not read.

"By Gosh! that's a blamed good bishop," remarked an unkempt smoker one evening from the
threshold, where his beef-hide shoes were covered
with fine snow. "I don't reckon Marse Robert could
ha' beat that."

"Marse Robert ain't never tried," put in a companion by the fire.

"Wall, I ain't sayin' he had," corrected the first
speaker, through a cloud of smoke. "Lord, I hope
when my time comes I kin slip into heaven on Marse
Robert's coat-tails."

"If you don't, you won't never git thar!" jeered
the second. Then they settled themselves again, and
listened with sombre faces and twitching lips.

It was during this winter that Dan learned how
one man's influence may fuse individual and op-
posing wills into a single supreme endeavor. The
Army of Northern Virginia, as he saw it then, was
moulded, sustained, and made effective less by the
authority of the Commander than by the simple
power of Lee over the hearts of the men who bore
his muskets. For a time Dan had sought to trace
the groundspring of this impassioned loyalty, seeking a reason that could not be found in generals
less beloved. Surely it was not the illuminated figure of the conqueror, for when had the Commander
held closer the affection of his troops than in that
ill-starred campaign into Maryland, which left the
moral victory of a superb fight in McClellan's

hands? No, the charm lay deeper still, beyond all the fictitious aids of fortune—somewhere in that serene and noble presence he had met one evening as the gray dusk closed, riding alone on an old road between level fields. After this it was always as a high figure against a low horizon that he had seen the man who made his army.

As the long winter passed away, he learned, not only much of the spirit of his own side, but something that became almost a sunny tolerance, of the great blue army across the Rappahannock. He had exchanged Virginian tobacco for Northern coffee at the outposts, and when on picket duty along the cold banks of the river he would sometimes shout questions and replies across the stream. In these meetings there was only a wide curiosity with little bitterness; and once a friendly New England picket had delivered a religious homily from the opposite shore, as he leaned upon his rifle.

"I didn't think much of you Rebs before I came down here," he had concluded in a precise and energetic shout, "but I guess, after all, you've got souls in your bodies like the rest of us."

"I reckon we have. Any coffee over your side?"

"Plenty. The war's interfered considerably with the tobacco crop, ain't it?"

"Well, rather; we've enough for ourselves, but none to offer our visitors."

"Look here, are all these things about you in the papers gospel truth?"

"Can't say. What things?"

"Do you always carry bowie knives into battle?"

"No, we use scissors—they're more convenient."

"When you catch a runaway nigger do you chop him up in little pieces and throw him to the hogs?"

"Not exactly. We boil him down and grease our cartridges."

"After Bull Run did you set up all the live Zouaves you got hold of as targets for rifle practice?"

"Can't remember about the Zouaves. Rather think we made them into flags."

"Well, you Rebels take the breath out of me," commented the picket across the river; and then, as the relief came, Dan hurried back to look for the mail bag and a letter from Betty. For Betty wrote often these days—letters sometimes practical, sometimes impassioned, always filled with cheer, and often with bright gossip. Of her own struggle at Uplands and the long days crowded with work, she wrote no word; all her sympathy, all her large passion, and all her wise advice in little matters were for Dan from the beginning to the end. She made him promise to keep warm if it were possible, to read his Bible when he had the time, and to think of her at all hours in every season. In a neat little package there came one day a gray knitted waist-coat which he was to wear when on picket duty beside the river, "and be very sure to fasten it," she had written. "I have sewed the buttons on so tight they can't come off. Oh, if I had only papa and Virginia and you back again I could be happy in a hovel. Dear mamma says so, too."

And after much calm advice there would come whole pages that warmed him from head to foot. "Your kisses are still on my lips," she wrote one day. "The Major said to me, 'Your mouth is very warm, my dear,' and I almost answered, 'you feel Dan's kisses, sir.' What would he have said, do you think? As it was I only smiled and turned away, and longed to run straight to you to be caught up in your arms and held there forever. O my beloved, when you need me only stretch out your hands and I will come."

Vol. 8—24.

A SOUTHERN HERO OF THE NEW TYPE.*

From The Voice of the People (1900).

AGAIN he was returning to Kingsborough. The familiar landscape rushed by him on either side—green meadow and russet woodland, gray swamp and dwarfed brown hill, unploughed common and sun-ripened field of corn. It was like the remembered features of a friend, when the change that startles the unaccustomed eye seems to exist less in the well-known face than in the image we have carried in our thoughts.

It was all there as it had been in his youth—the same and yet not the same. The old fields were tilled, the old lands ran waste in broomsedge, but he himself had left his boyhood far behind—it was his own vision that was altered, not the face of nature. The commons were not so wide as he had thought them, the hills not so high, the hollows not so deep—even the blue horizon had drawn a closer circle.

A man on his way to the water-cooler stopped abruptly at his side. "Well, I declar, if 'tain't the governor!"

Nicholas looked up, and recognizing Jerry Pollard, shook his outstretched hand. "When did you leave Kingsborough?" he inquired.

"Oh, I jest ran up this morning to lay in a stock of winter goods. Trade's thriving this year, and you have to hustle if you want to keep up with the tastes of yo' customers. Times have changed since I had you in my sto'."

"I dare say. I am glad to hear that you are doing well. Was the judge taken ill before you left Kingsborough?"

"The judge? Is he sick? I ain't heard nothin' 'bout it. It wa'n't more'n a week ago that I told him he was lookin' as young as he did befo' the war. It ain't often a man can keep his youth like that— but his Cæsar is just such another. Cæsar was an old man as far back as I remember, and, bless you, he's spryer than I am this minute. He'll live to be a hundred and die of an accident."

"That's good," said the governor with rising interest. "Kingsborough's a fine place to grow old in. Did you bring any news up with you?"

"Well, I reckon not. Things were pretty lively down there last night, but they'd quieted down this morning. They brought a man over from Hagersville, you know, and befo' I shut up sto' last evening Jim Brown came to town, talkin' mighty big 'bout stringin' up the fellow. Jim always did talk, though, so nobody thought much of it. He likes to get his mouth in, but he's right particular 'bout his hand. The sheriff said he warn't lookin' for trouble."

"I'm glad it's over," said the governor. The train was nearing Kingsborough, and as it stopped he rose and followed Jerry Pollard to the station.

There was no one he knew in sight, and, with his bag in his hand, he walked rapidly to the judge's house. His anxiety had caused him to quicken his pace, but when he had opened the gate and ascended the steps he hesitated before entering the hall, and his breath came shortly. Until that instant he had not realized the strength of the tie that bound him to the judge.

The hall was dim and cool, as it had been that May afternoon when his feet had left tracks of dust on the shining floor. Straight ahead he saw the garden, lying graceless and deserted, with the unkemptness of extreme old age. A sharp breeze blew from door to door, and the dried grasses on the wall stirred with a sound like that of the wind among a bed of rushes.

He mounted the stairs slowly, the weight of his tread creaking the polished wood. Before the threshold of the judge's room again he hesitated, his hand upraised. The house was so still that it seemed to be untenanted, and he shivered suddenly, as if the wind that rustled the dried grasses were a ghostly footstep. Then, as he glanced back down the wide old stairway, his own childhood looked up at him—an alien figure, half frightened by the silence.

As he stood there the door opened noiselessly, and the doctor came out, peering with shortsighted eyes over his lowered glasses. When he ran against Nicholas he coughed uncertainly and drew back. "Well, well, if it isn't the governor!" he said. "We have been looking for Tom—but our friend the judge is better—much better. I tell him he'll live yet to see us buried."

A load passed suddenly from Nicholas's mind. The ravaged face of the old doctor—with its wrinkled forehead and its almost invisible eyes—became at once the mask of a good angel. He grasped the outstretched hand and crossed the threshold.

The judge was lying among the pillows of his bed, his eyes closed, his great head motionless. There was a bowl of yellow chrysanthemums on a table beside him, and near it Mrs. Burwell was measuring dark drops into a wineglass. She looked up with a smile of welcome that cast a cheerful light about the room. Her smile and the color of the chrysanthemums were in Nicholas's eyes as he went to the bed and laid his hand upon the still fingers that clasped the counterpane.

The judge looked at him with a wavering recognition. "Ah, it is you, Tom," he said, and there was a yearning in his voice that fell like a gulf between him and the man who was not his son. At the moment it came to Nicholas with a great bitterness that his share of the judge's heart was the share of an outsider—the crumbs that fall to the beggar that waits beside the gate. When the soul has entered the depths and looks back again it is the face of its own kindred that it craves—the responsive throbbing of its own blood in another's veins. This was Tom's place, not his.

He leaned nearer, speaking in an expressionless voice. "It's I, sir—Nicholas—Nicholas Burr."

"Yes, Nicholas," repeated the judge doubtfully; "yes, I remember, what does he want? Amos Burr's son—we must give him a chance."

For a moment he wandered on; then his memory returned in uncertain pauses. He looked again at the younger man, his sight grown stronger. "Why, Nicholas, my dear boy, this is good of you," he exclaimed. "I had a fall—a slight fall of no consequence. I shall be all right if Cæsar will let me fast a while. Cæsar's getting old, I fear, he moves so slowly."

He was silent, and Nicholas, sitting beside the bed, kept his eyes on the delicate features that were the lingering survival of a lost type. The splendid breadth of the brow, the classic nose, the firm, thin lips, and the shaven chin—these were all downstairs on faded canvases, magnificent over lace ruffles, or severe above folded stocks. Over the pillows the chrysanthemums shed a golden light that mingled in his mind with the warm brightness of Mrs. Burwell's smile—giving the room the festive glimmer of an autumn garden.

A little later Cæsar shuffled forward, the wineglass in his hand. The judge turned toward him. "Is that you, Cæsar?" he asked.

The old negro hurried to the bedside. "Here I is, Marse George; I'se right yer."

The judge laughed softly. "I wouldn't take five thousand dollars for you, Cæsar," he said. "Tom Battle offered me one thousand for you, and I told him I wouldn't take five. You are worth it, Cæsar—every cent of it—but there's no man alive shall own you. You're free, Cæsar—do you hear, you're free!"

"Thanky, Marse George," said Cæsar. He passed his arm under the judge's head and raised him as he would a child. As the glass touched his lips the judge spoke in a clear voice. "To the ladies!" he cried.

"He is regaining the use of his limbs," whispered Mrs. Burwell softly. "He will be well again," and Nicholas left the room and went downstairs. At the door he gave his instructions to a woman servant. "I shall return to spend the night," he said. "You will see that my room is ready. Yes, I'll be back to supper." He had had no dinner, but at the moment this was forgotten. In the relief that had come to him he wanted solitude and the breadth of the open fields. He was going over the old ground again—to breathe the air and feel the dust of the Old Stage Road.

He passed the naked walls of the church and followed the wide white street to the college gate. Then, turning, he faced the way to his father's farm and the distant pines emblazoned on the west.

A clear gold light flooded the landscape, warming the pale dust of the deserted road. The air was keen with the autumn tang, and as he walked the quick blood leaped to his cheeks. He was no longer conscious of his forty years—his boyhood was with him, and middle age was a dream, or less than a dream.

In the branch road a fall of tawny leaves hid the

ruts of wheels, and the sun, striking the ground like a golden lance, sent out sharp, fiery sparks as from a mine of light. Overhead the red trees rustled.

It was here that Eugenia had ridden beside him in the early morning—here he had seen her face against the enkindled branches—and here he had placed the scarlet gum leaves in her horse's bridle. The breeze in the wood came to him like the echo of her laugh, faded as the memory of his past passion. Well, he had more than most men, for he had the ghost of a laugh and the shadow of love.

Passing his father's house, he went on beyond the fallen shanty of Uncle Ish into the twilight of the cedars. At the end of the avenue he saw the rows of box—twisted and tall with age—leading to the empty house, where the stone steps were wreathed in vines. Did Eugenia ever come back, he wondered, or was the house to crumble as Miss Chris's rockery had done? On the porch he saw the marks made by the general's chair, which had been removed, and on one of the long green benches there was an E cut in a childish hand. At a window above —Eugenia's window—a shutter hung back upon its hinges, and between the muslin curtains it seemed to him that a face looked out and smiled—not the face of Eugenia, but a ghost again, the ghost of his old romance.

He went into the garden, crossing the cattle lane, where the footprints of the cows were fresh in the dust. Near at hand he heard a voice shouting. It was the voice of the overseer, but the sound startled him, and he awoke abruptly to himself and his forty years. The spell of the past was broken—even the riotous old garden, blending its many colors in a single blur, could not bring it back. The chrysanthemums and the roses and the hardy zenias that came up uncared for were powerless to reinvoke the

spirit of the place. If Eugenia, in her full-blown
motherhood, had risen in an overgrown path he
might have passed her by unheeding. His Eugenia
was a girl in a muslin gown, endowed with immortal
youth—the youth of visions unfulfilled and desire
unquenched. His Eugenia could never grow old
—could never alter—could never leave the eternal
sunshine of dead autumns. In his nostrils was the
keen sweetness of old-fashioned flowers, but his
thoughts were not of them, and, turning presently,
he went back as he had come. It was dark when
at last he reached the judge's house and sat down to
supper.

He was with the judge until midnight, when, before going to his room, he descended the stairs and
went out upon the porch. He had been thinking of
the elections three days hence, and the outcome
seemed to him more hopeful than it had done when
he first came forward as a candidate. The uncertainty was almost as great, this he granted; but behind him he believed to be the pressure of the
people's will—which the schemes of politicians had
not turned. Tuesday would prove nothing—nor
had the conventions that had been held; when the
meeting of the caucus came, he would still be in
ignorance—unaware of traps that had been laid or
surprises to be sprung. It was the mark to which
his ambition had aimed—the end to which his career
had faced—that now rose before him, and yet in his
heart there was neither elation nor distrust. He
had done his best—he had fought fairly and well,
and he awaited what the day might bring forth.

Above him a full moon was rising, and across the
green the crooked path wound like a silver thread,
leading to the glow of a night-lamp that burned in
a sick-room. The night, the air, the shuttered
houses were as silent as the churchyard, where the

tombstones glimmered, row on row. Only somewhere on the vacant green a hound bayed at the
moon.

He looked out an instant longer, and was turning
back, when his eye caught a movement among
the shadows in the distant lane. A quick thought
came to him, and he kept his gaze beneath the heavy
maples, where the moonshine fell in flecks. For a
moment all was still, and then into the light came
the figure of a man. Another followed, another,
and another, passing again into the dark and then
out into the brightness that led into the little gully
far beyond. There was no sound except the baying
of the dog; the figures went on, noiseless and orderly
and grim, from dark to light and from light again
to dark. There were at most a dozen men, and they
might have been a band of belated workmen returning to their homes or a line of revellers that had
been sobered into silence. They might have been
—but a sudden recollection came to him, and he
closed the door softly and went out. There was
but one thing that it meant; this he knew. It meant
a midnight attack on the gaol, and a man dead before morning, who must die anyway—it meant
vengeance so quiet yet so determined that it was
as sure as the hand of God—and it meant the defiance of laws whose guardian he was.

He broke into a run, crossing the green and following the path that rose and fell into the gullies as
it led on to the gaol. As he ran he saw the glow of
the night-lamp in the sick-room, and he heard the
insistent baying of the hound.

The moonlight was thick and full. It showed the
quiet hill flanked by the open pasture; and it showed
the little whitewashed gaol, and the late roses blooming on the fence. It showed also the mob that had
gathered—a gathering as quiet as a congregation

at prayer. But in the silence was the danger—the determination to act that choked back speech—the grimness of the justice that walks at night—the triumph of a lawless rage that knows control.

As he reached the hill he saw that the men he had followed had been enforced by others from different roads. It was not an outbreak of swift desperation, but a well-planned, well-ordered strategy; it was not a mob that he faced, but an incarnate vengeance.

He came upon it quickly, and as he did so he saw that the sheriff was ahead of him, standing, a single man, between his prisoner and the rope. "For God's sake, men, I haven't got the keys," he called out.

Nicholas swung himself over the fence and made his way to the entrance beneath the steps that lead to the floor above. He had come as one of the men about him, and they had not heeded him. Now, as he faced them from the shadow he saw here and there a familiar face—the face of a boy he had played with in childhood. Several were masked, but the others raised bare features to the moonlight—features that were as familiar as his own.

Then he stood up and spoke. "Men, listen to me. In the name of the Law, I swear to you that justice shall be done—I swear."

A voice came from somewhere. "We ain't here to talk—you stand aside, and *we'll* show you what we're here for."

Again he began. "I swear to you——"

"We don't want no swearing." On the outskirts of the crowd a man laughed. "We don't want no swearing," the voice repeated.

The throng pressed forward, and he saw the faces that he knew crowding closer. A black cloud shut out the moonlight. Above the pleading of the sheriff's tones he heard the distant baying of the hound.

He tried to speak again. "We'll be damned, but we'll get the nigger!" called some one beside him. The words struck him like a blow. He saw red, and the sudden rage upheld him. He knew that he was to fight—a blind fight for he cared not what. The old savage instinct blazed within him—the instinct to do battle to death—to throttle with his single hand the odds that opposed. With a grip of iron he braced himself against the doorway, covering the entrance.

"I'll be damned if you do!" he thundered.

A quick shot rang out sharply. The flash blinded him, and the smoke hung in his face. Then the moon shone and he heard a cry—the cry of a well-known voice.

"By God, it's Nick Burr!" it said. He took a step forward.

"Boys, I am Nick Burr," he cried, and he went down in the arms of the mob.

They raised him up, and he stood erect between the leaders. There was blood on his lips, but a man tore off a mask and wiped it away. "By God, it's Nick Burr!" he exclaimed as he did so.

Nicholas recognized his voice and smiled. His face was gray, but his eyes were shining, and as he steadied himself with all his strength, he said with a laugh. "There's no harm done, man." But when they laid him down a moment later he was dead.

He lay in the narrow path between the doorstep and the gate where roses bloomed. Some one had started for the nearest house, but the crowd stood motionless about him. "By God, it's Nick Burr!" repeated the man who had held him.

The sheriff knelt on the ground and raised him in his arms. As he folded his coat about him he looked up and spoke.

"And he died for a damned brute," he said.

MARY JOHNSTON.

DREAMS OF A WESTERN EMPIRE.*

From Lewis Rand (1908).

JACQUELINE arranged the flowers, cut from her window stand, in the porcelain vase, and set the vase with care in the centre of the polished table. All was in order, from the heavy damask napkins and the Chelsea plates to the silver candlesticks and the old cut-glass. She turned her graceful head, and called to her husband, whose step she heard in the adjoining room. He came, and, standing beside her, surveyed the mahogany field. "Is there anything lacking?" she asked.

He turned and kissed her. "Only that you should be happy!" he said.

"If I am not," she answered, "he will never find it out! But when I see him, I shall hear that fatal shot!"

"He will make you quite forget it. All women like him."

"Then I shall be the exception. General Hamilton was Uncle Edward's friend. At Fontenoy they'll call it insult that I have talked with this man!"

"They will not know," Rand replied. "It was an honest duel fought nigh two years ago. Forget— forget! There's so much one must forget. Besides, others are forgiving. There is not now the old enmity between him and the Federalists."

"No?" said Jacqueline. "Why is that?"

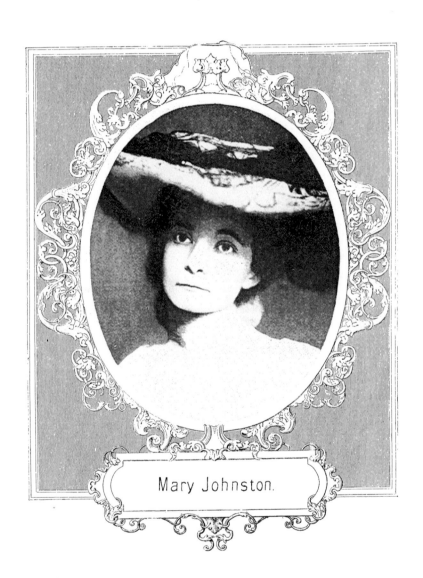

Mary Johnston.

"I cannot tell you, but old differences are being smoothed over. It is rather the Republicans who are out with him."

"I know that he is no friend to Mr. Jefferson."

"No, he is no friend to Mr. Jefferson. The room looks well, sweetheart. But some day you shall have a much grander one, all light and splendour, and larger flowers than these—"

His wife rested her head against his shoulder. "I don't want it, Lewis. It is only you who care for magnificence. Sometimes I wonder that you should so care."

"It is my mother in me," he answered. "She cared—poor soul. But I don't want magnificence for myself. I want it for you—"

"You must not want it for me," cried Jacqueline, with wistful passion. "I am happy here, and I am happy at Roselands—but I was the happiest of all in the house on the Three-Notched Road!"

There was a moment's silence, then Rand spoke slowly. "I was not born for content. I am urged on—and on—and I cannot always tell right from wrong. There is a darkness within me—I wish it were light instead!" He laughed. "But if wishes were horses, beggars might ride!—And you've cut all your pretty bright flowers! After supper, before we begin our talk, you must sing to him. They say his daughter is an accomplished and beautiful woman. But you—you are Beauty, Jacqueline!"

The knocker sounded. "That is he," exclaimed Rand, and went into the hall to welcome his guest. Jacqueline returned to the drawing-room, and waited there before the fire. She was dressed in white, with bare neck and arms and her mother's amethysts around her throat. In a moment the two men entered. "This is my wife, Colonel Burr," said Rand.

Jacqueline curtsied. A small, slight, black-eyed,

and smiling gentleman bowed low, and with much grace of manner took and kissed her hand. "Mr. Rand, now I understand the pride in your voice! Madam, I wish my daughter Theodosia were with me. She is *my* pride, and when I say that you two would be friends, I pay you both a compliment!"

"I have heard much of her," answered Jacqueline, "and nothing but good. My husband tells me that you have been in the South—and in Virginia we are welcoming you with a snowstorm!"

"The cold is all outside," said Colonel Burr. "Permit me—"

He handed his hostess to the green-striped sofa, and seated himself beside her with a sigh of appreciation for the warmth and soft light of the pleasant room, and the presence of the woman. "Your harp!" he exclaimed. "I should have brought a sheaf of Spanish songs such as the ladies sing to the guitar in New Orleans!—My dear sir, your fair wife and my Theodosia must one day sing together, walk hand in hand together, in that richer, sweeter land! They shall use the mantilla and wield the fan. Crowns are too heavy—they shall wear black lace!"

He spoke with not unpleasant brusqueness, a military manner tempered with gallantry, and he looked at Rand with quick black eyes. "Yes, they must meet," said Rand simply. He spoke composedly, but he had nevertheless a moment's vision of Jacqueline, away from the snow and the storm, walking in beauty through the gardens of a far country. He saw her with a circlet of gold upon her head, a circlet of Mexican gold. Crowns were heavy, but men— ay, and women, too!—fought for them. Hers should be light and fanciful upon her head. She should wear black lace if she chose,—though always he liked her best in white,—in her kingdom, in the kingdom he was going to help Aaron Burr establish.—No! in the kingdom Aaron Burr should help Lewis Rand establish! His dream broke. He was not sure that he meant to come to an understanding with Burr. It depended—it depended. But still he saw Jacqueline in trailing robes, with the gold circlet on her head.

Joab at the door announced supper, and the three went into the dining-room, where the red geraniums glowed between the candles. Jacqueline took her place behind the coffee-urn, and Joab waited.

The meal went pleasantly on. Colonel Burr was accomplished in conversation, now supple and insinuating, as a courtier, now direct, forceful, even plain, as became an old soldier of the Revolution, always agreeable, and always with a fine air of sincerity. The daughter of Henry Churchill did not lack wit, charm, and proper fire, and the Virginia hostess never showed her private feelings to a guest. She watched over the stranger's comfort with soft care, and met his talk with graceful readiness. He spoke to her of her family: of her grandfather, whose name had been widely known, of her father, whose praises he had heard sung, of Major Churchill, whom he had met in Philadelphia in General Washington's time. He spoke of her kinsmen with an admiration which went far toward including their opinions. Jacqueline marvelled. Surely this gentleman was a Democrat-Republican, lately the Vice-President of that party's electing. It was not two years since he had slain General Hamilton; and now, in a quiet, refined voice, he was talking of Federalists and Federal ways with all the familiarity, sympathy, and ease of one born in the fold and contented with his lot. She wondered if he had quarrelled with his party, and while he was talking she was proudly thinking, "The Federalists will not have him—no, not if he went on his knees to them!'' And then she thought, ''He is a man without a country.''

Rand sat somewhat silent and distrait, his mind occupied in building, building, now laying the timbers this way and now that; but presently, upon his guest's referring to him some point for elucidation, he entered the conversation, and thenceforth, though he spoke not a great deal, his personality dominated it. The acute intelligence opposite him took faint alarm. ''I am bargaining for a supporter,'' Burr told himself, ''not for a rival,'' and became if possible more deferentially courteous than before. The talk went smoothly on, from Virginia politics to the triumphal march of Napoleon through Europe; from England and the death of Pitt to the Spanish intrigues, and so back to questions of the West; and to references, which Jacqueline did not understand, to the Spanish Minister, Casa Yrujo, to the English Mr. Merry, and to Messieurs Sauve, Derbigny, and Jean Noël Destrehan of New Orleans.

Joab took away the Chelsea plates and dishes, brushed the mahogany, and placed before his master squat decanters of sherry and Madeira. The flowing talk took a warmer tone, and began to sing with the music of the South and the golden West; to be charged with Spanish, French, and Indian names, with the odour of strange flowers, the roll of the Mississippi, and the flashing of coloured wings. It was the two men now who spoke. Jacqueline, leaning back in her chair, half listened to the talk of the Territory of Orleans, the Perdido, and the road to Mexico, half dreamed of what they might be doing at Fontenoy this snowy night. The knocker sounded. ''That is Adam Gaudylock,'' exclaimed Rand. ''Joab, show Mr. Gaudylock in.''

Jacqueline rose, and Colonel Burr sprang to open the door for her. ''We may sit late, Jacqueline,'' said Rand, and their guest, "Madam, I will make court to you in a court some day!"

Gaudylock's voice floated in from the hall: "Is a little man with him?—a black-eyed man?" She passed into the drawing-room, and, pressing her brow against the window-pane, looked out into the night. The snow had ceased to fall, and the moon was struggling with the breaking clouds. The door opened to admit her husband, who came for a moment to her side. "It is not snowing now," he said. "A visitor will hardlly knock on such a night. If by chance one should come, say that I am engaged with a client, make my excuses, and as soon as possible get rid of him. On no account—on no account, Jacqueline, would I have it known that Aaron Burr is here to-night. This is important. I will keep the doors shut, and we will not speak loudly." He turned to go, then hesitated. "On second thoughts, I will tell Joab to excuse us both at the door. For you—do not sit up, dear heart! It will be late before our business is done."

He was gone. Jacqueline went back to the fire and, sitting down beneath the high mantel, opened the fifth volume of Clarissa Harlowe. She read for a while, then closed the book, and with her chin in her hand fell to studying the ruddy hollows and dropping coals. Perhaps half an hour passed. The door opened, and she looked up from her picture in the deep hollows to see Ludwell Cary smiling down upon her and holding out his hand. "Perhaps I should have drifted past with the snow," he said, "but the light in the window drew me, and I heard to-day from Fontenoy. Mr. Rand, I know, is at home."

"Yes," answered Jacqueline, rising, "but he is much engaged to-night with—with a friend. Did Joab not tell you?"

"Mammy Chloe let me in. I did not see Joab. I am sorry—"

He hesitated. There came a blast of wind that rattled the boughs of the maple outside the window. The fire leaped and the shadows danced in the corners of the room. Jacqueline knew that it was cold outside—her visitor's coat was wet with snow. Sitting there before the fire she had been lonely, and her heart was hungry for news from home.

"May I stay a few minutes?" asked Cary. "I will read what Major Edward says of Fontenoy."

She was far from dreaming how little Rand would wish this visitor to know of his affairs that night. Her knowledge extended no further than the fact that for some reason Colonel Burr did not wish it known that he was in Richmond. She listened, but the walls were thick, and she heard no sound from the distant dining-room. Cary would know only what she told him, and in a few minutes he would be gone. "I should like to hear the letter," she said, and motioned to the armchair beside the hearth. He took it, and she seated herself opposite him, upon an old, embroidered tabouret. Between them the fire of hickory logs burned softly; without the curtained windows the maple branches, moved by the wind, struck at intervals against the eaves. Jacqueline faced the door. It was her intention, should she hear steps, to rise and speak to Lewis in the hall without.

The letter which Cary drew from his breast pocket was from Major Churchill. That he did not read it all was due to his correspondent's choice of subjects and great plainness of speech; but he read what the Major had to say of Fontenoy, of the winter weather and the ailing slaves, of Mustapha, of county deaths and marriages, of the books he had been reading, and the men to whom he wrote. Major

Edward's strain was ironic, fine, and very humanly lonely. Jacqueline's eyes filled with tears, and all the flames of the fire ran together like shaken jewels.

"Almost all the rest," said Cary, "has to do with politics. I will not read you what he has to say of us slight, younger men and the puny times in which we live. But this will interest you—this is of general import."

He turned the page and read: "I have to-day a letter from G. Morris with the latest mischief from the North. Aaron Burr is going West, but with, I warrant you, no thought of the setting sun. The Ancient Iniquity in Washington smiles with thin lips and pronounces that all men and Aaron Burr are unambitious, unselfish, and peace-loving—but none the less, he looks askance at the serpent's windings. The friends of Burr are not the friends of Jefferson. There are Federalists—'tis said they increase in numbers—who do not wish the former ill; myself I am not one of them. Colonel Burr *desired* that duel; he lay in wait for the affront which should be his opportunity; he murdered Hamilton. He risked his own life—very true, the majority of murderers do the same. The one who does not is a dastard in addition—*voilà tout!*

"Burr quits the East, and all men know that the West, like Israel of old, is weary of an Idea and would like to have a King. If the world revolves this way much longer, the Man of the People will not be asked to write the next Declaration of Independence, and the country west of the Ohio will be celebrating not the Fourth of July but an eighteenth of Prairial. Aaron Burr and his confederates intend an Empire. 'Tis said there are five hundred men in his confidence here in the East, and that the chief of these wait but for a signal from him or from Wil-

kinson—whereupon they'll follow him and he'll make
them dukes and princes.

"Like Macbeth, he has done his murder and is on
his way to be crowned at Scone. He has not a wife,
but he has a daughter ambitious as himself. She
has a son. He sees his line secured. He has sub-
orned other murderers and made traitors of honest
men—and our Laputa philosopher at Washington
smiles and says there is nothing amiss!

"May I be gathered soon out of this cap-and-bells
democracy to some Walhalla where I may find Hamilton and General Washington and be at peace! This
world is growing wearisome to me.

"G. Morris speaks of the bulk of his news as report merely, but I'll stake my head the report is
true."

Cary ceased to read. Jacqueline sat motionless,
and in the silence of the room they heard the wind
outside and the tapping of the maple branches.

"If I were Mr. Jefferson," said Cary presently,
"I would arrest Colonel Burr this side of the Ohio.
He has been west too often; he is in the East now,
and I would see to it that he remained here. But
Mr. Jefferson will temporize, and Burr will make his
dash for a throne. Well! he is neither Cæsar nor
Buonaparte; he is only Aaron Burr. He is the adventurer, not the Emperor. The danger is that in all
the motley he is enlisting there may be a Buonaparte. Then farewell to this poor schemer and any
delusions he may yet nourish as to a peaceful, federated West! War and brazen clamour and the
yelling eagles of a conqueror!"

He spoke with conviction, but now, as though to
lighten his own mood, he laughed. "All this may
not be so," he said. "It may be but a dream of our
over-peaceful night."

Jacqueline rose, motioned him with a smile to keep

his seat, and, moving to an escritoire standing near the door, wrote a line upon a sheet of paper, then rang the bell and when Joab appeared, put the paper into his hand. "Give this to your master," she said, and came back to Cary beside the fire. She smiled, but he saw with concern that she was very pale, and that the amethysts were trembling at her throat. "I should not have read you this letter," he exclaimed. "It is over-caustic, over-bitter. Do not let it trouble you. You have grown pale!"

She bent over the fire as if she were cold. "It is nothing. Yes, I was troubled—I am always troubled when I think of Fontenoy. But it is over now—and indeed I wanted to hear Uncle Edward's letter." She straightened herself and turned to him a smiling face. "And now tell me of yourself! You are looking worn. Men work too hard in Richmond. Oh, for the Albemarle air! The snow will be white to-morrow on my fir tree, and Deb will have to throw crumbs for the birds. I have learned a new song. When next you come, I will sing it to you."

"Will you not," asked Cary,—"will you not sing it to me now?"

She shook her head. "Not now. How the branches strike against the roof to-night!"

As she spoke she moved restlessly, and Cary saw the amethysts stir again. A thought flashed through his mind. It had to do with Lewis Rand, of whom he often thought, sometimes with melancholy envy, sometimes with strong dislike, sometimes with unwilling admiration, and always with painful curiosity. Now, the substance of Major Churchill's letter strongly in his mind, with senses rendered more acute and emotions heightened as they always were in the presence of the woman he had not ceased to love, troubled, too, by something in her demeanor, intangibly different from her usual frank welcome, he suddenly and vividly recalled a much-applauded speech that Rand had made three days before in a public gathering. It had included a noteworthy display of minute information of western conditions, extending to the physical features of the country and to every degree of its complex population. One sentence among many had caught Cary's attention, had perplexed him, and had remained in his memory to be considered afterwards, closely and thoughtfully. There was one possible meaning—

Cary crumpled the letter in his hand. Rand's speech perplexed him no longer. That was it—that was it! His breath came quickly. He had builded better—he had builded better than he knew, when he wrote that paper signed "Aurelius"!

With fingers that were not quite steady he smoothed and refolded Major Churchill's letter. He was saying to himself, "What does she know? She grew pale. Thou suspicious fool! That was for thought of home. He will have told her nothing—nothing! Her soul is clear."

He pocketed his letter and, rising, spoke to her with a chivalrous gentleness. "I will go now. Do not let the thought of Fontenoy distress you. Do you remember the snow man we made there once, wreathing his head with holly? But I'll tell you a strange thing,—even on such a night as this, I always see Fontenoy bathed in summer weather!"

"Yes, yes," she answered. "I, too. Oh, home!"

He held out his hand. "You'll give my compliments to Mr. Rand?"

"Yes," she said. "He is busy to-night with a client from the country. He works too hard."

"Take him soon to Roselands and tie him there. Sing him To Althea and make him forget." He bent and kissed her hand. "Good-night—good-night!"

"Good-night," she answered, and moved with him

to the door. Standing there, she watched him through the hall and out of the house, then turned and, going to the window, pressed her brow against the pane and watched him down the street. The night had cleared; there was a high wind and many stars.

In Rand's dining-room the three men sat late over the wine and the questions that had brought them together, but at last the conference was somewhat stormily over. Burr and Adam Gaudylock left the house together, the hunter volunteering to guide the stranger to his inn. It was midnight, and Colonel Burr did not see his hostess. He sent her courtly messages, and he pressed Rand's hand somewhat too closely, then with his most admirable military air and frankest smile, thrust his arm through Gaudylock's and marched away. Rand closed the door, put down the candle that he held, and turned into the drawing-room.

Before the dying fire he found Jacqueline in her white gown, the amethysts about her throat, and her scarf of silver gauze fallen from her hand upon the floor. In her young face and form there should have been no hint, no fleeting breath of tragedy, but to-night there was that hint and that breath. The fire over which she bent and brooded seemed to leave her cold. The room was no longer brightly lighted, and she appeared mournfully a part of the hovering shadows. Her spirit had power to step forth and clothe the flesh. Almost always she looked the thing she felt. Now, in the half light, bent above the fading coals, she looked old. Her husband, with his hand upon the mantel-shelf, gazed down upon her. "It was wise of you to send me that note. Burr and I might have walked in here, or we might have spoken loudly. I heard Cary when he went out. How did you manage?"

"He asked for you. I told him that you were engaged with a client from the country. Oh, Lewis!"

Rand stooped and kissed her. "It was the best thing you could say. I would not have had him guess our visitor tonight. You are trembling like a leaf!"

"The best that I could say!—I don't know that. I feel like a leaf in the wind! I did not understand—but I was afraid for you. It is done, but I prefer to tell the truth!"

"I prefer it for you," said Rand. "To-night was mere unluckiness. And he suspected nothing?"

"He went without knowing who was in the dining-room. Lewis, what is there to suspect?"

He stood looking down upon her with a glow in his dark eyes and an unwonted red in his cheek. "Suspect? There is nothing to suspect. But to expect—there might be expectations, my Queen!"

"As long as you live you are my King!" she said. "To-night I am afraid for my King. I do not like Colonel Burr!"

"I am sorry for that. He is said to be a favourite with women."

"Lewis!" she cried, "what does he want with you? Tell me!"

So appealing was her voice, so urgent the touch of her hand, that with a start Rand awoke from his visions to the fact of her emotion. His eye was hawklike, and his intuition unfailing. "What did Ludwell Cary say to you?" he demanded.

She took her scarf from the floor, wound her hands in it, and clasped them tightly before her. "When I told him,—Mammy Chloe let him in,—when I told him that you were busy with your client, he thought no more of it. And then we talked of Fontenoy, and he read me a letter from Uncle Edward. Much of the letter was about Colonel Burr, and—and suspicions that were aroused. Uncle Edward called him a traitor and a maker of traitors. That is an ugly name, is it not? Ludwell Cary did not think the rumour false. He said that if he were Mr. Jefferson, he would arrest Colonel Burr. He, also, called him a traitor. I can tell you what he said. He said, 'But Mr. Jefferson will temporize, and Burr will make his dash for a throne. Well! he is neither Cæsar nor Buonaparte; he is only Aaron Burr. The danger is that in all the motley he is enlisting there may be a Buonaparte. Then farewell to this poor schemer and any delusions he may yet nourish as to a peaceful, federated West! War and brazen clamour and the yelling eagles of a conqueror!' That is what he said."

There was a silence, then Rand spoke in a curious voice, "Saul among the prophets! In the future, let us have less of Ludwell Cary."

"Lewis, why did Colonel Burr come here tonight?"

Rand turned from the fire and began to pace the room, head bent and hand at mouth, thinking rapidly. His wife raised her hands, still wrapped in the silver scarf, to her heart, and waited. As he passed for the third time the tall harp, he drew his hand heavily across the strings. The room vibrated to the sound. Rand came back to the hearth, took the armchair in which Cary had sat, and drew it closer to the glowing embers. "Come," he said. "Come, Jacqueline, let us look at the pictures in the fire."

She knelt beside him on the braided rug. "Show me true pictures! Home in Virginia, and honourable life, and noble service, and my King a King indeed, and this Colonel Burr gone like a shadow and an ugly dream!—that is the picture I want to see."

For a moment there was silence before the white

ash and the dying heart of the wood, then Rand with
the tongs squared a flaky bed and drew from top to
bottom a jagged line. "This," he said, "is the great
artery; this is the Mississippi River." He drew another line. "Here to the southwest is Mexico, and
that is a country for great dreams. There the plan-
tain and the orange grow, and there are silver and
gold—and the warm gulf is on this side, and the
South Sea far, far away, and down here is South
America. The Aztecs lived in Mexico, and Cortez
conquered them. He burned his ships so that he
and his Spaniards might not retreat. Here is the
land west of the Mississippi, unknown and far away.
There are grassy plains that seem to roll into the
sun, and there are great herds of game, and warlike
Indians, and beyond the range of any vision there
are vast mountains white with snow. Gold, too, may
be there. It is a country enormous, grandiose, rich,
and silent,—a desert waiting dumbly for the strong
man's tread." He turned a little and drew another
line. "To this side, away, away to the east, here
where you and I are sitting, watching, watching, here
are the Old Thirteen,—the Thirteen that the English
took from the Indians, that the children of the English took from England. It is the law of us all, Jacqueline, the law of the Three Kingdoms: the battle
is to the strong and the race to the swift. The Old
Thirteen are stable; let them rest! Together they
make a great country, and they will be greater yet.
But here is the Ohio—la belle Rivière, the French-
men call it. And beyond and below the Ohio, through
all the gigantic valley of a river so great that it
seems a fable, south to New Orleans, and westward
to the undiscovered lies the country that is to be!
And Napoleon, in order that he may brandish over
England one thunderbolt the more, sells it for a
song!—and we buy it for a song—and not one man

in fifty guesses that we have bought the song of the
future! The man who bought it knows its value—
but Mr. Jefferson cares only for Doric lays. He'll
not have the Phrygian. He dreams of cotton and
olives, of flocks and herds, rock salt and peaceful
mines, and the manors of the Golden Age,—all gathered, tended, worked, administered by farmers,
school-teachers, and philosophers! The plough-
share (improved) and the pruning-fork, a pulpit for
Dr. Priestley, and a statue of Tom Paine, a glass
house where the study of the mastodon may lead
to a knowledge of man, slavery abolished, and war
abhorred, the lion and the lamb to lie down together
and Rousseau to come true—all the old mirage—per-
fectibility in plain sight! That is his dream, and it
is a noble one. There is no room in it for the wicked
man. In the mean time he proposes to govern this
land of milk and honey, this bought-and-paid-for Par-
adise, very much as an eastern Despot might govern
a conquered province. The inconsistencies of man
must disconcert even the Thinker up in the skies.
Well—it happens that the West and this great new
city of ours, there at the mouth of the river, with her
levees and her ships, her merchants, priests, and
lawyers, do not want government by a satrap. They
want an Imperial City and a Cæsar of their own.
Throughout the length and breadth of this vast territory there is deep dissatisfaction—within and
without, for Spain is yet arrogant upon its borders.
The Floridas—Mexico—fret and fever everywhere!
It is so before all changes, Jacqueline. The very
wind sighs uneasily. Then one comes, bolder than
the rest, sees and takes his advantage. So empires
and great names are made.''

''So good names are lost!'' she cried. ''It is not
thus that you spoke one October evening on our way
from Albemarle!''

Rand dropped the iron from his hand. "That was a year and a half ago, and all things move with rapidity. A man's mind changes. That evening!—I was in Utopia. And yet, if we reigned,—if we two reigned, Jacqueline,—we might reign like that. We might make a kingdom wise and great."

"And Mr. Jefferson, and all that you owe to him? And your letter to him every month with all the public news?"

"That was before this winter," he answered. "We have almost ceased to write. I am not like James Madison or James Monroe. I cannot follow always. Mr. Jefferson is a great man—but it is hungry dwelling in the shadow of another."

"Better dwell in the shadow forever," cried Jacqueline, with passion, "than to reign with faithlessness in the sun!"

"I am not faithless—"

"So Benedict Arnold thought! Oh, Lewis!"

"You speak," said Rand slowly, "too much like the Churchills and the Carys."

In the silence that followed, Jacqueline rose and stood over against him, the scarf trailing from her hand and the amethysts rising and falling with her laboured breathing. He glanced at her and then went on: "Burr leaves Richmond to-morrow. He does not go West till summer, and all his schemes may come to naught. What he does or does not do will depend on many things, chiefly on whether or not we go to war with Spain. I am not going West with him—not yet. I have let him talk. I have brought him and Adam Gaudylock together; I have put a little money in this land purchase of his upon the Washita, and I have given him some advice. That is all there is of rebellion, treason, and sedition, —all the cock-a-hoop story! Ludwell Cary may keep his own breath to cool his own porridge. And you,

Jacqueline, you who married *me,* you have not a
soul to be frighted with big words! You and I shall
walk side by side."

"Shall we?" she said. "That will depend. I'll
not walk with you over the dead—dead faith, dead
hope, dead honour!"

"I shall not ask you to," he answered. "You are
not yourself. You are using words without thought.
It is the cold, the lateness, and this dying fire—Ludwell Cary's arrogance as well. Dead faith, hope,
honour!—is this your trust, your faith?"

"Lewis, Lewis!"

He rose, crossed the shadowy space between them,
and took her hands. "Don't fear—don't fear! We
two will always love. Jacqueline, there is that within
me that will not rest, that cries for power, and that
overrides obstacles! See what I have overridden
since the days beneath the apple tree! I am not idly
dreaming. Conditions such as exist to-day will not
arise again. Upon this continent it is the time of
times for the bold—the wisely bold. This that beck-
ons is no mirage in the West; it is palpable fact. Say
that I follow Burr—follow! overtake and pass him!
He has a tarnished name and fifty years,—a supple
rapier but a shrunken arm. He's daring; but I can
be that and more. He plans; I can achieve. I am no
dreamer and no braggart when I say that in the
West I can play the Corsican. What can I do here?
Become, perhaps, Governor of Virginia; wait until
Mr. Jefferson is dead, and Mr. Madison is dead, and
Mr. Monroe is dead, and then, if the world is yet
Republican, become President? The governorship I
do not want; the presidency is but a chance, and half
a lifetime off! But this—this, Jacqueline, is real
and at hand. Say that I go, say that I gain a throne
where you and I may sit and rule, wise and great and
sovereign, holding kingdoms for our children—"

"Oh!" exclaimed Jacqueline.

Rand drew her to him. "Don't fear—don't fear! The child will come—we want him so!"

"Promise me," she cried,—"promise me that you will see Colonel Burr no more, write to him no more! Promise me that you will put all this away, forever, forever! Oh, Lewis, give me your word!"

"I will do nothing rash," he said. "We will go back to Roselands,—we will watch and wait awhile. Burr himself does not go West until the summer. Ere then I will persuade you. That first July evening, under the mimosa at the gate, even then this thing was vaguely, vaguely in my mind."

"Was it?" she cried. "Oh me, oh me!"

"You are wearied," he said, "chilled and trembling. I wish that Ludwell Cary had aired his views elsewhere to-night! Put it all from your mind and come to rest—"

"Lewis, if ever you loved me—if ever you said that you would give me proof—"

"You know that I love you."

"Then, as I gave up friends and home for you, give up this thing for me! No, no, I'll not cease to beg" —She slipped from his arm to her knees. "Lewis, Lewis, this is not the road—this is not the way to freedom, goodness, happiness. Promise me! Oh, Lewis, if ever you loved me, promise me!"

From Rand's house on Shockoe Hill Ludwell Cary walked quickly homeward to the Eagle, where he and his brother lodged. As he walked he thought at first, hotly and bitterly enough, of Lewis Rand and painfully of himself, but at length the solemnity of the white night and high glitter of the stars made him impatient of his own mood. He looked at the stars, and at the ivory and black of the tall trees, and his mind calmed itself and turned to think of Jacqueline.

In the Eagle's best bedroom, before a blazing fire

and a bottle of port, he found Fairfax Cary deep in
a winged chair and a volume of Fielding. "Well,
Fair?" he said, with his arm upon the mantel-shelf
and his booted foot upon the fender.

The younger Cary closed his book and hospitably
poured wine for his brother. "Were you at the
Amblers'?" he asked. "It's a night for one's own
fireside. I went to the Mayos', but the fair Maria is
out of town. On the way I stopped at Bowler's Tavern to see his man about that filly we were talking
of, and I had a glass with old Bowler himself. He
let out a piece of news. Who d' ye think is in town
and under Bowler's roof?—Aaron Burr!"

There was a silence, then Cary said quietly,
"Aren't you mistaken, Fair?"

"Not in the least," answered the other. "He
came in a sloop from Baltimore yesterday. It is not
known that he's in town; he does not want it known.
He's keeping quiet,—perhaps he has another duel
on his conscience. I don't believe old Bowler knew
he had let the cat out. Burr leaves to-morrow. He
was out visiting to-night."

"How do you know that?" Cary demanded, with
sudden sharpness.

"Bowler's best bedroom in darkness—no special
preparations for supper—Burr's man idling in the
kitchen—mine host taking no care to speak low,—in
short, the wedding guest was roaming. I wonder
where he was!"

The elder Cary raised and drained the glass of
wine. He knew where Aaron Burr had supped and
passed the evening, and a coldness that was not of
the night crept upon him. As for Lewis Rand, he
cared not what he did nor why he did it, but for
Jacqueline Churchill. This had been the client from
the country! All the time she was keeping it secret

that Burr was there. She had turned pale. No wonder!—the faithful wife!

"Take care, that glass is thin—you'll break it!" warned the younger Cary, but the glass had snapped in the elder's fingers.

"Pshaw!" said Cary; "too frail for use! I'm off to bed, Fair. That bill comes up to-morrow, and it means a bitter fight. Good-night,—and I say, Fair, hold your tongue about Aaron Burr. Good-night!"

In his room he put out the candle, parted the window curtains, and looked upon Orion, icily splendid in the midnight sky. "What is there that is steadfast?" he thought. "Does she love him so?" He stood for a long time looking out into the night. He thought of that evening at Fontenoy when he had come in from the sultry and thunderous air and had found Rand seated in the drawing-room and Jacqueline at her harp, singing To Althea,—

> "Minds innocent and quiet take
> That for a hermitage."

The words and the vision of Fontenoy that night were yet with him when at last he turned from the window and threw himself upon the bed, where he finally fell asleep with his arm flung up and across his eyes.

THE WAY OF THE TRANSGRESSOR.

From the Same.

RAND closed the heavy ledger. "It is all straight," he said.

"It's as straight as if 't was a winding-up forever," answered Tom. "Are you going home now?"

"Yes."

"There's almost nothing on the docket. I've seen no such general clearance since you began to practise and took me in. You say you're going to refuse the Amherst case?"

"I have refused it."

"Then," quoth Tom, "I might as well go fishing. The weather's right, and every affair of yours is so cleaned and oiled and put to rights that there's nothing here for a man to do. One might suppose you were going a long journey. If you don't want me to-morrow, I'll call on old Mat Green—"

"Don't go fishing to-morrow, Tom," said Rand from the desk, "but don't come here either. Stay at home with Vinie."

"You won't be coming in from Roselands?"

"I won't be coming here." Rand left the desk and stood at the small window where the roses were now in bloom. "I shall send you a note, Tom, to-morrow morning. It will tell you what"— He paused for a moment. "What comes next," he finished. "There will be a message in it for Vinie." He turned from the window. "I am going home now."

"It's a good time for a holiday," remarked Tom, "and you needn't tell me that you don't need it, Lewis! I'll lock up and go to the Eagle for a while. What are you looking for?"

"Nothing," answered the other. "I was looking at the room itself. I always liked this office, Tom."

As he passed, he touched his subaltern upon the shoulder. There was fondness in the gesture. "Good-bye," he said, and was gone before Tom could answer.

Outside, in the bloom and glow of the May evening, he mounted Selim and rode out of the town. The people whom he met he greeted slightly, but with no change of manner which they afterwards could report. It was sunset when he passed the last houses, and turned toward the west and his own home. He rode slowly, with his eyes upon a great sea of vivid gold. By degrees the brightness faded, changing to an amethyst, out of which suddenly swam the evening star. The land rose into hills, the summits of the highest far and dark against the cold violet of the sky. From the road to Roselands branched the road to Greenwood. It was dusk when horse and rider reached this opening. Selim had come to know the altered grasp upon the rein just here, and now, according to wont, he fell into the slower pace. Rand turned in his saddle and looked across the darkening fields to the low hill, crowned with oaks, from which arose the Greenwood house. He gazed for a full minute, then spoke to his horse and they went on at speed. A little longer and he was at the gates of home.

His wife met him upon the doorstone. "I heard you at the gate—"

He put his arm around her. "What have you been doing all the long day?"

"I worked," she answered, "and saw to the house, and read to Hagar at the quarter. She's going fast. How tired your voice sounds! Come into the light. Supper is ready—and Mammy Chloe has said a charm to make you sleep to-night."

They went indoors to the lighted rooms. "You are wearing your amethysts," said Rand, "and the ribbon in your hair—"

She turned upon him a face exquisite in expression. "They are the jewels that you like—the ribbon as I wore it long ago. Come in—come in to supper."

The brief meal ended, they returned to the drawing-room. Rand stood irresolutely. "I have yet a line to write," he told her. "I will do it here at your desk. When I have finished, Jacqueline, then there is something I must say.''

He sat down and began to write. She moved to the window, then restlessly back to the lighted room and sat down before the hearth, but in a moment she left this, too, and moved again through the room. She passed her harp, and as she did so, she drew her hand across the strings. The sweet and liquid sound ran through the room. Rand turned. ''I have not heard,'' he said, in a low voice,—''I have not heard that sound since—since last August. Will you sing to me now?''

She touched the harp again. ''Yes, Lewis. What shall I sing?''

He rose, walked to the window, and stood with his face to the night. ''Sing those verses you sang that night at Fontenoy;'' then, as she struck a chord, ''No, not To Althea—the other.''

She sang. The noble contralto, pure, rich, and deep, swelled through the room.

''The thirst that from the soul doth rise
Doth ask a drink divine''—

Her voice broke and her hands dropped from the strings. She rose quickly and left the harp. ''I cannot—I cannot sing to-night. The air is faint— the flowers are too heavy. Come out—come out to the wind and the stars!''

Without the house the evening wind blew cool, moving the long branches of the beech tree, and rustling through the grass. To the west the mountains showed faintly, in the valley a pale streak marked the river. The sky was thick with stars. Behind them, through the open door, they heard the tall clock strike. ''I did not tell you,'' said Jacqueline, ''of all my day. Unity was here this afternoon.''

''Unity!''

"Yes. For an hour. She came with—with messages. My uncles send me word that they love me, and that Fontenoy is my home always—as it used to be. Whenever I wish, I am to come home."

"What did you answer?"

"I answered that they were all dear to me, but that my home was here with you. I told Unity to tell them that—and to tell it, too, to Fairfax Cary."

There was a silence; then, "It does not matter," said Rand slowly. "Whether it is done my way, or whether it is done his way, Fairfax Cary will not care. He is concerned only that it shall be done. You understood the message, Jacqueline?"

She answered almost inaudibly. "Yes, I understood."

"Seven months—and Ludwell Cary lies unavenged. I have been slow. But I had to break a strong chain, Jacqueline. I had fastened it, link by link, around my soul. It was not easy to break—it was not easy! And I had to find a path in a desert place."

She bowed her head upon her arms. "Do I not know what it was? I have seen—I have seen. O Lewis, Lewis!"

"It is broken," he said, "and though the desert is yet around me, my feet have found the path. To-morrow, Jacqueline, I give myself up."

She uttered a cry, turned, and threw herself into his arms. "To-morrow! O Love!"

He bent over her with broken words of self-reproach. She stopped him with her hand against his lips. "No, I am not all unhappy—no, you have not broken my heart—you have not ruined my life! Don't say it—don't think it! I love you as I loved you in the garden at Fontenoy, as I loved on our wedding eve, in the house on the Three-Notched Road! I love you more deeply now than then—"

"I have come," he answered, "to be sorry for almost all my life. Even to my father I might have been a better son. The best friend a young man ever had—that was Mr. Jefferson to me! and it all ended in the letter which he wrote last August. I was a leader in a party in whose principles I believed and still believe, and I betrayed my party. To-night I think I could give my life for one imperilled field, for one green acre of this land—and yet I was willing to bring upon it strife and dissension. Ingrate and traitor—hard words and true, hard words and true! I might have had a friend—and always I knew he was the man I would have wished to be—but, instead, I thought of him as my foe and I killed him. I have brought trouble on many, and good to very few. I have wronged you in very much. But I never wronged you in my love—never, never, Jacqueline! That is my mountain peak—that is my cleansing sea—that is that in my life which needs no repenting, that is true, that is right! Oh, my wife, my wife!"

The night wind blew against them. Fireflies shone and grey moths went by to the lighted windows; above the treetops a bat wheeled and wheeled. The clock struck again, then from far away a whippoorwill began to call. They sat side by side upon the doorstone, her head against his shoulder, their hands locked.

"What will you do?" he said. "What will you do? Day and night I think of that!"

"Could I stay on here? I would like to."

"I have put all affairs in order. The place and the servants are yours. I've paid every debt, I think. Mocket knows—he'll show you. But to live on here alone—"

"It will be the less alone. Don't fear for me—

don't think for me. I will find courage. To-morrow!"

"It is best," he said, "that I should tell you that which others may think to comfort you with. It is possible, but I do not consider it probable, that the sentence will be death. It will be, I think, the Penitentiary. I had rather it was the other."

After a time she spoke, though with difficulty. "Yes—I had rather—for you. For myself, I feel to-night that just to know you were alive would be happiness enough. Either way—either way—to have loved you has been for me my crown of life!"

"I have written to Colonel Churchill, and a line to Fairfax Cary. There was much to do at the last. Now it is all done, and I will go early in the morning. You knew that it was drawing to this end—"

"Yes, I knew—I knew. Lewis, Lewis! what will you do yonder all the days—the months—the—the years to come? Oh, unendurable! O God, have mercy!"

"I will work," he answered. "It is work, Jacqueline, with me—it is work or die! I will work. That which I have brought upon myself I will try to endure. And out of effort may come at last—I know not what."

They sat still upon the stone. The wind sank, the air grew colder; near and far there gathered a feeling of the north, a sense of loneliness and untrodden space. The whippoorwill called again.

Rand shuddered. "Our last night—it is our last night. Look!—a star shot over the Three-Notched Road."

Jacqueline slipped from his clasp and stood upright, with her hands over her ears. "Come indoors—come indoors! I cannot bear the whippoorwill!"

Early the next morning he rode away. Halfway down the drive he looked back and saw her standing under the beech tree. She raised her hand, her scarf fluttering back from it. It was the gesture of a princess, watching a knight ride from her tower. The green boughs came between them; he was gone, and she sank down upon the bench beneath the tree. It was there that Major Edward found her, an hour later.

Rand passed along the old, familiar road. He travelled neither fast nor slow, and he kept a level gaze. The May morning was fresh and sweet, the land to either side ploughed earth or vernal green, the little stream laughing through the meadow. He passed a field where negroes were transplanting tobacco, and his mind noted the height and nature of the leaf. At the Greenwood road he looked mechanically toward the distant house, but upon this morning he hardly thought of Cary. He thought of Gideon Rand, and of the great casks of tobacco which he and his father used to roll; of the old, strong horses, and of a lean and surly dog that they had owned; of the slow journeys, and of their fires at night, beneath the gum and the pine, beside wastes of broom sedge.

He came into Charlottesville and rode down Main Street to the Eagle, where he dismounted. A negro took his horse. "Put him up," directed Rand, "until he is called for." He kept his hand for a moment upon Selim's neck, then turned and walked down the street and into the Court House yard.

The shady place had always a contingent of happy idlers, men and boys lounging under the trees or upon the Court House steps. These greeted Lewis Rand with deference, and turned from their bountiful lack of occupation to watch him cross the grass and enter the Court House. "He's gone," remarked one, "straight to the sheriff's office. What's his business there?"

The next day and the next the idlers in the Court House yard knew all the business, and rolled it under their tongues. They loved a tragedy, and this curtain had gone up with promise. Had they not seen Lewis Rand walk into the yard—had they not spoken to him and he to them—had they not watched him enter the Court House? The boy who minded the sheriff's door found himself a hero, and the words treasured that fell from his tongue. It was true that he had been sent away and so had heard but little, but the increasing crowd found that little of interest. "Yes, sir, that's what he said, and just as quiet as you are! 'Is the sheriff in, Michael?' he asked. 'Tell him, please, that I want to see him.' That's what he said, and Mr. Garrett he calls out, 'Come in, Mr. Rand, come in!'"

Other voices claimed attention. "And when they dragged Indian Run yesterday, there was the pistol at the bottom of a pool—his name upon it, just as he told them it would be—"

"Fairfax Cary was in the court room yesterday when he was committed. He and Lewis Rand spoke to each other, but no one heard what they said."

The boy came to the front again. "I didn't hear much that morning before Mr. Garrett sent me away, but I heard why he gave himself up. I thought it wasn't much of a reason—"

The crowd pressed closer, "What was it, Michael, what was it?"

"It sounds foolish," answered the boy, "but I've got it right. He said he must have sleep."

Mrs. Burton Harrison.

MRS. BURTON HARRISON.

CROW'S NEST.*

From Crow's Nest and Bellhaven Tales (1892).

A fair May day in the spring of 1860 found two young men riding along a wood road of the borderland in Virginia, destined before long to echo with the ring of troopers' steel, with the tramp of hosts marching to war in mighty phalanx.

As yet, there was of the strife to come only a distant thunder growl in warning, and the ears that heard it were those of the watch-dogs of the nation! Hoyt and Newbold, formerly chums at college, had drifted hither in the course of a Southern journey undertaken after Newbold's serious illness at his home in New York. Hoyt, wide-awake, blue-eyed, alert and unimaginative, the mercantile element in his blood kept in check by the veneer of gracious Fortune, wondered at Newbold's vagrant fancy for byways and odd corners during their agreeably aimless jaunt. He would chaff his friend without ceasing over his fondness for lingering in churchyards, or losing his eyeglasses in dusty parish registers, while taking hieroglyphyic notes from some saffron page, dislodging for the purpose the filmy skeletons of veritable bookworms which had perished there, long since, of delightful satiety!

"And what if I love the seed-capsule and you the flower, Hoyt?" Newbold said, summing it all up. "You are a flower yourself, a splendid specimen, meant to bloom in the foremost *parterre* of our coming American Renaissance. Nature intended me for a nook or a niche somewhere, or else the bottom of a china jar in a corner cupboard.''

"I say!" Newbold continued, dreamily talking, somehow or other, I feel at home down here on the threshold of a world that is neither New England, with her high-pressure life of invention, enterprise, smartness, and general good repair, nor yet old England, with her storied memories. I like to think I'm not likely to encounter a rising capitalist south of the Potomac. I've a pet vision of these old grandees chipped out of colonial history, who will be found sitting beneath the umbrageous branches of their family trees, smoking good tobacco and sipping—what do they sip, Hoyt—Falernian?''

"For Falernian, read old rye," Hoyt answered. "Newbold, you are the most preposterous dreamer and dawdler. I don't see what you make it out of. Houses tumbling to pieces, old hats stuffed into the cabin-windows, the negroes along the road like scarecrows, their children little nudities. Not a decent farmhouse have we passed in three miles back; nothing but woods, woods, woods, before and behind.''

"One pardons any heresy in a hungry man," Newbold answered. "Cheer up, comrade! Think of what that dear, delightful fellow, Conway, who took us to his heart and club in Baltimore, promised us! A typical old border mansion (which should be hereabouts), and, for host, a relic of the pig-tailed gentry of a century ago. Conway, who is an eleventh cousin of these Hunters, felt himself quite free to bestow on us a letter of introduction to them. My knowledge of the topography of Fauquier County is limited, but, from the directions given by the hotel-keeper at Pohick, we must be somewhere near the

Aspen River, which bounds the Hunter property on this side. What a bit of road for a canter, Hoyt, this alley just ahead!''

They were off at a gallop through the long, green tunnel, made by oak and maple, sassafras and hemlock, sweet-gum and tulip-tree, blending their boughs in leafy communion. Vines of wild grape clambered everywhere upon their stout-shouldered neighbors, hanging out banners of close-woven greenery and tassels of luscious bloom. Here the light of the afternoon sun was filtered across the mossy ground, and from the hidden bowers of undergrowth came the song of many a sweet, unfrightened bird.

Beyond this dense tract of woodland the road came suddenly to a halt upon the steep bank of a rushing yellow. stream, churned to mad activity by a recent freshet. In the thicket of pines, upon the opposite shore, stood a weather-beaten red cottage, apparently deserted, with door and windows shut. A line stretched across the stream, and a rude attempt at ferry-tackle directed attention to the flatboat secured at the farther landing.

The two travelers sat their steeds and exhausted every known species of war-cry, whoop and yodel, but in vain. No answer, no sign of life from the ferryhouse. Only the mocking note of a crow, as he rose from a tree-top and sailed in tantalizing fashion across to the haven of their hopes.

"Confound the free-and-easy Virginian who undertakes this business!" Hoyt exclaimed, furiously flicking the mud from his trousers with his riding-whip. "It is all of a piece with the shiftless style of the neighborhood. Just let me get out of this box, and I'll expose him; I'll write to the papers about it; it's simply a disgrace to the state!"

Newbold had been sitting with slackened rein and dreamy eye, taking in all the candid beauty of an afternoon in spring in this remote and dewy spot. He started, looked at Hoyt, a quizzical gleam came into his eyes, and Hoyt laughed, albeit unwillingly.

Just then Hoyt, the more far-sighted of the two men, saw a slight figure detach itself from the black shadow of a belt of pines behind the ferryhouse, and, followed by another, come running to the bank. These were a boy and a girl, it soon appeared, and a shrill halloo across the swelling flood gave comforting assurance of relief at hand. To the surprise of the spectators, the creaking hulk of the ferryboat was at once boarded by the two children, and was swung out, not unskilfully, into the eddying stream.

"By jove!" Hoyt commented, admiringly, "the girl is doing the chief part of the work. There's pluck for you, and muscle too, Newbold! Look at the heave of that current, will you! Three cheers for the ferryman's daughter!"

Steadily the boat came on. Three cheers were given with a will, and, for answer, they could see the girl nod her head in quiet recognition.

"This is no ferryman's daughter," Newbold whispered as the boat touched shore.

She was about sixteen, slender and shapely. Her hat, trimmed with an oak-leaf wreath, had fallen back from her flushed face, and now, her task done, she stood, her beautiful bare hands clasped tightly across her waist, her breath coming quickened by exertion. The boy, her comrade, was a handsome, spirited creature, a few years younger. Both young people were of that luxurious type of beauty one sees on the mellow canvases of Lely and his fellows, having the rich coloring, the short upper lip that seems haughty when in repose, the cleft chin, the well-dilated nostrils; and both were clad in clumsily made garments of striped blue-and-white domestic cotton.

"Now, mind, Pink, I'm to ride your Bonnie Bess to-morrow, without the curb, for letting you have first turn," the lad exclaimed; and at once his fancy was taken by Hoyt's mare, who had begun to give every evidence in her power that she disliked boarding the ferryboat.

"Let me get on her, *please,* while you lead her on, sir," he pleaded. Hoyt laughed, and acquiesced. Quick as thought, the boy was in the saddle and had gathered up the reins. The mare entered a final protest by rearing violently, while her rider, deftly slipping from the saddle, stood, with one foot in the stirrup, neck to neck with the dancing beast. Before Hoyt could interpose, the mare had touched ground, and the boy was back again on his perch, a bright, wild gleam in his laughing eye. With some difficulty our travelers succeeded in obtaining permission to share the labor of ferrying the boat back.

"Well, if you want to," the girl said, with evident reluctance. "But Dolph and I so seldom get a chance. Old Stubblefield's afraid papa will hear of it, I suppose; but we made him show us how. Stubblefield's gone to mill, you know. Very few people come this way, and Dolph and I just happened to be in the woods over there when we heard you call. I suppose you came by way of Pohick?"

Here the boy broke in eagerly, with a certain pride: "My sister has been to Pohick once, when she went to the springs with Aunt Betty Alexander. I'm going some day."

Hoyt laughed his jolly laugh. Newbold smiled at the thought of the prim, sleepy little town upon the turnpike road, where the railway station and telegraph office seemed as much out of place as a staring new label on a worn leather trunk. "Each mortal has his Carcassonne," he murmured. And then came the bustle of getting ashore, of depositing the absent

Stubblefield's fee in a long-necked yellow gourd hung behind a broken pane in the window of the red cottage.

"Now add one more to your acts of friendship," Newbold said; "put us in the road leading to Colonel Hunter's house—I believe they call it Crow's Nest."

Dolph's laugh made the echoes ring. "Why, that's our house. You just keep along this wood road to the right for about three miles, and we'll meet you at the red gate. Come along, Pink; it's only a mile across the fields, our way. Let's see who'll be over that fence first."

They were off like a flash, and Newbold's eyes met Hoyt's.

"Original specimens of country gentry, aren't they?" Hoyt remarked. "I say, Newbold, it's getting deucedly on into the afternoon for a man who's had no lunch."

They plunged into the recesses of a cathedral-vaulted pine forest, and Newbold fell to musing and murmuring aloud.

"What did you say?" asked Hoyt.

"I was merely asking you a question."

"I didn't catch it."

"It is this," answered his companion:

"Have you seen a bright lily grow,
   Before rude hands have touched it?
Have you marked but the fall of the snow,
   Before the soil hath smutched it?
Have you felt the wool of the beaver,
   Or swan's-down ever?
Or have smelt of the bud of the brier,
   Or the nard in the fire?
Or have tasted the bag of the bee?
   O! so white, O! so soft, O! so sweet is she!"

"I call that a great many questions," Hoyt rejoined.

At the red gate Dolph was in waiting. His sister had gone on, he said, to announce their coming to

his father. Both men breathed freer on emerging
from the wide reach of dusky pine woods.

A low stone house, straggling along the summit
of a bleak hill, was Crow's Nest. A square porch in
front, built of heavy timbers; many small windows,
set with greenish panes of glass; a stack of outside
chimneys; and, on either side of the door, two grim
cedars, whose long arms year by year grew more
long and gaunt, until they tapped the garret window-
panes. Such were the distinguishing features of this
old Virginian house, around which hung an air of
pensive melancholy, as if it had long since become
resigned to settle down into the gray of declining
years. The visitors looked in vain for signs of feminine occupancy, a muslin curtain or a flower-pot.
All was chill, silent, and unsympathizing, quite out
of keeping with rosy Dolph, who was then engaged
in consigning their horses to a ragged negro groom.

"Pink scolded me," he said confidingly, as he
ushered his guests within. "She said I never
warned you about Black Jack."

"Black Jack! Is he a desperado who haunts
your woods?" Newbold naturally asked.

"It's our mud-hole," the boy answered innocent-
ly. "Just outside the red gate, don't you remember? You might have gone round, but it is right far
to go round. I expect you'd rather have come right
on, hadn't you? Black Jack's mighty bad in the
spring!" And he wistfully surveyed the nether garments of his guest.

The inner hall of Crow's Nest was long and narrow, the walls hung with fishing rods, with guns, with
foxes' pads and brushes, with bows and arrows rudely made. A few smoke-stained ancestors in red
coats, and their ladies in court-trains and toupets,
hung near the ceiling. Along the skirting-board was
ranged a row of men's boots, and a pair of antlers

held men's hats in every stage of disrepair. A half-dozen smiling negroes jostled one another in the background; and, starting from the wainscoting, it would seem, appeared an odd, old-time figure, in study-gown and cap, his hair worn in a queue, and his wrinkled face lit with cordial welcome.

"Welcome to Crow's Nest, gentlemen," he said heartily. "I am pleased to see that Black Jack has let you off the worse for a little mud only. Black · Jack is apt to be formidable at this season of the year. Come into the dining-room, pray, and take something after your ride. You, Trip, go tell your aunt Judy to hurry with her supper."

To present a letter of introduction seemed a mere matter of moonshine in the face of such a greeting. Our travelers were soon conducted to a chill dimity-draped chamber, with a bed of state in either end of it, where they found a small imp of darkness already blowing up a shovelful of embers beneath some light-wood knots upon the hearth. A couple of beaming black boys were on hand to brush and polish, and even Hoyt's reluctant spirit began to own the magic of hearty welcome. In a scanty room below, paneled with dark wood and dotted with profile likenesses cut from sticking plaster and pasted on a ground of white, together with faded Poonah paintings, pendent ostrich eggs, and many a smiling miniature, they presently found the daughter of the house. Pink had put on a muslin gown, and tied her truant locks beneath a scarlet brow. She received the two men without affectation, though a charming blush settled in each cheek. She did the honors by showing relics of the days of George and Anne that warmed the cockles of Newbold's antiquarian heart. In came the Colonel, in a well-brushed suit of black small-clothes; and a clanging bell announced the family meal.

"You will please hand Miss Hunter in to supper, sir," the old gentleman said, with a quaint wave of the hand. As Newbold obeyed, he fancied himself on tip-toe leading out a partner to the minuet!

[Then follow an account of a characteristic supper in an old-time Virginia home, various items of the history of the family, which included besides those already mentioned, six stalwart sons, and a mind portraiture of the father of the family, who figures as a typical Southern gentleman of the antebellum type.]

One who has encountered the pressure of Virginia hospitality knows that there is nothing for it but to submit, body and baggage. Hoyt and Newbold made a feeble stand against extending their stay at Crow's Nest; but, betimes next morning, a cart drawn by a large cream-colored mule and driven by a negro lad (whose garments, made of guano-bags, commended Smith's fertilizer to the public gaze), set off in pursuit of their luggage at the tavern in Pohick. Thus beset, our travelers resigned themselves to a fortnight's loitering. Hoyt, an enthusiastic sportsman, found his chief amusement in the saddle, under convoy of the stalwart six, or in roaming the woods and fields. Newbold derived endless entertainment from the life, the place, the people. Dolph and Pink led him captive everywhere. Aunt Judy was proud to show her various departments of baking, brewing, poultry-raising, hog-fattening, spinning, and weaving. He had called upon the new calf of the red-and-white cow; he had seen Judy make her wonderful "beat" biscuit; he had rifled her quince preserves in company with his allies. He liked best of all, perhaps, to pass hours in the old "office." In this retreat, common to most Virginian houses, the uncertain light came through small panes of glass, shadowed without by a massive clump of

box-bushes causing dusk to fall within at noonday,
and affording sanctuary where Aunt Judy dared not
pursue her fowls fleeing for their lives from block
and hatchet. Above the door, where, entering, the
visitor plunged headlong down an unsuspected step,
grew syringas, gnarled and ancient, with hoary bark
and sparse flowers. Sometimes a nest of young
chimney-swallows, loosened by the rain, would fall
upon the hearth, "pieping" for human sympathy.
Hounds wandered in and out the door; mice
sported on the book-shelves; not infrequently a
young heifer sauntered down the flagged walk to
set her forefeet on the mossy step and fix her serious gaze upon the occupant. Here Newbold liked to
sit, opening moldy envelopes, exploring mouse-eaten
documents, some bearing proud armorial seals, and
taking notes from a family correspondence extending back to the time of England's merry monarch.
The spring days glided by, till, on the eve of their
departure, Pink summoned both her guests to a final
round of "the quarter." Here, a number of whitewashed cabins, each boasting its separate patch of
garden, growing corn, sweet potatoes, tomatoes,
onions, and cabbage, were embowered in foliage and
connected by a broad walk swept as clean as the
deck of a man-of-war. A pleasant hum of business
struck the ear. Through open doors were seen
wheels, looms, hat-plaiting, basket-making. One or
two negro patriarchs, with heads like ripe cotton-
balls, sat blinking in the sun before their doors. On
the grass, on the walks, everywhere under foot, were
sportive piccaninnies clad in a single garment. As
the visitors passed down the line, smiles, bows, curt-
seys, and cordial good-bys were showered upon the
young men, who had won a host of admirers in "the
quarter."

Newbold lingered behind the others, and looked

back. It was a fine elastic day, full of sweet, homely
smells from wood and meadow and fresh-turned fur-
rows of the earth,—a day when the air "nimbly and
sweetly recommends itself unto the gentle senses."
From the farm-hands, at work on the slopes bordered by dark lines of pine forest, came cheerful
sounds mellowed by distance; in "the quarter" chat-
tering tongues were heard, with the crowing of
cocks and the clamorous joy of hens who had just
acquitted themselves of their diurnal duty to society.
It was all peaceful and pleasant enough. While
Newbold mused with regret over their approaching
departure, he heard a cry as if of pain from Pink,
who, with her two companions, Hoyt and Dolph, had
disappeared down a path leading to an isolated cottage. Newbold quickly followed, to be met by all
three of the missing young people, Dolph having
his arm around Pink, who looked pale and terrified.

"It is nothing," Hoyt explained. "We were idi-
otic enough to go into that old witch's cabin yonder
to have our fortunes told; and the woman was either
drunk or crazy, I don't know which, and frightened
Miss Hunter with some of her nonsensical sayings—
that's all."

"Oh! no," cried Pink. "Aunt Sabra never was
like that before—never." And she shuddered in-
voluntarily, clinging to her brother.

They had passed into the glen, a broad grassy valley, strewn with boulders of rock set in ferns, where
dogwood-trees in full blossom made a blaze of white
radiance in the shadow.

"Sit down upon one of these royal rocks," Newbold said to the young girl gently. "Tell me all
about your fortune-hunting, and we will laugh at it
together."

But Pink could not laugh. She looked from Hoyt
to her brother, but did not speak. Hoyt, strangely

enough for him, seemed to labor under a rare spell of embarrassment. Only Dolph laughed, like the light-hearted lad he was.

"All this because Aunt Sabra had what Mammy Psyche calls the highstrikes, Pink. It isn't worth worrying about. After all, I am the fellow to be worried, am I not, Mr. Hoyt?" and the lad looked up into his friend's face with a trustful smile.

"Oh! but she said—she said," Pink found voice to whisper, "that Dolph was—walking—across—his grave!"

"And that I, since Miss Hunter is too polite to continue the prophecy," Hoyt added, "that I am to be the grave-digger, or words to that effect. Pray, Miss Hunter, don't let this stupid accident mar the pleasure of our last day at Crow's Nest. Dolph here has shown that he believes in me. Won't you, too, be my friend?"

To Newbold's surprise, the color in Pink's face, as she placed her hand in Hoyt's, deepened to burning crimson.

[Three years later Newbold and Hoyt, now enlisted in the Northern army, are again in the vicinity of Crow's Nest. Newbold has heard from an old negro the story of the disasters that have come to the family—their extreme poverty, and the loss in battle of all the sons but Dolph. The heroine of the old negro's picturesque story is Pink, who has taken charge of the plantation—"it's dess a wonder her sperret ent bruck, wid de pore eatin' en de worrin' out in de hard work." Meanwhile Hoyt had married, but Newbold still cherished a love for the Virginia girl he had met years before.]

Once again upon the banks of the Aspen River our two friends came to a halt. This time it was no May-day pleasuring beneath the flowery arches of the wood. Hoyt was in command of a scouting ex-

pedition, which Newbold, out of the very restlessness
of his spirit, had volunteered to accompany. The
long winter of inactivity made an opportunity like
this a godsend to both men and officers. It was now
toward the end of March, and, by one of the co-
quetries of Virginia's climate at that season, a brisk
snow-storm had set in, driving Hoyt's party into
the shelter of a close growth of pine trees for their
noonday bivouac. Gathered round a tiny fire, whose
thin blue curl of smoke they would have hidden from
outside observation, they sat eating and chatting
merrily—their horses, tethered close at hand, comfortably munching provender beneath a thatch of
snow.

Suddenly the soldier on guard without gave a note
of warning to his comrades. In an instant every
man's hand was on his rifle. In the dead silence that
ensued, they could hear the long, even stride of
horses galloping on the far side of the river bank.
From their ambush they saw a party of Confederates down the steep descent to the ford. Their steeds
plunged into the stream and rioted with the swift
yellow current, waving his arm aloft in boyish pride
—joyous, gallant, and alert—good God! could this be
little Dolph?

"Fire!" came the ring of Hoyt's clear voice; and
the order was instantly obeyed.

Newbold was conscious of a mad movement of
protest. Before the smoke attending the deadly vol-
ley had scattered, the ranks of the rebel cavalry were
seen to split asunder. Two or three bodies plunged
heavily from their saddles to the ground. In the
skirmish that ensued the rest of them, surprised and
outnumbered, made desperate fight in vain. Those
not slain or captured on the spot turned back to
cross the ford, a rain of bullets following. More
than one succeeded in crossing unhurt; some sank

wounded on the far bank; and one poor fellow, struck
in midstream, sat his horse gallantly until he had
well nigh mastered the buffeting of the flood, then,
falling like a column, was lost to sight beneath the
angry tide. It was short work to look for Dolph.
The boy lay by the roadside, his fair face looking
heavenward, a bullet through his heart.

Hoyt, having a severe thigh-wound for his own
share of the encounter, was carried by his men into
the shelter they had recently quitted and laid on a
bed made of leaves and blankets, while a messenger,
accompanying the prisoners sent back under guard,
was dispatched to headquarters in search of a surgeon. Into this retreat, where the wounded of both
sides were lying, Newbold had caused Dolph's body
to be borne. A faint hope, too soon extinguished,
nerved him to continued efforts at resuscitation.
Hoyt, on discovering the object of his friend's solicitude, was beyond measure shocked and grieved. In
the intervals of his acute attacks of suffering, he
would ask impatiently if nothing could be done to
save the boy. From one of the wounded Confederates Newbold ascertained that this was young Hunter's first military service since his recent enlist-
ment; and that the party, at his request, had stopped
overnight at Colonel Hunter's house, whither it was
more than probable some one of the retreating men
had even now borne the news of the lad's fate.

"But I reckon I'd rather be here as I am, than
in his boots that tells the news," the soldier added,
between gasps of pain.

Newbold, having done what he could for the suf-
ferers, paced up and down the road in front of his
improvised hospital, a prey, for once in his life, to
blank uncertainty. As he strode back and forth, a
soldier on the outpost signaled him, pointing in the
direction of the far bank of the river. Going down

the steep path, Newbold saw through the mist of
swiftly falling snow the black hulk of the old ferryboat push out from the opposite shore.

"There are only two people aboard, sir," the sentry said. "They've a white flag up. It's a woman
and a nigger man, I guess."

Newbold's heart was filled with foreboding. He
could make no answer; he could only watch and wait.
The boat drew nearer. What he feared was realized. A gaunt old negro handled the ropes of the
ferryboat, and at his side a young girl stood direct-
ing him. A moment more, and Pink, her large eyes
fixed and staring, no tear upon the whiteness of her
cheek, sprang to the shore and came swiftly up the
bank.

"I have come to claim my dead," she said, in tones
so strange and sad that, instinctively, every man who
heard her doffed his cap and stood bareheaded in
the snowflakes. Newbold dared not answer; he
could not tell whether she recognized him or not. In
silence he led her, followed by old Jupiter, whose
shambling steps found it difficult to make a footing,
along the slippery path. Dolph's body had been removed a little apart from the others and laid on the
moss at the foot of a tree. Newbold hesitated for
a moment; then, drawing aside the sweeping bough
that veiled it from their sight, he motioned the young
girl to pass before him. He saw her swoop downward, like a mother-bird to its young, and then could
look no more. She came out presently, the same
marble creature who had entered there. Hoyt had
aroused from his benumbed condition, and, dimly
comprehending what had come to pass, begged Newbold to call her to his side.

"I must say—a word—you know. She may feel
more kindly to see me—in this state."

He had raised himself upon his elbow and looked

appealingly toward her. Pink's eyes met his. To Newbold's utter surprise, the young girl's face kindled with a momentary glow that was astonishment and joy and tenderness combined. She made a quick motion in Hoyt's direction, then as suddenly put both hands before her eyes and drew back.

"Pray speak to him, Miss Hunter," Newbold urged, in a voice that did not seem his own. "He is badly wounded, as you see, and your—sorrow—is the one disturbing thought he can't dismiss from his wandering brain. Surely, you will be merciful; surely, you will believe that this terrible day's work was one neither he nor I would have intentionally wrought."

As he spoke, the girl trembled pitiably; through her clasped hands he could see a stain of vivid carmine dye her cheek, then vanish, leaving it pale as before. With a sudden impulse, she crossed to Hoyt's side and bent down to him; but the wounded man, exhausted by his effort, had already fallen back in a stupor that might mean death.

Pink knelt for a moment gazing at him; then, rising, turned away. Newbold caught the murmur that escaped her lips.

"Better so," she whispered drearily.

"Better so," he echoed in his heart. "She will perhaps be spared a deeper pang."

Dolph's body was wrapped in his soldier's blanket; but, when the moment came to bear him forth, Newbold and the men who offered to assist were motioned back by the lean arm of Jupiter, who, mute and solemn, had kept watch beside the dead.

"I ax yer pardon, sir, but dis is *my* place, and I has my mistis' orders," the old man said; and, lifting the body tenderly to his breast, he walked with majestic tread along the path—the girl, erect and tearless, following.

A cloth laid over the boy's face fluttered back. Those who in silent awe looked after the sad procession till it passed from view saw the gleam of his golden curls nestling in the protecting arms of Jupiter, even as the ferryboat pushed out from shore. Midway in the stream Newbold caught his last glimpse of them: the girl at her old place by the ropes, battling with wind and current; the negro, on his knees beside her, striving to shield his burden from the storm. Then a mist came over the watcher's eyes; that and the falling snow blotted her forever from his sight.

GRACE ELIZABETH KING.

LA GRANDE DEMOISELLE.*

From Balcony Stories (1892).

THAT was what she was called by everybody as
soon as she was seen or described. Her name, besides baptismal titles, was Idalie Sainte Foy Mortemart des Islets. When she came into society, in the
brilliant little world of New Orleans, it was the
event of the season, and after she came in, whatever
she did became also events. Whether she went, or
did not go; what she said, or did not say; what she
wore, and did not wear—all these became important matters of discussion, quoted as much or more
than what the president said, or the governor
thought. And in those days, the days of '59, New
Orleans was not, as it is now, a one-heiress place,
but it may be said that one could find heiresses then
as one finds typewriting girls now.

Mademoiselle Idalie received her birth, and what
education she had, on her parents' plantation, the
famed old Reine Sainte Foy place, and it is no secret
that, like the ancient kings of France, her birth ex-
ceeded her education.

It was a plantation, the Reine Sainte Foy, the
richness and luxury of which are really well described in those perfervid pictures of tropical life,
at one time the passion of philanthropic imagina-
tions, excited and exciting over the horrors of slavery. Although these pictures were then often ac-

cused of being purposely exaggerated, they seem now to fall short of, instead of surpassing, the truth. Stately walls, acres of roses, miles of oranges, unmeasured fields of cane, colossal sugar-house—they were all there, and all the rest of it, with the slaves, slaves, slaves everywhere, whole villages of negro cabins. And there were also, most noticeable to the natural, as well as to the visionary eye—there were the ease, idleness, extravagance, self-indulgence, pomp, pride, arrogance, in short, the whole enumeration, the moral *sine qua non,* as some people considered it, of the wealthy slaveholder of aristocratic descent and tastes.

What Mademoiselle Idalie cared to learn she studied, what she did not she ignored; and she followed the same simple rule untrammeled in her eating, drinking, dressing, and comportment generally; and whatever discipline may have been exercised on the place, either in fact or fiction, most assuredly none of it, even so much as in a threat, ever attainted her sacred person. When she was just turned sixteen, Mademoiselle Idalie made up her mind to go into society. Whether she was beautiful or not it is hard to say. It is almost impossible to appreciate properly the beauty of the rich, the very rich. The unfettered development, the limitless choice of accessories, the confidence, the self-esteem, the sureness of expression, the simplicity of purpose, the ease of execution—all these produce a certain effect of beauty behind which one really cannot get to measure length of nose, or brilliancy of eye. This much can be said: there was nothing in her that positively contradicted any assumption of beauty on her part, or credit of it on the part of others. She was very tall and very thin, with small head, long neck, black eyes, and abundant straight black hair—for which her hair-dresser deserved

more praise than she—good teeth, of course, and a
mouth that, even in prayer, talked nothing but commands; that is about all she had *en fat d'ornements,*
as the modistes say. It may be added that she
walked as if the Reine Sainte Foy plantation extended over the whole earth, and the soil of it were
too vile for her to tread. Of course she did not buy
her toilets in New Orleans. Everything was ordered from Paris, and came as regularly through
the custom house as the modes and robes to the mil-
liners. She was furnished by a certain house there,
just as one of royal family would be at the present
day. As this had lasted from her *layette* up to her
sixteenth year, it may be imagined what took place
when she determined to make her *début.* Then it
was literally, not metaphorically, *carte blanche,* at
least so it got to the ears of society. She took a
sheet of note-paper, wrote the date at the top, added,
"I make my début in November," signed her name
at the extreme end of the sheet, addressed it to her
dressmaker in Paris, and sent it.

It was said that in her dresses the very handsomest silks were used for linings, and that real lace
was used where others put imitation—around the
bottoms of the skirts, for instance—and silk ribbons
of the best quality served the purposes of ordinary
tapes; and sometimes the buttons were of real gold
and silver, sometimes set with precious stones. Not
that she ordered these particulars, but the dress-
makers, when given *carte blanche* by those who do
not condescend to details, so soon exhaust the outside limits of garments that perforce they take to
plastering them inside with gold, so to speak, and,
when the bill goes in, they depend upon the furnish-
ings to carry out a certain amount of the contract in
justifying the price. And it was said that these
costly dresses, after being worn once or twice, were

cast aside, thrown upon the floor, given to the
negroes—anything to get them out of sight. Not an
inch of the real lace, not one of the jeweled buttons,
not a scrap of ribbon, was ripped off to save. And
it was said that if she wanted to romp with her dogs
in all her finery, she did it; she was known to have
ridden horseback, one moonlight night, all around
the plantation in a white silk dinner-dress flounced
with Alencon. And at night, when she came from
the balls, tired, tired to death as only balls can render one, she would throw herself down upon her bed
in her tulle skirts—on top, or not, of the exquisite
flowers, she did not care—and make her maid undress her in that position; often having her bodices
cut off her, because she was too tired to turn over
and have them unlaced.

That she was admired, raved about, loved even,
goes without saying. After the first month she held
the refusal of half the beaux of New Orleans. Men
did absurd, undignified, preposterous things for
her; and she? Love? Marry? The idea never occurred to her. She treated the most exquisite of her
pretenders no better than she treated her Paris
gowns, for the matter of that. She could not even
bring herself to listen to a proposal patiently;
whistling to her dogs in the middle of the most
ardent protestations, or jumping up and walking
away with a shrug of the shoulders and a ''Bah!''

Well! Everyone knows what happened after '59.
There is no need to repeat. The history of one is
the history of all. But there was this difference—
for there is every shade of difference in misfortune,
as there is every shade of resemblance in happiness.
Mortmarte des Islets went off to fight. That was
natural; his family had been doing that, he thought,
or said, ever since Charlemagne. Just as naturally
he was killed in the first engagement. They, his

family, were always among the first killed; so much
so that it began to be considered assassination to
fight a duel with any of them. All that was in the
ordinary course of events. One difference in their
misfortunes lay in that after the city was captured,
their plantation, so near, convenient, and rich in all
kinds of provisions, was selected to receive a contingent of troops—a colored company. If it had
been a colored company raised in Louisiana it might
have been different; and these negroes mixed with
the negroes in the neighborhood—and negroes are
no better than whites, for the proportion of good
and bad among them—and the officers were always
off duty when they should have been on, and on
when they should have been off.

One night the dwelling caught fire. There was an
immediate rush to save the ladies. Oh, there was
no hesitation about that! They were seized in their
beds, and carried out in the very arms of their enemies; carried away off to the sugar-house and deposited there. No danger of their doing anything
but keep very quiet and still in their *chemises des
nuit*, and their one sheet apiece, which was about
all that was saved from the conflagration—that is,
for them. But it must be remembered that this is
all hearsay. When one has not been present, one
knows nothing of one's own knowledge; one can only
repeat. It has been repeated, however, that although the house was burned to the ground, and
everything in it destroyed, wherever, for a year
afterward, a man of that company or that neighborhood was found, there could have been found also,
without search warrant, property that had belonged
to the Des Islets. That is the story; and it is believed or not, exactly according to prejudice.

How the ladies ever got out of the sugar-house,
history does not relate; nor what they did. It was

not a time for sociability, either personal or episto-
lary. At one offensive word your letter and you,
very likely, examined; and Ship Island for a hotel,
with soldiers for hostesses! Madame Des Islets
died very soon after the accident—of rage, they say;
and that was about all the public knew.

Indeed, at that time the society of New Orleans
had other things to think about than the fate of the
Des Islets. As for la grande demoiselle, she had
prepared for her own oblivion in the hearts of her
female friends. And the gentlemen—her *preux
chevaliers*—they were burning with other passions
than those which had driven them to her knees, encountering a little more serious response than
"bahs" and shrugs. And, after all, a woman seems
the quickest thing forgotten when once the important affairs of life come to men for consideration.

It might have been ten years according to some
calculations, or ten eternities—the heart and the al-
manac never agree about time—but one morning old
Champigny (they used to call him Champignon)
was walking along his levee front, calculating how
soon the water would come over and drown him out,
as the Louisianians says. It was before a seven
o'clock breakfast, cold, wet, rainy and discouraging.
The road was knee-deep in mud, and so broken up
with hauling that it was like walking upon waves to
get over it. A shower poured down. Old Champigny was hurrying in when he saw a figure approaching. He had to stop to look at it, for it was
worth while. The head was hidden by a green
barege veil, which the showers had plentifully be-
sprinkled with dew; a tall, thin figure. Figure!
No; not even could it be called a figure; straight up
and down like a finger or a post; high-shouldered,
and a step—a step like a plowman's. No umbrella;
no—nothing more, in fact. It does not sound so

peculiar as when first related—something must be
forgotten. The feet—oh, yes, the feet—they were
like waffle-irons or frying pans, or anything of that
shape.

Old Champigny did not care for women—he never
had; they simply did not exist for him in the order
of nature. He had been married once, it is true,
about a half-century before; but that was not reck-
oned against the existence of his prejudice, because
he was *célibatiere* to his finger tips, as any one could
see a mile away. But that woman *intrigué'd* him.

He had no servant to inquire from. He performed
all of his own domestic work in that wretched little
cabin that replaced his old home. For Champigny
also belonged to the great majority of the *nouveaux
pauvres*. He went out into the rice field, where were
one or two hands that worked on shares with him,
and he asked them. They knew immediately; there
is nothing connected with the parish that a field-
hand does not know at once. She was the teacher of
the colored public school some three or four miles
away. "Ah," thought Champigny, "some Northern
lady on a mission." He watched to see her return
in the evening, which she did, of course, in a blind-
ing rain. Imagine the green barege veil then; for
it remained always down over her face.

Old Champigny could not get over it that he had
never seen her before. But he must have seen her,
and, with his abstraction and old age, not have
noticed her, for he found out from the negroes that
she had been teaching four or five years there. And
he found out also—how, it is not important—that she
was Idalie Sainte Foy Mortemart des Islets. *La
grande demoiselle!* He had never known her in the
old days, owing to his uncomplimentary attitude toward women, but he knew of her, of course, and of
her family. It should have been said that his plan-

tation was about fifty miles higher up the river, and on the opposite bank to Reine Sainte Foy. It seemed terrible. The old gentleman had had reverses of his own, which would bear the telling, but nothing was more shocking to him than this—that Idalie Sainte Foy Mortemart des Islets should be teaching a public colored school for—it makes one blush to name it—seven dollars and a half a month. For seven dollars and a half a month to teach a set of—well! He found out where she lived, a little cabin—not so much worse than his own, for that matter—in the corner of a field; no companion, no servant, nothing but food and shelter. Her clothes have been described.

Only the good God himself knows what passed in Champigny's mind on the subject. We know only the results. He went and married *la grande demoiselle*. How? Only the good God knows that too. Every first of the month, when he goes to the city to buy provisions, he takes her with him—in fact, he takes her everywhere with him.

Passengers on the railroad know them well, and they always have a chance to see her face. When she passes her old plantation *la grande demoiselle* always lifts her veil for one instant—the inevitable green barege veil. What a face! Thin, long, sallow, petrified! And the neck! If she would only tie something around the neck! And her plain, coarse, cottonade gown! The negro women about her were better dressed than she.

Poor old Champignon! It was not an act of charity to himself, no doubt cross and disagreeable besides being ugly. And as for love, gratitude!

FRANCES LITTLE.

THE LADY OF THE DECORATION.*

October 2nd, 1901.

At last, dear Mate, I am started at my own work with the babies and there aren't any words to tell you how cunning they are. There are eighty-five high class children in the pay kindergarten, and forty in the free. The latter are mostly of the very poor families, most of the mothers working in the fields or on the railroads. There are so many pitiful cases that one longs for a mint of money and a dozen hands to relieve them. One little girl of six comes every day with her blind baby brother strapped on her back. She is a tiny thing herself and yet that baby is never unstrapped from her back until night comes. When I first saw her old weazened face and her eagerness to play, I just took them both in my lap and cried!

One funny thing I must tell you about. From the first week that I got here, the children have had a nickname for me. I noticed them laughing and nudging each other on the street and in the school, and whenever I passed they raised their right hands in salute, and gave a funny little clucking sound. They seemed to pass the word from one to another until every youngster in the neighborhood followed the trick. My curiosity was aroused to such a pitch that I got an interpreter to investigate the matter. When he came to report, he smilingly touched my

little enamelled watch, the one Jack gave me on my
16th birthday, and apologetically informed me that
the children thought it was a decoration from the
Emperor and they were saluting me in consequence!
And they have named me "The Lady of the Decoration." Think of it, I have a title, and I am actually
looked up to by these funny yellow babies as a
superior being. They forget it some time though
when we all get to playing together in the yard. We
can't talk to each other, but we can laugh and romp
together, and sometimes the fun runs high.

I am busy from morning until night. The two
kindergartens, a big training class in physical culture, two Japanese lessons a day and prayers about
every three minutes, don't leave many spare hours
for homesickness. But the longing is there all the
same, and when I see the big steamers out in the
harbor and realize that they are coaling for *home,* I
just want to steal aboard and stay there.

The language is something awful. I get my tongue
in such knots that I have to use a corkscrew to pull
it straight again. Just between you and me, I have
decided to give it up and devote my time to teaching the girls to speak English instead. They are
such responsive, eager little things, it will not be
hard.

As for the country, I wouldn't dare to attempt a
description. Sometimes I just *ache* with the beauty
of it all! From my window I can see in one group
banana, pomegranate, persimmon and fig trees all
loaded with fruit. The roses are still in full bloom,
and color, color everywhere. Across the river, the
banks are lined with picturesque houses that look
out from a mass of green, and above them are tea-
houses, and temples and shrines so old that even the
moss is gray, and time has worn away the dates engraved upon the stones.

We spent yesterday at the sacred Island of Miya-jima, which is about one hour's ride from here. The dream of it is still upon me and I wish I could share it with you. We went over in a sampan, a rude open boat rowed by two men in undress uniform. For half an hour we literally danced across the sea; everything was fresh and sparkling, and I was so glad to be alive and free, that I just sang for joy. Miss Lessing joined in and the boatmen kept time, smiling and nodding their approval.

The mountains were sky high, and at their base in a small crescent-shaped plain was the village with streets so clean and white you hated to walk on them. We stopped at the "House of the White Cloud" and three little maids took off our shoes and replaced them with pretty sandals. The whole house was of cedar and ebony and bamboo and it had been rubbed with oil until it shone like satin. On the floor was a stuffed matting with a heavy border of crimson silk, and in the corner of the room was a jar that came to my shoulder, full of wonderfully blended chrysanthemums. All the rooms opened upon a porch which hung directly above a roaring waterfall, and below us a dozen steps away stretched the sparkling sea, full of hundreds of sailing vessels and junks.

In the afternoon, we wandered over the island, visiting the old, old temples, listening to the mysterious wailing of the wind bells, feeding the deer and crane, and drinking in the beauty of it all. I felt like a disembodied spirit, traveling back, back over the centuries, into dim, forgotten ages. The dead seemed close about me, yet they brought no gloom, for I too was dead. All afternoon I had the impression of trying to keep my consciousness from drifting into oblivion through the gate of this magical dream!

How you would enjoy it all, and read its deeper meaning, which is hidden from me. But even if I can't philosophize like a certain blessed old Mate of mine, I can *feel* until every nerve is a tingle with the thrill.

Goodbye for a little while; I've stolen the time to write you this, and now it behooves me to hustle.

———

Christmas Day, 1901.

Had somebody told you last Christmas, as we trimmed the big tree and made ready for the family gathering, that this Christmas would find me in a foreign country teaching a band of little heathens, wouldn't you have thought somebody had wheels in his head?

And yet it is true, and I have only to lift my eyes to realize fully that I am really in the flowery kingdom. The plum blossoms are in full bloom and the roses too, while a thick frost makes everything sparkling white in the sunshine. The mountains have put on a thin blue veil trimmed in silver, and over all is a turquoise sky.

And best of all, everybody—I speak figuratively— is happy. It may be that some poor little waif is hungry, having had only rice water for breakfast, it may be some sad hearts are beating under the gay kimonos, and it *may* be, Mate dear, that somebody, a stranger in a strange land, can't keep the tears back, and is longing with all her mind and soul and body for home and her loved ones. But never you mind, nobody knows it but you and me and a bamboo tree!

This afternoon we are going to have tea for the Mammas and Papas, and I am going to put on my prettiest clothes and do my yellow locks in their most fetching style.

I shall lock up tight, way down deep, all heart-aches and longings and put on my best smile for these dear little people who have given to me, a stranger, such full measure of their sympathy and friendship, who, in the big service last month, when giving thanks for all the great blessings of the past year, named the new Kindergarten teacher first.

Do you wonder that I am happy and miserable and homesick and contented all at the same time?

The box I sent home for Christmas was a paltry offering compared to what I wanted to send, but the things were bought with the first money I ever earned. They are packed in so tight with love that I doubt if you ever get them out.

Our Christmas dinner was not exactly a success. We invited all the foreigners in Hiroshima, twelve in number, and everybody talked a great deal and laughed at everybody's stale jokes, and pretended to be terribly hilarious. But there was a pathetic droop to every mouth, and not a soul referred to *home*. Each one seemed to realize that the mere mention of the word would break up the party.

I tell you I am beginning to look with positive reverence on the heroism of some of these people! Tears and regrets have no place here; desire, ambition, love itself is laid aside, and only taken out for inspection perhaps in the dead hours of the night. If heartbreaks come, as come they must, there is no crying out, no rebellion, just a stiffer lip and a firmer grip and the work goes on.

I wish I was like that, but I'm not. If Nature had put more time on my head and less on my heart, she would have turned out a better job.

I put a pipe in the box for Jack. If you think I ought not to have done it, don't give it to him. As old Charity used to say, "I don't want to discomboberate nobody." Only I hope he won't think I am ungrateful and indifferent.

HIROSHIMA, February, 1904.

Dear old Mate:

I am breathless! For three weeks I have had a chase up hill and down dale, to the top of pine clad mountains, into the misty shadows of the deep valleys, up and down the silvery river, to and fro on the frosty road. For why? All because I had lost my "poise," that treasured possession which you said I was to hang on to as I do to my front teeth and my hair. So when I found it was gone, I started in full pursuit. Never a sight of its coat tails did I catch until Sunday, when I gave up the race and sat me down to fight out the old fight of rebellion, and kicking against the pricks.

It was a perfect day, the plum trees were white with blossom, the spice bushes heavy with fragrance, the river dancing for joy, and the whole earth springing into new, tender life. A saucy little bird sat on an old stone lantern, and sang straight at me. He told me I was a whiney young person, that it was lots more fun to catch worms and fly around in the sunshine than it was to sit in the house and mope. He actually laughed at me, and I seized my hat and lit out after him, and when I came home I found I had caught my "poise."

To-day in class I asked my girls what "happiness" meant. One new girl looked up timidly and said, "Sensei, I sink him just mean *you*." I felt like a hypocrite, but it pleased me to know that on the outside at least I kept shiny.

I tell you if I don't find my real self out here, if I don't see my own soul in all its bareness and weakness then I will never see it. At home, hedged in by conventionality, custom, and the hundred little interests of our daily life, we have small chance to see ourselves as we really are, but in a foreign land, stripped bare of everything in the world save *self*, in a loneliness as great sometimes as the grave, face to face with new conditions, new demands, we have ample chance to take our own measurement. I cannot say that the result obtained is calculated to make one conceited!

I fit into this life out here, like a square peg in a round hole. I am not consecrated, I was never "*called* to the foreign field," I love the world and the flesh even if I don't care especially for the devil, I don't believe the Lord makes the cook steal so I may be more patient, and I don't pray for wisdom in selecting a new pair of shoes. When my position becomes unbearable, I invariably face the matter frankly and remind myself that if it is hard on the peg, it is just as hard on the hole, and that if they can stand it I guess I can!

You ask about my reading. Yes, I read every spare minute I can get, before breakfast, on my way to classes, and after I go to bed. Somebody at home sends me the magazines regularly and I keep them going for months.

By the way, I wish you would write and tell me just exactly how Jack is. You said he was working too hard and that he looked all fagged out. Wasn't it exactly like him to back out of going South on account of his conscience? He would laugh at us for saying it was that, but it was. He may be unreligious, and scoff at churches and all that, but he has the most rigid, cast-iron, inelastic conscience that I ever came across. I wish he would take a rest. You see out here, so far away from you all, I can't help worrying when any of you are the least bit sick. Jack has been on my mind for days. Don't tell him that I asked you to, but won't you get him to go away. He would curl his hair if you asked him to.

Preparations for war are still in progress and it makes a fellow pretty shivery to see it coming closer and closer. Hiroshima will be the center of military movements and of course under military law. It will affect us only as to the restrictions put on our walks and places we can go. With the city so full of strange soldiers, I don't suppose we will want to go much. Two big war ships, which Japan has just bought from Chili, are on their way from Shanghai. Regiment after regiment has poured into Hiroshima and embarked again for Corea. I am terribly thrilled over it all, and the Japanese watch my enthusiasm with their non-committal eyes and never say a word!

My poor little sick girl grows weaker all the time. She is a constant care and anxiety, but she has no money and I cannot send her back to her wretched home. The teachers think I am very foolish to let the thing run on, and I suppose I am. She can never be any better, and she may live this way for months. But when she clings to me with her frail hands and declares she is better and will soon get well if I will only let her stay with me, my heart fails me. I have patched up an old steamer chair for her, and made a window garden, and tried to make the room as bright as possible. She has to stay by herself nearly all day, but she is so patient and gentle that I never hear a complaint. This morning she pressed my hand to her breast and said wistfully, "Sensei, it makes sorry to play all the time with the health."

Miss Lessing tried to get her in the hospital but they will not take incurables.

Somehow Jack's hospital scheme doesn't seem as foolish as it did. If there are other children in the world as friendless and dependent as this one, then making a permanent home for them would be worth all the great careers in the world.

YOKOHAMA, July 5, 1905.

Do you suppose, if people could, they would write letters as soon as they got to Heaven? I don't know where to begin nor what to say. The only thing about me that is on earth is this pen point, the rest is floating around in a diamond-studded, rose-colored mist!

I will try to be sensible and give you some idea of what has been happening, but how I am to get it on paper I don't know. I got here yesterday, the 4th of July, on the early train, and rushed down to the hatoba to meet the launch when it came in from the steamer. I had had no breakfast and was as nervous as a witch. Your letter had not come, and my fears were increasing every moment.

Well I took my place on the steps as the launch landed and waited, with very little interest I must confess, for your young missionary to appear. By and by I saw a handkerchief tied to a sleeve, but it was a man's sleeve. I gave one more look, and my heart seemed to stop. "Jack!" I cried, and then everything went black before me, and I didn't know anything more. It was the first time I ever fainted; sorrow and grief never knocked me out, but joy like that was enough to kill me!

When I came to, I was at the hotel and I didn't dare open my eyes. I knew it was all a dream, and I did not want to come back to reality. I lay there holding on to the vision, until I heard a man's voice close by say, "She will be all right now, I will take care of her." Then I opened my eyes, and with three Japanese maids and four Japanese men and two ladies off the steamer looking on, I flung my arms about Jack's neck and cried down his collar!

He made me stay quiet all morning, and just before tiffin he calmly informed me that he had made all the arrangements for us to be married at three o'clock. I declared I couldn't, that I had signed a contract for another year at Hiroshima, that Miss Lessing would think I was crazy, that I must make some plans. But you know Jack! He met every objection that I could offer, said he would see Miss Lessing and make it all right about the contract, that I was too nervous to teach any more, and last that I owed him a little consideration after four years of waiting. Then I realized how the lines had deepened in his face, and how the gray was streaking his hair, and I surrendered promptly.

We were married in a little English church on the Bluff, with half a dozen witnesses. Several Americans whom Jack had met on the steamer, a missionary friend of mine, and the Japanese clerk constituted the audience.

It is all like a beautiful dream to me still, and I am afraid to let Jack get out of my sight for fear I will wake up. It was Fourth of July, and Christmas, and birthday, and wedding day all rolled into one. The whole city was celebrating, the hotel a flutter of flags and ribbons, the bay full of every kind of pleasure craft. At night there was a grand lantern fête and fireworks, and a huge figure of Uncle Sam with stars in his coat tails. Thousands of Japanese in their gayest kimonas thronged the Bund, listening to the music, watching the foreigners and the fireworks.

Jack and I were like two children; he forgot that he was a staid doctor, and I forgot that I had ever been a Foreign Missionary Kindergarten teacher. We were boy and girl again and up to our eyes in love. It was the first Fourth of July for fifteen years that I did not have some unhappiness to conceal. As one of my girls said about herself: "My little lonely heart had flewed away!"

All the loneliness, the heartaches, the pains are justified now. I do not regret the past for through it the present is.

Do you remember the lines: "He shall restore the years that the locust hath eaten?" Well, I believe that while I have been struggling out here, He has restored them, and that I will be permitted to return to a new life, a life given back by God.

Of course you know we are going on around. It seems rather inconsistent to say I am glad of it after all my wailing for home. The truth is, home has come to *me!*

Jack says we are to meet you and Dr. Leet in Paris. You needn't try to persuade me that Heaven will be any better than the present!

There is no use in my trying to thank you for your part in all this, dear Mate. I have been a chronic state of gratitude to you ever since I was born! I can only say with all my heart and soul, "God bless you and Good-bye."

P.S. In my wedding ring is engraved M.L.O.T.D. Can you guess what it means?